PUBLICATIONS OF THE
COUNCIL ON FOREIGN RELATIONS

CHARLES P. HOWLAND
DIRECTOR OF RESEARCH

SURVEY OF AMERICAN
FOREIGN RELATIONS

1929

PREVIOUSLY PUBLISHED

SURVEY OF AMERICAN

FOREIGN RELATIONS

1928

SURVEY OF

AMERICAN FOREIGN RELATIONS

PREPARED UNDER THE DIRECTION OF

CHARLES P. HOWLAND

DIRECTOR OF RESEARCH
OF THE COUNCIL ON FOREIGN RELATIONS
RESEARCH ASSOCIATE IN GOVERNMENT AT YALE UNIVERSITY

PUBLISHED FOR THE COUNCIL ON FOREIGN RELATIONS

NEW HAVEN · YALE UNIVERSITY PRESS

LONDON · HUMPHREY MILFORD · OXFORD UNIVERSITY PRESS

1929

COUNCIL ON FOREIGN RELATIONS

THE purpose of the Council on Foreign Relations is to study the international aspects of America's political, economic, and financial problems.

In addition to holding general and group meetings, the Council publishes *Foreign Affairs*, a quarterly review; the annual *Survey of American Foreign Relations*; the *Political Handbook of the World*, issued annually; and individual volumes on special international questions.

OFFICERS

ELIHU ROOT
Honorary President

JOHN W. DAVIS
President

PAUL D. CRAVATH
Vice-President

EDWIN F. GAY
Secretary and Treasurer

WALTER H. MALLORY
Executive Director

DIRECTORS

HAMILTON FISH ARMSTRONG
ISAIAH BOWMAN
NORMAN H. DAVIS
STEPHEN P. DUGGAN
ALLEN W. DULLES
JOHN H. FINLEY
OTTO H. KAHN

R. C. LEFFINGWELL
GEORGE O. MAY
WESLEY C. MITCHELL
FRANK L. POLK
WHITNEY H. SHEPARDSON
PAUL M. WARBURG
GEORGE W. WICKERSHAM

OWEN D. YOUNG

COMMITTEE ON RESEARCH

EDWIN F. GAY
Chairman

GEORGE W. WICKERSHAM
WHITNEY H. SHEPARDSON

ISAIAH BOWMAN
WESLEY C. MITCHELL

PREFACE

IN this SURVEY, the purpose of the Council on Foreign Relations is to make an objective study of America's present-day foreign relations, not to write history; at the same time, the work is not intended to be a gazetteer or summary of a year's happenings. The date of each volume thus marks the year of publication and is not indicative of a period under review. As was said in the preface to the SURVEY for 1928, the topics selected for each volume "will be those in which a culmination of some sort has thrown the questions involved into high relief, or those which have come to a stage of temporary arrest and so allow of deliberate examination." On this basis the subjects have been chosen for this volume.

Immigration, although constantly iterated to be solely a matter for domestic control, is a subject of international import, for whatever action is taken by any nation affects emigration from other nations, not to speak of issues directly raised between governments, as, for example, by the Oriental exclusion acts. Another aspect of the immigration or population question bears directly upon the position of the United States in the world of nations. Surplus land is no longer available in the United States for settlement by any considerable number of people; this fact, with a growing population and an increased mechanization of agriculture, are factors in a steady movement of population cityward, and a consequent restriction policy. The situation thus arising has international consequences, as stated by Dr. Bowman:

The withdrawal from a fast-growing population of its accustomed frontier and free or cheap land has already had consequences of public concern. We can (1) limit the population; (2) develop our industries at an accelerated pace; (3) increase the yield of the land, in part by intensive methods and in part by further reclamation of swamp and desert. But all three affect our foreign policy either directly or indirectly, through immigration, labor, trade, and the tariff. One eighth of our agricultural land is required to produce the farm products that we ship abroad, and it is largely this surplus that is the foundation of existing standards of farm living. When our population becomes stationary through the operation of forces that eventually limit any nation's growth, we shall tend strongly toward European standards of living. Before that point is reached our social structure will necessarily be strained to the utmost and our foreign policy will become of acute public interest, for its relation to the standard of living will then be more generally recognized.[1]

Much of the material contained in this volume and some of the text has been supplied by scholars who have been willing to merge their identity in a collaborative enterprise. It has continued to seem, on the balance of advantage, that the contributions should not be published as signed articles, and this for several reasons. In a symposium, responsibility would attach to the individual author, not to the Council's editorial staff. Since changes, generally in style, but sometimes in essential substance, are made by the editor, whether on his own decision or on the advice of experts in the respective fields, a chapter is often the product of several minds, and also may have a tone not intended by the original writer. In some cases data are assembled by several persons, none of whom shares in coördinating them. Finally, the SURVEY should have unity of outlook, cohesion of treatment, and harmony of style. For these reasons the editor assumes responsibility for the volume.

The editor desires to express his profound gratitude to the contributors to whose unselfish efforts is mainly due whatever value the book possesses. The primary collaborators in this volume are Professor Herbert L. Briggs, who drafted the Note on the Protection of Nationals Abroad; Edna Cers, whose work is the section on Immigration; Professor Joseph P. Chamberlain, who wrote the bulk of the chapter on the World Court; Professor Charles E. Chapman, who supplied the material for the chapter on Cuba; Colonel Clifford D. Ham, who provided most of the data for the chapter on Nicaragua; Professor Clarence H. Haring, who compiled the chapters on Panama, Costa Rica, Salvador, Guatemala, and Honduras; Judge Otto Schoenrich, who supplied the substance of the chapter on Santo Domingo and an outline for that .

---

[1] Isaiah Bowman, *The New World,* 4th edition, pp. 690-691.

on Haiti; and Clarence K. Streit, who furnished material on Haiti.

Those who have given of their time and patience, with meticulous attention to detail, sometimes to the extent of contributing substantially to the text, include Professor Edwin M. Borchard and Professor Philip C. Jessup, as well as several persons of official position, whose criticisms and suggestions have been of great value. Others who have made helpful suggestions and whose assistance the editor gratefully acknowledges are: Victor C. Cutter, Professor Paul H. Douglas, Professor Leland H. Jenks, A. C. Millspaugh, Professor Edward Alsworth Ross, William L. Schurz, and Professor Walter F. Willcox.

The Research Committee of the Council have given their wholehearted assistance. In particular, the Chairman of the Committee has not stinted time or energy.

The editor's staff associates, Martha Anderson and Herbert B. Elliston, have collaborated with him in the preparation of the entire volume. It has been a joint labor of ideas and writing, and to describe their respective shares would be impossible. To Mr. Elliston, however, may be attributed the major portion of the economic data.

Footnotes, irksome to the general reader, are limited to the instances where a reference is necessary to support the text, to acknowledge the source of an idea, or to establish a quotation not generally familiar. For purposes of reference the Tables of Contents will be reprinted in each volume cumulatively for a number of years. Bibliographical lists on international relations appear in each issue of *Foreign Affairs*, published by the Council. The London Conference of the Institutions for the Scientific Study of International Affairs requested at its March meeting that the Council on Foreign Relations publish these bibliographical lists in reprint form for official distribution in the different countries represented at that conference. The Council has decided to do this and these bibliographical lists can be obtained upon request.

C. P. H.

New Haven,
August 1, 1929.

CONTENTS

CONTENTS

THE REPUBLICS OF CENTRAL AMERICA

I.

THE CARIBBEAN[1]

General considerations of policy, strategic and economic, arising out of what President Taft called "the logic of our geographical position," determine in the large the political relations of the
United States to the Caribbean. The succeeding chapters give an
account of the events out of which each of these individual relations
is composed; the narrative is brief, for the purpose of this SURVEY
is to describe the present-day foreign relations of the United
States and not to rewrite familiar history. The concluding chapter of the section attempts to state the questions of policy which
the Caribbean region presents to the United States, whether general, or arising out of the specific incidents described in the individual countries. Here there is no narrative of events; the theme
is policy only. As to policy, a Survey could scarcely hope to find
a new and ultimate truth on a subject on which thousands of books
have been written. The material is familiar to most readers; the
main effort has therefore been in the direction of compactness and
detachment.

---

[1] The relations of the United States with Mexico will be considered in a future
volume.

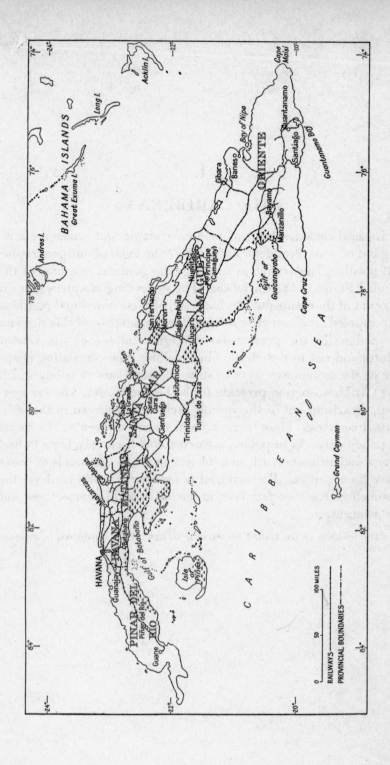

THE CARIBBEAN

Scale: 0 — 100 — 200 — 300 — 400 — 500 MILES

ons and leaseholds of the United States in red ————

positions owned or leased by the United States ■

positions controlled in effect by the United States through treaty provisions ▲

positions owned by European Powers ◆   Capital cities ●

International air mail and passenger routes

operation, August, 1929   Under mail contract and in course of organisation - - - - - - - - - -

Routes under survey

Railways

Plata

Samana Bay

CAN LIC

Santo Domingo

Mona Passage

MONA I.   San Juan

PORTO RICO

Ponce

VIEQUES I. (US)

STA CRUZ (U.S.)

VIRGIN ISLANDS (U.S.)

CULEBRA (U.S.)

ST THOMAS (U.S.)

ST JOHN (U.S.)   ANGUILLA (BR.)

ST MARTIN (FR.)

ST BARTHOLOMEW (FR.)

BARBUDA (BR.)

ST EUSTATIUS (NETH)

ST CHRISTOPHER (ST KITTS) BR.

NEVIS (BR)

ANTIGUA (BR.)

MONTSERRAT (BR.)

LEEWARD

GUADELOUPE (FR.)   16

ISLANDS

MARIE GALANTE (FR.)

DOMINICA (BR.)

MARTINIQUE (FR.)

WINDWARD   ST LUCIA

ST VINCENT (BR.)   BARBADOS (BR.)

ISLANDS

GRENADA (BR.)

S E A

ARUBA (NETH)

CURAÇAO (NETH.)

BONAIRE (NETH.)

TOBAGO (BR.)

MARGARITA (VEN.)

Pto Cabello   Caracas   Port of Spain

TRINIDAD (BR.)

Maracay

ENEZUELA

66   60

THE ISLAND REPUBLICS

CHAPTER ONE

CUBA

PRE-INDEPENDENCE RELATIONS

FEW regions of the world have given the United States more concern than the Island of Cuba. The reason is epitomized in the seal of the republic. This represents Cuba in the form of a key to the Americas, stretching out from Florida on the one hand to Yucatan on the other. Cuba was in fact early marked down as an object of international rivalries; many a project was devised in England for filching the island from Spanish control, but Spain clung to it tenaciously, realizing that the rest of its western empire depended on its continued possession.

The American colonies were fully aware of the importance of Cuba in their affairs. Its strategic importance to them is defined in the following description:

Cuba, lying at important crossroads of Caribbean and Gulf trade routes, commands the only two entrances to the Gulf of Mexico and one of the chief passages to the Caribbean Sea. . . . Thus it is in a position to bottle up the Gulf ports of the United States and to jeopard that nation's control of interoceanic canal routes. Furthermore, its many large and easily defensible harbors could serve as unexcelled bases for enemy ships engaged in blockading the ports or hampering the commerce of the United States.[1]

Or, to adopt picturesque language, "Cuba lies in Uncle Sam's front yard, with a short waterway to his kitchen door."[2] The newly-founded western settlements had no outlet for their goods to compare with the Mississippi route down to New Orleans and thence through the Gulf of Mexico. The acquisition of New Orleans at the time of the Louisiana purchase in 1803 served to re-

---

[1] D. S. Whittlesey, "Geographic Factors in the Relations of the United States and Cuba," *Geographical Review*, XII, 241, April, 1922.

[2] Frank G. Carpenter, Monthly *Consular and Trade Reports*, July, 1905, p. 239.

lieve the situation, but only in part, for the west was still at the mercy of any power holding Florida or Cuba.

In 1807 Jefferson, who was among the earliest advocates of acquisition, remarked that in the event of war with Spain, Cuba might "add itself to our confederation." In a letter of 1809 to Madison he suggested that Napoleon might be willing to give Cuba to the United States to keep this country from interfering with French plans elsewhere in Latin America. "That would be a price," said Jefferson, "and I would immediately erect a column on the southernmost limit of Cuba, and inscribe on it a *ne plus ultra* as to us in that direction." The same wish was often expressed by leading American statesmen of the next fifty years. It was not so much that they desired Cuba for itself; they were afraid some European power, as Madison put it, "might make a fulcrum of that position against the commerce and security of the United States."

The purchase of Florida in 1819, after the acquisition of West Florida, added to the peace of mind of the western states, but made the Cuban question the more acute, as the only surviving problem of its kind. For the next quarter century reports were circulated that England would give Gibraltar and cash for Cuba, that Spain would turn over Cuba as security for a loan from England, that the British and French fleets which constantly appeared in Cuban waters were bent on seizing the island, and that the Spanish Bourbons might cede it to the Bourbons of France in return for military or financial assistance.

The United States was unceasingly vigilant to oppose these designs. On the whole it was satisfied to see Cuba remain in the possession of Spain, a country too weak to threaten the United States, and eventually England and France were constrained to adopt a similar policy. Both wanted it, but preferred Spain's retention of the island to acquisition by either of the other two powers. The British Government for a while tried to persuade the American and French governments to join it in a self-denying ordinance, guaranteeing the island to Spain, but the United States would at no time agree to these suggestions; aside from the "no entangling alliance" principle, there were few American statesmen who did not believe that Cuba would some day be a part of the United States.

Cuba served as a base for Spanish attacks against the rebellious colonies during the Spanish American wars of independence. The Spanish colonies sought to revolutionize the island or to send expeditions from Colombia or Mexico to overwhelm the Spanish forces there, but they were frustrated by France, England, and the United States. France was opposed, as ally of the Spanish Bourbons; England and the United States, believing that a Colombian or Mexican occupation could not be permanent, feared that Cuba might fall into other hands. The American people were enthusiastically in sympathy with the patriot cause on the mainland of Spanish America, but Cuba occupied a special position calling for a different point of view. Cuban opinion itself was not in favor of independence; many wanted a separation from Spain, but desired to join Colombia, Mexico, or the United States. Cuban agents urged union upon the American Government, and it was discussed in Cabinet meetings. Some Americans, including John C. Calhoun, wished to "take the goods the gods provide us," but the view of John Quincy Adams prevailed; he was unwilling to risk British opposition, for in the event of war the British fleet was strong enough to capture Cuba for England.

Meantime the situation in the Mississippi Valley was changing rapidly. While a large part of western commerce still made its way through the Gulf, direct communication with the east by way of the Great Lakes, the canals, and the new railroads, was in course of development. The west was therefore relieved to a great extent of its fear that it might be at the mercy of a strong power in control of Cuba; furthermore, it was no longer felt that England or France entertained annexationist designs. But other factors came into play. The addition of Texas in 1845 and further annexation resulting from the Mexican war, 1846-1848, aroused nation-wide interest in southward expansion, which was intensified by the demand for a transisthmian route to the Pacific Ocean, particularly to the newly-won golden California. Through its relation to the proposed canal Cuba occupied the same position with respect to the far west and the Pacific coast that it had held earlier to the

Mississippi Valley. These years were filled with projects for the acquisition of Cuba, ranging from filibustering expeditions to purchase.

Another factor may have decided the issue against American acquisition of Cuba: the slavery dispute in the United States. The southern states regarded "manifest destiny" as a medium for slavery extension, through which they might build up their political strength against the onslaughts of the abolitionists. Cuba was ideally suited to their purposes, not only because of its close connection with the United States, but also because it was one of the few remaining regions where slavery existed. The question came to be the line of cleavage over the scheme to annex Cuba; before long the early enthusiasm of the north began to dwindle and at length it was entirely dissipated. The outcome of the Civil War made this feeling national. Slavery in Cuba, once a reason for annexation, was now its outstanding obstacle. Other issues once uppermost in men's minds had also changed complexion. Direct communication with the trans-Allegheny west had long since developed, and a few years after the war a railway to the Pacific coast was completed. Furthermore, by the Clayton-Bulwer Treaty of 1850 the United States was assured of participation with England in the building and use of a transisthmian canal.

A country so close and disturbed as Cuba, however, could not long remain out of the range of American policy. Commercial America was quietly linking itself with a country which was the biggest sugar-producing region of the world. The Ten Years War, beginning 1868, which Cuba engaged in for its independence, brought back American concern.

Animated partly by the damage occasioned to American interests, the United States in 1869 proposed the following terms as the basis for American mediation: an acknowledgment of Cuban independence by Spain; in return therefor, payment of an indemnity to Spain by Cuba; the abolition of slavery in Cuba; and an armistice, pending negotiations. The first of these provisions was the stumblingblock, and the war dragged on, domestic troubles in the peninsula keeping Spain from exerting its full force in Cuba. The United States, unwilling to suffer prolongation of a state of affairs so harmful to American interests, began at length to consider intervention. In 1876 Secretary Fish suggested a better observance by Spain of treaty relations, the establishment of a more liberal and less corrupt government in Cuba, the gradual emancipation of the slaves, and an improvement of commercial facilities, together with a removal of the obstructions that hampered trade with the United States. The Spanish authorities agreed to all of these suggestions, but the fighting continued; and it was not until 1878 that an agreement was reached in the Peace of Zanjón. Three years later, in 1881, it was followed by a law for gradual emancipation, and in 1886 slavery came altogether to an end. Another Spanish promise, to introduce good government in Cuba, one feature of which was to be Cuban representation in the Spanish Cortes, was also tardily fulfilled, but more in appearance than in fact.

With the return of peace, commerce with Cuba developed fast, and was furthered by the mechanization of the sugar industry which was partly encouraged by American engineers and capitalists. The importance of the economic relation with Cuba as early as 1881 is testified by a United States consular report of that year quoted by Professor Leland Jenks in *Our Cuban Colony*, "Cuba has become commercially a dependency of the United States, while still remaining a political dependency of Spain."

THE WAR OF 1898

Economic stress was at the bottom of the revolution of 1895. Cane sugar had to compete in world markets with "protected" beet sugar whose production in Europe increased from two hundred thousand tons in 1850 to four million in 1894. In the latter year the United States in the Wilson tariff bill, in order to benefit Louisiana cane and western beet sugar producers, placed duties on sugar imports; the effect was hurtful to the Cuban industry. Meantime Spain would in no way relax the discriminatory tariffs on Cuban imports, so severe that it was cheaper to ship from the United States to Spain and back to Cuba, paying as well a profit to the Spanish trader, than to ship direct from the United States.

The combination of circumstances was disastrous. As Mr. Woodford, the United States Minister to Spain, said:

When exposed without mitigation to two systems of hostile tariffs, at a time when the price of cane sugar had been reduced by competition to a very low point, the Cuban producers threw up their hands in despair and the bands of laborers thus deprived of work were the first to swell the ranks of the insurgents.

Under the leadership of Máximo Gómez and Antonio Maceo the Cubans carried the war into every province of the island. Gómez declared that if the Spaniards would not give up Cuba, he would make it worthless to them; that might induce them to leave, he said, since they were in the island only for what they could get out of it. In keeping with this policy he issued two orders in 1895 to the effect that nobody was to engage in any commerce with towns in Spanish possession or raise any sugar, since these things would in fact redound to the advantage of Spain. Laborers were forbidden to work in sugar mills, and other properties that might be of aid to the Spaniards were put to the torch. A policy of destroying capital would damage Spanish landlords and at the same time spur American owners to bring pressure to bear on Washington for an intervention that would pacify the island.

The Spaniards were not behindhand in severe measures, though less shrewd in considering their effect in the manufacture of popular opinion in the United States. The keynote of General Weyler's methods was his so-called *reconcentrado* (reconcentration) policy. Men, women, and children, under penalty of death and forfeiture of property, were ordered to move into garrisoned Spanish towns or concentration camps, and no civilian was allowed to go into the rural districts without a passport. People crowded into the cities or camps, where no provisions were supplied to keep them alive, and they died by the thousands. It is said that fifty-two thousand perished in the province of Havana alone. Weyler had not taken into account the fact that he was creating sympathy for the Cuban cause in other countries. To the vast body of the American people Spanish retention of the island became as unacceptable as to the Cubans themselves, and demands for intervention in the name of humanity were made long before President McKinley finally took action.

American sympathy at first contented itself with various resolutions in Congress—for an inquiry into conditions in Cuba, for a recognition of belligerency, for intervention, and even for recognition of Cuban independence. In April, 1896, Congress passed a resolution recognizing Cuban belligerency and proposing a tender of American good offices on the basis of independence, leaving it to the President's decision whether the resolution should be carried into effect or not. President Cleveland, however, felt that there was as yet no basis in international law for a recognition even of belligerency; he began negotiations with Spain for the enactment of reforms satisfactory to the Cubans, but Tómas Estrada Palma, the Cuban agent in New York, subsequently first president of Cuba, let it be known that the Cubans were not interested in anything short of independence.

The United States elections were held in the fall of 1896. The Republicans, the party out of power, put a plank in their platform stating that since Spain had "lost control of Cuba" and was "unable to protect the property or lives of resident American citizens," the Government of the United States "should actively use its influence and good offices to restore peace and give independence to the Island." The Democratic platform simply extended "sympathy" to the Cubans in their struggle for independence, but Cleveland, the retiring President, devoted a long paragraph to Cuban affairs in his annual message of December, 1896. After mentioning a number of reasons for American concern, including the nearness of Cuba to the United States, an American investment of from thirty to fifty million dollars in the island,[3] and a volume of trade that had reached $103,000,000 in 1893 and $96,000,000 in 1894, he continued:

When the inability of Spain to deal successfully with the insurrection has become manifest, and it is demonstrated that her sovereignty is extinct in Cuba for all purposes of its rightful existence, and when a hopeless struggle for its reëstablishment has degenerated into a

[3] The total value of American investments in Cuba was estimated by Secretary of State Olney in his 1896 report as $45,000,000.

strife which means nothing more than the useless sacrifice of human life and the utter destruction of the very subject-matter of the conflict, a situation will be presented in which our obligations to the sovereignty of Spain will be superseded by higher obligations, which we can hardly hesitate to recognize and discharge.

Weyler's harsh policies occupied the attention of the press during 1897, and animosity toward Spain and sympathy for the insurgents were at fever heat. The new President, McKinley, in his first annual message, in December, 1897, remarked that the "near future will demonstrate" whether the United States should take action, holding that this must work out in a recognition of belligerency or independence, or in an intervention against both sides, or in favor of one side against the other. "I speak not of forcible annexation," he added, "for that cannot be thought of. That, by our code of morality, would be criminal aggression."

Yielding to this clamor in the United States, Spain recalled Weyler, and his successor announced a program of reform, including the establishment of Cuban home rule, with most of the functions of government in the hands of an elected legislature; but since "the supreme government of the colony shall be exercised by a governor-general," appointed by the crown, it was improbable that Spain meant to institute any comprehensive autonomy. In any event the law, which went into effect on January 1, 1898, came too late to alter the course of affairs. The Autonomists and the Reformists (a Spanish group) accepted it, but the die-hard Spaniards in the Constitutional Unionist party were uncompromising in their opposition; they organized demonstrations against home rule, and even against the United States and the Americans in Cuba. The American consul-general became alarmed, and requested that as an emergency measure a war vessel be sent to Havana to protect American citizens. Some days later, on February 15, 1898, this boat, the *Maine*, was mysteriously blown up in Havana harbor with a loss of 264 men. Whosever the act, its effect was to embroil Spain and the United States, and it was not possible from this time on to stem the American demand for the overthrow of Spanish rule.

The *Maine* incident was the incitement rather than the inevitable cause of the United States entry into war. McKinley's efforts to hold back American impatience received little help from the Spanish Government, which indulged in the maneuvering normal to peace-time diplomacy, as if unaware of the imminence of a crisis; offers of an armistice, of the sort of self-government that Canada enjoyed, and of an amnesty were offset by reservations that the powers of the central government under a Cuban constitution should not be lessened, that an amnesty be restricted to a period fixed by the Spanish Government, and that the *Maine* affair be arbitrated. Yielding at last to the pressures upon him, of which that created by Roosevelt's influence was not the least, McKinley remitted the whole question to Congress on April 11, 1898:

The long trial has proved that the object for which Spain has waged the war cannot be attained. The fire of insurrection may flame or may smoulder with varying seasons, but it has not been and it is plain it cannot be extinguished by present methods. The only hope of relief and repose from a condition which can no longer be endured is the enforced pacification of Cuba. In the name of humanity, in the name of civilization, in behalf of endangered American interests which give us the right and the duty to speak and to act, the war in Cuba must stop. In view of these facts and of these considerations, I ask the Congress to authorize and empower the President to take measures to secure a full and final termination of hostilities between the government of Spain and the people of Cuba, and to secure in the island the establishment of a stable government, capable of maintaining order and observing its international obligations, insuring peace and tranquillity and the security of its citizens as well as our own, and to use the military and naval forces of the United States as may be necessary for these purposes.

Congress passed a Joint Resolution on April 20 which meant a declaration of war on Spain. The Senate wished to recognize the Cuban Republic, but the House, on the personal intervention of the President, refused to concur; the resolution was, however, amended as follows:

That the United States hereby disclaims any disposition or intention to exercise sovereignty, jurisdiction, or control over said island except for the pacification thereof, and asserts its determination, when that is accomplished, to leave the government and control of the island to its people.

The war ran swiftly to an inevitable conclusion; by midsummer Spain was ready for peace, and on July 26, through the French Government, asked for conditions of peace. The President named the following terms as preliminary to negotiations:

1. "Relinquishment" by Spain of all claim of sovereignty over or title to Cuba, and immediate evacuation.

2. In lieu of indemnity, cession to the United States by Spain of "Porto Rico and other islands now under the sovereignty of Spain in the West Indies, and also the cession of an island in the Ladrones."

3. Retention of Manila by the United States until the disposition of the Philippines should be determined in the peace treaty.

Spain unwillingly accepted these terms, which were embodied in more ample form in a protocol of August 12; a new article made more ample provision for the evacuation of Spain's possessions in the West Indies.

In the negotiations Spain was ready, as the Spanish Minister of State said, to accept conditions for Cuba providing "absolute independence, or independence under an American protectorate, or annexation to the United States, preferring annexation, because this would guarantee better the security of the lives and property of Spaniards who resided or had estates there." The United States did not share Spain's apprehensions over Cuban independence, but in the disturbed condition of the island felt that Cuba might need the aid which it was disposed to give. For the time being the United States was to act as a trustee of the island and take responsibility "for the protection of life and property." Another clause of the treaty provided that on the termination of American occupancy the United States was to "advise any government established in the island to assume the same obligations." None of the Cuban debt, which had been incurred by Spain largely as the result of the war in Cuba, was to remain on Cuban shoulders. Among non-Cuban features of the treaty was the acquisition by the United States of Porto Rico, Guam, and the Philippines for a payment of twenty million dollars. The treaty was proclaimed on April 11, 1899.

MILITARY GOVERNMENT UNDER GENERAL WOOD

FROM the close of 1898 to the spring of 1902, the independence of Cuba was postponed, and the country was under a military government of the United States. During most of 1899 General John R. Brooke was in command, but in December of that year he was succeeded by General Leonard Wood, with Elihu Root, Secretary of War, in ultimate direction from Washington. Brooke relieved suffering, disbanded the army, provided revenue by reorganizing the customs service, took a census, pacified the island, and in general did the preliminary spade-work for General Wood, whose main task was to prepare Cuba for self-government.

In his message to Congress of April 11, 1898, McKinley made no reference to a Cuban "government," but spoke of the war between "Spain and the Cuban people," for the insurrectionists had not as yet been recognized even as belligerents. Naturally this attitude was not received with enthusiasm by the Cubans in the field; they had endured terrible hardships in behalf of independence, and saw no reason why they should not have it at once. They were suspicious of American intentions, despite the promise contained in the Joint Resolution of April 20, 1898, and it was clear that steps must be taken promptly to allay these suspicions. A law of elections must be promulgated. General Wood called an informal meeting of leading Cubans, at the same time submitting a plan prepared by Cuban officials under his direction. A majority of the notables favored a sweeping democratic suffrage, but the Governor adopted the opinions of the minority which accorded with his own. His plan provided that all native-born Cuban men who were at least twenty-one years old might vote, if they could read and write, or had $250 worth of property, or had served in the Cuban army during the war. The secret ballot and other familiar American features were also called for in the new law.

The first, a municipal, election under this law met with fair success. General Wood then announced a fresh step in the direction of independence. Acting on orders from Washington, he issued an order, July 25, 1900, for the election of a convention "to frame and adopt a Constitution for the people of Cuba, and, as a part thereof, to provide for and agree with the Government of the United States upon the relations to exist between that Government and the Government of Cuba."

The requirement for determining the nature of relations with the United States "as a part" of their own Constitution did not escape the notice of the Cuban politicians, but on assurances that the terms of the order would be modified they elected delegates. The Convention met at Havana on November 5, 1900, when General Wood read an order setting forth that the "first" duty of the delegates was to "frame and adopt a Constitution," and then "formulate what, in your opinion, ought to be the relations between Cuba and the United States." Afterward, "the Government of the United States will doubtless take such action on its part as shall lead to a final and authoritative agreement between the people of the two countries to the promotion of their common interests." So the delegates prepared a Constitution and signed it on February 21, 1901.

Mr. Root's Proposals.

Although the new Constitution paid slight attention to relations with the United States, Mr. Root interposed no objection to it. In his annual report for 1901 he remarked:

I do not fully agree with the wisdom of some of the provisions of this constitution; but it provides for a republican form of government; it was adopted after long and patient consideration and discussion; it represents the views of the delegates elected by the people of Cuba; and it contains no features which would justify the assertion that a government organized under it will not be one to which the United States may properly transfer the obligations for the protection of life and property under international law, assumed in the Treaty of Paris.

But strong as was his desire to prepare Cuba for self-government, Mr. Root was equally anxious to see Cuban-American relations formalized. The nature of United States requirements had already been made known in a dispatch which Secretary Root had sent to General Wood on February 9, 1901. This had been communicated to members of the Convention on February 15. After reciting the self-imposed duty assumed by the United States under the Joint Resolution of April 20, 1898, and the obligations toward Spain derived from the Treaty of Paris to provide for "protection of life and property" during the American occupation and upon its termination to "advise any government established in the island to assume the same obligations," Mr. Root discussed the kind of government that should be set up in Cuba, and made the following comment:[4]

It seems to me that no one familiar with the traditional and established policy of this country in respect to Cuba can find cause for doubt as to our remaining duty. It would be hard to find any single statement of public policy which has been so often officially declared by so great an array of distinguished Americans authorized to speak for the Government of the United States, as the proposition stated, in varying but always uncompromising and unmistakable terms, that the United States would not under any circumstances permit any foreign power other than Spain to acquire possession of the island of Cuba.

Jefferson and Monroe and John Quincy Adams and Jackson and Van Buren and Grant and Clay and Webster and Buchanan and Everett have all agreed in regarding this as essential to the interests and the protection of the United States. The United States has, and will always have, the most vital interest in the preservation of the independence which she has secured for Cuba, and in preserving the people of that island from the domination and control of any foreign power whatever. The preservation of that independence by a country so small as Cuba, so incapable, as she must always be, to contend by force against the great powers of the world, must depend upon her strict performance of international obligations, upon her giving due protection to the lives and property of the citizens of all other countries within her borders, and upon her never contracting any public debt which in the hands of the citizens of foreign powers shall constitute an obligation she is unable to meet. The United States has, therefore, not merely a moral obligation arising from her destruction

4 See Elihu Root, *The Military and Colonial Policy of the United States,* Ed. Robert Bacon and James Brown Scott, for references to the passages quoted.

of Spanish authority in Cuba and the obligations of the Treaty of Paris for the establishment of a stable and adequate government in Cuba, but it has a substantial interest in the maintenance of such a government.

We are placed in a position where, for our own protection, we have, by reason of expelling Spain from Cuba, become the guarantors of Cuban independence and the guarantors of a stable and orderly government protecting life and property in that island. Fortunately the condition which we deem essential for our own interests is the condition for which Cuba has been struggling, and which the duty we have assumed toward Cuba on Cuban grounds and for Cuban interests requires. It would be a most lame and impotent conclusion if, after all the expenditure of blood and treasure by the people of the United States for the freedom of Cuba and by the people of Cuba for the same object, we should, through the constitution of the new government, by inadvertence or otherwise, be placed in a worse condition in regard to our own vital interests than we were while Spain was in possession, and the people of Cuba should be deprived of that protection and aid from the United States which is necessary to the maintenance of their independence.

Mr. Root proceeded to recite five provisions which the United States felt that "the people of Cuba should desire to have incorporated in her fundamental law." Though in somewhat different phraseology, they were virtually the same as Articles one, two, three, four, and seven of the Platt Amendment, which was passed without giving the Cuban Convention much opportunity of discussing Mr. Root's suggestions. It passed the Senate on February 27 and the House on March 1.

THE PLATT AMENDMENT

CUBA was administered by the War Department, and the resolution which came to be known as the Platt Amendment was an amendment not to the Cuban Constitution, but to the army appropriation bill before the United States Congress. It was named after Senator Platt, chairman of the Committee on Foreign Relations of the Senate. Its terms are as follows:

Provided further, That in fulfilment of the declaration contained in the joint resolution approved April twentieth, eighteen hundred and ninety-eight, entitled "For the recognition of the independence of the people of Cuba, demanding that the Government of Spain relinquish its authority and government in the island of Cuba, and withdraw its land and naval forces from Cuba and Cuban waters, and directing the President of the United States to use the land and naval forces of the United States to carry these resolutions into effect," the President is hereby authorized to "leave the government and control of the island of Cuba to its people" so soon as a government shall have been established in said island under a constitution which, either as a part thereof or in an ordinance appended thereto, shall define the future relations of the United States with Cuba, substantially as follows:

I. That the government of Cuba shall never enter into any treaty or other compact with any foreign power or powers which will impair or tend to impair the independence of Cuba, nor in any manner authorize or permit any foreign power or powers to obtain by colonization or for military or naval purposes or otherwise, lodgment in or control over any portion of said island.

II. That said government shall not assume or contract any public debt, to pay the interest upon which, and to make reasonable sinking fund provision for the ultimate discharge of which the ordinary revenues of the island, after defraying the current expenses of government, shall be inadequate.

III. That the government of Cuba consents that the United States may exercise the right to intervene for the preservation of Cuban independence, the maintenance of a government adequate for the protection of life, property, and individual liberty, and for discharging the obligations with respect to Cuba imposed by the Treaty of Paris on the United States, now to be assumed and undertaken by the government of Cuba.

IV. That all acts of the United States in Cuba during its military occupancy thereof are ratified and validated, and all lawful rights acquired thereunder shall be maintained and protected.

V. That the government of Cuba will execute, and, as far as necessary, extend, the plans already devised or other plans to be mutually agreed upon, for the sanitation of the cities of the island, to the end that a recurrence of epidemic and infectious diseases may be prevented, thereby assuring protection to the people and commerce of Cuba, as well as to the commerce of the southern ports of the United States and the people residing therein.

VI. That the Isle of Pines shall be omitted from the proposed constitutional boundaries of Cuba, the title thereto being left to future adjustment by treaty.

VII. That to enable the United States to maintain the independence of Cuba, and to protect the people thereof, as well as for its own defense, the government of Cuba will sell or lease to the United States lands necessary for coaling or naval stations at certain specified points, to be agreed upon with the President of the United States.

VIII. That by way of further assurance the government of Cuba will embody the foregoing provisions in a permanent treaty with the United States.

In Cuba only the most conservative elements accepted the Amendment. Cubans in general complained bitterly that it allowed them less than independence and was therefore a violation of the promise contained in the Teller Amendment to the Joint Resolution. On this point it may be said that no promise of unconditioned sovereignty had been made. John Bassett Moore has succinctly stated the relation between the two documents in a communication to Professor Chapman:

The Spanish Commissioners, . . . early in the negotiations, proposed to cede Cuba to the United States; and I think they were surprised as well as chagrined when President McKinley declined to entertain the proposal. President McKinley, . . . in effect compelled the omission from the resolution of intervention, in April 1898, of a clause recognizing the insurgent organization called the Republic of Cuba, and the fact is well known that his reason for so doing was his belief that the United States, in intervening to expel by force the government of Spain, should, in the interest of all concerned, preserve its freedom to deal as might seem best, during the war and at its close, with conditions as they might then be found to exist. This was not conceived to be incompatible with the Teller resolution. Among the grounds on which the intervention of the United States was justified, abroad as well as at home, that which was most generally accepted was the need of putting an end to the disorders that had more or less prevailed in the island during the preceding thirty years. It is a very common thing, as the events of even the past few years have shown, for the period succeeding the establishment, by war, of the independence of a new state, to be characterized by tumults, by disregard of life and property, and by revolutionary activities, growing out of inexperience in government and the personal rivalries of political or military chieftains. It is equally notorious that such conditions have repeatedly given rise to foreign intervention, armed as well as unarmed, without other justification than that which international practice affords. It was considerations such as these that inspired the Platt Amendment; and they were reinforced by the further consideration that the United States would, in conformity with declarations repeatedly made in the course of the preceding hundred years, stand ready to protect the island's independence against attack. . . .[5]

Seeing that Mr. Root had at least the share of a joint draftsman of the Amendment, his contemporaneous observations are of particular value. On March 29, 1901, he wrote General Wood:[6]

It only signifies the formal action of the government of the United States, based on the just grounds of disaster or imminent peril, and in fact is no more than a declaration or recognition of the right of action which the United States had in April, 1898, as a result of the failure of Spain to govern Cuba. It does not give the United States any right which she does not already possess and she has not exercised, but it gives her, to the benefit of Cuba, a position between Cuba and foreign nations in the exercise of that right which can be of immense value in qualifying the United States to protect the independence of Cuba.

He thereupon instructed General Wood to convey to the Cuban Constitutional Convention the following communication:

You are authorized to state officially that in the view of the President the intervention described in the third clause of the Platt amendment is not synonymous with intermeddling or interference with the affairs of the Cuban Government, but the formal action of the Government of the United States, based upon just and substantial grounds, for the preservation of Cuban independence, and the maintenance of a government adequate for the protection of life, property, and individual liberty, and adequate for discharging the obligations with respect to Cuba imposed by the treaty of Paris on the United States.[7]

[5] *A History of the Cuban Republic*, pp. 643-645.
[6] *Cuba, Senado Memoria*, 1902-1904, p. 457.   [7] *Ibid.*, pp. 455-456.

Responding to the outburst of feeling in Cuba, the Constitutional Convention of Cuba rejected the Platt Amendment by a vote of twenty-four to two, and sent commissioners to Washington; to them Mr. Root reiterated that the Platt Amendment conveyed no limitation of Cuba's independence. The main points of the Root statement were:[8]

. . . By virtue of this clause (III) the European nations will not question the intervention of the United States in defense of Cuban independence. The first and third bases preserve the United States from seeming to be the aggressor when it faces other nations to defend the independence of Cuba. These clauses signify, further, that no nation may menace Cuban independence without preparing to combat the United States. Any nation which attempts to intervene in Cuba will have to declare war on the United States, thus becoming the aggressor, a position which gives the United States obvious advantages under international law. . . . Good diplomacy consists in so handling the way in which a conflict arises between two nations that it is the adversary which has violated the law. These clauses place the United States on the side of the law with respect to every other nation that attempts to endanger the independence of Cuba. . . . Clause III does not grant new rights, but it does give to the United States better facilities than those inherent in the Monroe Doctrine for the defense of Cuban independence. The letter to General Wood and the telegram with reference to said Clause III indicate that said clause does not signify either interference or intervention of any sort in the Government of Cuba. . . . Intervention in Cuban affairs will be resorted to only in case of great disturbances, similar to those which occurred in 1898, and with the sole and exclusive object of maintaining Cuban independence unimpaired. Intervention will only take place to protect the independence of the Cuban Republic from foreign attack, or when a veritable state of anarchy exists within the republic. This clause does not diminish Cuban independence; it leaves Cuba independent and sovereign under its own flag. The United States will come to the rescue only in extreme cases to help Cuba to preserve its absolute independence, and God grant that this extremity may never be presented. . . . The spirit, the tendency, the substance of the Platt Amendment is to establish in Cuba an independent and sovereign nation. . . .

[8] *Cuba, Senado Memoria,* 1902-1904, pp. 469 ff.

Meanwhile, until the proposals should be adopted, the military government would be maintained.

The Constitutional Convention again considered the Amendment and, in accepting it by the bare margin of fifteen to fourteen, added its own interpretation, to which the United States Government replied that acceptance could not be qualified. On June 12, 1901, by a vote of sixteen to eleven, with four members absent, the Amendment was at length adopted, and in due course was added as an "appendix" to the Constitution, together with the Permanent Treaty, which consists of the first seven articles of the Amendment which was signed at Havana on May 22, 1903.

The election of a Cuban government to take over control of the island's affairs was the next step of the military government. General Wood issued an order fixing the date of a presidential election on December 31, 1901. The Nationalists would have been glad to support the veteran and patriot Máximo Gómez as their candidate for the presidency, but Gómez declined to run. "Men of war, for war," he said, "and those of peace, for peace." With Gómez out of the running, the two leading candidates were Tómas Estrada Palma and Bartolome Masó, veterans both of the two Cuban wars. Estrada Palma had won general respect by his conduct as Cuban delegate abroad during the '95-'98 revolution. He had the support of Máximo Gómez, the most popular man in Cuba, the backing of the Nationalist and Republican parties, the two most powerful political groups in the island, and the good will of the United States. Masó and his friends, foreseeing defeat, objected to the constitution of the Central Board of Scrutiny, an electoral board which contained Nationalists and Republicans but no partisans of Masó, and refused to go to the polls. Estrada Palma was thus elected first president of the Republic of Cuba, and the military government wound up its work and turned over the administration on May 20, 1902, in the same room where three and a half years before Spanish authority had been surrendered to the American forces. The last civil order of the military government was the promulgation of the Constitution of the new republic.

Wood's Achievements.

The work of Leonard Wood in Cuba has been extolled by opinion of all shades. His liking for autocratic forms has been scored but has not blinded judgment of his monumental achievements, which have earned for him a rank among colonial administrators with Cromer and Lyautey.

Writing at the close of the United States intervention of 1906-1909, but with the work of 1899-1902 more particularly in mind, a well-known Englishman, Sir Harry Johnston, said:

The impartial traveler cannot but feel sincere admiration for the results of American intervention in Cuba. Nowhere has the work of the Anglo-Saxon been better done or with happier results. In fine, all has been carried out quietly, unostentatiously, honestly, and in a manner to attract and conciliate the Cuban people. It has been an achievement in the best "Anglo-Saxon" style.[9]

Sir Harry Johnston is known to approve of imperial administration, but Martínez Ortiz,[10] a notable Cuban scholar, shares his view:

Very rarely will history offer twenty-four months of administration more fruitful than his. . . . If the government of General Wood was very notable from an administrative point of view, from a political point of view it was even more remarkable. It may be said that Cuba owes to him the constitution of its government in the form in which it was established—a form which permits it to go on strengthening itself. . . . Beyond a doubt the permanent relations between Cuba and the United States were prepared in the first place by Secretary Elihu Root, but without the very effective aid of Mr. Wood things might have taken a quite different course. . . . He maintained himself relatively aloof from intimate association with Cubans, but was accustomed to do justice to the personal qualities of prominent and virtuous sons of the country.

Among Wood's main achievements were: prison reform; reform of the courts; adjustment of relations between church and

[9] "An Englishman's Impressions of American Rule in Cuba," *McClure's*, Sept., 1909, p. 496.

[10] *Cuba: los primeros años de independencia*, I, 387-397. This work is an outstanding history of the period, 1899-1909.

state; extermination of yellow fever; provision for the care of the sick and insane; establishment of an educational system; erection of public works, including harbor improvements; road building; the installation of sanitary systems; railway development and regulation; assistance to agriculture; suppression of banditry and maintenance of law and order; improvement of the customs service, including a new tariff law; establishment of a national library; installation of municipal governments, with election of officials; establishment of a Cuban government.

These were all solid accomplishments, and none was more noteworthy than the fight against yellow fever,[11] with which the name of Dr. Walter Reed is inseparably associated. Yellow fever had had a long and fearsome history in the Americas. Endemic in Havana, it was epidemic in the United States, and Havana was considered its focal point for the whole western hemisphere. So successful was the campaign against the disease that as compared with the 103 deaths in Havana in 1899 and the 310 in 1900, 1901 presented the following record of deaths: January, 7; February, 5; March, 1; April, May, and June, none; July, 1; August, 2; September, 2; the following nine months, none.[12]

The New Treaties.

Estrada Palma put through the conventions which were to determine Cuba's relations with the United States. The Reciprocity Treaty[13] was negotiated by Tasker H. Bliss, representing President Roosevelt, in the early fall of 1902, and signed on December 11, 1902. The treaty caused much skirmishing in Congress, but was eventually ratified late in 1903; Cuba ratified it on March 28, 1903. In November, 1902, the United States Government had suggested the cession of the bays of Guantánamo, Cienfuegos, Bahía Honda, and Nipe, but the diplomacy of Estrada Palma was successful in limiting the transaction to the rental of naval sta-

11 The full story has been written by Russell H. Fitzgibbon, *Relations between the United States and Cuba, 1900-1917*, Univ. of Indiana, 1928 (MS.).

12 Also see Leonard Wood, "The Military Government of Cuba," in *Annals of the American Academy*, Vol. XXI, Philadelphia, 1903; and Albert Gardner Robinson, *Cuba and the Intervention*.

13 The Reciprocity Treaty is discussed on pp. 54 ff.

tions in the bays of Guantánamo and Bahía Honda for such time as the United States might need them. By a later treaty of December 27, 1912 the United States gave up its rights at Bahía Honda for increased advantages in the bay of Guantánamo, and now has virtually complete control over a tract of land at Caimanera in this bay. This treaty still remains unratified.

In a treaty signed July 16, 1903, the United States surrendered to Cuba all claim to sovereignty over the Isle of Pines. This treaty was not ratified within the time prescribed; so a new treaty was signed on March 2, 1904, without any limitations as to date of ratification, stating that the "relinquishment" was "in consideration of the grants of coaling and naval stations" already made by Cuba to the United States. The Senate failed to ratify it. In April, 1907, in a case involving payment of customs duties, the Supreme Court of the United States held that the island was *de facto* Cuban territory, since the United States had never taken possession, yet on a vote in the Senate in 1908 the treaty was rejected. After repeated attempts of various presidents to revive it, the treaty was ratified in 1925. During the whole period the Isle of Pines was administered as a part of Cuba.

INTERVENTION UNDER ROOSEVELT

The Revolt of 1906.

The new Republic showed from the first the characteristic weakness of Caribbean politics in the subordination of public duty to private interest. Little difference in principle existed between the two principal parties in Cuba, Moderates and Liberals. "Ins" and "outs" contested violently for control of elections. The Moderates at first represented the "ins," and since Estrada Palma leaned to the Moderates, he accepted from them nomination for a second term. The Liberals nominated a soldier-politician, José Miguel Gómez.

The Moderates made up a registry of 432,313 voters, of whom at least 150,000 represented fraudulent names, in consequence of which the Liberals abstained from voting, proclaiming at the same time that their party "declines to be responsible for the future."

In Caribbean politics this usually means that the offended party intends to seek its rights through revolution. So it happened in Cuba in 1906, and the Government proved unable to defend itself; the rebel "armies" threatened the capital itself. Not much loss of life was sustained but the outbreak aroused a general feeling of insecurity and fear. Business came to a standstill, and the problem of subsistence in the capital was serious.

On September 8, 1906, Consul-General Steinhart, who was in charge during the absence of the United States Minister, telegraphed to the State Department:

Absolutely confidential. Secretary of State, Cuba, has requested me, in name of President Palma, to ask President Roosevelt send immediately two vessels; one to Havana, other to Cienfuegos; they must come at once. Government forces are unable to quell rebellion. The Government is unable to protect life and property. President Palma will convene Congress next Friday, and Congress will ask for our forcible intervention.[14]

Two days later he sent another message:

President here worried because no reply received my message, and asks war vessels be sent immediately.

The same day Acting Secretary of State Bacon, in the absence of Secretary Root (then in South America), replied that two ships were being sent, but remarked "the President directs me to state that perhaps you do not yourself appreciate the reluctance with which this country would intervene," following this up with a letter of the 11th, saying that President Roosevelt believed "actual, immediate intervention to be out of the question." On succeeding days Steinhart sent more and more urgent messages. On the 12th he transmitted a memorandum by the Cuban Secretary of State to the effect that the government was unable to withstand the revolutionists, also saying

President Estrada Palma asks for American intervention and begs that President Roosevelt send to Habana with the greatest secrecy and rapidity 2000 or 3000 men.

14 Dispatches and documents quoted and not otherwise indicated are to be found in Taft and Bacon, *Report,* U.S., 59th Cong., 2d Sess. (1906-1907), Ser. 5105, H.D. 500.

In his cablegram of the 13th Steinhart said

President Palma, the Republic of Cuba, through me officially asks for American intervention because he can not prevent rebels from entering cities and burning property.

He further stated that Estrada Palma was resolved to resign and turn over the government to any representative whom the President of the United States might designate. Next day he cabled that Estrada Palma, the Vice-President, and all the Secretaries proposed to resign, which would mean a condition of anarchy, since there would be no legally constituted power to convoke Congress.

It was an inauspicious moment for United States action. Secretary Root was just completing a tour of South America in an attempt to allay suspicions of United States policy; furthermore, it had long ago been decided in Washington that the interests of the United States were best served by the existence of an independent republic of Cuba. Yet it seemed that something had to be done. As a first step Roosevelt sent an open letter on September 14 to the Cuban minister to Washington urging the Cubans to sink their differences. He announced his intention of sending his Secretary of War, Mr. Taft, and the Assistant Secretary of State, Robert Bacon, to Havana to aid the Cubans to that end. The letter created an excellent impression both in Cuba and in the United States, and possibly saved the revolution from entering a dangerously destructive stage.

The Taft Mission.

Taft and Bacon, accompanied by the American Minister, reached Havana on September 19. They were the last hope for a solution of the problem without formal intervention, but though they spared no effort to bring about an adjustment of affairs, they were foredoomed to failure. In his first conversation with the commissioners the Cuban President made a statement of

his efforts to teach his people the knowledge of self-government which by twenty years of residence in the United States he had acquired from association with the American people, of his successful handling of the finances of the Cuban Government, of the economy of expenditure in his administration, of the encouragement he had given to the investment of foreign capital, and of the consequent prosperity which had come to Cuba during the four years of his incumbency as President. He manifested an intense interest in the large balance which there was in the treasury, and the greatest regret that that balance was likely to be much reduced by the extravagance of expenditures required in the efforts made and making to suppress the insurrection. He said that he had insisted upon the maintenance of all the guaranties of civil liberty under the constitution, and had declined to suspend them until the insurrection had proceeded to a point where it could not be avoided; that for six months he had been made aware of the plotting which was going on against the government, but that so great was the prosperity and the comfort of the people, and so successful had his government been in arts of peace, he declined to take rigorous steps against the conspirators, for he had not supposed that such an insurrection as had occurred was possible. He deplored what he regarded as a lack of gratitude and patriotism on the part of those who were supporting the insurrection, and gave us a number of instances tending to show that the leaders of the insurrection were moved only by the basest of purposes—by a pecuniary greed and for office. His demeanor was dignified and earnest, the evidences of his sorrow were touching, and what he said made a deep impression on us.

It was his privately expressed view that

from the moment the Government treated with the rebels it placed itself on an inclined plane of interminable concessions, initiating an era of successive insurrections, and putting the stability of future governments on a frail basis. I could never consent to be an accomplice in such evil in exchange for being permitted to continue to occupy the Presidential chair of the Republic.[15]

The commissioners early in the inquiry came to the conclusion that the government procedure in the 1905 elections had been fraudulent. On September 21 Taft reported to Roosevelt

if the present government could maintain itself, or if it had a moral support or following which would be useful in case of interven-

[15] *Report of Provisional Administration from October 13, 1906 to December 1, 1907*, pp. 13, 14, and 15.

tion, Bacon and I would be strongly in favor of supporting it as the regular and constitutional government, because the election was held under forms of law and has been acted upon and recognized as valid, but the actual state of affairs is such that we would be fighting the whole Cuban people in effect by intervening to maintain this government.

The Moderates agreed to accept the arbitration of the American commissioners, provided the insurrectionists would first lay down their arms; and gave assurances that all the issues in dispute could be adjusted if the dignity of the government were conserved by its not being required to treat with armed rebels.

Zayas was empowered by the Central Revolutionary Committee of the Liberal party and by the insurrectionist generals to act on behalf of the opposition. The commissioners' stand on the election had been interpreted as a great Liberal victory, and Zayas therefore was eager to accept their suggestions for the resignation of all officials elected in 1905 except the President and Vice-President, for the needed electoral, municipal, and judiciary laws and a civil service law covering government employees in general, and for a specified date in the near future for new elections. He would not consider, however, a prior laying down of arms by the Constitutionalist forces; he continued the negotiations thenceforth on the basis of a compromise without reference to the arms question. Since Estrada Palma and the Moderates were adamant on this point, the conversations were fruitless, and the President reiterated his decision to resign, expecting that his resignation and that of all executive officials and the dissolution of Congress without electing a successor would force the appointment of a provisional government by the United States. The Liberals also generally favored intervention, because, as Taft declared, "they can earn their victory in the holding of new elections." Each side was eager to make it appear that the other had caused the intervention.

Those who took the field in this insurrection were the least stable elements in Cuban society. Mr. Taft's comment was:

The even remote possibility suggested in your telegram of last night that under any possible hypothesis the Platt Amendment may require the present insurrectionary force to be treated as a government *de facto* makes me shiver at the consequences. It is not a government with any of its characteristics, but only an undisciplined horde of men under partisan leaders. The movement is large and formidable and commands the sympathy of a majority of the people of Cuba, but they are the poorer classes and the uneducated. The Liberal party, which is back of the movement, has men of ability and substance in it, but they are not titular leaders of the insurgent forces in whom such a government *de facto* must vest if in anybody.[16]

He was horrified at the thought that the creation of a "provisional government . . . would probably have involved the immediate appointment of insurgent generals to office."

Taft as Governor.

The Cuban Congress assembled on September 28. The President offered the resignations of his Secretaries and his own, and then the Vice-President resigned. The Moderates, by deciding not to attend, left Congress without a quorum. Cuba was thus without a government; nobody would take control. In consequence, on September 29, 1906, Taft published the following proclamation, approved by President Roosevelt, taking over the government on behalf of the United States:

To the people of Cuba:

The failure of Congress to act on the irrevocable resignation of the President of the Republic of Cuba, or to elect a successor, leaves this country without a government at a time when great disorder prevails, and requires that, pursuant to a request of President Palma, the necessary steps be taken in the name and by the authority of the President of the United States to restore order, protect life and property in the Island of Cuba and islands and keys adjacent thereto, and, for this purpose, to establish therein a provisional government.

The provisional government hereby established by direction and in the name of the President of the United States will be maintained only long enough to restore order and peace and public confidence, and then to hold such elections as may be necessary to determine those persons upon whom the permanent government of the Republic should be devolved.

[16] *Report of Provisional Administration from October 13, 1906 to December 1, 1907,* p. 477.

In so far as is consistent with the nature of a provisional government established under the authority of the United States, this will be a Cuban government, conforming, as far as may be, to the constitution of Cuba. The Cuban flag will be hoisted as usual over the Government buildings of the island. All the executive departments and the provincial and municipal governments, including that of the city of Habana, will continue to be administered as under the Cuban Republic. The courts will continue to administer justice, and all laws not in their nature inapplicable by reason of the temporary and emergent character of the government will be in force.

President Roosevelt has been most anxious to bring about peace under the constitutional government of Cuba, and has made every endeavor to avoid the present step. Longer delay, however, would be dangerous.

Taft's proclamation made it clear that the country was to have a Cuban government, under the Cuban flag, though temporarily in the hands of the United States. The action of the United States met with general approval; it had obviously been undertaken unwillingly, and it promised a respite from strife and insecurity.

For the time being Taft acted as governor, and busied himself in solving the more immediate problems connected with the reestablishment of order. Two thousand United States marines were landed and most of them were stationed seven miles west of the center of Havana. Later fifty-six hundred more men were distributed in various parts of the island. It was the plan to employ them "as a background to give confidence," using the rural guards for the suppression of disorder. The most pressing problem Taft had to settle concerned the disarming and disbanding of the insurrectionist forces and the no less difficult task of discharging the national militia, which in some instances was "even more unruly and less disciplined than the insurgents." The insurgents agreed to lay down their arms, restore any property they had taken, and return to their homes, on the understanding that the United States provisional government would carry out the settlement that Taft and Bacon had suggested in so far as it might then be applicable. In two weeks the disarming was well under way.

Mr. Taft released all political prisoners on the day of his proclamation, and followed this up a few days later with an amnesty. In the distribution of political patronage the insurrectionist leaders wanted Mr. Taft to put Moderates out of office and replace them with Liberals; they were advised "that it was not the intention of the provisional government to oust faithful public servants to make places for Liberals," but were assured that Liberals would be preferred whenever vacancies occurred, "until an equality was restored."

The Magoon Government.

After completing these tasks looking to an immediate settlement Mr. Taft was recalled to Washington and replaced by Charles Edward Magoon. Assurance that Magoon would follow the course that Taft had marked out was provided by making him subject to the United States Secretary of War, an office that Taft continued to hold. At the same time it was decided to regard affairs in Cuba as civil and not military.

The program of the provisional government seemed simple: to hold an honest election and turn the island back to its people as soon as possible. It was expected that this would take only a few months, but an examination of Cuban law revealed that the government would have to undertake a considerable amount of legislation before it could liquidate its program. The great body of Cuban law consisted of provisions enacted for the Spanish peninsula, modified for Cuba by royal orders or by orders of the military government of the United States or laws of the Cuban Congress. Most of it was monarchical in form and directly contrary to the spirit of the excessively liberal Cuban Constitution. The Cuban Congress, however, was too little informed about legislative matters and too busy with political discussions to enact the supplementary laws needed to give full effect to the Constitution. This failure of Congress was one of the important causes of the revolution of 1906. It was impossible to do the work through the medium of the Cuban Congress, since the commission had stated that the elections to Congress in 1905 had been vitiated by fraud, and had made the resignation of the members one of the tenets in their peace compromise. That left but half a Congress, not enough for the legal quorum of two-thirds, and it was decided that the provisional government should dispense with Congress. On December 3, 1906, Governor Magoon formally vacated the places of the congressmen elected in 1905, and himself took over responsibility for legislation. An Advisory Law Commission, consisting of nine Cubans and three Americans, was appointed to prepare new laws; its chairman was Colonel Enoch Herbert Crowder, who was destined to play a great part in Cuban affairs. The commission, which entered upon its duties on December 24, 1906, was first charged with the preparation of five laws suggested by Taft and Bacon, concerning elections, provinces, municipalities, the judiciary, and the civil service, but it proved necessary to make other enactments.

Elections were held in the fall of 1908, with General Menocal the candidate of the newly formed Conservative party, a successor of the Moderates, and José Miguel Gómez the standard bearer of the Liberals. In what has by common consent been regarded as a well-handled, honest election, Gómez obtained the victory. No doubt desirous of winding up the intervention before his term expired in March, 1909, Roosevelt gave orders early in 1908 that Cuba should be turned over to its own officials not later than February 1, 1909; and this took place on January 28, 1909.

Comment on Intervention.

This was the only intervention which the United States has formally and constitutionally made. In similar circumstances in 1917 and in 1924 the United States upheld the constituted power, because this seemed the simplest way both to avoid complications and to check civil war. In 1906 the United States was experimenting with a new Caribbean policy growing out of the construction of the Panama Canal. If the Taft inquiry had never begun the State Department might have supported Estrada Palma, right or wrong, but commissioners on the ground could hardly simplify the problem in this fashion. Moreover, they quickly found themselves in *de facto* possession of internal responsibility. "Had the legislators chosen the first man who passed the door," said a Cuban publicist, "intervention would have been averted."

The operation of the intervention government has been much criticized. The Magoon government tried to satisfy the place-hunters in order to keep turbulent spirits from stirring up trouble. The politicians were allowed to fill vacancies, Liberals receiving the preference on the theory that they had not previously been accorded their fair share of the spoils. The policy was calculated to keep the peace, but it gave the Cubans a handle that they were not slow to grasp; in recent years they have been prone to excuse existing corruption on the ground that Magoon introduced the *botella*,[17] ignoring the fact that the *botella* under other names had been employed almost from the day the Spaniards set foot in Cuba. As to the provisional government's prodigality in this respect Martínez Ortiz says:

The governor defended himself from his critics by saying he was doing nothing but accede to the requests of the great Cuban politicians. He washed his hands of the matter; he could not stop to be proper when those who were most interested were desirous of throwing the house through the window.[18]

Magoon yielded too easily to the importunings of politicians in granting pardons. But he had some excuse in the disorder of the times, and especially in the severity of the Spanish law, which gave a trial judge no option for leniency in imposing sentence after technical guilt had been established. And, in general, it must be said that the blunders of the second intervention were mostly of the sort inevitable in American administration at a distance. They sprang from the necessity of governing Cuba with an eye upon Washington politics. They were affected by the difficulties of fulfilling a major obligation intact to Cuba, under a constitutional scheme which enabled Congress to hold up appropriations for an army of pacification at any time, or to impose additional guaranties, fresh Platt Amendments, as a condition for its withdrawal.[19]

17 The word *botella*, or bottle, is used in the sense of a nursing-bottle containing rich milk for the political baby.

18 Martínez Ortiz, *op. cit.*, II, 853.

19 Leland H. Jenks, *Our Cuban Colony*, pp. 102-103.

CHANGING BASES OF RELATIONS

Gómez and Menocal.

Though Gómez's improprieties were well known and generally admitted, he was the most popular of Cuban presidents, because, as Professor Chapman says, he was "a *simpático* in the full sense of that delightful Spanish word." His policy, if such it could be called, was to give the country an administration favorable to business; in his message to Congress, November 1, 1909, he said, "In my program of government I put economic interests above every other public question." He proceeded to build up a strong military establishment, making sure that nobody would do to him what he and the other Liberal leaders had done to Estrada Palma. He allowed the Magoon-built roads to go to ruin, he built a number himself which were in turn abandoned by his successor, and he revived the Spanish tradition of handing out political plums. Gómez several times recommended the enactment of laws to supplement the Constitution, but the request received little attention from Congress, the nature of whose interest in national affairs may to some extent be measured by its first four items of legislation. One was a political spoils act which deprived mayors (*alcaldes*) of their proper and legitimate functions; another restored cockfighting; the third was a notorious amnesty bill; and the fourth was an even more notorious lottery law.

Gómez and Zayas had been bitter rivals for the Liberal nomination in 1908, and when force of circumstances compelled the latter to give way he did so only on the promise of Gómez to support him for the presidency in 1912. When the time came Gómez vigorously opposed the Zayas candidacy on the ground of Zayas' lack of respectability as a candidate, hoping to succeed himself, despite his single-term preëlection promise. But Zayas won the nomination, whereupon Gómez and his most partisan followers threw their influence to the Conservative candidate, General Menocal, who came off victorious.

Menocal had close American affiliations. At the age of two he had been taken to the United States, whither his father emigrated when forced to leave Cuba at the time of the Ten Years' War.

Menocal spent much of his boyhood on a plantation in Mexico, but was educated in the United States, attending the Maryland College of Agriculture and eventually obtaining a degree in engineering at Cornell in 1888. He worked at his profession, at first in Nicaragua in connection with interoceanic canal projects, and then in Cuba. At the outbreak of the war in 1895 he enlisted as a private, rose quickly, and attained the rank of major-general. Under the United States military government Menocal was for a time chief of police of Havana, then inspector of lighthouses, but resigned in 1899 to go into business with the Cuban American Sugar Company. For that company he set up the Chaparra sugar plantation, which under his management became the largest estate of its kind in the world. While popular generally among his countrymen, he was accused by many Liberals of being an annexationist because of his long stay in the United States and his close relations with American business.

During most of Menocal's first administration, 1913 to 1917, the government was in difficulties. Gómez left only a million and a half dollars in the treasury, along with unpaid debts enough to cause a substantial deficit. The 1913-1914 and 1914-1915 crops were poor. The World War for a time upset normal foreign trade; Cuban tobacco, for example, was virtually outlawed in European markets as a luxury which did not contribute toward victory. It was the war need for sugar that for good or ill put Cuba's economy on a one-crop basis. The 1915-1916 sugar crop was a good one, and the high prices for the product ushered in a period of abounding prosperity. In 1914 Menocal established a Cuban monetary system on the same basis as that of the United States, and established United States money as legal tender. In 1915 he permitted sugar brokers to quote their commodity in American money and in cents per pound, replacing the former system of Spanish weights and money.

Taft-Knox "Preventive Policy."

The basis of United States relations with Cuba has changed since 1909, when the first use of the Platt Amendment in active form came to an end. Then, as we have seen, the United States was reluctant to intervene at all, still more to establish a provisional government as it felt obliged to do. Toward the close of the intervention this reluctance produced the injunction to the administrators in Cuba to "keep things quiet." The injunction in its turn produced the Taft-Knox "preventive policy," a sort of police power for Cuba, like that which President Roosevelt had applied to the rest of the Caribbean. Its purpose was to keep peace in Cuba and to stay out of Cuba, and the reconciliation of this dual policy led to what its critics called "continuous intermeddling." President Taft knew how easy it was to start a revolution in Cuba and therefore how difficult it was to avoid intervention. In explaining the preventive policy in an interview with the Cuban Minister to Washington, March 12, 1912, he said[20] that it "consisted in doing all within its (the United States') power to induce Cuba to avoid every reason that would make intervention possible at any time." Thus, fearing that a given incident might turn out to be the germ of another revolution, his administration was quick to "view with alarm," even though the sequel often proved that the origin of the trouble had been of trivial import. In nearly all these affairs the object of admonition was to try to prevent any development of a situation that might cause intervention.

The United States soon had occasion to apply the new policy in connection with a revolutionary threat by an organization known as the Veteranists. Secretary Knox notified the Government of Cuba that the situation caused the United States "grave concern," intimating that the laws should not be "defied" (in the way threatened by the Veteranists), and remarking that Cuba ought to prevent any development which might compel the United States Government "to consider what measures it must take." Clearly this was a threat of intervention. Fearing that the United States, once in, might never retire again, the veterans' organization in March, 1912, reached an agreement with the government whereby the campaign against officeholders was dropped and the veterans consented to act merely as a benevolent association and to aid the authorities as supplementary guardians of the peace.

Mr. Knox made use of the same policy, though with less success,

[20] Jenks, *op. cit.*, p. 325.

in "somewhat steadying the situation and thereby assisting the government of Cuba" to put down the uprising of a negro political party under Estenoz, in 1912. A race war broke out on May 20, the tenth anniversary of the republic, and though it was soon well in hand everywhere except in Oriente, the whole island was alarmed, and these fears communicated themselves to the Government of the United States. The American Minister, insisting that "this ought not to be considered as an intervention," announced certain United States naval dispositions in Cuban waters and, notwithstanding the protests of Gómez, a body of marines was landed at Daiquiri near Santiago. Mr. Knox,[21] in reiterating that protection is not intervention, asserted that the spirit of the measures taken "has been well called a 'preventive' policy."

The American forces remained on Cuban soil for several weeks, affording protection to foreign-owned mines and sugar estates. In June, over the objections of the Cuban Government, two American war vessels were sent to Havana, which by this time was in a state of panic. The Cuban Government got the upper hand over the rebel forces, and by mid-July the revolt was over, to the great relief of the nervous Taft government. The revolution cost the lives of Estenoz himself and some three thousand of his followers.

In the field of finance the preventive policy was expressed by a declaration to the Cubans that in the opinion of the United States Article II of the Permanent Treaty[22] prohibited Cuba from assuming or contracting without American consent any public debt in excess of or in addition to the debt already contracted or authorized.[23] Article III was even made the support of an objection to the Zapata Swamp concession to a Cuban company, charged by the United States Minister to be "a specious pretext for giving away incalculable millions in timber and charcoal woods." The right of intervention under Article III, said the United States Government,

. . . entitles this government to caution the Cuban Government against adopting an improvident or otherwise objectionable fiscal

---

[21] *For. Rel.*, 1912, p. 248.
[22] For text of Treaty and Platt Amendment, see pp. 16 ff.
[23] Final message of Governor Magoon, January 28, 1909, *Supplemental Report, Provisional Governor of Cuba*, p. 9.

policy on the ground that such policy might ultimately, either by itself or in connection with general conditions in Cuba, produce a situation there requiring the United States to intervene for any of the purposes recited in this article. . . .

The timber proved of little value, and this, together with the alteration in the concession terms, led to the State Department's withdrawal of its objections.

On the same ground the United States expressed disapproval[24] of the exchange of the "Arsenal" lands, government property along Havana harbor, for the Villanueva tract, belonging to the United Railways, an English company, an exchange which created a scandal in Havana on account of the belief that a stupendous amount of political graft was involved. The theory seems to have been that the exchange might make the Cuban Government not "adequate for the protection of life, property, and individual liberty," because of the injury to its credit.[25]

Extension of Policy under Wilson.

The Wilson administration, already in office when Menocal came to power, continued the "preventive policy" and was soon enveloped in entanglements. A day after its assumption of office Secretary Bryan cabled the American Minister in Havana to secure the presidential veto of an amnesty bill which had just been passed by the Cuban Congress. The State Department took the stand that the object of the bill was to shield officials of the Gómez administration from prosecution for graft and other offenses, and the argument apparently was that if these prosecutions did not take place Cuba's credit would be affected. In spite of the uproar which this suggestion aroused in Cuba, Menocal eventually vetoed the amnesty bill.

Another entanglement was the Ports Company affair. A plan for dredging and otherwise improving Cuban harbors brought in United States and British capital. The Cuban Government's decrees were so variable and arbitrary that the owners of the bonds of the Ports Company enlisted American support. The United States represented to Cuba that its failure to give compensation

[24] *For. Rel.*, 1912, p. 315.
[25] Articles on "Cuba," in *New International Yearbook.*

for the company's claims amounted to a violation of Article III of the Permanent Treaty. A compromise was later arranged which permitted the United States to end its connection with the affair.

The "preventive policy" involved an active interest on the part of the United States in the presidential elections—always a low spot in the Cuban political weather map. Trouble early began to brew over the 1916 election. The current turned against Menocal from the time he decided to run for reëlection in 1916 in violation of a one-term promise. Opposed by leading men of his own party, he nevertheless gained the nomination, making use of the conventional corrupt and forcible methods. Meanwhile Gómez and Zayas had temporarily buried the hatchet, and Zayas became the Liberal candidate. The normal campaign of violence ensued. The Liberals made it clear that they intended to win, if not at the polls, then through the medium of revolution; the Conservatives swore they would carry the election at all costs. So the episode of 1905-1906 repeated itself.

The number of votes cast was nearly double the number of eligible voters. The Liberals would probably have won in a fair election, and the Menocal government hesitated to appropriate the victory; not for two months was a Conservative success declared. Protests under the law brought matters eventually before the Supreme Court, which called for new elections in a few precincts of Santa Clara and Oriente provinces, as the vote of those precincts, which were reputedly Liberal, had "disappeared." The gain of either Santa Clara or Oriente would have decided the issue in the Liberal favor.

We have already observed that when opposition parties in certain Latin American countries are convinced that the government will not give them fair treatment, they withdraw from any attempt at securing victory at the polls, holding that it would be of no avail, and concede the legal victory to the government party. Revolution being their only redress, they engage in civil war. This was what happened in 1917 in Cuba. The Liberals had no doubt of their ability to win in a revolution and on February 10, several days before the date set for the first of the partial elections, Gómez raised the standard of revolt in the province of Santa Clara.

During the time between the elections of November and the outbreak of the revolution in February the United States had by no means been an indifferent spectator of the Cuban scene. Indeed, the Washington authorities were more than usually interested in the maintenance of peace, for it was becoming increasingly clear that the United States must enter the war against Germany. In this enterprise the Cuban sugar crop would be indispensable, and, in consequence, the State Department was not disposed to see it destroyed by civil war. As early as November, 1916, the United States Minister announced that all should respect the law, attaching special responsibility to those in high places.

Upon the outbreak of hostilities in February, 1917, this attitude became more and more insistent. On February 11 in a long note to the Cuban Government Secretary Lansing urged both parties to compose their differences by lawful methods, calling attention to a similar controversy in the history of the United States, the Hayes-Tilden election, which had been settled peacefully, "even though the decision favored the candidate that received a minority of the votes."

The note was published after the Liberals had taken the field. This prompted another statement, February 14, saying that the United States gave its "confidence and support" only to constitutional governments. There was also a vague statement to the effect that the United States would oppose such governments as came to power through revolution or other illegal means. Five days later, on the 19th, a third note was given to the press in which the United States announced that it supported the government and that the insurrection, which was characterized as "lawless and unconstitutional," would "not be countenanced." The United States would hold the leaders of the revolt responsible for damage to the persons and property of foreigners and would study what attitude should be adopted toward those who were participating in the disturbances.[26]

The strong tone of these communications was partly explained by the approach of war between the United States and Germany; Liberal action at a time when the United States was about to de-

[26] *For. Rel.,* Feb. 19, 1917.

clare war on Germany was in some quarters looked upon as a pro-German maneuver. Another explanation was that American public opinion favored Menocal, not only because of his American connections, but also because much had been written about the corruption of the Gómez administration and the uprightness of the government of Menocal. Furthermore, the Liberals were regarded as more hostile to the United States than the Conservatives.

The notes virtually settled the issue in Cuba; the Liberals could not expect to win in the face of United States opposition. So they tried to force Menocal into an acceptance of their views as the only means of avoiding intervention, which had been fatal to the government party in a similar situation in 1906. Menocal, however, took the opposite course. He announced that there was no need for intervention, that he would put down the revolution without help, and that he had purchased ten thousand rifles and five million rounds of ammunition from the United States Government;[27] and he issued a call for volunteers.

The main army of the Liberals under Gómez was caught in a trap on March 7, and Gómez himself was taken with almost his entire command. Soon the province of Oriente was overrun by government troops, and by May the fighting was virtually over.

Meanwhile the supplementary elections in Santa Clara were held on February 14. The Liberals made no effort to participate; any action on their part would probably have been ineffective since the government had its own methods of vote counting. The Conservative success was striking; in a normally Liberal district where there were 2,401 voters on the official voting list the Conservatives polled 2,427 votes to 33 for the Liberals. The elections in Oriente were as halcyon as those in Santa Clara: the full list was voted.

At the request of the Liberal commander in Oriente, Commodore Belknap, commanding the United States naval squadron, landed a body of marines at Santiago on condition that the Liberal forces would evacuate the city. Some American forces also occupied Guantánamo, Manzanillo, and Nuevitas, and a body was also sent inland to protect the mines of El Cobre.

The closing days of the revolt were inextricably involved in the

27 Merino and Ibarzábal, *La revolución de febrero*, p. 98.

larger question of the World War. There was no reason to connect the revolution or the Liberal party with German designs, but Menocal was shrewd enough to use the charge in Cuba and also in the United States, and to declare war on Germany on April 7, one day after the United States. The State Department was in no mood to let local difficulties interfere with larger plans for war-making. Vigorous messages were sent to Cuba pointing out that any deviation from public order tending to obstruct the sugar output would be considered a hostile act and that the United States would consider and treat insurrectionists as its own enemies.

On May 20, 1917, Menocal was inaugurated for a second term, and the phenomenal prosperity which came to Cuba during the last year of his first administration ran over the first three years of his second administration. This was due to the soaring of sugar prices, which not only transformed Cuba but also strengthened its economic tie with the United States, for the climb of sugar prices brought in a continuing wave of American investment. United States capital in Cuba in 1914 amounted to two hundred million dollars; there was almost as much other foreign capital, and about seven hundred millions in Cuban holdings. Under Menocal these amounts, and especially the figures for United States capital, were increased many times over.

THE CROWDER REFORMS

THE idea had developed, especially among the Liberals, that some sort of help from the United States was necessary if they were to have a fair chance of victory in the coming 1920 elections, and eventually both Conservatives and Liberals concurred in the issue of an invitation to General Crowder early in 1919 to come to Cuba and assist in revising the election law he had devised in 1908. Crowder accepted, and at once caused a census to be taken, and studies to be made of the elections since 1909, so as to know what varieties of fraud had been practiced. In the new enactment greater reliance was placed on the judiciary than had been the case under the old law, so much so that it was virtually impossible for a man legally to become President of Cuba without the acquiescence of the Supreme Court.

A change in leadership had taken place within the Liberal party. Zayas, having lost caste with the Liberals, tried to secure nomination from a party of his own called the *Populares*. Not succeeding in his aim, he allowed himself to be nominated, with Menocal's support, by the Conservatives, his opponents in 1916. José Miguel Gómez, by risking his life and his fortune in 1917, had recovered and even enhanced his former prestige, and he received the Liberal nomination.

Fearing the usual election trouble, the State Department on August 30, 1920, announced that the United States would not favor either party, and would appoint observers to guard against intimidation or fraud. The observers came and observed, but could not prevent the employment of evil methods or the spilling of blood; Zayas lost only the province of Havana.[28]

Appeals were taken to the Supreme Court in accordance with the provisions of the electoral law, but the introduction of technicalities into the preliminary hearings delayed a decision, and it appeared as if Menocal intended to carry the election in the usual manner or keep the presidency for himself in default of a legal election. The Liberals appealed for United States interposition, and the Wilson administration at once took steps to meet a situation which had in it all the elements of danger. On January 6, 1921, without formal prior notice to the Cuban authorities, General Crowder appeared again in Havana as President Wilson's personal representative. The Liberals, who were convinced that Menocal would yield the election only to force, welcomed him; indeed, as early as November 7, 1920, they had suggested the appointment of a United States provisional government pending the holding of new elections. Some Conservatives resented General Crowder's visit, but the followers of Zayas dissembled any concern they may have felt; only a speedy, legal settlement would make their victory real.

On January 10, 1921, Crowder addressed a long communication to Menocal, objecting to the delays in the decision of disputed elections, and pointing out how matters might be expedited. The

28 For an observer's account of the 1920 election see Herbert J. Spinden, "America and Her Duty in Cuba," *Boston Transcript,* Aug. 7, 1923.

situation was "one of great gravity," which when considered with the existing financial crisis constituted "a menace to the national life, calling for extraordinary remedial measures." The Supreme Court was immediately allowed to take action, and, as in 1916, on the whole favored the Liberal contentions, annulling the elections in 250 voting districts, or about 20 per cent of the total. Partial elections were fixed for March 15 and were to be held simultaneously. As usual General Crowder set to work methodically, visiting and inspecting all the expected "battle grounds"; he induced Menocal, Gómez, and Zayas to sign a "pact of honor" in which Menocal agreed not to use military supervisors, but to rely on inspectors representing the Central Electoral Board.

The stage was set for what might have been an honest election, when Gómez and the Liberals for some reason or other took fright, and, fearing that they would not receive fair play, refused to go to the polls, thus giving Zayas a walk-over.

If the Liberals had gone to the election they might have seen Gómez inaugurated president on May 20. Gómez hurried to Washington to plead his case before the State Department. He wanted new elections under American supervision, but a charge of fraud from a party which had given its opponents a walk-over made small appeal. The United States had not been invited to intervene by the constituted authorities as it had been in 1906, and it could not act *sua sponte* on the possibility that the Conservatives would have stolen the elections of March 15 if the Liberals had gone to the polls. There was not a shadow of a case under the Permanent Treaty, so the United States on April 17 formally recognized Zayas as President. Disorder gradually subsided, and the Liberals, recognizing the futility of protesting the American attitude, took their seats in Congress, and Zayas was duly inaugurated on May 20. A few weeks later Gómez died in New York, a hero and a martyr in the eyes of the Cuban nation, and the once esteemed Menocal retired to private life.

The Zayas Administration.

Even before Zayas became President it was apparent that United States help would be necessary to save the country from bankruptcy and the possibility of intervention. Menocal was about to retire, leaving nothing in the treasury and a huge floating debt, a seriously impaired government income, and a heavy debt service on foreign-held bonds. Since it was clear that the administration would find it difficult to obtain enough money for running expenses, and would have none of the usual perquisites, Zayas was ready to accept the suggestions of Crowder for reforms necessary to set Cuba's house in order.

An emergency loan of five million dollars was obtained from J. P. Morgan and Company which enabled the republic to resume payments on the funded debt. From the external standpoint the next most pressing immediate problem was the handling of the floating debt, which included the left-over contracts in the Department of Public Works. Since it was known that many of the agreements were tainted with fraud, Crowder brought pressure to bear on Zayas to clean up these Augean stables, and the President, on August 13, 1921, issued a decree covering contracts on which work had not been completed; all illegal contracts were to be annulled, and readjustment in unit prices or cancellation was to be provided on legal contracts. The necessary investigation was undertaken under the direction of the United States military attaché, who found that out of contracts worth $49,000,000, $37,000,000 had not been executed; prices were far in excess of prevailing rates; appropriations were much greater than had been authorized by Congress; and some contracts had never had congressional sanction. The total of 354 contracts involved obligations far beyond Cuba's ability to pay. Zayas' effort to correct these evils was half-hearted; in some cases he annulled contracts, but gave the contractors a bonus; and in various ways a "goat"[29] was maintained in the department's affairs.

Crowder's Fifteen Memoranda.

General Crowder's ideas for the renovation of Cuban public life were embodied in a series of communications which he sent direct

[29] Edward L. Conn, *The Crisis in Cuba: III, The Goat in the Treasury, Philadelphia Public Ledger*, Nov. 21, 1923. In various Hispanic American countries the word *chivo*, or goat, is used as a synonym for graft, on the analogy of a goat's giving milk.

to Zayas and which are known as the "Fifteen Memoranda." The Crowder memoranda were issued on authority which the General considered inherent in the Platt Amendment. He apparently considered that the United States had the right to investigate any department of the Cuban Government under a supposed relation between Article II and Article III, but the Cuban Senate protested that the Platt Amendment "was not synonymous with interference or intervention in the affairs of the Cuban Government." Only one of the memoranda, number thirteen, has been published in full, but much authentic information has been published about them. The series began in February or March, 1922, and ran on for some months. Number three made suggestions for the constitutional amendments already proposed in Zayas' inaugural. Number five asked for information on revision of contracts in the Department of Public Works as well as on the actual indebtedness of the government. Number six urged the passing of a budget, suggesting what the budget should contain. Number seven stated that the maximum of the budget should be $55,000,000, pointing out methods of retrenchment. Number eight reminded Zayas of the graft and corruption still prevailing which Crowder said undermined Cuban credit and made government action imperative. Number nine related to the floating debt, pointing out that additional debt had accrued since the national audit; Crowder said it would have to be met either by drastic cuts in expenditures or by a loan and that before this could be discussed a reliable audit would be necessary. Numbers ten and eleven discussed the state lottery reforms which Crowder considered an essential preliminary to negotiations for a stabilization loan.

To obtain an accurate understanding of the financial situation Crowder had caused William P. G. Harding, recently a member of the Federal Reserve Board of the United States, to be invited to Cuba in 1921. After two months' work Mr. Harding reported that it would take a large staff of experts several years to make an accounting, and suggested that a fresh start be made with a good accounting system. He drew up a plan for a national banking law, including a National Reserve Bank based on United States capital and United States control; Americans, he said, would not invest in the bank on any other basis. Crowder made this plan the subject of memorandum number twelve, but more than suggestions of reform were necessary to get positive results. Nobody realized more than General Crowder that the men in power were not fit instruments for a "moralization" program, and he was therefore eager to replace them. Zayas responded to pressure, for the loan which was so badly needed was not yet forthcoming, and an "Honest Cabinet" was appointed and quickly began to earn its title. The budget was further reduced; unnecessary employees were detached from the pay rolls, and bonuses to others were abolished. Zayas annulled 98 out of 354 contracts in the Public Works Department, though often to the accompaniment of improprieties, and the Honest Cabinet disposed of all but 95 of the remainder, at the same time laying bare fraudulent contracts entered into under Zayas and wasteful favoritism toward his and his supporters' relatives and protégés.

The appointment of the Honest Cabinet marked the influence of Crowder at its height. Up till this time he had been successful in getting his policy accepted by both Washington and Cuba. It would seem that the only conditions precedent to a loan which the bankers had laid down were the acquiescence of the State Department and a guarantee that the proceeds would be used to liquidate the floating debt. For this and other purposes $50,000,000 was suggested as the amount of the loan. What more was required of Cuba? The answer was furnished by Crowder in memorandum number thirteen, dated July 21, 1922. In this memorandum he pointed out that the resumption of payments on the bonded debt had taken place out of the proceeds of the Morgan emergency loan of $5,000,000, not out of ordinary revenues, while the domestic loan of 1917 was still some $3,000,000 in arrears, and the floating debt was said to be about equal to the total expected annual receipts. On account of its rights under the Permanent Treaty the United States needed assurances that the Cuban Government would take adequate steps to secure prompt payment of interest and sinking fund charges on its bonds; Congress should therefore pass laws providing for an external loan, assigning a new gross sales tax for service upon it. The retrenchment provided for in the new budget must be realized, and the graft alluded to in memorandum number eight done away with, in part through the removal of certain officials from office. Charges of extensive frauds in the customhouse and the internal revenue bureau must be proved false or the evils corrected as a condition precedent to a loan. The memorandum alluded to corruption in the judiciary, mentioned the improprieties still surrounding the award of government contracts, such as the failure to call for competitive bids or to insist on reasonable unit prices, and, while not demanding any radical reform, pointed out that some steps should be undertaken to remedy these conditions.

While the Cubans denounced vehemently the corruption which the memorandum had uncovered, they were equally wrathful with General Crowder, and protested against his "unwarranted interference in Cuban affairs"; but the memorandum had its effect, and the loan was issued early in 1923, yielding over $48,000,000 to the Cuban treasury. The price was 96.77, with a 5½ per cent coupon rate and 1953 was fixed as the date of maturity. About $7,000,000 was devoted to payment of the war debt to the United States, $6,000,000 was turned over to the Department of Public Works for use for sanitation schemes only; and the remainder, $35,000,000, was specifically earmarked for application to the floating debt.

Meanwhile the economic prospects of the country had improved. The 1922-1923 sugar crop brought a good price, and the returns were reflected in government receipts, which eventually proved to be nearly $73,000,000 for 1922-1923.

Disregard of General Crowder.

Zayas' restiveness under the Crowder restraints was shared by his associates and by some of the prominent newspapers. The Cuban Congress had already adopted a resolution calling upon the United States Government to adjust itself to the spirit of the Platt Amendment as embodied in Mr. Root's letter to General Wood of April 3, 1901, stating that United States rights were not to be interpreted as amounting to a privilege of interfering in Cuban affairs; but the reverse of the political medal appeared in the preamble to an amnesty bill passed by the Senate on October 9, 1922, which asserted that graft should not be prosecuted as a crime, since it had developed naturally by being "introduced" under the American administration of Governor Magoon! The resolution went on to recite the various forms of corruption in Cuban political life and to argue that graft had become customary and therefore permissive; the bill proposed a blanket immunity for all grafters. The United States objected to the resolution, and that part of the bill was killed in the House.

Not a few non-political leaders were opposed to the Crowder mission, even though they approved of his measures, for they were afraid it might result in a loss of independence, and were confident of the emergence of good government without foreign aid. For the present, in their opinion, the worst Cuban government was better than the best foreign government.

Zayas saw the time was ripe to take advantage of this anti-Crowder feeling. Declaring that his Cabinet were representative of the United States rather than of Cuba, on April 3, 1923, he dismissed four of his Secretaries for "high reasons of state," and brought back his former satellites. For a few months Cuba was rampant with "nationalism."[30]

No reproval came from Washington; the Harding administration, tired of interference which boded more and more complications, was anxious to retire from the Cuban imbroglio. General Crowder, who had been appointed Ambassador to Cuba in January, 1923, watched in silence the tearing up of his Fifteen Memoranda. The evil features of the lottery were either sanctioned or made worse and the bill was passed by a great majority. Zayas vetoed it, complying with his promise, but his message praised Congress for its noble sentiments and invited passage over his

[30] In Zayas' final message to Congress in April, 1925, he put special emphasis upon his assertion of "nationalism," saying that this amounted to a "cult" with him. Referring to Cuban relations with the United States, he said:

"Perhaps my greatest reward on leaving the duties which I discharge is in having the full consciousness of having brought about a rectification of an erroneous concept about our capacity for the life of an independent nation and of our qualities as citizens, and, in consequence, of having caused a change from a status of an annoying and belittling tutelage to that of a correct, adequate, and reciprocal conduct where our dignity does not suffer."

veto. The measure passed by 96 to 3 in the House on July 23 and unanimously in the Senate next day, and Zayas affixed his signature on August 4.

Sugar continued to be the Lady Bountiful of the Cuban treasury, begetting corruption and official extravagance. For 1923-1924 government receipts were about $91,500,000, about $93,-500,000 in 1924-1925, not taking account of revenues that never reached the treasury.

The United States Government during a resurgence of corruption remained quiescent save for several mild protests. The overthrow of the government party spelled revolution, for revolution was the only method by which it could be accomplished, and revolution invited complications.

It was left to the Cuban people to rouse themselves. A public conscience against political corruption, stimulated by Crowder's Fifteen Memoranda, showed itself in newspaper attacks on Zayas. Civic organizations, led by intellectual leaders such as Fernando Ortiz, produced *manifiestos* denouncing government corruption and calling for the enactment of the moralization program. The Veterans' Association, the most highly respected group in the country, standing more than any other for patriotism, came out for reform. Unfortunately the movement, in its turn, was manipulated by politicians who were lying in wait to appropriate a reform movement as a means to raise themselves to power. General Carlos García y Vélez, son of the famous Calixto García of independence days, finding that the Veterans' Association preferred a conservative pace, formed a new organization under the name of the Veterans' and Patriots' Association, and on April 30, 1924, a revolt broke out near Cienfuegos.

What would the United States do? Support the Veterans and Patriots who espoused the Crowder reforms, or support the constituted power in Zayas who had rejected the reforms and corrupted the administration? President Coolidge, following the Wilson policy, decided to support Zayas. An embargo was placed on the sale of munitions to the insurrectionists, while Zayas was allowed to purchase needed equipment from the United States Government itself. Apart from this, García Vélez proved himself unequal to his task and the revolt misfired. The fiasco, coupled with the evidence of United States support of the constituted power, gave Cuba over to the politicians. There was no further need to restrain themselves in the pursuit of private fortune at the expense of the state. Public opinion against them had expressed itself, and had failed ignominiously; for the next year, the last of the Zayas administration, corruption became the chief business of state. For weeks there would be no meetings of either chamber, except to pass notorious legislation; practically nothing was done to get rid of illegal contracts in the Public Works Department, and a number of the national services were sadly neglected.

Downfall of Zayas.

The presidential election came round again in November, 1924. Zayas had entered office on a one-term platform, and had frequently expressed himself as opposed to reëlection, but in May, 1924, with the campaign of the Veterans and Patriots now dead, he announced that he would run again, presumably as in 1920, as the Conservative candidate, with the support of the *Populares*, or those who had split from the Liberals as Zayistas. He was still "opposed to reëlection," but Congress had "five times" neglected his requests to take action on the matter; so it was apparently their wish that he should again offer his services to the nation.

The campaign within the Liberal party between General Machado and Colonel Mendieta, allies of 1916, commanded the major share of attention during the summer of 1924. The latter was favored by the regeneration element but not by the powerful American business interests; he had taken part in the demonstrations against Zayas and was believed to be a man of unimpeachable honesty. Machado, who had been out of politics since 1917, was not so well known, though he had been a leading soldier and had held a high place in the Liberal councils. Mendieta did little campaigning, thinking his nomination was certain if the delegates to the Liberal assembly voted as the people wanted them to vote. He also lost votes by giving out an interview in which he asserted that Cuba's future lay in her going hand in hand with the United States. Machado, on the contrary, adapted himself to existing conditions, went to the Liberal assembly, made frequent speeches elsewhere, gave a number of promises, and won many friends by his agreeable personality. He finally carried off the nomination.

At the Conservative assembly Zayas lost the nomination to Menocal. The army officers were hostile to Zayas; but in general the opposition to him was so great that his election on any basis would probably have provoked revolution. Zayas for a time contemplated a separate candidacy, but after a number of conferences with Machado he withdrew his own candidacy in the latter's favor. The return of the *Populares* to the Liberal fold thus reunited the party.

Cuba is normally liberal. The word "Liberal" had an appeal that gave the party its start, and the habit of voting that ticket had passed from father to son. Although the Liberals had triumphed only once since the party was formed in 1905, they had represented a majority in each of the five elections—a split in their ranks in 1912 had given the Conservatives an honest victory—and the unfair treatment the Liberals had received in 1916 and 1920 had added to their numbers, and strengthened their loyalty to the organization. Machado's vote was increased by the unpopularity of his opponent. Menocal, though the strongest man in the inner councils of the Conservative party, and possibly the only one who could have beaten Zayas for the nomination, was detested because of his eight years' rule and because he was an aristocrat. It was evident that on an honest vote Machado was sure to win, and the government was therefore under no necessity of manufacturing votes. Machado had an immense majority, carrying every province except Pinar del Río. For a while it seemed likely that Menocal would dispute the election and keep the country in turmoil for several months until a revolution or the intervention of the United States should come along to effect a readjustment. On November 2, the day after the election, he issued a statement asserting that the election had been illegal and "declining responsibility for the future." It was the usual prelude to disturbance, but several days later he acknowledged defeat, apparently after a long conference with General Crowder. It was an event unique in Cuban annals and did much to redeem the past delinquencies of the former president.

General Machado.

Inducted to the presidency on May 20, 1925, and reëlected for a six-year term beginning May 20, 1929, General Machado has shown himself a stronger man than his predecessors. Like them he repeatedly declared that he would never seek reëlection; and also like them he bowed before the pressure of his followers. Unlike them, however, he can find justification for not keeping his promise in the fact that this is not his second term but his first under the amended constitution. In 1927 the Cuban Congress proposed the extension of the presidential term to six years, and to the proposal a three-party convention agreed, subject to application after the expiration of General Machado's four-year term. At the presidential elections of November, 1928, the three parties combined to reëlect him, and no candidate appeared to oppose him. General Machado thus begins his new term with overwhelming support.

Such opposition as there is to the Machado *régime* has to work underground because of a condition of things which has curtailed freedom of speech and given the President firm control of Congress and party machines. Congress's amenability is explained partly by the link established through the President's control of the State lottery. Tickets are sold to the public through two thousand collectorships at an advance averaging 50 per cent over the legal price. The President distributes the collectorships, and it would be flying in the face of Cuban political experience if he did not exchange them for support. At the same time Machado, by a combination of strong-man rule and political sagacity, has succeeded in nourishing nationalism in Cuba while maintaining good relations with the United States.

General Crowder, the lawgiver of Cuba, retired from the ambassadorship in the year of General Machado's reëlection.

ECONOMIC INTERESTS

Sugar—the Nexus.

Cuba produces a fourth of the world's cane sugar and a fifth of the world's cane and beet supply. Tobacco is also a well-known Cuban product, but ten times more sugar than tobacco is sold abroad; in fact, sugar represents 85 per cent of the country's exports. Thus Cuba is a supreme example of a single-crop economy, exhibiting all the symptoms of dependence on a world price in business fluctuations, private extravagance, public waste when sugar prices are high, and bankruptcies, distress, and unrest when sugar prices are low. Sugar markets and a remunerative sugar price are the principal desiderata of Cuban foreign policy.

Cuba's dependence on sugar has become a dependence on conditions in the American sugar market, partly because the United States takes three-quarters of the Cuban export, and partly because of the unique preferential duty accorded by the terms of the Reciprocity Treaty of 1902.

The history of reciprocity with Cuba dates back to 1884, when the United States negotiated a treaty with Spain looking to mutual tariff concessions in the Cuban and Porto Rican trade. It was not signed by the United States because of a change of administration, but a second reciprocity treaty went into effect in 1891-1892, and stimulated trade. Up to this time both Americans and Cubans had been gravely concerned over the restrictive commercial policy of Spain and its annoying methods of enforcing trade regulations. Seventy-five per cent of Cuba's exports went to the United States, and were paid for mostly by bills on London, because the Spaniards, holding to the mercantilist conception of colonial rule, hindered Cuban purchases of American goods. In sixteen years, 1876 to 1891 inclusive, the United States bought Cuban products to the value of $924,000,000, and sold an amount valued only at $189,000,000. It was cheaper to ship flour from the Mississippi Valley to Spain, pay a duty there and ship it back to Cuba, than to send it direct to Havana. Burdensome duties existed on other commodities that had to be imported by the Cubans, such as butter, lard, shoes, and calicoes, and shipments were subject to the further handicap of extra-tariff exactions. The termination in 1894 of the Reciprocity Treaty, coupled with the fixation through the Wilson tariff of a duty on raw sugar of 1.05 cents a pound, was a severe economic setback to Cuba.

The Dingley tariff of 1897 fixed the sugar duty at 1.685 cents a pound. Cuban production costs were two cents a pound. Prior to the Dingley tariff the world price was four to five cents a pound. Deprived of the American preference, Cuban sugar producers were thrown on the open market, but here conditions were becoming chaotic, for the bounties to European beet sugar producers had brought on overproduction and a rapidly falling price level. Beet sugar, amounting at that time to two-thirds of the entire world output, depressed prices below the Cuban cost of production, and Cuba's plight became extreme.

McKinley, Roosevelt, Root, and Wood constantly and energetically urged the parlous state of the Cuban sugar industry and "the weightiest reasons of American public policy" as making advisable a return to reciprocity in connection with the new relations to be established with the Cuban Republic. In his first presidential message to Congress, Roosevelt said:

There are weighty reasons of morality and of international interest why the policy of reciprocity would be held to have a peculiar application in the case of Cuba. We are bound by every consideration of honor and expediency to pass commercial measures in the interest of her material well-being.

Later he said:[31]

I urge the adoption of reciprocity with Cuba not only because it is eminently for our interests to control the Cuban market and by every means to foster our supremacy in the lands and waters south of us, but also because we of the giant republic of the north should make all our sister nations of the American continent feel that whenever they will permit it, we desire to show ourselves disinterestedly and effectively their friend.

The campaign was one of the most strenuous in Roosevelt's eventful life, for he had to face the massed attack of the domestic beet and cane sugar interests. Instead of waiting for the Senate's action, which had protracted discussion unconscionably, a reciprocity treaty was negotiated with the newly-established Cuban Republic on December 11, 1902. The Senate ratified it, but inserted the unusual provision that it was not to have effect until both houses had registered approval. This was given by a special

[31] For. Rel., 1902, p. xx.

session of Congress November 19, 1903, and the measure was finally repassed by the Senate December 16, 1903.

The 1902 treaty admitted dutiable Cuban goods into the United States at a reduction of 20 per cent from the regular tariff rates; Cuban sugar under the Fordney-McCumber Act pays a duty of 1.7648 cents per pound, whereas sugar from other foreign countries has to pay 2.206 cents.[32] In return for this privilege dutiable American goods enter Cuba at preferential rates between 20 and 40 per cent off the regular tariff.

A detailed study of prices[33] shows that at least in 1904-1909 the larger part of the duty which the United States Government remitted in accordance with the treaty went into the pockets of Cuban producers. In these years the United States imported from Cuba over sixteen billion pounds of sugar, on which the differential amounted to over fifty-four million dollars; these millions played a considerable part in the establishment of the Cuban state. Since 1910, however, the reciprocity arrangement has ceased to accrue to the Cuban producers, because of the elimination of full-duty sugar from the American market. The percentage of full-duty sugar consumed in the United States dwindled from 23 per cent in 1909 to 7.1 per cent in 1910, and steadily fell away until in 1928 it was only 1 per cent. Thus it has ceased to govern the American price, which since 1910 has been determined by the world price and the duty on Cuban sugar. The United States Tariff Commission[34] concludes that the differential now inures "wholly to the benefit of the American purchaser of Cuban sugar," or the American sugar refiner.

Mr. Culbertson observes[35] that the advantages which a country derives from a reciprocity treaty are ordinarily to be found in increased exports. In the first twenty-one and a half years in which the Reciprocity Treaty was in effect, Cuba exported to the United States merchandise to the value of $4,666,167,044;[36] or virtually

[32] This rate is now in process of alteration in the Hawley-Smoot bill, which, however, confirms the preference.

[33] U.S. Tariff Commission: *Reciprocity and Commercial Treaties*, 1918, pp. 320-335, quoted by Culbertson, *International Economic Policies.*

[34] U.S. Tariff Commission, *Effects of the Cuban Reciprocity Treaty*, 1929, p. 78.

[35] *Op. cit.*, p. 131.　　　　　　　　[36] *Foreign Affairs*, 1928, p. 236.

80 per cent of its total. During the same period it imported from the United States goods to the value of $2,902,359,002, or slightly over 67 per cent of all its imports. In 1928 the figures were: exports to the United States, $202,678,000; imports from the United States, $127,860,000. When the Reciprocity Treaty first went into effect, it was anticipated that its fruits for Cuba would be mainly economic and for the United States mainly political. The figures given would seem to bear this out, showing a relatively larger increment to Cuban exports. Other factors disturb this simple arithmetical deduction. While Cuba's exports to the United States have been larger than Cuba's imports from this country, the average profit on the latter trade is much larger than that on Cuba's sugar exports. Cuban sugar is governed by a world price, in consequence of which the Cuban producer gets for his sugar the same price he receives in other markets, and this price nowadays borders on the cost of production. Moreover, a large part of the profits of sugar exportations from Cuba are enjoyed (or, as is nowadays the case, the losses are borne) by American companies in Cuba, and, if made, are returned to the United States in the form of dividends.

Sugar as the economic link between the United States and Cuba has been prolific of so many other links that American interests permeate the entire Cuban economy. In trade Cuba last year stood seventh among suppliers of goods to the United States and eleventh among its customers; in both exports to and imports from the United States it is ahead of any other Latin American country. As a debtor to the United States Cuba is exceeded only by Canada. The foreign debt of the Cuban Government, amounting to $83,-000,000, is all held in the United States; in addition, Americans participate in the ownership of sugar, tobacco, mining, and fruit enterprises, railways, public utilities, telephone systems, docks, warehouses, banks, and hotels. Two thousand miles of public and four thousand miles of private railroad are American controlled; the American Foreign Power Company owns the light and power business in nearly all of the important towns of the island, including the Havana Electric Company. The Cuban Telephone Company is a subsidiary of the International Telephone and Telegraph Company; its wires extend the length and breadth of Cuba. The Havana Dock Company is in American hands. Approximately two-thirds of the entire output of sugar is produced by American-owned mills. Altogether the American investment in Cuba at the end of 1928 was estimated at about a billion and a half dollars.[37]

The Gyrations of Sugar.

In the early days of the industry methods of cultivation were poor and capital expenditures slight; the industry was in the hands of small farmers, each possessing a primitive grinding mill (*ingenio*). A thousand of these mills were in operation in 1827 and over two thousand in 1860. These conditions prevailed until about 1878, when the industry began to be mechanized. The impulse to mechanization came partly from the abolition of slavery but principally from conditions in the world market. The European beet-sugar industry, especially in Germany, had begun to challenge the cane sugar of Cuba. In the eighties more sugar was produced from beet than from cane, beet sugar was making headway in the United States, and Hawaiian sugar was beginning to appear on the market. The price fell until in 1894 it reached 3.2 cents a pound. The Cuban industry was saved from ruin by the introduction by American *entrepreneurs* of machinery which was able to get a high percentage of sucrose content out of the cane, to produce sugar in volume, and to produce it much more cheaply than under the old methods.

The machinery constituting the *central*, or sugar mill, was brought to Cuba by an army of American engineers and capitalists. The less efficient among the Cuban estates became subordinate to the nearest mill, selling their cane to the mill owners. Centralization was furthered by the so-called *colono* system, which came at length to be the principal basis for the production of sugar. The *colonos*, whether on their own land, a hired plot, or that of the mill, raised cane at their own risk, and turned it over to the mill. At first the transaction was an outright sale, but eventually a profit-

[37] Finance and Investment Division, U.S. Department of Commerce, $1,435 millions; Cuban-American Chamber of Commerce, in *Commercial and Financial Chronicle*, January 21, 1928, $1,505 millions; Leland H. Jenks, *Our Cuban Colony*, $1,150 millions. Mr. Jenks's figures are based on ascertainable bank values of plant.

sharing plan was evolved whereby the *colono* got a certain percentage of the sugar (in practice, of the price it brought) from the cane he delivered to the mill. The *central* spelled the end of the small, independent proprietor; in his place large estates were created, owned by corporations or absentee landlords and operated by wage-earners or tenant farmers. The two thousand grinding mills were gradually replaced by 180 *centrales*. The revolution saved Cuban sugar, introduced American investment as a controlling force, and started a system which forced output to tremendous heights.

By 1914 there were already some two hundred millions of United States dollars in Cuba, and under President Menocal the figure was increased several times over. In July, 1914, sugar was in the doldrums, selling for 1.93 cents per pound. The war demand brought a quick advance to three cents, and in 1916-1917 to four cents; this was the magnet for American capital. Fears of a world shortage through increased consumption and the lessened production of beet sugar in the belligerent countries drove sugar up until it sold for 6.75 cents a pound. The United States and allied countries felt that the price must be checked as a war measure, and, having the power to withdraw shipping facilities from the island, induced Cuba to accept price control. A price of 4.60 cents was agreed upon and later was advanced to 5.50 cents—a generous price as measured by pre-war standards, though much less than could have been obtained without control.

This large margin of profit brought money pouring into Cuba, where the post-war speculation came to be known as the "dance of the millions." The importance of credit and its expansion to an exaggerated degree in Cuban life was a new phenomenon. A few small banks had been established in the Spanish period, but they were unimportant, and foreigners came in to cater to the banking needs of a flourishing country. The great foreign houses entered Cuba after 1898: the Royal Bank of Canada in 1902, the National City Bank of New York in 1914, followed by the First National Bank of Boston and the Chase National Bank. Another important bank was the North American Trust Company, founded by a number of Americans in 1899, which in 1901 became the National

Bank (*Banco Nacional*) of Cuba. Banks of the mushroom variety also sprang up, among them the International Bank (*Banco Internacional*) of Cuba, with 102 branches. Out of the obvious fact that large sums were needed to move the sugar crops, now greater than ever and more expensive to handle, a cloudburst of credit was created on what seemed to be the unlimited future wealth of Cuba; for a time the security for loans was sugar at 15 to 20 cents a pound.

Cubans had prospered under the sugar control prices of 4.60 to 5.50 cents a pound, and when sugar control was given up at the close of the 1918-1919 crop and European beet sugar did not revive, the demand sent the price to much higher levels. On February 18, 1920, sugar was quoted at 9⅛ cents, on March 18 at 11, April 17 at 18½, and May 19 at 22½. American companies bought not only sugar but also estates, paying enormous prices in order to assure themselves of an unfailing supply. The Rosario estate whose owner had determined upon selling out at four and a half million dollars was sold to an American chocolate concern for eight millions.

The owners of sugar and sugar estates were not the only ones to profit. The *colonos* also became rich, being able to demand a greater percentage of the value of the crop, sometimes as much as two-thirds, and, in consequence, graduated into the landowning class (*haciendados*), blossoming out with palatial homes in the Vedado district of Havana. The smaller *colonos* had their share in the general orgy of wealth, if only in the form of hitherto unknown luxuries.

Business for the first time in Cuba's history rated ahead of politics in social esteem, and it became the fashion for the patrician class not only to go into business but in some cases even to become *colonos*. Groups were formed in political life to protect business and to exercise pressure upon the government to defend sugar, and public opinion exerted itself in the same direction because the entire island was implicated. New conditions developed among the working classes. Foreign labor poured in, but the whites did not stay long at the plantations, being drawn to the cities, where they introduced radical labor ideas, and produced an almost unending series of usually successful strikes.

Havana was more visibly transformed than any other part of the island. It became a city of millionaires, with the splendid Vedado homes as an outward manifestation of their wealth. The opulence of the city was augmented by American prohibition. Thirsty Americans began to visit Havana in great numbers, introducing a constant flow of ready cash into an already rich city. New hotels were erected, the Jockey Club established, the far-famed Casino built, and through these and other ways Havana advertised her readiness to enjoy life with the fortune that the war effort of sugar had given her.

But the war had come to an end and the beet sugar industry was rapidly regaining its pre-war position. High prices also encouraged sugar production elsewhere. The shortage was overcome and the price dropped. Sugar, raised for less than 10 cents and in early 1920 selling at 20 cents, had received bank loans on a 15 cent basis. The price was $22\frac{1}{2}$ cents on May 19, $18\frac{1}{2}$ on June 18, $16\frac{1}{2}$ on July 20, 11 on August 19, 7 on October 13, $5\frac{1}{4}$ on November 18, and $3\frac{3}{4}$ on December 13. When the price fell to 8 cents the piling up of losses brought on the stage of ruin. Banks called their loans, debtors were unable to pay, and their security was now worth less than the loan; depositors started a run on the banks, and the banks began to close their doors. The first to go was the overgrown International. The "dance of the millions" ended in a moratorium on October 11, 1920, and when two of the greatest banks of the island, the Spanish Bank (*Banco Español*) and the National itself, took advantage of the temporary relief thus afforded, public confidence became completely undermined. In April, 1921, the National Bank closed its doors; it was found to have liabilities of over sixty-seven million dollars, as against a million and a half in cash on hand; there were other assets, but many of them were worthless. The Spanish Bank and other institutions of less note soon followed the National into oblivion, and the National City Bank of New York and the Royal Bank of Canada replaced them as the leading banks of Cuba. Foreign banks now control the Cuban money market.

The sugar industry in due course found a new equilibrium, but the recovery of European beet and the stimulation of production in American and other fields have brought about an oversupply and a consequent low price. The world's production in the season 1928-1929 is estimated by Willett and Gray at 26,710,000 tons, which is 45 per cent more than the output in 1913-1914. Consumption cannot maintain such a pace, and the surpluses are responsible for the fact that the price of duty-paid Cuban sugar in New York averaged only 4.2 cents a pound in 1928, as compared with 4.1 cents for the five years ended December 31, 1913, when the general level of commodity prices was 50 per cent less than it is today. The price of sugar, exclusive of the United States duty, averaged 2.957 cents in 1927, 2.459 cents in 1928 and was 1.68 cents on May 23, 1929.

Great efforts are being made to persuade consumption to march with production. Cuba at first thought the remedy for overproduction lay in crop limitation. Quotas were fixed for the 1926-1927 and 1927-1928 crops, and in November, 1927, Cuba obtained an agreement with Germany, Poland, and Czechoslovakia to seek a national apportionment of sugar exports. This movement, however, failed; Cuba decided to lift its control of output; and the Economic Committee of the League of Nations has taken up its problem. Meanwhile production continues to advance because of the sheltered position which home industries enjoy through protective tariffs.

The Politics of Control.

No writers acknowledge more readily than serious-minded Cubans that the wealth of their country is based on its relations with the United States. But they consider that the reciprocity feature of those relations is antiquated, not because the preference no longer inures to the Cuban producer but because the present duty on sugar is inordinately high, working out at over 100 per cent when reduced to an *ad valorem* basis. Of the approximate $600,000,000 customs duties collected annually by the United States, the products of Cuba pay to the American treasury about $150,000,000; 25 per cent of the customs revenue of the United States, in other words, is contributed by Cuba. In 1927 this worked out at 55 per cent of the entire value of Cuban products imported into the United States; whereas in the same year the proportion of duties to total value of American products imported into Cuba was 15 per cent.

Two factors must be borne in mind when considering the United States tariff on sugar, first, the relative costs of production between Cuba and the United States, and, second, the political pledges to Cuba inherent in treaty relations. American tariff legislation is based in theory on equalizing the lower costs of production in exporting countries with those obtaining in the United States. In the last statement of production costs by the United States Tariff Commission on July 31, 1924, the majority report stated that the difference in costs of production in Cuba and the United States was 1.2307 cents a pound; since the existing duty on Cuban sugar was 1.76 cents, they recommended a reduction in the tariff. The minority report stated the difference to be 1.8525 cents, but did not recommend an increase in duty because they considered the data inadequate. Before the Tariff Commission concluded its studies the Institute of Economics, Washington, D. C., had initiated an investigation under the direction of Professor Philip G. Wright.[38] Professor Wright came to the conclusion that the difference between costs in Cuba and in the principal beet-sugar areas in the United States ranged from $1\frac{1}{4}$ to $1\frac{1}{2}$ cents a pound.

The second point is bound up with the theory of Cuban-American relations. The exclusion of Cuban sugar was obviously not intended, and the question is therefore one of determining what part of United States consumption it is desirable to have supplied from Cuba. Higher duties would mean an encroachment by domestic producers and by the Philippines, Porto Rico, and Hawaii, whose sugar enters the United States free, on the market now enjoyed by Cuba. It would also mean the diminution of the customs revenue from Cuban sugar, a higher price to the American consumer, and the crippling of American sugar enterprises in Cuba.

Cuba considers the present duty so lacking in reciprocity that a writer says, "The reduction of this duty is the great desideratum

[38] Cf. *Sugar in Relation to the Tariff.*

of Cuban foreign policy. It is regarded as the only certain guarantee for the future prosperity of their too exuberant sugar industry."[39] Specifically the Cubans are working for a new commercial agreement to supplant the old treaty. According to a note presented to Secretary Kellogg on December 15, 1927, they proposed that Cuba be granted free entry of a limited quantity of its sugar, the other part to be subject to the present tariff.

Cuban feeling is exercised over the broader question of so-called foreign exploitation. The scholar Enrique José Varona has repeatedly reminded the Cubans that their best lands are foreign owned, growing sugar (and to a less extent, tobacco) for export; while the Cubans have to import from abroad almost everything they consume, even food and other commodities that might be produced at home. "Our tendency," he says,[40] "is to live from the budget and not from the land." Another writer of note, Jorge Roa, remarks bitterly[41] that the Cubans won their independence from Spain only to turn the country over to alien business interests, and were allowed merely to retain a national hymn, a national flag, and the right to pay taxes.

Cuban arguments might give the impression that American capital in Cuba is a unit which has American diplomacy constantly at its beck and call in the exploitation of Cuba. For the most part the facts do not support this impression. The United States Government has consistently taken the stand that it is not a claims agency, and American business men have usually adapted themselves to local conditions of which the principal feature is vigorous competition, not with Cubans or Europeans, but with other American business men. It generally happens that in any controversy involving American capital, American companies will be found on both sides. A case in point was the dispute over the Tarafa law which sought, *inter alia*, to consolidate Cuban railroads so as to reduce freight rates. The complexity of American interests in the island insured disharmony of feeling toward this measure.

The situation in regard to sugar lands is that the sugar *cen-*

[39] *Foreign Affairs,* January, 1928, p. 237.
[40] *De la Colonia a la Republica,* p. 208.
[41] "Del Ambiente actual," in *Diario de la Marina,* May 13, 1924.

trales secure their cane either from "administration" farms—lands cultivated by wage earners under the immediate supervision of the *central*—or from *colonos*. Sometimes the *colono* owns his own land, but in the majority of cases he leases land from the *central*. The *central* advances money, usually at 8 per cent, to the *colono* for the purpose of buying tools, oxen, and other products necessary for cane cultivation. The company agrees to pay to the *colono* the equivalent in money of 5½ *arrobas* of sugar for each 100 *arrobas* of cane delivered, minus the advances made and rent for the land. A *colono's* contract usually runs for five or ten years. The *colono* is almost always hopelessly in debt to the *central*, and this means that ownership is sacrificed. This type of one-crop agriculture, in which the tenant works upon a five-year or a ten-year contract, has not been regarded as conducive to either diversification or productivity. The *colono* has little incentive to improve his land or even to erect a suitable dwelling. The cultivation of cane is so exacting that few *colonos* attempt to raise foodstuffs; in fact, the *colono* is restricted by contract to cultivate either cane exclusively or cane and vegetables in certain designated plots.

It is untrue to suggest that Americans "own" Cuba in the sense that they have gained a majority title to Cuban lands. While 60 per cent of the sugar industry is in American hands, at least 95 per cent of the *colonos'* plantations are still under Hispano-Cuban control. Fernando Ortiz thinks that American ownership of Cuban lands does not amount to more than 16.72 per cent, though Professor Jenks[42] gives the proportion of arable land under American control at 22 per cent. Even so, the figures show that the Cubans still "own" their country. Far from being exploited in the sense of being bled to poverty, Cuba is wealthy; its national wealth is estimated at four billion dollars, though Americans own 40 per cent of it. From the standpoint of national wealth the opulence of Cuba may be unduly concentrated in Havana, but this does not detract from its influence on the national economy.

The fact is that without American capital Cuba would be considerably reduced from its place as one of the richest of the countries of Latin America relatively to its population. American cor-

[42] *Our Cuban Colony*, p. 286.

porations, too, are not uncognizant of their responsibilities toward the people who help them reap their profits. They help cane farmers with loans and in other ways to keep up their cultivation; some of the best schools in Cuba are provided by them, free of charge; trades are taught to Cubans through their agency; money is expended in the provision of sanitation; hospitals are furnished; aid is rendered to townships for municipal improvements; roads are kept in repair.

American capital makes its contribution to the cost of Cuban government, but even with that help the burden on the Cubans is painfully heavy. Most of the revenue is derived from customs duties on trade with the United States, and this is reflected in a high cost of living. In 1909 Cuba was paying $12.10 *per capita* in customs duties, as compared with the United States, $3.55; France, $2.22; Italy, $1.72; Germany, $1.22; and Austria, $.51. Customs receipts in one year of the Menocal *régime* amounted to $30 per inhabitant, and averaged about $17 for the whole Menocal period. They averaged about $23 under President Zayas. The system has frankly been called "extortion for revenue only," for duties are levied not so much on luxuries or on products for which Cuba has an "infant industry," as on necessities which, in view of the giving over of Cuba to sugar, have mostly to be imported. Thus the burden on the poorer classes is heavy.

CONCLUSION

THE Platt Amendment attempted to prescribe a new relation for an indefinite future, a relation based on "ties of singular intimacy and strength," and it had therefore to employ vague terms. These terms have generated opposing schools of loose and strict constructionists. Hershey[43] sees no reason why the term "protectorate" should not be used frankly. "Client state" in the sense of "protectorate" is the designation adopted by some authorities; others prefer "quasi-protectorate," "part sovereign," and "half sovereign." Wheaton[44] holds that Cuba is a "protected state,"

[43] A. S. Hershey, *The Essentials of International Public Law and Organization*, p. 169.

[44] Henry Wheaton, *Elements of International Law* (Atlay Ed.), pp. 66-67.

though not in the sense that the principalities of India are protected states. Hall[45] speaks of the "imperfect independence of Cuba resulting from its treaty relations with the United States." Dickinson[46] maintains that "several of the obligations of a guarantor are involved in the responsibilities which the United States has assumed," though he says that the relationship is not strictly speaking an international guaranty. Oppenheim,[47] on the other hand, controverts assertions that Cuba is only part sovereign. Independence does not mean boundless liberty for a state to do what it likes without restriction. It is a question of degree, and it is therefore also a question of degree whether the independence of a state is destroyed or not by certain restrictions. It is generally admitted that states under suzerainty or under protectorate are not so much restricted that they are fully dependent, but are half sovereign; but Oppenheim would not place Cuba in this category, since the United States does not enjoy a protectorate over Cuba.

Most Cubans regard the right to intervene as reserved to meet only extraordinary emergencies; to them the "preservation of Cuban independence" means such a guaranty as that undertaken by the European powers for the neutrality of Belgium, whereby the right of intervention accrues only in case of a direct foreign attack. As for the "maintenance of a government adequate for the protection of life, property, and individual liberty," they adopt the thesis that intervention is justified under the treaty not by turbulence and disorder, rebellion, or even revolution, but only by such a continuing state of trouble as might be described as anarchy. In support of this thesis Cubans invoke Mr. Root's interpretation of the Platt Amendment given to the Cuban commissioners in 1901, and the course of events between 1902 and the 1906 intervention when no attempt was made to read into the Platt Amendment any warrant for general interference in Cuban affairs, and when Cuba's protests at United States activities were carefully heeded. The 1906 intervention came from events of another scale, and, as Professor Jenks has pointed out, little doubt

45 W. E. Hall, *A Treatise on International Law* (Higgins Ed.), p. 31.
46 E. D. Dickinson, *The Equality of States in International Law*, p. 251.
47 L. Oppenheim, *International Law* (McNair Ed.), I, 252-253.

exists that at that time "The Platt Amendment saved the independence of Cuba"; there was a hiatus in government which no Cuban would fill.

Intervention in Cuba has proved to bring in its train a host of minor complications and these have prompted hasty withdrawals. To avoid the serious commitment of an intervention the "preventive policy" of the Taft administration was ushered in, and broadened under war pressure by the Wilson administration into something which seemed to give a new significance to the Platt Amendment. It worked out in the "intermeddling," now admonitory, now interfering, for which its exponents found shelter under the ample wing of the Platt Amendment. Even though supervision has since been relaxed, the measure of it exercised by the United States Ambassador in Havana goes beyond the terms of the Platt Amendment, and is a process of what Cubans call "Plattization."

The fact is that the basis of Cuban-American relations resides in the special interest which the United States has asserted in the Caribbean. President Coolidge was the latest President to say "toward the government of countries which we have recognized this side of the Panama Canal we feel a moral responsibility that does not attach to other nations." The Platt Amendment attempts to codify this duplex interest and "moral responsibility." Its refinements therefore must be sought in the United States' interpretation of "moral responsibility," and this makes the question one of behavior: will "intermeddling" work as an encouragement of the vital forces in Cuba, peacefully manifested, or will it serve as the shield of corruption? To the suggestion that disputes holding the seeds of intervention might be referred to arbitration, whether under the Pan-American arbitration treaty of January, 1929, signed by both Cuba and the United States, or by voluntary agreement, the answer is that, so handled, the shadow of intervention with its admonitory effect would disappear, and that no United States administration has as yet shown a willingness to arbitrate any feature of Caribbean policy, whether in interpretation of a treaty or otherwise.

CHAPTER TWO

SANTO DOMINGO

CONDITIONS AND EARLY HISTORY

AT a distance of 1,225 miles south of New York, between Cuba
and Porto Rico at the gateway of the Caribbean, lies Hispaniola, the first land touched by Columbus, now divided between
the Republics of Haiti and Santo Domingo. A treaty defining
their common boundary which had been pending for fifty years
was signed January 21, 1929. The strategic value of Mole St.
Nicholas on the northwestern and of Samaná Bay and Peninsula
on the northeastern extremity have given Haiti and Santo Domingo an importance disproportionate to their resources and
population.

Occupying the eastern two-thirds of the island, Santo Domingo covers 19,332 square miles. Its inhabitants, now estimated
at approximately nine hundred thousand, are less than one-third
of the island's population. About 95 per cent of the people of
Haiti are pure blacks; the remainder mulattoes of all shades. Of
the Dominicans probably one-fourth are pure blacks; one-third,
white; and the remainder mulattoes, quadroons, octoroons, and
near-whites. No social or political discrimination is made on racial
lines, but a desire for the ascendancy of the white race is expressed
in the aid given Spanish, Italian, and north European immigrants. Even more than in race the people of the two countries
differ in language and traditions; for since the Treaty of Ryswick,
by which in 1697 Spain recognized the western third of the island
as French, the Haitians have looked to France for inspiration, and
French is the official language; in Santo Domingo a good Spanish
is spoken and the predilections are Spanish.

With a twelve-month growing season, the island is verdant and
potentially fertile. About 8,000,000 acres are cultivable, 3,000,-
000 are suitable for grazing, and 9,500,000 acres are forest land.
The products are similar to those of the other West India isles,
except that Santo Domingo exports also cacao; the United States
absorbs almost the entire crop, which in 1927 was worth $7,322,-

607 and was second in value of products. The total foreign commerce[1] for that year amounted to $58,962,783, of which $27,-784,014 represented imports, and $31,178,769 exports. In 1905 Santo Domingo had a so-called favorable balance of trade of $4,159,270. The balance fluctuated about this level until the War; in 1919 it reached a peak of $17,582,765. In 1921 the balance fell to $3,971,279 against the Republic. This was recovered the next year, and in 1924 the favorable balance was $8,682,325, decreasing to a little over a million for each of the next two years, then rising to $3,394,722 in 1927, and falling to $1,966,588 in 1928.

The chief export is raw sugar, of a total value in 1927 of $16,-668,385, and since 1914 constituting over 50 per cent of the total value of exports. Formerly the United States took the greater part but the sugar tariff of 1922 has driven the Dominican sugar output to other markets, in 1927 divided principally among Ireland, $5,198,908; England, $3,393,293; Canada, $3,379,034, and The Netherlands, $1,435,014. Tobacco is third in export value, $2,582,486 in 1927, of which $1,299,944 went to Germany; for this crop also the United States market is limited by a protective tariff. Coffee is fourth, $1,749,522, of which the largest portion is absorbed by Cuba. Dominican coffee and cacao exports have met competition from countries with low wage levels. In 1927 the United States received 28 per cent of Dominican exports, Ireland 17 per cent, England and Canada each 11 per cent.

Of the imports, consisting principally of rice, wheat, and manufactures—cotton, silk, and their manufactures, leather products, machinery, tools, iron and steel—the United States furnished 64 per cent in 1927 and Germany 8 per cent.

A weekly passenger, freight, and mail service was established between New York and Santo Domingo *via* San Juan, P. R., June 14, 1927. Vessels carrying the United States flag transported 44 per cent of the imports, Norwegian 20 per cent, Dutch 12 per cent, German 9 per cent. Of the exports Norwegian ships carried 24 per cent, British 21 per cent, United States 19 per cent, Dutch 9 per cent, and German 6 per cent.

[1] Figures for commerce taken from *Report of Dominican Customs Receivership*, 1927.

Transportation on the island is chiefly by road, the two public railways in Santo Domingo together having a length of only 147 miles. One is owned by the Government and gives useful service; the other is a white elephant to its owner and motor competition is now serious. Neither is standard gauge and as the gauges are different, cars and locomotives cannot be interchanged. About 225 miles of railway run through private estates.

Colonial Days.

After its discovery Santo Domingo enjoyed a brief period of prosperity. Under Don Diego Columbus, son of the famous Admiral, Santo Domingo City was the capital of the Spanish possessions in America; but accounts of other newly found lands attracted the Spanish adventurers more than the mechanical processes of sugar production and they went forth again in their search for gold. In 1586 Sir Francis Drake honored the capital by one of his raids; and in the next few years British and French attacks had so ruined Hispaniolan trade that in 1606 the Spanish Government closed all the ports except that of Santo Domingo City. The island entered upon a long decline, its quiet unbroken save by occasional attacks of English expeditions or the incursions of buccaneers. Settling in the western part some French buccaneers laid the foundations for the French colony of Saint Domingue, which later became the Republic of Haiti. At the end of the eighteenth century the Spanish part of the island was again becoming settled and prosperous, but it was engulfed in the uprising of the French section, and in 1795, by the Treaty of Basle, the entire island was ceded to France. In 1809, when Spain and England were at war with France, the Spanish colonists revolted, and aided by British forces captured the city of Santo Domingo, reëstablishing Spanish rule. In 1821 Santo Domingo attempted to proclaim its independence, but was overrun by the Haitians and annexed to Haiti. To the succeeding twenty-two years of Haitian domination may be attributed major responsibility for the anarchy, unrest, and civil disturbance which have ever since plagued the Dominican Republic.

During the years when other Latin American Republics were afforded the opportunity of learning to govern themselves, Santo Domingo was prostrate under the domination of a tyranny which had for its chief object not only the eradication of the Caucasian race but also the obliteration of all the foundations of European culture and civilization upon which the institutions of the American world have been builded.[2]

In this subjugation may be found the roots of Dominican antagonism toward the Haitians, and of the present policy of refusing opportunity for settlement to the negroes who come for the annual harvesting.

On February 27, 1844, the inhabitants of the Spanish section rose against their Haitian rulers and proclaimed the Dominican Republic. But the struggle to maintain its existence gave the Dominicans little opportunity to gain experience in constitutional government and practice or to establish traditions of democratic government. During the first twenty-five years of national life, some of the political leaders believed that the happiness of Santo Domingo depended upon securing the protection of a strong power capable of preserving order, and the years of revolutionary turmoil and border warfare with Haiti, which did not recognize Dominican independence until 1874, confirmed them in their opinion. The party out of control was usually willing to offer annexation to a foreign power as the price of aid in the domestic conflict. France and Spain were preferred for reasons of identity or similarity of language, customs, and religion. Immediately after the declaration of independence a vain attempt was made to obtain a French protectorate, and in 1846 a Spanish protectorate. Although the existence of slavery and of prejudice against the colored race inspired misgivings, many Dominicans favored the United States because of its republican form of government and the probability of commercial advantages. Accordingly an appeal was made on January 24, 1850, for a protectorate. Upon its rejection, because of French and British opposition, Santo Domingo requested a tripartite mediation to put an end to the

2 Sumner Welles, *Naboth's Vineyard* (1928), p. 900. All quotations not otherwise credited are taken from this work.

struggle with Haiti. Under Daniel Webster as Secretary of State a special agent was appointed to join with the representatives of France and England in notifying the Haitian negro "emperor" Faustin that he must recognize the Dominican Government and cease constant warfare. These efforts came to naught, and in 1852 the French Minister of Foreign Affairs informed Haiti that France and England were disposed to maintain Dominican independence.

Relations with the United States.

Upon the failure of another attempt, in 1854, to secure a Spanish protectorate, President Santana sought closer relations with the United States, opening negotiations with General William L. Cazneau, special agent appointed by President Pierce with instructions to obtain by treaty a lease of the Samaná Peninsula. A survey of Samaná Bay by Captain (later Major General) George B. McClellan, aroused the opposition of the British and French governments, whose representatives threatened withdrawal of protection over Santo Domingo; Santana thereupon promised that the Dominican Government would never sell, lease, grant, or alienate in any way any portion of Dominican territory to any foreign government. The treaty originally agreed upon by the Dominican President and Cazneau had expressed its motive as "the acquisition of a strategic tract as a coaling depot in Samaná Bay." Owing to pressure, during almost two years of negotiations, from the French and English governments, this was revised and a simple commercial treaty was laid before the United States Senate. Washington was not interested in any treaty which did not include the lease of Samaná Bay, and the Senate refused to ratify it. Thereupon Santana resigned, May 26, 1856.

Exhausted by continual uprisings and the constant menace of invasion from Haiti, the agricultural and commercial classes desired peace more than independence. Consequently, in 1861, on the invitation of Santana, who had been inaugurated president for the third time, January 31, 1859, Isabella II of Spain annexed Santo Domingo. Although at the insistence of the Spanish Government that its troops would not occupy Santo Domingo without the unanimous consent of the Dominican people, an expression of support had been obtained, six weeks after the proclamation revolts began, and in 1863, when the Spanish penal code was substituted for the more enlightened Napoleonic Code, and increased taxes were levied, an insurrection broke out which caused Spain to withdraw from the island in 1865. Dissensions which had been rife among Dominican leaders while fighting Spain continued after the reëstablishment of the Republic. Santo Domingo had to begin its sovereignty anew for Spain left it deprived of either an executive head or representative or judiciary bodies.

The Dominican Republic had been recognized as an independent state by the United States Government prior to 1861 through the sending of diplomatic representatives and by the reception of Dominican diplomatic agents in Washington. In 1866 a commercial treaty was proclaimed, and in 1883 a regular diplomatic representative was accredited to Santo Domingo. From then until 1905 the United States minister to Haiti was also *chargé d'affaires* in Santo Domingo and occasionally visited that country. The office of Minister to Haiti was one of the United States foreign service posts reserved for colored men. In 1905 for the first time a separate diplomatic agent was sent to represent the United States in Santo Domingo.

INDEPENDENCE TO 1904

With the abolition of slavery in the United States, and the ending of the revolution against Spain, Cazneau recognized his opportunity to renew bargaining for concessions. Secretary Seward, a convinced expansionist, was known to believe that the United States should acquire a West Indian naval base. With Cazneau's support, Cabral, after his inauguration as constitutional president in September, 1866, made an earnest attempt to lease Samaná Bay to the United States for $2,000,000; but as complete control was not offered, Secretary Seward at length became discouraged. The negotiation for the purchase of the Danish West Indies ended that for the cession of Samaná, and a commercial treaty was ratified by the United States Senate on April 30, 1867, and by the Dominican Congress on May 16.

Baez, Cabral's successor, then resumed negotiations for the annexation of Santo Domingo to the United States. Conceiving that possession of the Dominican Republic might serve to solve the negro problem by affording a place for emigration, President Grant sent one of his military aides, General Babcock, to ascertain the feeling in regard to annexation provided the public debt of $1,500,000 were assumed. Apparently sentiment was favorable, for, upon his return from Santo Domingo, Babcock reported having pledged $100,000 in cash and $50,000 worth of arms as a first instalment; despite Secretary Fish's opposition, Grant chose to consider his government bound and sent Babcock back with power to negotiate a treaty. Accordingly, on November 29, 1869, alternate agreements were signed for a lease of Samaná Bay and for annexation, and Babcock took possession, under the United States flag, of a coaling station. As a government-conducted plebiscite the vote of sixteen thousand in favor of annexation to eleven against it, the next February, might be asserted, on the logic of numbers, to be fifty times as successful as Louis Napoleon's vote in 1852 of 7,824,129 to 253,149 in favor of a re-establishment of the French empire.[3]

Both treaties lapsed, but the annexation treaty was revived, and President Grant urged its passage. Led by Senator Sumner, powerful opposition developed in the Senate, and the treaty failed of ratification. Under a Congressional resolution of January 12, 1871, the President sent a commission of inquiry to Santo Domingo—Benjamin F. Wade, Andrew D. White, and Samuel G. Howe, the head of the Samaná Bay Company—and he interpreted their report[4] on the productiveness and healthfulness of Santo Domingo, on the assimilability of the people, and on their desire for annexation, as favorable to his views, but Congress took no action.

[3] For a similar instance, see p. 144.

[4] *Report of the United States Commission of Inquiry to Santo Domingo*, 42d Congress, 1st Session, Senate Document, Washington, 1871. See also Samuel Hazard's *Santo Domingo, Past and Present, with a Glance at Haiti*, New York, 1873. Hazard was a newspaperman who accompanied the commission.

Samaná Bay Company.

As a halfway measure, the Baez administration, on December 28, 1872, rented Samaná Bay for ninety-nine years to an American corporation. President Baez did not lose hope in the ultimate goal of annexation, but was overthrown a year later by a revolution. A new generation which had grown up since independence had been declared and had come to look upon civil disorder as a normal condition, came into power, and foreign annexation ceased to be an issue. The new administration rescinded the contract of the Samaná Bay Company on the ground of failure to make the contractual payments.

Ten years of anarchy followed, with a wearisome succession of military presidents. At times a president would be in office for only a few weeks before being ousted by a revolution, and occasionally his term of office would be one long war. The rapid succession of Dominican presidents in 1876 and again in 1878 recalls Rome's year of the four emperors.

In 1882 power was assumed by an energetic negro revolutionist, a former bandit, Ulises Heureaux, who either directly or through his lieutenants ruled with a rod of iron for almost twenty years. The peace he imposed was an apparent tranquillity based on terror, and his epigram that he did not care what history recorded of his conduct as he would not be here to read it was a costly one for his country. With his death in 1899 the chaotic undercurrents which ended in bankruptcy in 1904 broke loose.

Financial Condition.

The politics of Santo Domingo are so closely related to its financial condition, as is the case with so many Caribbean countries, that a brief statement of its financial history is necessary. The growth of the Dominican debt to 1904 may be divided into three periods:

1. In 1869, President Grant's Commission reported a debt of $1,565,831.59. In that year Baez made the first foreign loan, the Hartmont Loan. Falling into the hands of sharpers, Santo Domingo was mercilessly fleeced. Bonds were issued in London to an amount of £757,700 but the Republic received only £38,095. In

1870 the loan contract was repudiated by the Dominican Senate, and until 1887 the floating debt steadily accumulated from unpaid salaries, claims, bills for war supplies, etc.

2. Between 1888 and 1898 the bonded debt rose from $3,850,-000 (scaled valuation, $770,000) to $19,426,750. Heureaux interested an Amsterdam banking house, Westendorp and Company, which in 1888 floated a second loan for £770,000 at 6 per cent, and in 1890 a third for $900,000. A railroad from Santiago to Puerto Plata is the only tangible result which remains of all the loans contracted by Heureaux. To provide for the service of these loans the bankers organized a collection agency called the "regie" which was given the right to administer and control the customs. But in the rôle of fiscal agents Westendorp and Company were not successful, and as a result of the interest of two Americans the San Domingo Improvement Company of New York, organized under New Jersey State Laws, took over the "regie" and the management of the railroad, and at the instance of Heureaux bought out a French bank in May, 1892. The refunding operations, which were the condition of the transfer, were the occasion of a fourth bond issue of £2,035,000 in 1893. Three more issues aggregating $4,250,000 were floated, but as the customs receipts were not sufficient for the interest on all of them the 1893 loan defaulted in 1897. Ruinous in its conditions, the eighth bond issue, together with Heureaux's recklessness and wastefulness, brought about a crisis.

Foreign Pressure.

By reason of the tyranny and corruption of his *régime* and his issues of paper money, popular hatred of Heureaux became bitter, crystallizing in the Junta Revolucionaria de Jovenes organized by General Vasquez and ending in the assassination of Heureaux by Ramón Cáceres; Vasquez was then unanimously elected provisional president by the revolutionary generals. Upon the expiration of his term, Jiménez was inaugurated president. Thereupon the French creditors became insistent for payment of the debts contracted by Heureaux. A French flagship and two other men-of-war entered Santo Domingo Harbor, a United States warship following. The French assumed a conciliatory attitude, and the United States Minister pressed a private American claim. Rising anti-American feeling demanded the cancellation of the Improvement Company's concession. Jiménez shilly-shallied with the Company, and when the Belgian and French bondholders repudiated the new agreement he issued a decree excluding the Company from the customhouses. He then made a separate agreement with the Franco-Belgian bondholders specifically pledging the income from the ports of Santo Domingo and San Pedro de Macorís for the service of their bonds. Subsequent negotiation of contracts caused political friction: less money was available for the creditors than formerly and default again took place.

Settlement of Claims.

Upon being ousted from the customhouses, the San Domingo Improvement Company appealed to the State Department in Washington, which counseled a private settlement. The Company claimed $11,000,000 for such bonds as it still held, its interest in the Santiago–Puerto Plata Railroad, and other rights. Provisional President Vasquez, who had overthrown Jiménez in 1902, finally offered to recognize a round sum of $4,500,000, and signed a protocol with United States diplomatic representatives, designating this sum as the amount due and leaving details of payment to be settled by a board of arbitrators appointed by the American and Dominican Governments. The board, consisting of two Americans and one Dominican, met in Washington and rendered its award in 1904. It designated the customhouses of Puerto Plata, Monte Cristi, and those of Samaná Bay as specific security and appointed the Vice-President of the Improvement Company as Financial Agent. In the event of failure by the Dominican Government to pay any of the monthly instalments he was to take over the customhouse first of Puerto Plata, and if these revenues were insufficient, of the other northern ports.

Italy and Germany pressed their claims and the Dominican Government signed protocols with Italy defining the claims and guaranteeing their payment by certain customs receipts; nothing was paid on any of the foreign protocols and the bonded debt likewise remained in default.

FISCAL ASSISTANCE

Toward the latter part of 1904 Santo Domingo fell into bankruptcy. In the civil turmoils the account books had been improperly kept and not even the amount of the debt was accurately known, being estimated at various sums between $25,000,000 and $50,000,000. Every item had been in default for many months, and interest, often 2 per cent a month or more, was accruing at such a rate that the whole income of the country would hardly have sufficed for its payment. Commerce was handicapped by high wharf and harbor charges collected by private individuals, principally Italians and British, under government concessions, and by prohibitive port dues imposed on foreign vessels in accordance with the Clyde Line concession. The Government was devoting almost three-fourths of its income to combating insurrectionists, who were little more than bandits and had the habit of raiding ports when a foreign steamer was expected and retreating to the woods after collecting the customs duties.

More than three-fourths of the debt was held by foreigners who were clamoring for payment. The same revenues and customs were pledged several times over to different governments: in general, the ports of the northern coast were pledged primarily to Americans and secondarily to Italians, those of Samaná Bay primarily to Italians and secondarily to Americans, and those of the southern coast primarily to French and Belgians and secondarily to Italians; the export tax on cacao was mortgaged to the Italian Government. Only one of the international agreements specified when and how the customhouses to which it referred were to be turned over; the others made pledges in general terms. The exception was the arbitral award in favor of the San Domingo Improvement Company. No payments had been made to it, and in October, 1904, the Financial Agent was placed in possession of the Puerto Plata customhouse; in February, 1905, the Monte Cristi customhouse was also turned over to him. The success of United

States collections led the other foreign creditors to press their claims more vigorously. In December, 1904, the French representative in Santo Domingo, acting for French and Belgian interests, threatened to seize the customhouse of Santo Domingo City, the mainstay of the Government. The Italian creditors also demanded compliance with their agreements. Foreclosure of these European mortgages would obviously mean indefinite occupation and the destruction of the Dominican Government, as no revenue would be left to sustain it.

United States Control.

In this difficulty the Dominican Government proposed that all ports be taken over by the United States. Accordingly, on February 7, 1905, a treaty was signed providing that all Dominican customs duties be collected under United States direction, that 45 per cent of the receipts be delivered to the Dominican Government for its expenses, the remaining 55 per cent to be reserved as a creditors' fund, and that a commission be appointed to ascertain the true amount of Dominican indebtedness and the sum payable to each claimant. But there was no desire in the United States for intervention in Dominican matters, and the tension then existing between the Senate and President Roosevelt endangered many of the President's measures. Consequently, the Senate adjourned in March, 1905, without action on the Dominican treaty.

The Dominican Government could find no solution for its problem. The creditors, tired of waiting, were in no mood to permit further delay, and the Government, being without resources, was not able to appease them. President Morales had been forced to use customhouse receipts to meet governmental expenses. Fearful that the European creditors would seize the customhouses to pay their claims, he appealed to the United States. The appeal offered President Roosevelt an opportunity for that intervention which, he thought, "in America as elsewhere," might be required by "an impotence which results in a general loosening of the ties of civilized society," and which at the same time might check German ambition for a foothold in the Western Hemisphere. Using his position as Commander-in-Chief of the Navy, Roosevelt arranged a *modus vivendi* with Santo Domingo, and, unable to gain the consent of the Senate, justified executive action as follows:

It has for some time been obvious that those who profit by the Monroe Doctrine must accept certain responsibilities along with the rights which it confers; . . . the justification for the United States taking this burden and incurring this responsibility is to be found in the fact that it is incompatible with international equity for the United States to refuse to allow other Powers to take the only means at their disposal of satisfying the claims of their creditors and yet to refuse, itself, to take any other steps. . . .

The conditions in the Dominican Republic not only constitute a menace to our relations with other foreign nations, but they also concern the prosperity of the people of the Island, as well as the security of American interests, and they are intimately associated with the interests of the south Atlantic and Gulf States, the normal expansion of whose commerce lies in that direction. . . .[5]

Improvement under Modus Vivendi.

Under the *modus vivendi* the President of the United States was to designate an American to collect the revenues of all Dominican customhouses and disburse the receipts in a manner similar to that determined by the pending treaty. This temporary arrangement came into being April 1, 1905. The effects were immediate. The creditors ceased their pressure, confidence returned, interior trade revived, smuggling was diminished, exports and imports increased, and receipts covered budget appropriations. On December 31, 1905, a deposit of $815,000 gold stood to the Government's credit in the National City Bank of New York; on January 1, 1907, $2,317,607.40. Nevertheless "during 1905 an average of eleven vessels, mostly of the gunboat and cruiser type, was continuously maintained in Dominican waters throughout the twelve months of the year."[6] In order to obtain more positive information with respect to the Dominican debt, the United States Government commissioned a financial expert, Professor Jacob H.

[5] Message from the President of the United States to the Senate, February 15, 1905.

[6] *Inquiry into Occupation and Administration of Haiti and Santo Domingo*, Washington, 1922, p. 91.

Hollander of Johns Hopkins University, to make an investigation of financial conditions. In an elaborate report[7] Professor Hollander found the amount of the claims pending against the Dominican Government on June 1, 1905, to be about $40,000,000.

It was believed that Senate opposition to the treaty would be diminished if the Dominican Republic made a direct settlement with its creditors and the United States merely undertook to administer the customs for the service of the debt as adjusted. The Dominican Minister of Hacienda, Don Federico Velasquez, came to the United States in June, 1906. In two months he and Dr. Hollander evolved a plan, contingent upon the completion of a treaty with the United States, of which the essential features were: (a) an arrangement with Kuhn, Loeb & Company for the issue of fifty-year 5 per cent bonds of the Dominican Republic to the amount of $20,000,000; (b) an offer to adjust recognized debts and claims at rates varying from 10 to 90 per cent of the nominal values specified in the offer. The nominal aggregate as recognized by the Republic, exclusive of accrued interest, was about $32,000,000, which it was proposed to settle for about $17,-000,000. The proposed scaling down provoked opposition and remonstrance, but by the beginning of 1907 holders of credits had signified their assent in sufficient number to assure the success of the readjustment.

1907 Convention.

In the new convention, signed February 8, 1907, and ratified by the United States Senate and by the Dominican Congress, the United States did not try to adjust or determine the Dominican debt but administered the customs for the service of a new loan. It was provided that the United States President should appoint a General Receiver to collect all customs duties until payment or redemption of the entire bond issue of $20,000,000. From the receipts he was to pay (a) the expenses of the receivership, (b) $100,000 per month to the fiscal agent of the loan, and (c) the balance to the Dominican Government; whenever the collections

[7] J. H. Hollander, *Report on the Debt of Santo Domingo*, Fifty-ninth Congress, First Session, Senate Executive Document, Washington, 1905.

exceeded $3,000,000 in any year, one-half of the excess was to be applied to the sinking fund for the further redemption of bonds.[8] The Dominican Government agreed not to increase its "public" debt, or to "modify" its import duties, without the consent of the United States.

The many defaults on its bond issues had destroyed Dominican international credit, but the virtual guaranty by the United States made the new bonds a good investment. As the agreement with Kuhn, Loeb & Company could not be carried out owing to the panic of 1907, the creditors' claims were paid direct, 80 per cent in bonds and 20 per cent in cash from the fund accumulated under the *modus vivendi*. Furthermore, the onerous wharf and harbor concessions and the restrictive concession of the Clyde Line were canceled, and the funds remaining devoted to public improvements. The financial and economic conditions of the country continued to improve as if by magic. Imports and exports, and with them the income of the Government, quickly reached higher figures than had hitherto been attained, the revenues for 1907 being $4,000,000. The Government established a Bureau of Public Works under the supervision of an American engineer, and with the assent of the United States Government obtained $500,-000 for its construction program. The Cáceres Administration continued the policy of government ownership of public utilities. Sanitary conditions in the large cities were greatly improved.

Communication.

Mountain ranges traversing Santo Domingo horizontally and separating north and south hindered commercial development. This barrier was aggravated by inadequate means of communication; and the resulting immobility of the residents of each section created intense local prejudices. The exercise of virtual control by the local governor in each of the twelve provinces and frequent defiance of the weak central government prevented national unity. At this time trails, traversable only on horseback, connected the principal towns. In the rainy season communication was so difficult that the journey from the capital to Santiago often took

---

[8] Receipts increased so that the loan of 1908 was liquidated February 1, 1927.

three days. Even in dry weather the usual way to go from one of these cities to the other was *via* the railroad to or from Puerto Plata and by steamer around the eastern extremity of the island. To remedy this condition road construction was undertaken. The highroad between the capital and Azua was completed as far as San Cristóbal; and the northern highroad, to connect the capital with the cities of the Cibao, as far as Los Alcarrizos.

During this period Washington looked upon the Dominican receivership as a trusteeship. So far as the Dominicans were concerned the Convention of 1907 was negotiated with delicacy and had benefited Santo Domingo in three ways: (a) it had established Dominican credit; (b) it had assured the Government of revenue; (c) it had removed the danger of European intervention.

PERIOD OF INCREASING INTERVENTION

The assassination of President Cáceres on November 19, 1911, interrupted a period of stability and prosperity. The youthful military commander of the city, General Victoria, seized the reins of power and compelled the election of his uncle, a Senator of the same name. Almost at once uprisings took place in all parts of the country; civil war soon became general and the country was devastated by contending factions.

Within ten months the Victoria Government had exhausted the surplus accumulated by President Cáceres, and had increased the public debt by $1,500,000, thus, according to State Department interpretation, infringing the Convention of 1907. The advice of the newly appointed Minister, Mr. W. W. Russell, proposed a control far beyond that provided for in the Convention as a consequence of its breach:

Only complete control by our Government would permanently insure order and justice, but any degree of control would be beneficial; indeed, without our effective control, one administration here would be as good as another. Once having landed men for protection of the custom-houses, in accordance with our rights under the convention, we might be able to dictate a policy beneficial to the country. The main evils to be remedied are: the absolute subservience of the courts;

forced recruiting for the army; wholesale imprisonment without trial; peculation of public funds.[9]

Two commissioners, a member of the Bureau of Insular Affairs of the War Department, and the Chief of the Latin American Division of the State Department, were sent with 750 marines to investigate the situation. In return for some of the concessions demanded by them upon their arrival in October, 1912, President Victoria urged the United States Government to consent to the flotation of a new bond issue to cancel the indebtedness which his Government had created. This the United States Government refused unless the Dominican Government would agree to assume responsibility for the misappropriation of public funds, and to appoint a financial adviser. President Taft's Commissioners offered the Victoria Government the alternative of resigning or of forfeiting its share of the customs revenues, and made it known that the Department of State would consider loans to the Dominican Government as a violation of the Convention. Though the United States Government would not recognize a revolutionary government, the Commissioners promised United States support to a constitutionally elected government and control of the customhouses then held by the revolutionists; also, following the appointment of a financial adviser designated by the United States, they said they would favor a loan.

Victoria thereupon found it expedient to resign. Archbishop Nouel, unanimously elected provisional president for two years, proposed to give an impartial administration. But the pressure applied for favors he could not grant, criticism of his appointments, and the menacing attitude assumed by some of the military leaders disgusted him; ill and discouraged, he resigned after three months. Upon the retirement of Archbishop Nouel in March, 1913, the Dominican Congress elected a compromise candidate, General Bordas. The designation was not popular, uprisings were renewed, and soon the country was again devastated by civil war.

Changing Attitude of State Department.

During the early part of this period United States policy was

[9] Mr. Russell to Secretary Knox, Sept. 19, 1912.

determined by Secretary of State Knox, who undertook to treat the Dominicans in the same paternal manner that President Roosevelt adopted toward the Cubans: "I am doing my best to persuade the Cubans that if only they will be good they will be happy; I am seeking the very minimum of interference necessary to make them good." The imposition of a native government too weak to maintain itself unaided expresses the character of the unsettled conditions between 1908 and 1916.

In the second half of this period Mr. Bryan as Secretary of State used the office of Receiver General to reward one of his campaign workers, Mr. Vick, to whom he addressed his famous inquiry: "Can you let me know what positions you have at your disposal with which to reward deserving Democrats?" A new Minister, James M. Sullivan, continued the policy of taking an active part in the internal affairs of the Dominican Republic.

Arriving in Santo Domingo in the midst of civil warfare, Minister Sullivan engaged in parleys with the revolutionists and promised them a "fair ballot and free elections" if they would disarm. When they accepted his terms the State Department sent observers from Porto Rico to watch the ensuing elections for a constitutional convention, though this action was authorized by no agreement with the Dominican Government, and indeed, was engaged in over its protest.

Financial Expert Appointed.

On January 12, 1914, the United States Minister was authorized to audit the daily expenses of the Dominican Government, and on March 20 the Bordas Government agreed to the appointment of a "financial expert" to supervise the receivership, the Department of Public Works, and any bureau of public accounts.

This growing encroachment by the United States undermined the prestige of President Bordas. In April civil war was renewed and Bordas took the field in person against Arias, an habitual revolutionist. By June the contest had narrowed down to a government attack on Puerto Plata, which was held by the revolutionists. The commander of the United States warships in the port proclaimed, as a protection of foreign life and property, that a bombardment of Puerto Plata would not be permitted. As Bordas disregarded this establishment of a neutral zone, the U.S.S. *Machias* fired upon the government forces, an action which was construed as evidence that the United States favored the revolutionists.

Bordas' term expired on April 13, but because of the civil war elections were not held until June. These elections were rendered abortive through fraud, and while Bordas remained *de facto* president, the Financial Adviser refused to advance funds to the Dominican Government on the ground that his position was no longer constitutional. Bordas' concessions to the United States had brought him for a time day-to-day funds from the Receiver of Customs, but these were now stopped and new debts piled up.

In August, 1914, President Wilson sent two commissioners to insist upon peace and the selection of a provisional president until an election could be held under United States supervision. Meeting with the political leaders they agreed upon Rámon Baez, a son of former President Buenaventura Baez, and on August 27 he was inaugurated provisional president. Early in November former President Jiménez was reëlected and inaugurated on December 5. The Vasquez faction refrained from voting, charging that partiality was shown the Jimenistas, and demanding annulment of the election on the ground that the distribution of electors was not in proportion to the population and that fraud was rife in spite of the presence of United States observers.

Assumption of Customs Collections.

Needing money for overdue salaries, the Dominican Government early in 1914 had pledged the alcohol and tobacco taxes to the Receivership, reserving the right of collection to itself. Although bound to recognize Jiménez as constitutional president, the State Department delayed action until he had agreed to the collection of internal revenue taxes under the Receivership. This assumption of the right of collection by the Receivership was a serious infringement of Dominican sovereignty and offended the local politicians because it deprived them of a lucrative source of profit. Moreover it involved the gradual assumption of general public administration: a foreign government may collect and transmit customs duties without interfering in the domestic affairs of a country, but once internal revenues are taken over, the control of the police, road construction, public improvements, and other tasks follows inevitably. Efficient and honest administration in fiscal matters at the hands of the United States is part of the price received by a Caribbean country for surrender of its independence.

Fiscal conditions improved rapidly under this extended control. In 1919 the alcohol tax which had averaged only $210,000 from 1909 to 1916 produced $809,270.21. The total internal revenue collections increased from $450,000 in 1915 to $2,998,686 by 1924.

Secretary Bryan attempted to continue his policy of giving United States representatives complete control in Santo Domingo. Before their inauguration Jiménez and Velasquez had committed themselves to retain the Financial Adviser who had been appointed June 1, 1914, but President Jiménez could not obtain the consent of his Congress to recognize Mr. Johnston as Comptroller. Embarrassed, he sent a delegation to Washington to protest; as a result Johnston was placed on the Receiver General's pay roll. Secretary Bryan resigned a few days after the conference, and not long afterward Minister Sullivan followed him into retirement.

In September W. W. Russell was reappointed with instructions to warn the Dominican Government that further violation of Article III of the 1907 Convention against increase of the public debt must cease. The Dominicans reasoned that "public" debt meant "bonded debt" and supported their contention by precedents from civil law jurisdictions. Washington interpreted "public" debt to include "floating" debt, that is, all outstanding indebtedness. Inasmuch as any increase in indebtedness in backward countries may produce internal disorders and make claims which have to be funded, especially if these increase too rapidly to be paid in cash, the same evils may be created whatever the nature of the indebtedness.

On November 19 Mr. Russell presented the Dominican Government with a formal note stating that its violation of the Convention gave the United States the right (a) to insist upon the immediate appointment of a financial adviser, and (b) to provide for a constabulary, organized and commanded by an American.

The Dominicans refused both demands, and an appeal to President Wilson brought a noncommittal reply. Opposition to Jiménez became more pronounced; in April, 1916, General Arias seized command of the fortress in the Capital, gaining control of the city, and on May 1 the Chamber of Deputies took a vote of impeachment against Jiménez. United States marines were landed on May 4, ostensibly to protect the Legation, and the United States offered the President troops, but Jiménez wanted rifles and ammunition for his own soldiers and hesitated to impose his authority with foreign bayonets. Sick in body and depressed in mind, he resigned on May 7 and went to Porto Rico.

The Occupation.

United States marines continued to land at different seaports during June until a total of about eighteen hundred had disembarked. They proceeded into the interior, taking over duties of preserving public order and disarming the inhabitants; they met with no serious opposition except in the north, where the following of Arias was strongest. All the insurgents eventually dispersed or surrendered, and Arias himself submitted to the military control which became complete throughout the country. Total marine losses in occupying the country were 3 officers killed and 3 wounded and 4 enlisted men killed and 12 wounded; the losses of the insurgents are estimated at between 100 and 300 killed and wounded. On June 18 the United States authorities directed the Receivership to collect the internal revenues as well as the customs.

The Dominican Congress on July 25, 1916, elected Dr. Francisco Henriquez y Carvajal, a distinguished physician, provisional president for five months, until general elections could be held. Washington, however, declined to recognize him unless measures were adopted similar to those contained in the treaty of September, 1915, between Haiti and the United States.

Jealous of his country's sovereignty, fearful that the arrangements proposed would make the Dominican Government sub-

servient to insufficiently responsible United States officials, and
knowing that opposition to the proposed treaty would be general,
Henriquez refused to accede to the demands. Thereupon the
United States authorities declined to pay over any of the Republic's revenues to the Dominican Government. Since they collected both the customs duties and the internal revenues, the Government was thus left penniless and no salaries were paid. Some
services, such as the mail, were discontinued almost entirely, and
the whole governmental machinery was paralyzed, yet many officials continued to perform their duties without compensation. This
manner of exerting pressure united the Dominicans, and their
determination was strengthened by clashes between marines and
the populace, overbearing behavior on the part of some of the
marine officers, and a rigorous censorship. On August 25 and September 14, the Provisional President suggested compromises, but
the United States Minister, on instructions from Washington, refused to discuss halfway measures, and on September 30 presented
another set of demands. The Dominican Minister in Washington,
Don Armando Pérez Perdomo, made a final plea for an agreement
that "would not imply the complete obliteration of Dominican
sovereignty." This was answered in effect by Secretary Lansing's
memorandum of November 22, 1916, to President Wilson:

The situation has now reached a very serious point, in view of the
fact that according to telegrams from the Legation at Santo Domingo the President has issued a decree convoking the electoral college for the purpose of electing senators and deputies. It is apparent
that the majority of the senators and deputies will be from the Arias
faction, hence giving Arias, who has been the disturbing element in
Santo Domingo for many years, complete governmental control,
even in the event of the election of Henriquez as constitutional president.

This new phase of the situation, coupled with the fact that the
provisional government will not meet the views of the United States
in regard to the establishment of financial control and constabulary,
brings the Government of the United States face to face with a serious
problem.

The withholding of the funds by the United States Government,
on account of the fact that recognition has not been granted to

Henriquez, has brought an economic crisis in the country which is daily growing worse and for which this Government would not wish to be placed in such a position that it would be held responsible.

After a careful consideration of the matter, in conference with the Navy Department, it was thought that the only solution of the difficulty would be the declaration of martial law and placing of Santo Domingo under military occupation, basing this on the interpretation which the United States has given to the Dominican Convention of 1907 and also upon the present unsettled conditions in the Republic.

Captain Knapp, who has gone in command of the cruiser squadron of the Atlantic fleet as Commander of the Forces in Dominican waters, is understood to have arrived today in Santo Domingo and it is felt that no time should be lost in instructing him to put into effect the proclamation declaring military control and to immediately commence the disbursement of the funds under martial law.[10]

Enclosed with this memorandum was a copy of the proclamation which President Wilson, his entire attention occupied with the European situation, reluctantly[11] approved except for one clause which he thought too arbitrary. Serious as the situation was in its financial and international aspects, other factors must be considered: (1) the *modus vivendi* and the 1907 Protocol had removed the danger of European intervention; (2) the claims asserted for $16,000,000 were later reduced by the Claims Commission to about one-fourth of this sum; (3) the increase in internal debt was partly due to the withholding of funds by the Financial Adviser as a means of bringing pressure to bear on the Dominican Government; (4) a constitutional government did exist in Santo Domingo which the United States was ready to recognize upon accession to its demands; and (5) the landing of troops and the proclaiming of martial law in a country at peace is an evidence of dissatisfaction with some event or condition other than a debt increase.

[10] *For. Rel.*, 1916, p. 240.

[11] President Wilson's reply, November 26, 1916, to Secretary Lansing's communication:

"It is with the deepest reluctance that I approve and authorize the course here proposed, but I am convinced that it is the least of the evils in sight in this very perplexing situation. . . ."

MILITARY GOVERNMENT

On November 29, 1916, Captain (later Rear Admiral) H. S. Knapp issued a proclamation declaring the Dominican Republic under United States military administration and in a state of occupation. The proclamation recited that the Dominican Republic had failed to live up to the terms of the Convention of 1907, that his Government had patiently tried to aid the Dominican Government, but that the latter was not inclined or able to adopt the measures suggested. For these reasons the United States Government believed the time had come to take steps to assure the execution of the Convention and to maintain domestic tranquillity in the Dominican Republic. Admiral Knapp declared that the object of the occupation was not to destroy Dominican sovereignty, but to restore order; that Dominican laws were to continue in effect so far as they did not conflict with the objects of the occupation or the decrees of the military government; that the Dominican courts were to continue in their functions, except that offenses against the military government were to be judged by military courts; and that all Dominican revenues were to be paid over to the military government for administration.

Five days after the proclamation of occupation, Don Armando Pérez Perdomo filed a protest:

A state of war which alone could have justified such a proceeding on the part of the Government of the United States toward the Dominican Republic has never existed between the two Nations.

And therefore by acting as it has with the Dominican Republic, Your Excellency's Government plainly violated in the first place the fundamental principles of public international law which laid down as an invariable rule of public order for the nations the reciprocal respect of the sovereignty of each and every one of the other states of the civilized world, and in the second place, the principles which guide the doctrine of Pan-Americanism which hallow the inviolability of American nationalities; principles which may be said to have found their highest virtues in the many official declarations of the learned President of the United States.

The practical grounds which impelled the occupation and later the taking over of government administration are indicated in a

Navy Department memorandum prepared August 5, 1921, for the Senate Investigation Committee:[12]

Our international relations were now rapidly approaching a critical stage. It was highly desirable to have peaceful conditions close to our own boundaries, and the United States Government therefore stipulated that a new treaty be drawn with the new Dominican Government guaranteeing the maintenance of law and order and further assuring the payment of Dominican financial obligations. This treaty was in reality the price of recognition, and Dr. Henriquez refused to accede to the terms. Thereupon the United States authorities refused to pay over any of the revenues of the Republic. There being no surplus in the treasury, government salaries ceased throughout the Republic. This deadlock continued from early August, 1916, until late November of the same year, when, all efforts to induce the Dominican authorities to conduct their Government in a manner conducive to the maintenance of internal peace and to the satisfactory conduct of foreign relations having proved of no avail, the United States Government on November 29, 1916, proclaimed a state of military occupation of the Dominican Republic by the naval and marine forces of the United States and made the Republic subject to military government.

Military Administration.

Except for the portfolios of Interior and of War and Marine to which Dominican citizens were declared ineligible, the Military Governor apparently expected the Dominican chiefs of executive departments to coöperate with him, but as they failed to appear at their offices their posts were declared vacant and filled by Navy officers. In his report[13] Admiral Knapp says that although he had not had the "prevision" to put Americans in control, "the advantage of having officers actually administering, instead of observing and checking the administration of others, has been evident." The theory of an independent state under temporary occupation was carefully observed, and the United States Minister continued to represent the State Department. Dr. Henriquez left the country.

[12] *Inquiry into Occupation and Administration of Haiti and Santo Domingo,* p. 93.

[13] *Ibid.,* p. 95.

The military government proceeded to organize the finances and to pay arrears of salaries (excepting those of the Provisional President and his Cabinet Ministers which were withheld on the ground that they had participated in a government unrecognized by the United States), to subdue several non-complying bandits, and to confiscate all arms. We may describe its achievements under categories.

Finances.

By Executive decrees, June 26 and July 9, 1917, a Claims Commission was appointed composed of two members of the United States Marine Corps, two able Dominicans, and a Porto Rican lawyer. The number of claims filed was 9,038 for a total of $16,-960,513.48; $4,292,343.52 was allowed by the Commission. The claims under $50 were paid in cash and the larger creditors received bonds of an issue authorized by the United States Government in 1918. These had no market in Santo Domingo but after arrangements had been made were salable in the United States at prices ranging between 87½ and 92. The accounting and auditing systems were greatly improved and simplified. Steps were taken to provide a proper check on the purchase of materials, supplies, and other property, which had often been purchased in large quantities and had later disappeared. Pay-roll graft was eliminated. Numerous measures were taken to insure efficiency and honesty in conducting the public business and handling public funds. Much attention was given to the improvement of the internal revenue laws under the advice of a tax expert.

An impartial tariff commission of five experts made a study of the customs tariff, and on their recommendation a new tariff went into effect January 1, 1920, which reduced the general level of duties about 38 per cent. It gave liberal treatment to foodstuffs, chemical and pharmaceutical products, manufactures of iron and steel, and building materials, and lowered the rates on articles having to do with agriculture and transportation. Many manufactured commodities were on the reduced or free lists, and since these were imported mostly from the United States, benefit accrued to United States enterprises from the new schedule. Revenues immediately rose to a sum far greater than that of any previous time, but in the autumn occurred the crash in sugar and tobacco and the business crisis which was felt throughout the world. Santo Domingo recovered by 1924, when its revenues reached their former figures, though the low tariff still remained in effect.

Land Titles.

Sparseness of population makes the Dominicans essentially a landowning people; like the New England farmer, the Dominican is capable when hired but prefers to do his own work. The original titles to land consisted of grants issued in the name of the Spanish monarch; later, titles of communal lands were based on occupation. A law of 1885 waived the required thirty years of continuous occupation for validation of squatting but did not give definitive title. Boundaries were drawn to give access to water, for Santo Domingo was a grazing country. In the successive occupations by France, Haiti, and Spain, and during the civil wars, the few titles which may have been registered were lost. An old custom had divided lands on the death of a landowner, not cadastrally but by setting a money value on them and then giving each heir a portion of this valuation; upon the death of the heir his shares would again be distributed, and this process continued for generations. The sale of these "peso titles" not specifying a physical part of the general estate and without any record of the total number of peso titles in the estate increased the general confusion.

In an effort to resolve this situation, the military government established a land court, and also inaugurated a land tax, the first direct tax on the people. This aroused severe protest, and under the reorganized Dominican Government was almost dropped, despite the fact that 50 per cent was paid by foreigners. By 1924 the land tax had shown itself to be far from lucrative, decreasing from a yield of $1,011,002.09 in 1920 to $350,000. The provision of the land registration law which gave clear title to land possessed for ten years up to January 1, 1921, relieved large estates of litigation by claimants who showed no interest in the land until the plantation became prosperous. In 1925 the assessed value of the principal sugar estates was $40,894,135.78, chiefly owned by

Americans and secondarily by Italians, with less than $2,000,000 in Dominican hands.

Inasmuch as native workers are scarce, part of the labor necessary to harvest the sugar crop has to be imported. The directors of the enterprises are for the most part foreigners, and company stores furnish employees with necessities. Though good sugar years make for general prosperity, and though the economic status of the inhabitants has rapidly risen, the immediate profit derived by Dominican business from the presence of the large industries and the labor influx is relatively small. A similar condition, more marked in degree, exists in Egypt where the advantage from the greatly improved position of cotton goes much more to the Greek, Syrian, and Italian business men than to the fellahin.

Education.

The school system of Santo Domingo was in a deplorable condition with a limited number of schools in the larger towns and none in the rural districts. The teachers were grossly underpaid, and the schools were installed in miserable quarters usually consisting of a small earth-floored room with two or three board benches for the pupils and a broken desk for the teacher. The total number of pupils enrolled was estimated at about 18,000, and the average daily attendance at about 21 per cent. There was no real school administration. Soon after the military government took charge a commission of prominent Dominicans was established which prepared a series of new school laws; every effort was made to increase the number of schools, provide proper equipment, and improve the quality and efficiency of the teachers. Within two years the school enrolment had grown to 100,000, with a daily attendance of 85 per cent; the schools were neat and well equipped. Opportunities for agricultural instruction were also provided.

Pacification and Police.

Pacification was accomplished, although the means adopted were sometimes drastic. The army was reorganized into a police force under United States officers. For the first time all parts of the country became subject to a central authority, and the almost universal habit of carrying arms was ended by a thorough disarming of the population. Insurrections no longer occurred, the countryside was not subject to devastation, and people were able to attend to their affairs in peace.

Sanitation.

Prior to the establishment of the military government, little attention had been given to sanitation or public health. Steps were now taken to clean the towns, remove garbage, close polluted wells, report and control transmissible diseases, vaccinate against smallpox, remove the leper asylum from the center of Santo Domingo City to the country, regulate the practice of medicine and midwifery, and promote hospital work.

Postal Department.

The post-office system was reorganized, and although very soon twice as much mail was handled as formerly, the time for sending a letter across the island was reduced from twelve days to four. The national telephone system was merged with the post-office system and a twenty-four-hour service provided.

Roads and Other Public Works.

The military government built about 150 kilometers of new macadam roads, 150 kilometers of second-class roads, 300 kilometers of third-class roads, and a number of fine bridges over the most turbulent streams. The road building program thus inaugurated has been industriously extended by the succeeding Dominican Government. Santo Domingo now has an excellent highway system with 1,010 kilometers of surfaced roads, and 339 kilometers of unsurfaced roads. For 1929 the estimate of maintenance is $606,700. The military government also repaired public buildings, extended wharves, dredged harbors, erected school buildings, and made many other improvements. Two factors must be taken into account when it is said that the military government has little to show for the large sums which were budgeted for public improvements: (a) Road building is difficult and expensive alike on account of the nature of the land and climate. Because of torrential rains roads must be solidly constructed, and stone had often to be hauled over long stretches of miry land. (b) Lack of policy delayed needed funds; the Navy Department could not undertake long-time projects when withdrawal was pending. For example, an extensive public works program calling for an expenditure of $10,000,000 was planned[14] but when the Dominican Government approached the State Department for its approval of a loan, a change of policy was announced. After six months' delay $2,500,000 was granted.

Other Accomplishments.

The military government took measures to promote commerce, and during the World War saved millions of dollars for exporters by securing shipping for Dominican exports, sometimes having them carried on naval transports. It modernized the port law; established a meteorological service; instituted a more careful supervision of immigration; enacted laws for the care of abandoned children; simplified criminal procedure and cleared the jails of prisoners awaiting trial; cleaned the jails; established higher salaries for judges; enacted a civil service law; took the first reliable census of the Republic, and made a general geological survey.

Reasons for Opposition.

In spite of the material benefits, the Dominicans found many grounds for opposition to the occupation. First, during the World War the State Department paid little attention to Santo Domingo, and the Navy Department, having no division to study the problem, gave almost complete authority to military men as governors. The Navy Department considered itself the "steward" of the State Department in carrying out policies, the General Receiver was responsible to the Bureau of Insular Affairs of the War

[14] This plan was approved by the second Pan-American financial conference in January, 1920.

Department, and the Minister reported to the State Department. Confusion in administration naturally arose.

In every army there are some ruffians, and the excesses of one rascal attract more attention than the proper actions of many honorable men. Many of the best marine officers in the lower ranks had been sent to France and their places filled by raw recruits who were inclined to be rough, especially when looking for concealed arms. Cases are recorded of oppression, acts of cruelty and occasional rowdyism of drunken officers or marines, very irritating to the average Dominican; the stories and rumors of excesses were repeated and grossly magnified in Santo Domingo and abroad.

Secondly, no explanation of the occupation was given. If the Washington officials had a policy they did not impart it to the military governors, and orders were given on a hand to mouth basis. This was accompanied by a censorship of the press which forbade every criticism of the military government, and exhibited the characteristics common to all censorships. It was aggravated by the war mentality of 1917-1918; ironical stories were told of the censoring of a speech delivered by the Chief Justice, the prohibition of a reference to Kant as a great German philosopher, the rejection of an article on the Red Cross because the author had formerly written about Bolshevism, the removal of the electric sign "Independencia" from the cinema theater of that name. What was satisfactory to the censor of one province might be suppressed in another. The indignation of Latin America eventually spread to the United States and the Navy Department in 1920 ordered the relaxation of the censorship rules.

Thirdly, the military government, maintaining an attitude of aloofness, made little attempt to secure the coöperation of representative Dominicans in legislative and administrative fields, and governed by executive order since, after December 26, 1916, the Dominican Congress was not allowed to meet. The provost courts, constituted by United States officers, generally ignorant of Spanish and indifferent to Dominican sentiment, had jurisdiction "over offenses against the occupation." The phrase was elastic and the country absorbed stories of injustice or harsh sentences, though just decisions attracted no attention.

Increasing Hostility.

In consideration of the growing hostility to the military government, the State Department finally instructed Admiral Snowden to appoint a Junta Consultiva to give expression to the Dominicans' point of view. Accordingly on November 12, 1919, a committee composed of four Dominicans made a series of reports which included a protest against the new foreign loan of $5,000,-000 proposed by the military governor. Six days after the last memorandum an increased rigor in the censorship convinced the Dominicans that the military governor did not intend to keep faith with them. Censorship is all the more precarious as an institution of government from the fact that in the eyes of authority the most seditious criticism is that which is unanswerable. The members of the Junta Consultiva resigned January 9, 1920, and in March the Union Nacional Dominicana was formed to agitate for the withdrawal of United States troops. In July an internationally known Dominican poet, Fabio Fiallo, published a versified outburst against the "chains" and "outrages" and was sentenced by a provost court to three years' imprisonment, later commuted to one year. Dominican publicists went on lecture tours in Latin America and Europe condemning the conduct of the United States.

Because of his illness President Wilson did not know of the Dominican situation. The attention of Secretary Colby, about to start on a journey to Brazil, Uruguay, and Argentina to better South American relations, chanced upon Santo Domingo; realizing that the occupation of Santo Domingo had no valid reason for continuing and was creating ill-will, he instructed Admiral Snowden to issue a proclamation of withdrawal, December 24, 1920. But it was easier to assume control than to return their sovereignty to a people whose training for its exercise was imperfect according to American conceptions. The difficulties came partly from the military authorities, who desired prolonged occupation, and partly from the Dominicans, who demanded immediate, unconditional evacuation. Attempts on the part of the military authorities to stifle such demands by invoking censorship regulations increased popular discontent. The uncertainty, the abandonment of all projects except those already under way and the consequent disorganization of working forces caused an economic depression and increased Dominican resentment.

A commission, composed of the members of the original Junta Consultiva and some others, was formed to amend the Constitution, generally to revise the laws and to draft a new election law, but they resigned when the military governor refused to accept the reservations which they made upon accepting office. To remedy this unauthorized act of the Governor, the Department of State, after many negotiations, again appointed a commission.

Change in Military Governor.

With the change of administration in the United States in March, 1921, Rear Admiral Samuel S. Robison was appointed military governor with instructions to issue a proclamation setting forth a program of evacuation. Unfortunately public sentiment had been so antagonized during the preceding two years by the practices of the military government that this proclamation met with general opposition. Some persons continued to demand unconditional evacuation; others distrusted elections under military auspices; others charged that the officering of the national police by Americans was a trick to continue the military government. The political leaders brought about a deadlock by announcing that their followers would not participate in the proposed elections.

The military governor was authorized on July 27 to announce that the elections would be postponed and the program of evacuation delayed until the Dominicans should be willing to coöperate. The military government was at this time also faced with financial embarrassments by reason of the post-war economic crisis and the refusal of the Department of State to authorize a loan.

Up to this time the State and Navy Departments had given scant heed to the complaints about conditions in Santo Domingo, but by July, 1921, the inflamed reports of excesses and the attitude of Latin America brought about an inquiry by a Senate Committee.[15] The next February Secretary Hughes made new proposals, including one for a loan of $10,000,000, but the refusal of the Dominicans to consider them or to coöperate caused him to proclaim the continuance of the military government at least until July 1, 1924.

However, when a portion of the bonds, issued[16] to relieve the financial difficulties in which the military government found itself, had been sold, Don Francisco J. Peynado went to Washington and was able to reopen negotiations and prepare the way for a new committee. The chief compromise of the new evacuation program formulated in coöperation with this committee was the paragraph which read:

A Provisional Government, composed of Dominican citizens and selected by representatives of the Dominican people, will be installed to enable the citizens of the Dominican Republic to carry out such legislative reforms as they may desire, and to make such amendments to their Constitution as they may deem appropriate, and to hold general elections for the installation of a subsequent permanent Government without the intervention of the authorities of the United States.

A revision of the 1919 tariff and preferential treatment similar to that accorded Cuba, for which Peynado had pleaded, were not accorded.

The State Department withdrew demands for a financial adviser, control of the internal revenues, a police force under United States officers, a legation guard, etc. The withdrawal of United States forces was to be as nearly unconditional as it could be made without creating confusion and injustice. A convention between the United States and Santo Domingo was to be approved pro-

[15] *Inquiry into Occupation and Administration of Haiti and Santo Domingo.* Hearings before a Select Committee on Haiti and Santo Domingo, United States Senate, Sixty-seventh Congress, First and Second Sessions, pursuant to Senate Resolution 112.

[16] The amount issued was $6,700,000, to repay the advances received the previous year and other outstanding obligations and to continue the public works program. Using the unissued $3,300,000 of bonds as security the Dominican Government made a loan of $2,500,000 in 1924, and when this was paid off, in two years' time, the unissued bonds were offered to the public, in 1926.

viding for the ratification of such acts of the military government as tax levies, expenditures, or rights created in favor of third persons; thereupon an executive would be formally elected. Immediately thereafter United States forces would leave the Dominican Republic.

Facilitation of Withdrawal.

To facilitate the carrying out of the plan President Harding appointed Sumner Welles, formerly Chief of the Latin American Division of the State Department, as special envoy to Santo Domingo. A "Commission of Representatives" was also appointed, composed of Mr. Welles, General Horacio Vasquez, chief of the Partido Nacional, Don Federico Velasquez, chief of the Partido Progresista; Don Elias Brache, of the Jimenista party; Don F. J. Peynado, unaffiliated with any party, and Archbishop Nouel. Owing largely to the tact of Mr. Welles and the continuous understandings made possible by the Commission's contacts, the plan was not wrecked by the unsympathetic attitude of some of the military authorities and by the jealousies of the Dominican politicians.

At uninterrupted sessions during August and September the details of withdrawal were elaborated, provision made for the arbitration of all disputes between the two governments which might arise from differences in the interpretation of the Convention, and the text of the evacuation treaty agreed upon.

The Dominican members of the Commission chose a neutral in politics, Juan Bautista Vicini Burgos, as provisional president, selected a cabinet to assist him, and continued in the character of an executive council until a constitutional president was inaugurated. On October 21, 1922, the provisional government was installed; United States forces were concentrated at various points and took no further administrative part. Their commander remained on good terms with the provisional president, and the marine officers performed excellent work in training Dominicans to take charge of the new national police, which is now well organized and disciplined.

CURRENT PERIOD

PROVISIONAL PRESIDENT VICINI BURGOS ruled by executive decree as the military governors had done, and proved a good administrator. In 1923 the provisional government decreed a new electoral law modeled closely upon the Cuban Electoral Code, but instead of agreeing on the necessary changes in the electoral law and hastening the elections, the Dominican political leaders devoted themselves to building up their political fences. Intense rivalry developed, and all the tact of Mr. Welles was required to prevent an open rupture. The general election was not held until March, 1924, when a large majority was given to the alliance between the National and Progressive parties, which favored the selection of former President Horacio Vasquez as president of the Republic and Velasquez as vice-president.

President-elect Vasquez made a brief trip to the United States to confer about a revision of the 1907 Convention, and upon his return was inaugurated, July 12, 1924. Embarkation of United States forces of occupation had begun in June, and the last marine left on September 18, 1924; on the 29th, the Dominican Republic became a member of the League of Nations.

1924 Convention.

A new fiscal convention, signed December 27, 1924, and ratified by both countries, authorized the Dominican Government to borrow a maximum amount of $25,000,000. Under its terms the President of the United States appointed a General Receiver of Dominican Customs to collect the customs duties, apply them to the service of outstanding bond issues, and pay over the balance to the Dominican Government. If in any year the customs revenues exceed $4,000,000, 10 per cent of the excess is to be applied to the redemption of outstanding bonds. The Dominican Government promises not to increase its public debt except by agreement with the United States, and not to modify its customs duties unless the altered rates may be calculated to provide one and one-half times the amount necessary for the service of the public debt.

Article II (identical in wording with the same clause in the Convention of 1907) provides that:

The Dominican Government will provide by law for the payment of all customs duties to the General Receiver and his assistants, and will give to them all needful aid and assistance and full protection to the extent of its powers. The Government of the United States will give to the General Receiver and his assistants such protection as it may find to be requisite for the performance of their duties.

Its vagueness, like that of the Platt Amendment in the case of Cuba, makes the United States arbiter as to what obligations and privileges are permitted. The potential authority admitted under the clause may avert an actual resort to it.

During the twenty-three years of the receivership, April 1, 1905, to December 31, 1927, the following sums were paid on loans:

1. To Guaranty Trust Co. of N. Y. for service of $20,000,000 loan
   of 1908 $31,366,609.18
2. To National City Bank of N. Y. for service of $1,500,000 loan
   of 1912   1,746,806.5c
3. Deposited with International Banking Corporation (a subsidiary
   of the National City Bank of N. Y.) to the credit of the Dominican Republic 5 per cent bond issue of 1918 ($4,161,300)   4,746,213.45
4. To Equitable Trust Co. of N. Y. for service of $2,500,000 loan of
   1921   428,125.00
5. To Lee, Higginson and Co. of N. Y. for service of
   a. $6,700,000 issue of 1922   2,149,583.10
   b. $3,300,000 issue of 1926   605,000.00
   c. $5,000,000 issue of 1926   274,999.92

The National City Bank loan of 1912 was represented by Treasury Notes of a total nominal amount of $1,500,000 purchased at 97½, bearing interest at 6 per cent per annum and redeemable not later than January 1, 1919. The 1918 loan, which was raised to settle claims, was retired by January, 1926, twelve years before the date fixed for maturity. Unfavorable financing conditions in New York were responsible for the 8 per cent interest rate on the issue underwritten by the Equitable Trust Co. and for the fact that it was sold below par. As improvement in conditions was expected, this issue was made for only a four-year period and was regarded as an advance to be paid out of a later issue. In fact, the bonds were paid out of the 1922 Twenty-Year Customs Administration Sinking Fund Gold Bond Issue of $10,000,000, bearing interest at 5½ per cent. The amount issued in 1922 was $6,700,000, which, besides paying off the 1921 advance, was used to liquidate other outstanding obligations and to continue the public works. In 1924 the balance of these bonds, $3,300,000, was used as security for a loan of $2,500,000, represented by Two-Year 5½ per cent Collateral Trust Gold Notes. After the maturity of these Two-Year Notes in 1926 the $3,300,000 Twenty-Year Bonds were offered to the public.

Of the $10,000,000 which was issued under the 1924 Convention, $5,000,000 was put out in 1926 in the form of 14-Year Customs Administration 5½ per cent Sinking Fund Gold Bonds, and $5,000,000 in January, 1928. The loans of 1922 and 1926 constitute a total funded debt of $20,000,000; both are secured by a charge on the customs revenues, the lien of the 1926 loan being junior to that of the 1922 loan. Both loans are listed on the New York Stock Exchange and both carry sinking funds sufficient to retire the entire issues by maturity. Prior to 1930, when payments for the sinking fund of both loans begin, the annual requirement for the service of both issues of bonds is for interest alone. After 1930 the annual debt service requirement will be $550,000 for interest on each loan, $841,667 for sinking fund on the 1922 loan, and $1,010,000 for sinking fund on the 1926 loan, or a total of $2,951,667. The Convention provides for the continuance of the collection of customs duties by the General Receiver

until the payment or retirement of any and all bonds issued by the Dominican Government in accordance with the plan and under the limitations as to terms and amounts hereinbefore recited.

Present Administration.

According to the revised Constitution of January 9, 1929, the president, vice-president, and Congress are elected for four years. A cabinet of seven assists the president. The Senate is composed of twelve members, representative in theory of the twelve provinces, and the Chamber of Deputies consists of one deputy for every

30,000 inhabitants or fraction of more than 15,000 inhabitants; no province can have less than two deputies. The president cannot be reëlected or elected as vice-president in the period following his term of office. The Constitution prohibits capital punishment, export taxes, the issue of paper money, and membership of foreigners in the constabulary.

The administration of President Vasquez has continued the public works program initiated by the military government, particularly in connection with roads and harbors, and has concerned itself with the stimulation of agriculture, diversification of crops, development of natural resources, irrigation, and colonization. A grave problem confronts the Dominican Government in the regulation of foreign capital so that it may serve as a progressive force in the country and yet not impinge upon Dominican sovereignty.

In April, 1929, President Vasquez invited Sumner Welles to bring a commission to Santo Domingo "to recommend a scientific budget system to control all expenditures and methods of improving administrative organization." Under the chairmanship of General Dawes an unofficial commission in three weeks of intensive labor drew up a detailed report of conditions with recommendations as to economies to be brought about by governmental control of all expenditures, sale of certain public utilities owned and operated by the Government at a deficit, and reorganization of some departments. The report recommended the adoption of a system similar to a civil service for governmental posts and contained in codified form ready for enactment a budget law and several others regulating projected improvements which would provide funds for the $10,000,000 budget proposed and make resort to additional loans unnecessary.

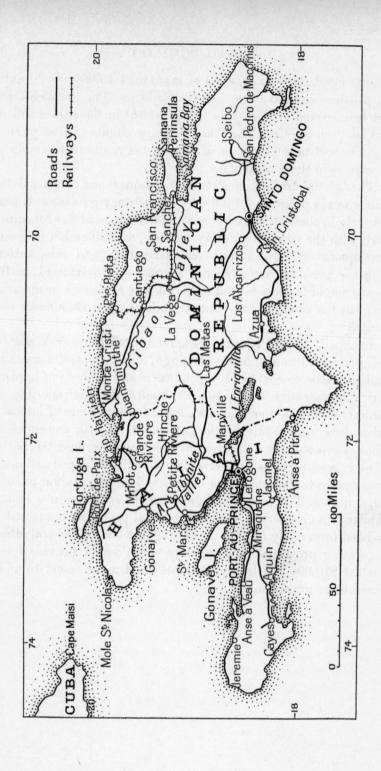

gap between the tribal customs inherited from Africa and a feeling of civic and social responsibility has not been bridged.

Early History.

The scarcity of labor resulting from the virtual extermination of the native Indian led to the introduction of negroes from Africa, and in 1512 their importation to Hispaniola was recognized by the Spanish crown as a legitimate business. This was the inception of the slave trade which was to affect so profoundly the economic life of the Americas.

The Spaniards were adventurers, seekers for gold and quick profits, and made little attempt to develop the resources of the island, but, determined to restrict trade with and settlement in the New World to their nationals, they maintained a fleet of guard ships. This prerogative was contested by English, French, and Dutch adventurers, who established several bases. In 1529 a Spanish fleet destroyed these settlements, and a few desperate refugees found their way in open boats to Tortuga, an island close to the northern shore of Haiti and now one of its possessions.

This little island became the headquarters of all refugees from Spanish oppression in the Americas; banded together in a society which they called the Brethren of the Coast, they became the terror of the "Spanish Main." Most of their children were of mixed blood with negro mothers captured from the slave ships, for few white women came to the island, and here developed the mulatto caste which was primarily responsible for the first Haitian revolution. By the end of the century these people had spread to the mainland; the English, outnumbered by the French, had been expelled and a number of settlements had grown up under the French flag. While Spain until 1697 did not recognize the right of France to any part of the island, these settlements under the efficient rule of French governors rapidly developed into a prosperous colony and toward the end of the eighteenth century over one-third of the merchant marine of France was employed in trade with St. Domingue, the richest colonial possession of the time. Over five hundred thousand slaves imported from Africa were employed on more than eight thousand plantations, covering approximately three million acres. On the rich alluvial plains grew sugar, indigo, cotton, and tobacco, and on the hillsides coffee. Rich as a Creole was a common expression in Paris where the colonial planters spent several months each year.

The administration of the French colonial possessions in the West Indies, directed by the Minister of Marine, was far more tyrannical than was English rule over its American colonies. Just complaints against heavy taxation and harsh ordinances ruthlessly administered by French agents had created a feeling of bitterness between the colonial proprietors and the mother country. A class of bureaucrats grew up who neither understood nor sympathized with the Creole population. Among the French-born bureaucrats, the Creoles, and the poor whites the only bond was the common desire to keep their position secure against the mulattoes and blacks, who together then as now outnumbered them nine to one.

In 1795 the Estates General promulgated the "Rights of Man" and declared that "not a single part of the nation shall ask in vain for its rights from the assembly." The Jacobin colonial policy threatened the basic foundation of economic life in the colony, dependent as it was on the complete subjection of the blacks and mulattoes to the despotic rule of the white proprietors. The policy of the Jacobin agents in the colony toward the white "aristocrats," whom they hated, culminated in open rebellion and ultimately in an attempt by the mulattoes to gain their promised privileges by force. These attempts failed, but the supremacy of the whites had been questioned, and during the struggle the slaves, who had been ruthlessly exploited by both sides, came to realize the power of their numerical strength, and finally rose against their masters, indiscriminately massacring white men, women, and children. After years of horrors, Toussaint L'Ouverture, a slave of slave parents, became their leader.

With an army of ex-slaves, Toussaint rid the country of English and Spanish invaders, and by his political sagacity and powers of leadership completely dominated the French government agents and the mulatto element which had initiated the revolution. By 1800 Toussaint was undisputed master of the French

colony of St. Domingue and within a year had brought the
Spanish part of the island under his control. Under a liberal constitution he assumed the title of "Governor General for Life." Realizing the necessity of organized control over agricultural enterprises Toussaint invited the return of some of the French planters,
and by stringent laws compelled the former slaves to work. Prosperity returned and a negro state seemed about to be permanently established. But a lull in his European wars left Napoleon
Bonaparte free to turn his attention to the reëstablishment of
French commerce and the expansion of his empire. By treaty
with Carlos IV he had gained Louisiana from Spain, and dreaming
of a huge colonial empire he dispatched his brother-in-law, General Leclerc, with fifty-four vessels and an army of twenty thousand veterans to recover St. Domingue, the logical base for his
proposed operations in the Americas.

After months of heroic fighting against these well-trained and
well-equipped troops, Toussaint was forced to surrender. In May,
1802, after making terms with Leclerc, he retired to his plantation in the interior, whence he was enticed to a coast town, and in
spite of definite promises of safe conduct was arrested and deported to France where he died in solitary confinement in the
Fortress de Joux about a year later. This treacherous arrest of
Toussaint and the growing suspicion that the French planned to
restore slavery alienated the black leaders who had joined forces
with Leclerc; many of them deserted and took to the hills. Con-
firmation of a rumor that Napoleon had reëstablished slavery in
Guadeloupe infuriated the blacks and the revolt became general;
Leclerc found himself deserted by his black allies and cooped up
in the town of Cap Haitien with a fever-stricken and rapidly
diminishing army, unsupported by supplies and replacements
from home. He died of fever in October, 1802, and was succeeded
by Rochambeau, who, on November 19, 1803, capitulated to the
blacks under Dessalines and, sailing out of the harbor of Cap
Haitien with the pitiful remnant of a magnificent army, surrendered to a waiting English fleet. In this ill-fated expedition
Napoleon had permanently lost to France its richest colony, and

of the total 43,000 veterans who had been sent some 8,000 survived to be transported to English military prisons.

On January 1, 1804, Dessalines assembled his victorious chiefs at the port of Gonaives, and standing on the seashore, proclaimed the independence of his people; tearing the French tricolor into three parts, he united the red and blue, creating the flag of Haiti, and restored the aboriginal name for this island.

INDEPENDENCE TO INTERVENTION

When independence was established, Haiti was in economic ruins, and the country was devastated; the poverty-stricken population was composed of ex-slaves, many less than a generation from African jungles, few literate or with a background which would give them a conception of citizenship, few experienced in self-directed labor, and none trained in the administration of civil affairs. The abolition of slavery had been interpreted by the blacks as freedom from labor; indeed the prosperity achieved under Toussaint was possible only because, with keen foresight, he returned their plantations to the *émigré* proprietors and inaugurated a system of enforced labor. Little removed from slavery, although freed, the blacks were practically serfs, forbidden to leave without written permission the plantations to which they were attached.

The autocracy of the self-constituted rulers and years of subjection to military power had destroyed all respect for authority not based on force. Dessalines, who was proclaimed emperor on October 8, 1804, came to power as a lone "tiger." The constitution he promulgated prohibited white people from acquiring property of any kind and adopted the generic term "black" for all of his subjects. While a man of extraordinary courage and genius for leadership Dessalines was as unfitted by training and temperament to rule as were his people for freedom to work out their own destiny. After a general massacre of the few remaining French, and an indiscriminate killing of mulattoes who had opposed him, he ruled despotically less than two years before he was himself assassinated.

After his death, the black general, Christophe, and the educated mulatto, Pétion, each of whom had served under Dessalines, contested for leadership. Christophe, an ex-slave, fully believed in perpetuating the despotism which he had helped to establish. He had no illusions as to the capacity of this people for self-government and planned to make himself dictator of the country. Pétion had seen military service in Europe and imbibed the Jacobin spirit as he had known it in the days preceding the French Revolution. He dreamed of a utopian republic and proposed a liberal constitution based on the theories of the "rights of man."

The mulatto element which supported Pétion was in a decided minority but was intelligent and experienced in affairs. Fearing to oppose Christophe openly they resorted to the clever expedient of electing him president under a constitution so restrictive of the presidential powers that the black leader's refusal to accept it was a foregone conclusion. Christophe promptly refused to recognize the new constitution or accept his election, and gathering his followers in the north, marched on the Capital. After initial successes, during which Pétion's forces were routed, Christophe returned to the North, established the "State of Haiti," and was later crowned king. Pétion was elected president of the Republic of Haiti, and the country remained divided until the death of Christophe in 1820.

Under Christophe's despotic rule the North prospered. He built a magnificent palace, *Sans Souci*, near Cap Haitien, and started another at Dessalines with 365 doors, the ruins of which bear evidence of his ambitions. Fearing a return of the French, he erected the tremendous citadel, *La Ferrière*, on a mountain top towering above *Sans Souci* as a refuge in the event of a foreign invasion which never materialized.

Pétion's utopian ideals and liberal government were unsuited to a people just released from slavery. The division of the North and South, to which may be traced much of the internal conflict which has since marked Haitian history, resulted in constant border warfare, and in the far south bandit chiefs refused for years to recognize Pétion's authority. Huge sums, sorely needed for the economic developments which he had planned, were spent in the maintenance of an army, agriculture was neglected, and the people, knowing no ruling force but fear, and fearing the president not at all, reverted to the leisurely existence and license which had marked the days before Toussaint organized his government.

Although Pétion had materially aided Bolivar in his struggle to free the South American countries from Spanish rule and was largely instrumental in the final success of the "Liberator," his own republic was not recognized by the foreign powers, and France, the chief market for Haitian products, was most unfriendly, repeatedly demanding a huge indemnity as a price for recognition of Haitian independence. Thoroughly disillusioned and embittered by the ingratitude of his people, Pétion died in 1818 and on his deathbed chose as his successor Jean Pierre Boyer, another mulatto who also had served with the French armies in Europe.

Two years later, when Christophe was stricken by paralysis, his people revolted. Christophe retired to *Sans Souci* and shot himself, ending a despotic reign of thirteen years as dramatically as he had inaugurated it. After his death the North and the Spanish part of the island united with the South under Boyer, and the whole island was incorporated in the Republic of Haiti. In 1825 Boyer was forced by a naval demonstration to agree to an ordinance of the French Government under which the independence of Haiti was recognized on the most exacting and onerous terms. In addition to a 50 per cent reduction in custom duties on French goods, Haiti agreed to pay 115,000,000 francs as an indemnity to the former colonial proprietors, and to the French Government 30,000,000 francs for the public buildings and fortifications most of which were now in ruins.

The Spanish section of the island refused to participate in this indemnity claiming that it was properly chargeable only to the area once owned by France. Revenues derived mostly from customs duties were greatly reduced by the French trade preferential, and the Government was forced to contract loans under unfavorable conditions to meet the first indemnity payments. Thus immediately after its inauguration the Haitian state was loaded with a debt for which it had no means of payment, and although more favorable terms were negotiated in 1838 the burden of this debt has ever since been detrimental to stability.

Boyer was forced to resign in 1843 after twenty-five years in office and thirty-six years of mulatto control. Within three years, four presidents were elected, three of whom were deposed by revolutions. In 1847 Faustin Solouque, an ignorant, illiterate negro general, chosen by a clique of politicians, was made president. Solouque proved to be anything but the complaisant tool his sponsors had expected, and caused himself to be crowned Faustin, First Emperor of Haiti. After his overthrow in 1859, seven presidents were elected during the next twenty-two years, six of whom were deposed by revolutions. In the following eighteen years of comparative peace, Hippolyte, Simon Sam, and Nord Alexis held office, and although Sam and Alexis were deposed by revolutions, the country made decided progress. Nord Alexis fell largely on account of his fearless determination to prosecute a clique of grafters who had systematically looted the Government. The election of Antoine Simon in 1908 inaugurated the *Epoque des Gouvernements Ephémères* which with insurrections, revolutions, assassinations, and spoliation of government funds, completed the political, moral, and financial bankruptcy of Haiti.

Relations with the United States.

During Haiti's struggles toward sovereignty the question of slavery was paramount in internal and external affairs of the United States. Pro-slavery sentiment was strong enough in the nation and in Congress to prevent recognition of Haitian independence until after the Civil War. The southern representatives and their sympathizers were bitterly opposed to the recognition of negro republics, both because of their belief that this would acknowledge the equality of the black, and because after 1840 they thought to make the Caribbean an outpost slave colony. But after the removal of southern influence from Congress Haiti was recognized in 1864. Negotiations were undertaken from time to time to secure Mole St. Nicolas and a treaty similar to that which the United States made with Santo Domingo in 1907. Conditions in Haiti from 1910 to 1915 were therefore watched with grave concern by the United States. As administration succeeded administration, and the individual in power focused his attention on raising money to maintain himself in office or to reward the chiefs who had put him there, Haitian foreign relations became seriously involved. Several European governments exerted pressure to secure settlement of their nationals' claims, even to the extent of landing forces. Both government and revolutionary leaders were careful not to kill or molest foreigners or destroy their property, and the Government managed to pay interest on external debts, but fell behind in the amortization of French bonds consisting of loans floated in 1896 and 1911. During this period a series of internal loans floated in Haiti were taken by German merchants at discounts varying from 20 to 40 per cent, in return for which they received valuable concessions, including electric light franchises, ice plants, wharfing privileges, and certain railroad franchises.

In 1910 the "consolidation scandal," involving French, German, and Haitian officials of the national bank and prominent government officials, resulted in the organization of the Banque Nationale de la Republique d'Haiti. To the German demand for participation in this bank the French objected unless American interests were also represented. Following his policy of reducing the preponderance of European capital in the Caribbean, Secretary Knox participated actively in the matter and through his intervention about eight thousand shares of a total of forty thousand shares of the Banque Nationale were subscribed for by American banking houses.

Foreign claims against the Government included thirty-six French claims, fourteen German, ten American, six British, four Italian, two Dominican, one Danish, one Dutch, one Spanish, and one Belgian. In December, 1910, a collective note, signed by the British, French, German, and Italian Ministers, proposed to the Haitian Government a commission for the settlement of these claims; on the rejection of this proposal, a collective note, which was signed also by the United States Minister, stated that an international commission would be organized if settlement of outstanding difficulties were not made within three months.

The more pressing of these claims were gradually disposed of and in 1913 arbitration agreements with France and Germany were concluded. In the same year a concession for a railroad system to traverse the island from Port-au-Prince to Cap Haitien, 140 miles distant, was obtained by an American, James P. MacDonald. The Haitian Government agreed to guarantee 6 per cent interest on bonds issued to meet the cost of construction up to a maximum of $35,000 per mile. Three short unconnected sections were completed, but in 1913 work was suspended and operation interfered with by revolutionary disturbances. In September, 1914, the Government refused to pay interest on the bonds, asserting non-fulfilment of contract. The company contended that construction and even operation was impossible owing to political conditions, and although the contract specifically provided that "in no case and for no reason shall disputes that may arise as to the interpretation of the clauses of the present contract give occasion for diplomatic recourse," Secretary Bryan intimated that the power of the United States would be invoked if the rights of the company were not safeguarded.

First Draft of Convention Proffered.

Earlier in 1914 Secretary Bryan had instructed the United States Minister in Haiti to suggest to the Haitian Foreign Minister

that the United States is, as is natural, on account of the vested interests of American citizens in the Republic of Haiti, interested in the proper administration and collection of the customs, and would be well disposed toward lending its aid in any practical way to the Government of Haiti if such were desired.[3]

Secretary Bryan went on to suggest that in view of the opening of the Panama Canal the United States was interested in having lighthouses erected throughout the Caribbean and that if desired it would lend expert aid to the Haitian Government in selecting appropriate locations. On July 2, 1914, he followed this offer with a draft of a convention between the United States and Haiti modeled largely on the Dominican Treaty of 1907. A dispatch

[3] *For. Rel.*, 1915, p. 541.

from the United States legation in Port-au-Prince to the State Department on the 30th emphasized the fact that the political situation in Haiti was "subordinate to and embodied in the financial situation."[4]

In January, 1914, President Oreste had been deposed by a revolution, and British, French, German, and American warships landed troops to protect foreign interests. The State Department feared German dominance in the Caribbean and was strengthened in its resolution to control Haiti by the joint representation at Washington of European governments that any reorganization must be under international auspices. An opportunity for intervention occurred in October when the Government of Zamor, Oreste's successor, fell and the principal officials took refuge in various foreign legations. On the same day, Acting Secretary Lansing wired the United States legation that the "Department is contemplating convention along the lines of its instruction of July 2." The next day he instructed the United States Minister to impress on all Haitian leaders that the United States "views with utmost concern" the existing situation and "might be compelled to take steps necessary to prevent a period of disorder and anarchy which would harm the rights and property of Americans and other foreigners," wiring two days later that upon the establishment of a *de facto* government the Department contemplated conversations looking toward a customs convention and free elections under American supervision. The Minister reported that the city was perfectly calm and there was no need to land troops. In a memorandum of November 4, Mr. Lansing suggested that all candidates for the presidency should meet and choose a provisional president; if agreement were reached the United States would recognize and support the man chosen. "If they cannot agree, the Government of the United States will itself name a provisional president, sustaining him in the assumption of office, and support him in the exercise of his temporary authority. The provisional president will not be a candidate for president."

---

[4] All quotations not otherwise cited are from the *Hearings before a Select Committee on Haiti and Santo Domingo,* United States Senate, Sixty-seventh Congress, pursuant to S. Res. 112.

Thereafter free elections were to be held under American supervision. If these elections were apparently unfair, the United States would hold new elections "in which the mistakes observed will be corrected." After a government had been set up, the United States

would feel at liberty thereafter to insist that revolutionary movements cease, and that all subsequent changes in the Government of the Republic be effected by the peaceful processes provided in the Haitian Constitution. By no other course can the Government of the United States fulfil its tacitly conceded obligations as the nearest friend of Haiti in her relations with the rest of the world.

Conditions for Recognition of Theodore.

The suggestions in this memorandum were not put into effect, and on November 7, President Theodore was quietly elected in the absence of contesting candidates. On November 12, Secretary Bryan wrote to the United States Minister stating that if the Theodore Government were believed to be a *de facto* government the Minister should inform him that he would be recognized by the United States "as provisional president" when a commission of three persons should be appointed by the Haitian Government with full powers to negotiate at Washington a convention governing the following points: customs control as previously outlined; settlement of outstanding questions between the Haitian Government, the American railroad and the Bank; agreement by Haiti to give full protection to all foreign interests; and lastly an agreement by Haiti never to lease to any European government any portion of Haitian territory for use as a naval or coaling station.

The United States Minister seems to have been somewhat startled by Mr. Bryan's conditions relative to the recognition of the constitutionally elected president of Haiti. He telegraphed to Washington that Theodore had been regularly elected in accordance with the Constitution and wondered whether in view of this fact it were really desired that he should carry out the instructions he had received. Mr. Bryan replied in the affirmative and that there should be added as a further condition the signing of a protocol for the settlement by arbitration of pending claims of American citizens against Haiti.

Meanwhile, in accordance with the 1910 Loan Contract, the Bank was acting as the state treasury, receiving all customs and other governmental revenues. It had had difficulty with the Haitian Government over the use of funds. On June 9, 1914, the United States Minister cabled to the State Department:

If at the end of the fiscal year . . . the bank shall not have renewed the convention, the government will find itself without funds of any sort and with no income and undoubtedly will find it most difficult to operate. It is just this condition that the bank desires, for it is the belief of the bank that the government when confronted by such a crisis would be forced to ask the assistance of the United States in adjusting its financial tangle and that American supervision of the customs would result.[5]

The convention was not renewed on October 1, and a few days later the United States Minister approached the Government on the subject of a new treaty with the United States. Continuing in financial straits, the Haitian Government authorized the issue of sixteen million gourdes[6] in paper money; the issue of two million of this amount was protested by the Bank as a violation of its contract. Fearing that the Government might attempt forcibly to take its funds which the Bank held and refused to pay out, the Bank decided to transfer them to the National City Bank in New York. For this purpose it enlisted the support of the United States Government and a marine guard escorted $500,000 in gold to a warship which transported it to New York. In 1919 the National City Bank returned the sum with 2 per cent interest. The Haitian Minister in Washington protested that an article of the bank contract had formally prohibited diplomatic intervention and had provided for the arbitration of all differences in the interpretation of the contract. Secretary Bryan, having previously advised with the Vice-President of the Haitian National Bank and a representative of the National City Bank and arranged that at least half a million dollars should be brought to New York, replied that the Bank had acted within its powers, that the gold was still available

5 *For. Rel.*, 1914, p. 346.

6 A gourde, the unit of Haitian currency, was equal to 96.5 United States cents at par of exchange. It has now been stabilized at 20 cents.

for redemption purposes, that if the Haitian Government merely wanted it for that purpose there was no reason why it should not be in New York drawing interest, and that the bank was justified in protecting the reserve from possible theft by lawless revolutionists. A little later in December, Haitian soldiers removed $67,000 in gold under authority of a judgment of a lower Haitian court.

During the War the German shares of the National Bank were seized by the French interests, and in 1917, after repeated suggestions by Secretary Bryan, the National City Bank purchased the shares held by American banking interests. Since France, after entering the War, had not been able to attend to the management of the National Bank, it had been administered from New York. In 1919 the National City Bank bought all the French shares, including those seized from the Germans, and has since been the sole owner. In 1928 the bank was incorporated as a Haitian institution.

In the spring of 1915 two commissions were sent to Haiti to negotiate a treaty. The first failed because the Haitians held the commissioners to be without proper credentials, and the second because a revolution interrupted discussion on certain proposals with which Haiti had disagreed. President Theodore having left the country, Guillaume Sam was elected president March 4. On the twenty-fourth he was recognized by Germany and Italy, and France later followed suit.

In June, at the outbreak of another revolution, the French cruiser *Descartes* landed a small force at Cap Haitien to protect its consulate. Admiral Caperton, then in Mexican waters, was ordered to proceed to Cap Haitien, "thank the French commander and take the necessary steps to protect property and preserve order." The French thereupon withdrew, Admiral Caperton ordered that no fighting should occur in the city, and lay off the Cape waiting developments.

At Port-au-Prince President Sam, who had been only four months in office, realizing that plots against him were maturing in the capital, had arrested and incarcerated in the national prison about two hundred men whom he suspected of designs against him.

He had also brought to the Capital a *caco* army under the command of a general who, only a few months before, had proclaimed Sam chief of the provisional government.

For some time diplomatic asylum, no longer sanctioned by international law, had been giving Haiti trouble. The Government stated that it could not guarantee the preservation of quiet in the capital if foreign legations continued to harbor political refugees. With the exception of the United States legation which had refused to harbor political refugees, all legations were now crowded with prominent men who feared arrest. In these legations plans for the overthrow of the president were being formulated.

Sam and some of his adherents, anticipating an attack, had spent the night of July 27 on the porch of the palace. Early the next morning the palace was attacked by a small body of citizens led by Charles de Delva, the present mayor of Port-au-Prince. The palace guard made an attempt at resistance, but Sam's *cacos* failed him and took to the hills; Sam took refuge in the adjoining French legation. Learning of the attack on the palace, Charles Oscar, the commandant of the *Arrondissement* and a close friend of the President, ordered the massacre of the political prisoners. At daylight the streets were thronged with frantic men, women, and children. The prison was opened, and from the heaps of corpses such bodies as could be identified were claimed by their relatives. The French legation was surrounded by a threatening mob but no active violence was attempted until the following morning when the people, returning from the burial of the victims of the massacre, saw the smoke of Admiral Caperton's flagship in the outer harbor; fearing that Sam would escape them, a number of prominent men entered the French legation, secured Sam and threw him over the fence to the mob which tore his body apart and dragged the pieces through the streets.

The American *chargé* sent word to Admiral Caperton that the President had been murdered, two foreign legations violated, and 167 prominent citizens massacred. He explained that no government existed in the city, that thousands of *cacos* were waiting in the hills ready to attack the defenseless city, and that a general massacre of the mulattoes was imminent. The Admiral was preparing a landing force when he received from Washington the following cable:

State Department desires that American forces be landed at Port-au-Prince and that American and foreign interests be protected; that representatives of England and France be informed of this intention; informed that their interests will be protected, and that they be requested not to land.

Admiral Caperton immediately occupied the capital, and reported on the thirty-first that all was calm, the city being controlled by a committee of citizens acting "practically" under his directions.[7] Caperton's cable continued: "Chamber of Deputies asked permission elect president, but deferred in compliance my request. Time for election president not propitious for maintaining law and order."

On August 2 Admiral Caperton reported to the Secretary of the Navy that a stable government in Haiti was not possible until the *cacos* were disbanded and their power broken. "Such action," his dispatch continued, "is now imperative at Port-au-Prince if the United States desire to negotiate treaty for financial control of Haiti." On the same day the French landed a legation guard at Port-au-Prince about which Caperton had already, on July 31, reported to the Secretary of the Navy:

French minister informed me had received dispatches from Paris, French Government, stating that French Embassy, Washington, had been directed inform United States Government that France considered landing legation guard at Port-au-Prince necessity for national honor. French minister repeated his conviction that we were ably protecting life and property and assured his guard would be confined to legation and that arms of French guard would not be carried by them outside of legation. He further stated that he wishes it understood he does not intend interfering in any way my actions in town.

Election of Dartiguenave.

On August 7 the Admiral telegraphed that "the immediate

---

[7] This was the usual procedure at the time of an overthrow of government; a "committee of safety" administered affairs until a president was elected.

election of a President is clamored for by all classes of Haitians."
Mr. Leger, a distinguished and able administrator to whom all
parties would have rallied, refused to have his name considered,
saying:

Tell the Admiral I will do everything in my power for Haiti, but I
must watch and see what the United States will demand of Haiti, and
be in a position to defend Haiti's interests in case the demands should
be unreasonable. At this time I could not possibly accept the Presidency. I am for Haiti, not for the United States.

Dartiguenave, the president of the Senate, was therefore considered the likeliest candidate, having stated that "Haiti must
and will accede gladly to any terms proposed by the United
States." Caperton's dispatch continued:

Now, they say they will cede outright without restriction St.
Nicholas Mole, granting us the right to intervene when necessary;
customs house control, and any other terms. Only they beg to avoid
as far as possible, humiliation. They insist that no government can
stand except through protection of the United States.

The Admiral stated that he would permit Congress to elect a
president on the twelfth, unless otherwise directed.

On August 10 the Secretary of State informed the *chargé* as
follows:

First: Let Congress understand that the Government of the
United States intends to uphold it, but that it cannot recognize action which does not establish in charge of Haitian affairs those whose
abilities and dispositions give assurances of putting an end to factional disorders.

Second: In order that no misunderstanding can possibly occur
after election, it should be made perfectly clear to candidates as soon
as possible and in advance of their election, that the United States
expects to be entrusted with the practical control of the customs, and
such financial control over the affairs of the Republic of Haiti as the
United States may deem necessary for an efficient administration.

The Government of the United States considers it its duty to support a constitutional government. It means to assist in the establishing of such a government, and to support it as long as necessity

may require. It has no design upon the political or territorial integrity of Haiti; on the contrary, what has been done, as well as what will be done, is conceived in an effort to aid the people of Haiti in establishing a stable government and in maintaining domestic peace throughout the Republic.

On August 12 Dartiguenave was elected under the protection of United States marines. According to the instructions received by the *chargé* three days later the conditions of recognition were to be ratification of a treaty with whose terms the Haitian Government had been familiar "for more than a year." In view of assurances that the Haitian authorities were willing "to go farther than before, including the cession to the United States of Mole St. Nicholas," the Secretary of State wished to renew negotiations.

Military Intervention.

In a cable of August 19 to the Secretary of the Navy, Admiral Caperton described the situation:

United States has now actually accomplished a military intervention in affairs of another nation. Hostility exists now in Haiti and has existed for a number of years against such action. Serious hostile contacts have only been avoided by prompt and rapid military action which has given United States control before resistance has had time to organize. We now hold capital of country and two other important seaports. Total force at my disposal now, one armored cruiser, two gunboats, one converted yacht, and 1,500 marines. This force now deployed at maximum extension consistent with maintaining control of occupied territory and prompt concentration for defense. Department now desires that custom houses in seven other cities be occupied. Custom houses can not be taken charge of unless cities in which they are located are occupied with sufficient military force to protect our customs officers and preserve order. Further extension of present force imperative to avoid. No forces should be without support and communication facilities of naval vessels for the present at least. To occupy these seven additional ports means practically military occupation of seacoast of Haiti, which is extensive. No attempt must be made to accomplish this until there are available sufficient force and sufficient officers and organization completed for assuming customs service.

The Admiral called for additional forces and personnel from the Navy to organize and administer the customs service, and asked that the plans be kept secret, "pending treaty negotiations. While at later date, after constabulary is organized, our forces may be withdrawn, yet at present moment United States should take no chance of injury to its dignity and prestige."

Secretary Lansing instructed the *chargé* on August 22:

For your guidance in informal conversations with the *de facto* President, you may use the following as your views of the motives and purposes of the Government of the United States:

To establish a stable government and lasting domestic peace so that the Haitian people may safely enjoy their full rights of life, liberty and property and all patriotic citizens may be encouraged to participate in the development of their country, the treaty submitted ought to be ratified immediately, and at the same time the Haitian Government should invite this Government to enter into a modus vivendi embodying the same terms as the treaty and to operate thereunder until the United States Senate has acted upon the treaty.

You might express the conviction that, in case such a request for a modus was made, the Haitian Government would not find this Department unsympathetic toward any proper effort which might be made to place the Haitian finances on a sound basis so that the Haitian Government may be able to pay promptly adequate salaries to its officials; to establish a good school system; to build roads and generally facilitate the transportation and marketing of the products of the country; to extend and perfect the present telegraph lines and erect and maintain wireless stations; to undertake harbor improvements and municipal sanitation; and, by carrying on public works of this nature, to furnish employment to the people and furnish them opportunities to improve their industrial and intellectual condition.

To the end that this economic development may be freely and safely undertaken by the Haitian people, it seems indispensable to organize and maintain a trained constabulary which will take the place of the Haitian army and which, well officered and properly equipped and disciplined, will possess sufficient power to preserve order, suppress insurrections, and protect life and property throughout the Republic.

With the great resources of Haiti undeveloped because of the frequent political disorders and the constant danger to life and property, the *de facto* President must desire to adopt measures which will remove these obstacles. Believing him to be inspired by patriotic motives and the sincere purpose to improve the conditions of the Haitian people by maintaining peace and securing to them their individual rights, he will undoubtedly aid in carrying out the steps suggested. In his efforts he may confidently expect the United States, which seeks only the welfare of Haiti and its people, to give him such protection and assistance as it may properly render.

On August 23 the *chargé* informed the Secretary of State that the Haitian Minister of Foreign Affairs had said that the Government would have to resign if the United States insisted on its demand that the treaty should be accepted without modification. The Secretary of State replied that if the Government did not secure prompt ratification of the treaty as the Department had been led to suppose it would, the United States would have either to set up a military government until honest elections could be held, or permit the control of the Government to pass to some other political faction which would fall in with the American plans. On the next day Admiral Caperton reported that the chances for the successful negotiation of the treaty would be increased if for the moment he ceased seizing the customhouses and conducted "no further military operations except those necessary for preserving peace and order and for other important military reasons." He recommended the establishment of military government in case the Haitian Government resigned, adding:

Present is most critical time in relations with Haiti, and our decisions now will, to a great extent, determine future course. If military government is established, we would be bound not to abandon Haitian situation until affairs of country are set right and predominant interests of United States of America secured.

Martial Law.

On September 3, Admiral Caperton proclaimed martial law "in accordance with the law of nations," indicating that he was proceeding on the theory of military occupation, and one by one he assumed charge of all the customhouses. The State Department, desirous of receiving a request from the Haitian President for the taking over of the customhouses, had prompted Admiral Caperton to that effect, but received from the President a protest instead of the hoped-for invitation.

As Admiral Caperton had been ordered to place his collections of customs revenues in private accounts under his own name "in trust for the Haitian Government," making disbursements only for a constabulary, public works, and "the maintenance of the customs and port services and such military government as the United States may establish" and the Government had no other income, conditions soon became serious. The destitution was so great that Caperton appealed to the Red Cross. Finally the State Department authorized him to use funds "for the organization and maintenance of an efficient constabulary for conducting such temporary public works as will afford immediate relief through employment for the starving populace and discharged soldiers." Several times Caperton had suggested to the State Department that it authorize a loan, and on September 14 cabled to the Secretary of the Navy:

In order to assure prompt ratification Haitian Government desires immediate assurances in such shape as to be effective for use in Chamber of Deputies to the effect that the United States will exercise its good offices to obtain a temporary loan of $1,500,000.

The loan was not authorized but as President Dartiguenave seemed to have become more amenable, he was recognized two days later and the Treaty was signed by the United States *chargé d'affaires* and the Haitian foreign minister.

Means to Secure Treaty Ratification.

On October 3, Admiral Caperton's appeal was followed by a report from the *chargé d'affaires* as to the weapon which the withholding of funds gave the opposition, and that the President and his cabinet

will resign rather than attempt the fight in the senate under this handicap. . . . It is most important that the present administration remain in power as it is not believed that one more favorable to the United States could be obtained and in view of all facts as they appear here that a military government would probably have to be established should this Government fall.

Instead of assurance of a loan or payments in accordance with recommendations of both Admiral Caperton and the *chargé d'affaires*, Secretary Daniels instructed Admiral Caperton to furnish the Haitian Government with a weekly allowance of $25,000. "Question payment back salary will be settled by department immediately after ratification of treaty." The Chamber of Deputies voted ratification the next day, but the Senate continued its opposition. The weekly allowance was less than that needed for salaries and other necessary expenses of the Haitian Government but was all that could be assured from the customs receipts "in view of expenditures contemplated for constabulary, public works, etc."

Admiral Caperton believed that the President of Haiti and his cabinet were doing their utmost to expedite ratification and that any interference with their methods only hindered matters, but the State Department instructed him to tell the Cabinet that he was confident that if the Treaty were not ratified, his "Government (had) the intention to retain control in Haiti until the desired end (was) accomplished."

On the day on which the Admiral delivered his message to the Cabinet, the Haitian Senate passed the Treaty with a number of interpretative reservations. In February, 1916, the United States Senate consented to the Treaty and on May 3, 1916, ratifications were exchanged.

FIRST YEARS UNDER THE TREATY

The chief provisions of the Treaty were:

1. Appointment by the President of Haiti, upon the nomination of the President of the United States, of a General Receiver to collect, receive, and apply all customs duties, and of a Financial Adviser to be attached to the Ministry of Finance.

2. Article V. All sums collected and received by the General Re-

ceiver shall be applied first to the payment of the salaries and allowances of the General Receiver, his assistants and employees and expenses of the Receivership, including the salary and expenses of the Financial Adviser, which salaries will be determined by previous agreement; second, to the interest and sinking fund of the public debt of the Republic of Haiti; and, third, to the maintenance of the constabulary referred to in Article X, and then the remainder to the Haitian Government for the purposes of current expenses.

3. Article VI. The expenses of the Receivership shall not exceed five per centum of the collections and receipts from custom duties, unless by agreement by the two Governments.

4. Article VIII. The Republic of Haiti shall not increase its public debt, except by previous agreement with the President of the United States and shall not contract any debt or assume any financial obligation unless the ordinary revenues of the Republic available for that purpose, after defraying the expenses of the government, shall be adequate to pay the interest and provide a sinking fund for the final discharge of such debt.

5. Article XI. The Government of Haiti agrees not to surrender any of the territory of the Republic of Haiti by sale, lease or otherwise, or jurisdiction over such territory, to any foreign government or power, nor to enter into any treaty or contract with any foreign power or powers that will impair or tend to impair the independence of Haiti.

6. Article XII. The Haitian Government agrees to execute with the United States a protocol for the settlement by arbitration or otherwise, of all pending pecuniary claims of foreign corporations, companies, citizens or subjects against Haiti.

7. Article XIII. The Republic of Haiti, being desirous to further the development of its natural resources, agrees to undertake and execute such measures as in the opinion of the high contracting parties may be necessary for the sanitation and public improvement of the Republic, under the supervision and direction of an engineer or engineers, to be appointed by the President of Haiti upon nomination by the President of the United States, and authorized for that purpose by the government of Haiti.

8. Creation of a native constabulary which is a combined army and police force, rural and urban, officered by Americans.

9. For "the proper and efficient development of its agricultural, mineral and commercial resources and in the establishment of the

finances of Haiti on a firm and solid basis, . . . the High Contracting Parties shall have authority to take such steps as may be necessary to assure the complete attainment of any of the objects comprehended in this treaty; and should the necessity occur, the United States will lend an efficient aid for the preservation of Haitian independence and the maintaining of a government adequate for the protection of life, property, and individual liberty."

10. Article XVI. The present treaty shall remain in full force for the term of ten years, to be counted from the day of exchange of ratifications, and further for another term of ten years if, for specific reasons presented by either of the high contracting parties, the purpose of this treaty has not been fully accomplished. . . .

Administration by Naval Officers.

On November 29, 1915, the *modus vivendi* was signed, and until the United States ratified the Treaty on February 28, 1916, Haiti was administered by naval officers appointed pending the installation of Treaty officials. Port-au-Prince was on the verge of starvation, business was at a standstill, and conditions throughout the country were distressing. As soon as Admiral Caperton secured control of revenue receipts he used them to pay wages to the peasants whom he set to work repairing roads, cleaning streets, making gutters, reconstructing telegraph and telephone lines, installing hand-pumps, covered wells, and street lanterns, and renovating the water-works and the prisons. At first the peasants were distrustful as they were not accustomed to paid employment, but after discovering that wages were forthcoming at the end of each day, too many applied for the amount of money available.

Admiral Caperton's authority to use the funds collected from the customhouses for the constabulary and public works did not permit of paying interest on foreign or internal debts. This created dissatisfaction among the holders of Haitian bonds in France and caused distress for those Haitians for whom internal loans had been practically the only method of local investment. As late as March 20, 1920, the American Consul at Port-au-Prince reported that commerce was suffering because interest on the internal debt had not been paid; sales of imported goods were materially reduced thereby, and the people were financially embarrassed. Admiral Caperton could find work for peasants but for the upper- and middle-class families, some of whom held bonds, he could do nothing. Their "antagonism and animosity" hindered him; he needed their support and this he could not gain without funds to pay the interest due them. Government salaries were in arrears, and school teachers were especially badly off, some not having received their pay for over eighteen months. Several times Admiral Caperton urged a loan, as the Haitian Government had inherited

months of unpaid debt and has incurred expenses in educating country to realize necessity of ratifying treaty. Salaries, debts, and obligations amounting to $500,000 must be paid before December 20. Otherwise Government prestige will be lost amongst Haitians and serious conditions will result.

Toward the end of December, 1915, as certain activities under the Department of Public Works and military and civil government were to be turned over to the Haitians, Admiral Caperton recommended an allowance in addition to the weekly $25,000 at that time given the Haitian Government; but the Department of State, considering such expenditure unwise, requested Caperton to retain control of the departments which he proposed to relinquish, and personally pay salaries to minor officials who were in the greatest need.

Admiral Caperton continued to urge Secretary Daniels to authorize a loan for the purpose of giving relief to the railroad company and settling many other pressing claims, and to advance the $100,000 promised upon ratification of the treaty, stating that American prestige was involved in the matter. Secretary Daniels replied:

Loan of $1,500,000 cannot be arranged until after arrival of commission and settlement of difficulties with bank. . . . Weekly payment of $25,000 was authorized in lieu of this proposed advance and was intended to supersede it. If, however, Haitian authorities still consider $100,000 due upon ratification of treaty, the amount may, in order to maintain prestige, be paid from funds in your hands, provided advance from this source is agreeable to Haitian government.

He added certain instructions with regard to receipts in order "to place entire responsibility on Haitian Government."

"Caco" Uprising.

By the fall of 1916, Haiti had been pacified and the first object of the Treaty, namely, to secure the tranquillity of the country, had for the time being been accomplished. It is generally believed that this condition would have prevailed and that no further military measures involving the use of United States marines would have been necessary if it had not been for the revival and the abuse of an obsolete law which required that citizens should work on road construction and maintenance in the communities in which they lived.

Only remnants of the magnificent system of highways built in the French colonial period were visible. The need for roads connecting the capital with the commercial centers and with the insurgent North, not only for military purposes but for economic development, was obvious. The first Treaty engineer, a commander in the United States Navy, did not arrive in Haiti until January, 1917, and as no funds were then available, many months passed before the Department of Public Works started to function. Meanwhile such public works as were undertaken were administered by the *gendarmerie*, organized in February, 1916, under the command of a marine officer. Construction work on the principal highways was started by the marines shortly after the intervention, and had also been carried on by the *gendarmerie* with paid labor although little money was available. Therefore the suggestion that an old law, dating from 1864, should be enforced was accepted by the chief of the *gendarmerie* as a solution of the road building problem. With the consent of the President and the approval of the commanding officer of the American expeditionary forces in Haiti, the *corvée* law was put into effect.

In the beginning little opposition developed and some of the roads through well-populated districts were made passable for automobiles without serious trouble with the people. The most important road in Haiti, from a military standpoint, is the highway from Port-au-Prince to Cap Haitien, long stretches of which are through sparsely settled districts. Here the American officers of the *gendarmerie* had difficulty in filling their *corvée* quota, and inspired by urgent orders from headquarters to rush road construction, a number abused the *corvée* law or countenanced its abuse by subordinates. Thousands of Haitian peasants were forced to labor long after the time fixed by law, and other thousands were kept in the moving *corvée* gangs and taken miles beyond the limits of their communes. The officers in charge were insufficiently supplied with money even to feed their men properly, and certain of the *corvée* gangs were handled with brutality. Tickets issued by road foremen certifying that the stipulated work had been performed were torn up and the holders forced to return to work. Resentment against the *corvée* was intensified by propaganda of enemies of the American intervention and of the Dartiguenave Government to the effect that the whites had come to reënslave the peasants, and able-bodied men in districts through which roads were being built took to the hills.

The situation became so serious that in October, 1918, orders were issued to discontinue the *corvée*, but unfortunately in certain northern districts which had for years been the center of *caco* activities, these orders were disregarded and by the time the *corvée* was finally stopped a strong anti-American feeling prevailed. In the fall of 1918 Charlemagne Peralte, an influential *caco* chief, escaped from the Cap Haitien prison and, taking to the hills, proclaimed himself chief of an army of liberation. This uprising was at first handled by the *gendarmerie* but in the spring of 1919 thousands of *cacos* were in the field, and by the fall the situation became serious. Charlemagne had organized a "government" and commissioned officers to "fight against the Americans." To oppose the scattered bands under his command, totaling between 15,000 and 17,000 men, only about 1,000 marines and 2,000 gendarmes were available, and most of them were necessarily assigned to police duties and garrisons in the principal towns. In October, 1919, Charlemagne was killed by a marine attached to the *gendarmerie*, and a few months later the *caco* uprising collapsed with the surrender of many of the most prominent chiefs. Officials' reports estimated that more than 1,800 *cacos* were killed in the field. The American casualties were one officer killed and two wounded, twelve enlisted men killed and twenty-six wounded.

Extension of Treaty.

The treaty posts were gradually filled: The Financial Adviser assumed his duties in July, 1916, the General Receiver took over the administration of the customs service in August, the Public Works Engineer arrived in January, 1917, and the Sanitary Engineer the following October. Confusion arose from lack of direct superior central control in Haiti, and silence in Washington as to policy and division of administration there. The three chief elements in the government and administration of Haiti from 1916 to 1922 were:

I. The Government of Haiti: President, Cabinet, Council of State, and, until 1918, either national legislature or a constituent assembly.

II. The Military Occupation under the Marine officer commanding the United States expeditionary forces in Haiti and responsible to the Navy Department.

III. The treaty officials, appointed by the United States State and Navy Departments, each, in his relations to the others, independent:

(a) A Financial Adviser, a civilian, under the State Department. Mr. McIlhenny considered the chief of the Latin American Division his superior officer, and during two years the holder of the latter office changed five times. Owing to the lack of coöperation between the executive and legislative branches of the Haitian Government existing laws could not be changed; the undefined powers of the Financial Adviser could not be effective; hence, without the coöperation of the judiciary, no legislation could be enforced.

(b) A General Receiver, a civilian, under the State Department. Under the Treaty the General Receiver is disbursing officer for customs receipts, but in 1918 a military order directed the "depository of internal revenues to make no payments authorized by the Haitian Government unless the warrants of payment were viséed by the Financial Adviser." Later a Haitian law made the General Receiver disbursing officer for all receipts.

(c) A Chief of the *gendarmerie*, a Marine officer, under the Navy Department.

(d) A Chief Engineer for Public Works, a Navy officer, under the Navy Department.

(e) A Chief Sanitary Engineer, a Navy officer, under the Navy Department.

Business with the Haitian Government on matters regarding investment of capital involved treating with: (a) the military government, (b) the treaty officials, (c) the Haitian Government, (d) the United States minister.

Each official carried on his office as he saw fit, with little direction from Washington or understanding of what it intended, and no common program or coöperation to a common end. The powers of each were for the most part left ambiguous, authority and responsibility were not clearly defined, and means for the coördination of their activities were not provided. Coördination by the Haitian Government was impracticable, chiefly because the Treaty officials were installed for the purpose of checking, controlling, and guiding it. In any case, without definite organization and firm supervision, there is likely to be friction between military and civilian officers. Owing to these conditions, there was disagreement, inefficiency, confusion, and delay. The possibility of a direct conflict of authority between the Haitian and American administrations, which might have caused delays in administration and in the accomplishment of the Treaty aims, was obviated by the President's failure to call elections for the National Assembly. The Haitian Constitution of 1918 contained transitory provisions which provided that elections for the Senate and Chamber of Deputies are to be called in January 16 "of an even-numbered year. The year shall be fixed by decree of the president." Meanwhile, under the same transitory provisions, legislative functions are exercised by a Council of State appointed by the president whose measures become law: that is, the president names the Council; then, as the election of the president is a prerogative of the National Legislature and the Council is its successor, the Council in turn names him. The provisions of the Constitution were not mandatory in form, and as President Dartiguenave had not exercised the discretionary powers conferred on him by this clause of the Constitution, the Council of State continued to function as the legislative body and elected Louis Borno president on May 10, 1922, upon the expiration of Dartiguenave's term.

By an exchange of notes during 1918 the Haitian Government agreed to submit all proposed legislation to the United States legation for approval. On several occasions the legation has refused to recognize legislative acts as valid and binding, especially those which deal directly with treaty provisions, such as laws reducing the revenues of the State, as it had not approved them before they were put into effect.

A little more than ten months after the exchange of ratifications Foreign Minister Borno and the United States Minister signed an agreement extending the Treaty to 1936. Mr. Borno tried vainly to use the granting of the ten year extension as a lever for having Haitians appointed in the customs service. On the ground that Article XIV of the Treaty empowered the executive departments of the two governments "to take such steps as may be necessary to insure the complete attainment of any of the objects of the treaty," this extension was not submitted for ratification on either side, notwithstanding Article 2 of the extension which reads:

The present act shall be approved by the High Contractng Parties in conformity with their respective established procedures and the approvals thereof shall be exchanged in the city of Port-au-Prince as soon as may be possible.

The reason given for the extension of the Treaty in 1917 was the Haitian Government's need of a loan to meet the large amount of foreign claims pending, and to provide funds for public improvements, and the opinion of Washington that a loan could not be floated unless the United States should guarantee conditions in

Haiti for the duration of the loan. The President of Haiti, not wishing to exteriorize internal debts, wanted a loan for foreign indebtedness only. Since all important sources of revenue remaining after deduction of the 5 per cent for receivership expenses were pledged to various loans, the security for the new loan was a general pledge of all revenues. The Financial Adviser, Mr. McIlhenny, spent the greater part of his time in the United States trying to obtain a loan. In November, 1918, a project of an internal revenue law, proposed by the Financial Adviser, was rejected by the Haitians chiefly because it placed the administration of the internal revenue system under American control. On October 3, 1919, an agreement was signed which provided for a claims commission to determine the total government obligations, and for a bond issue of not more than $40,000,000. The negotiations still going on as late as April, 1922, the High Commissioner suggested that in view of the fact that the loan would cause an annual deficit of $1,000,000 the United States stood ready to help the Haitian Government draft new tax laws to impose higher taxes. Finally in 1922 thirty-year bonds were issued to an amount of $16,000,000. Twelve million dollars proved sufficient to cover all outstanding foreign obligations, the depreciation of the franc permitting a refunding of the foreign debt of 80,000,000 French francs at about $6,000,000, while $2,660,000 refunded the National Railway bonds, and $3,526,170.08 the total other claims allowed by the Claims Commission. An agreement provides for the continuance of United States supervision of the collection and allocation of pledged customs revenues for the duration of the loan, regardless of the expiration of the Treaty on May 3, 1936. If present rates of payment are maintained amortization will be completed by 1942 or 1943.

The Claims Commission made its report in June, 1926, having examined 5,482 claims which had accumulated since 1899. Internal funded debts were removed from its jurisdiction. The following table[8] shows the awards; one-third of which were paid in cash and two-thirds in Series B Haitian 6 per cent bonds:

[8] *Report* of High Commissioner, 1926, p. 8.

	Number of claims	Amount claimed	Amount allowed
American	157	$ 6,037,675.73	$ 455,729.90
Haitian and various	72,133	14,888,728.29	1,615,154.39
French	572	16,307,642.65	756,071.53
British	177	1,345,634.45	176,638.51
Italian	52	186,054.57	21,004.21
German	178	1,163,492.27	501,571.54
Total	73,269	$39,929,227.96[9]	$3,526,170.08

In May, 1920, Mr. McIlhenny endeavored to gain Haitian approval of the modification of the bank contract and of a measure prohibiting the importation and exportation of non-Haitian money except under certain conditions, and the enactment of a territorial law. The Haitian Government agreed to the first point, made a counter-memoir in regard to the others and rejected Mr. McIlhenny's recommendations for the repeal of certain laws passed in disregard of the agreement of August 24, 1918, that projects of law were to be presented to the United States minister for his consideration and, if necessary, for discussion. One of these laws had been with regard to the return of alien enemy property, and the Minister and the State Department held that prior approval was required; Mr. McIlhenny wished this sequestrated property sold, and the Haitians refused. The French and British legations, the Royal Bank of Canada, and the American Foreign Banking Corporation protested against the power which would reside in the hands of the Financial Adviser if the recommendations in regard to the importation and exportation of non-Haitian currency and the drawing up of long-term leases were carried out. In view of the attitude of the Haitian Government, Mr. McIlhenny in July, 1920, suspended consideration of the 1920-1921 budget.

Preparation of a New Constitution.

Prior to the occupation interest payments on all debts had been met by the Haitian Government although amortization payments had lapsed. In 1916 when the revenues were insufficient to cover

[9] The jurisdiction of the Commission having been limited to May 3, 1916, $10,-443,326.91 of the total represents claims that the Commission was not competent to adjudicate.

the 5 per cent allowed for receivership expenses, interest on foreign debts and expenses of the Haitian Government, the State Department authorized the Receiver General to give the maintenance of the Haitian Government the first claim against the funds after the 5 per cent had been deducted. Accordingly the interest due November 15, 1915, was not paid and all payments on debts were suspended until April, 1920. Mr. McIlhenny's view was:

> So long as the Haitian Government evinced its willingness to accept the advice and the assistance of the American officials . . . there was no serious objection to a continuance of the waiver of the strict application and interpretation of Article V of the treaty. But when it became clear . . . that the Government of Haiti had determined upon an obstructive attitude, that it refused to do those things which were patently and clearly for its own benefit—it refused to put in operation any of the recommendations of the financial adviser, no matter how worthy—then I conceived that it was entirely within the province of the American administration to see that the application of the treaty was carried out. . . .

As the Haitian Government continued its opposition, Mr. McIlhenny in August, 1920, recommended that the salaries of the president, his cabinet and his council and of the principal state executive officers be suspended without notice. After three months, President Dartiguenave, in direct negotiation with Washington, agreed to certain compromises; thereupon payment was resumed.

The Treaty once in force, the United States desired that the Haitian Government should change its Constitution to make it consistent with provisions of the Treaty; clauses prohibiting the ownership of real property by foreigners were to be eliminated and an appendix was to be added similar to the Cuban "Platt Amendment." Several commissions were sent to take up formally or informally the modification of the Constitution.

Dissolution of Congress.

Opposition to the proposed changes crystallized in the Haitian Senate, and as President Dartiguenave feared impeachment on the charge that he had betrayed his country to the Americans, he dissolved the Senate by decree on April 5, 1916, and the next day had the doors to its building locked. The presidential decree also convened the Chamber of Deputies exclusively as a constituent assembly for constitutional revision. On April 27 members of the Senate and of the Chamber met in a rented house and organized as a national assembly. Meanwhile the President appointed a Council of State of twenty-one to prepare the changes in laws to conform to the Treaty. As the life of the Chamber of Deputies expired on January 10, 1917, an election, to be supervised by American officers, for another constituent assembly was called. This newly elected body was presented with a constitution which was the result of protracted negotiations in which the Haitian President and his ministers, the Navy Department and the Department of State took part; several drafts were prepared in Haiti and forwarded to Washington for consideration. This constitution altered the presidential term from seven to four years and substituted a *gendarmerie* for the old military establishment. Besides the clause granting to foreigners the right to hold real property, the Haitians feared those which ratified the acts of the American Occupation and permitted diplomatic intervention to safeguard the acts of foreigners.

The Haitian Government transmitted this draft and the accompanying correspondence to the Assembly. Already hostile both to the intervention and the suggested constitutional changes, the Assembly proceeded to draw up a constitution of their own which failed to include the provisions on which Washington had insisted.

On June 18, General Cole, the new commanding officer of the Occupation who had "received instructions to exert every endeavor to prevent the passage of such a project," notified Washington that "unless contrary instructions received, if necessary to prevent passage proposed constitution (i.e., with amendments the Haitians proposed to make) I intend to dissolve National Assembly through President, if possible, otherwise direct." He was informed in reply that "the Department vests you with full discretionary power. Endeavor to accomplish desired end without military force." General Cole then obtained the signature of President Dartiguenave to a decree dissolving the National Assembly under warning "that in case the President did not sign the decree, [he] would suppress the National Assembly [him]self and would recommend the establishment of a military government." As the President of the Assembly refused to accept the decree unless presented by a cabinet member, Major Butler, the head of the *gendarmerie*, proclaimed the dissolution of the National Assembly.

First Plebiscite.

According to Haitian law, constitutions have to be ratified by the National Assembly. With the National Assembly dissolved, the desire of the Treaty officials to have a constitution adopted in form by the Haitians prevailed over the theory that the mass of the Haitians were incapable of voting intelligently on such a question, and a plebiscite to legalize the new Constitution was decided upon. A proclamation issued by the marine officer in charge of Port-au-Prince declared that "any abstention from such a solemn occasion will be considered an unpatriotic act." The polling places were in charge of either the United States marines who were officers in the Haitian *gendarmerie* or members of the Marine Corps itself. The peasants, herded in from rural districts, were bashful and self-intimidated and quite unaware of what was going on. In some places, voters were given ballots of a color which signified approval, while ballots of disapproval could be had only on request. In favor of the Constitution 98,294 votes were cast; there were 769 negative ballots.

CENTRALIZED CONTROL

PROGRESS of the country was very slow during these first seven years of the Occupation. For the first time customs were collected honestly and government funds were disbursed in accordance with the budget, yet there was much criticism. Those who had lived by government graft were disgruntled and their stories, together with tales of the unsatisfactory conditions in Haiti and of excesses committed by marines, led to an investigation by a board of inquiry of the Navy Department, and finally in 1921 to a Senate Committee investigation.

The Committee condemned the blunders of the *corvée* as errors "of commission like those of omission arising from failure to develop a definite and constructive policy under the treaty"; it blamed "the departments in Washington" for not appreciating the need of selecting for service in Haiti men sympathetic to the Haitians who would work with them on a cordial personal and official basis. Some outrages had been committed by marines, especially when seeking arms or when they were excited by atrocious acts of Haitian insurgents; the offenses may in large part at least be laid at the door of the new recruits sent down to replace men withdrawn for service in France. The Senate Committee found that offenders had been summarily punished.

The Senate report resulted in the reorganization and centralization of United States authority in Haiti as follows:

I. A High Commissioner, a personal representative of the United States president, takes the place of the United States minister and ranks over all treaty officials, receiving his instructions from the State Department. His function is to supervise, coördinate, and report upon the work of the Treaty officials. The Haitian Government can enact no law nor grant any important contract without his sanction. Treaty officials who meet with him regularly as a sort of Cabinet are:

   (a) All the Treaty officers named under the 1915-1922 *régime*. (Consolidation in 1924 of the offices of Financial Adviser and General Receiver added to administrative efficiency.)

   (b) A new Treaty official, a civilian, Chief Agricultural Engineer, a post created in 1923.

   (c) A Legal Adviser (an American civilian), a post created in 1923.

   (d) The commander of the expeditionary forces, a Marine Colonel. (The present force consists of one skeleton brigade of the United States Marine Corps, to which are attached an aviation unit, motor transport corps, etc.)

II. The Government of Haiti: The President, his Cabinet and his Council of State, a provisional body of 21 members appointed by the President and electing him in turn, and vested with legislative power.

The High Commissioner's salary and the expenses of the marine expeditionary force are borne by the United States. The marine and navy officers in the service of Haiti under the Treaty receive their ordinary salaries from the United States and an extra stipend from Haiti. The civilian officials appointed under the Treaty are paid by Haiti.

Aside from the marine brigade, the number of American officials, both military men and civilians, in the Haitian service totals about 250. The American personnel in the offices of the Financial Adviser-General Receiver and of the agricultural engineer is entirely civilian. Some of the American assistants of the public works engineer are naval officers and some civilians. The American sanitary staff is composed almost entirely of naval officers. With the exception of a small number of officers and non-commissioned officers of the United States Navy Medical Corps, the American *garde* officers are drawn from the Marine Corps. All in all, 80 per cent of the treaty officials are drawn from the Navy and the Marine Corps, and more than half of these are connected with the *garde d'Haiti*.

A high turnover has resulted, for the navy and marine officers are detached for Haitian duty for a period of not more than three years. That period ended, they are transferred elsewhere no matter how well fitted for the peculiar work in Haiti they may have proved or how deeply interested they have become; new and inexperienced men are sent to replace them. The exceptions to this rule have been rare and are balanced by exceptions on the other side—officers who do not remain even three years.

Although civilian officials are not subject to this rule, their turnover has been high for a variety of personal reasons. Between 1922 and 1928 five Financial Advisers, four sanitary engineers, three chiefs of the *gendarmerie*, and two chief engineers for public works served.

The Second Plebiscite.

President Borno, in defending his refusal to call legislative elections for January 10, 1926, proclaimed that nine-tenths of the Haitians were illiterate peasants, "incapable of exercising the

over cases involving the United States military establishment; martial law, while still technically in force, is not exercised, and its existence seems to have aroused less antagonism than the recently enacted press law which prohibits criticism of the Haitian Government or of the Occupation. Moreover, although the Department of Justice was not placed under American direction, the Haitian civil and criminal codes were translated into English by a *gendarmerie* officer in order that they might be applied by American officers attached to the *gendarmerie*. In the first years of the intervention the misunderstandings which resulted from these interpretations would have been ludicrous had they not been tragic.

Corruption has been due partly no doubt to the inadequate salaries of judges. A Haitian judge in the Court of Appeals now receives $140 a month, while a Haitian captain in the *gendarmerie* receives $150. In his report for 1926, General Russell said: "The courts are, if such could be possible, less effective than ever and their inefficiency and incompetency more notorious;" in 1927 he reported "no improvement" and that none had been expected.

Garde d'Haiti. The former *gendarmerie*, organized along military lines, serves as rural constabulary and urban police and also has charge of communal fire departments, trails, the insane, prisoners, issue of automobile and arms licenses, and the radio, and acts as agent for other treaty departments in such services as collecting information regarding land titles, road censuses, etc. Officers act as Communal Advisers throughout the country. Wherever there is a justice of the peace, a non-commissioned officer or specially trained private of the *garde* acts as public prosecutor. On January 1, 1929, 16 per cent of the captains, 29 per cent of the first lieutenants, and 53 per cent of the second lieutenants were Haitians. The tardiness in appointing native officers has been due to several causes: the *élite* dislike manual labor and are prejudiced against leaving the towns; Haitian officers are disinclined to take commands in districts where they have lived because of the civil functions attached to *garde* duty in which relatives and friends may bring pressure to bear; the enlisted personnel have more confidence in American commanders, and there is still a considerable percentage of illiteracy and disease among them. When General Butler started to organize the *gendarmerie* he found from blood tests taken from 1,200 *gendarmes* selected at random among 50,-000 Haitians that 95 per cent had blood diseases and 85 per cent intestinal worms, a condition which had to be cured before *gendarmes* could stay awake long enough to do sentry duty. In 1927, 62 per cent were reported as having yaws as against 75 per cent in the civilian population.

Whatever may have been the justice of complaints against both marines and *gendarmes* in the past, especially in the early days of the intervention, one now sees no evidence of popular fear of either and hears almost no Haitian complaints of brutality. Some of the difficulties of the early period may have arisen from the fact that the *gendarmerie* was drilled in English. American officers then knew neither the local patois nor French, although now most *garde* officers speak creole. To the maintenance of the *garde* about 15 per cent of total revenues is devoted.

Prisons. According to General Butler, the prisons were "vile beyond description" when turned over to the Americans. With a monthly allotment of $8,000 from the Financial Adviser, the military government started two industrial schools which the prisoners built themselves, and reorganized the prison system so that prisoners were classified according to offenses, were well fed, taken care of, and taught trades. Making all the clothing for the *gendarmerie*, the prisoners not only made the prison nearly self-supporting, but could save some money themselves. The penitentiary, which is under the *garde*, has become in nearly all respects a model institution with a sunny workshop. In 1927 the death rate at Cap Haitien prison was 38.1 per thousand, a great decrease over former years.

Public Works. Before 1915 most of the country was inaccessible except on horseback, as the magnificent system of roads which had been built when Haiti was a flourishing French colony had been allowed to go to ruin. The evidences of the grading, bridges, and culverts were still observable, and in the early road building of the occupation little new engineering was required. The road from Cap Haitien to the capital, rebuilt by the *corvée*, was finished in the summer of 1917. Between July 16, 1916, and March 9, 1918, about 470 miles of road were made passable for motors, and to date about 900 miles of highway have been constructed. As a means of communication and transportation, a highway system is undoubtedly necessary for the use of the many motor cars which afford an elastic means of passenger and freight transportation well adapted to a small mountainous country, where short hauls predominate, but in its present state of development Haiti needs also a network of passable trails connecting the interior with the markets and coördinating with the highway system. In 1928, the highway construction program emphasized the building of trails.

The antiquated telegraph system has been replaced by local and long distance telephone facilities connecting the commercial centers; in the capital and at Cap Haitien, automatic telephone exchanges have been installed. The service is operated by the Government at a profit.

Old French colonial irrigation systems have been repaired and new projects for the irrigation of large areas of potentially productive agricultural land have been studied and initiated; much has been accomplished toward the solution of the municipal water supply problem and the proper housing of government activities, especially in the capital.

Public Health. Sanitary conditions in Haiti in 1915 were barbarous. Even to induce the superstitious peasants to accept free treatment offered for the many diseases that have retarded Haitian progress was no small task, yet syphilis, one of the three main diseases, has been successfully fought and it is gradually becoming a less important economic factor. Peasants have been won away from the voodoo "doctors" by American "miracles"—such as making the blind see by the operation for cataract. In addition to a general "clean-up" campaign, including the draining of swamps, in which great strides have been made toward exterminating the malaria-carrying mosquito, ten general hospitals have been provided and over forty free rural clinics, in which approximately a million treatments were given in 1928; there is no district so difficult of access that it does not receive a regular visit from doctors of the sanitary service. Haitian doctors and nurses have been trained and have been promoted to responsible posts. Under the direction of American Red Cross nurses, a training school for Haitian nurses is maintained. With the aid of the International Health Board of the Rockefeller Foundation a medical survey has been made and a free medical college established, and several Haitians are sent to Canada and Europe each year for graduate training. Port-au-Prince has been made into a sanitary city.

Service Technique has come to cover all the agricultural and educational work carried on under American direction. Public instruction was one of the two departments which were not included in the Treaty provisions. As a result, no preliminary expert survey of educational opportunities and needs was made, no program, including coördination of construction with teacher-training, was laid out, and enrolment in the recently established vocational schools has increased so slowly that they can exert little influence before the expiration of the Treaty. Haitian educational legislation has not been revised, and the educational system has not been organized on a unified and permanent basis so as to insure, as far as possible, the continuance of educational effort on sound lines after the expiration of the Treaty.

Up to the time of the American intervention the entire school system of Haiti, from the primary grades up, emphasized classical studies almost to the complete exclusion of industrial education. As a consequence, the children and young men of Haiti have been guided *from*, rather than *toward*, productive industry. This is the primary cause of the low productivity of Haiti as contrasted with neighboring countries with soil no more fertile nor climate more favorable than that of Haiti. This emphasis of classical studies and practical exclusion of agricultural and industrial education has necessarily led to the creation of a class of young men who desire to take up professions such as law and medicine, or commercial and clerical occupations, a great portion of the latter seeking governmental positions. The members of this class do not know how to use their hands and have no idea of the dignity of labor. As a result there is a regrettable shortage of agriculturists and skilled workers. It is among such a class that revolutions are bred.[10]

Without directly administering the Department of Education, the American authorities, through their control of appropriations, have centralized educational developments in the *Service Technique*, devoted essentially to vocational training. The Financial Adviser reported in 1926-1927 that his policy is "to maintain

[10] Fourth Annual Report of the American High Commissioner, 1925, p. 6.

expenditures for classical education at about their present level while devoting as large resources as are available to the extension of agricultural and vocational training."

To this end the *Service Technique* in charge of the chief agricultural engineer was started in 1923. Included in this service is the *Ecole Centrale* for the training of agricultural and industrial school teachers and technicians. Young Haitians, after one year's intensive training,[11] are sent to conduct rural schools at a minimum salary of $40 a month, which is larger than the salary received by 95 per cent of the teachers in the Haitian Department of Public Instruction. A secondary agricultural school has been established at Plaisance to bridge the gap between the rural farm schools and the *Ecole Centrale*. The rural farm schools form complete substitutes, as far as they have been installed, for the Haitian schools. Over five thousand children are enrolled in these schools for elementary instruction with an attendance of 62 per cent in 1927-1928. A second industrial school for girls was opened at St. Marc on November 3, 1927, and one for boys at Cap Haitien on April 1, 1928, making six. In 1928-1929 sixty-five vocational schools, urban and rural, were reported. The eighty-one teachers in these schools receive an average salary of $464 a year.

Toward its end of increasing productivity, the American agricultural service, in addition to maintaining the above schools, seeks to reach the peasant through its twenty demonstration farms, seven demonstration coffee mills, agricultural and industrial fairs, veterinary clinics, free moving pictures and the establishment of radio receiving sets in the market places of the principal towns. Work is being done to inoculate livestock against disease and to improve breeds. Research work showing the possibilities of growing sisal, cotton, pineapples, etc., has been carried on and some progress made toward the development of these crops.

Economic Conditions. Haitian financial difficulties arise mainly from the following causes:

1. A one-crop country, annual revenues are severely curtailed

---

[11] This is provisional owing to the lack of trained men; only 173 were enrolled in 1927-1928. Since its organization in 1924, 340 students have been enrolled of whom 129 are now employed in the *Service Technique.*

and money for ordinary consumer's needs is lacking if the coffee crop is poor or the price falls on the world market. The coffee grows almost wild, in small and badly cultivated patches. Efforts are now being made to teach the peasants better methods of cultivation and handling. To eliminate the "dead season" which sends surplus labor to Cuba and Santo Domingo, an attempt is being made to increase complementary products such as cassava, poultry, livestock, honey, tropical fruits, corn, and rice, and to stimulate interest of large producers in the growing of sisal in the North. If successful this will prove of great benefit, because sisal can be grown on land useless for agriculture or grazing.

2. Haiti is one of the four countries out of thirty-four, recently studied by an American banking house, whose customs receipts exceed all other revenues, the others being its neighbors, Santo Domingo and Cuba, and El Salvador. In 1911-1912 (a fairly typical year) customs constituted more than 97 per cent of total revenues; 60 per cent of the customs receipts came from export taxes, almost entirely on coffee; 23.14 per cent is derived from emigration fees.

Most of the improvement in this respect, and also in an increase in revenues making funds available for constructive expenditure, began when Dr. Cumberland became Financial Adviser-General Receiver in January, 1924. A general example of honest and efficient financial administration was set up. Taxes under the old law bore most heavily upon the peasants, who directly or indirectly paid practically all export taxes and almost all the import taxes on foodstuffs, cotton manufactures, and soap. Duty on wheat flour is still one of the highest fixed by any country, although Haiti does not produce grain, and flour is one of the peasant's chief foodstuffs. The duty (fixed per kilo) is roughly $1.50 a hundred pounds, and even more on cheaper flours, that for corn meal being $2.00 and rye flour $3.00. The tariff applies a higher duty on kerosene, which goes chiefly to the peasants, than on gasoline which is used more by foreigners, and until a recent amendment exempted certain agricultural implements, a high tax was assessed on the importation of machinery. While increasing total customs receipts, Dr. Cumberland so shifted their sources that since then import revenues are more than double those from exports. An excise-tax law, passed on August 14, 1928, authorized the president to reduce or abolish export duties; this has already been done on bananas. The internal revenue service has also been reorganized and the receipts from this source so increased that customs duties now furnish less than 87 per cent of total revenues. Dr. Cumberland recommended that eventually not more than 50 per cent of revenues should be derived from customs receipts, but as Haitian traditions, like those of most Latin American countries, are against direct taxes this adjustment of revenues may take some time.

Owing to "an officially announced prohibition of emigration under date of July 13, 1928," only 14,098 emigrants left Haiti as compared with 22,970 in 1925-1926. Therefore emigration fees, which have constituted about 25 per cent of internal revenues, were materially reduced in 1927-1928, and since only four emigration agents were active against twenty-five the previous year, income from license fees also declined. In the past a large number of laborers emigrated annually to Cuba and the Dominican Republic of whom only about two-thirds returned. Restriction of the Cuban sugar crop and unsatisfactory industrial conditions, besides reducing Haitian emigration, are reflected also in the increase in the number of emigrants who returned to Haiti during 1927-1928; 11,844 emigrants returned as compared with 2,956 for the preceding fiscal year.

3. Haiti has had and probably will continue to have few industries; its investments abroad are negligible; as the commercial, industrial, and agricultural enterprises are financed chiefly by foreign capital there are heavy remittances abroad not directly compensated for by credit items; finally, as the public debt too is largely in foreign hands, interest and amortization payments flow out of the country.

Financial order is now established; in 1922 the external debt was converted from francs to dollars; paper money has been retired and reserves created for the nickel subsidiary currency and for the National Bank notes which constitute government currency; the gourde, which had declined to a low point, has been stabilized at 20 cents, the budget balanced. The public debt was

$18,887,623 on September 30, 1928, consisting of three bond issues, each bearing 6 per cent interest and secured and administered alike. Series A for $16,000,000 were floated by the National City Company of New York under the auspices of the State Department in 1922 to cover the external debt; they are held mostly by foreigners. Series B, amounting to $6,234,041.94, were floated in 1923 to refund the internal debt and pay the awards of the Claims Commission; on March 31, 1929, bonds of this issue aggregating $861,000 were held by foreigners and $1,462,500 by Haitians. Series C, for $2,660,000, originally bonds of the National Railroad, became in 1924 a direct obligation of the Haitian Government at a 25 per cent discount; the majority bondholders are foreigners. Series A mature in 1952, Series B and C in 1953. The annual amortization and interest payments absorb about 21 per cent of the revenues as against 75 per cent prior to 1915.

For the entire period of the receivership 82.01 per cent of total imports have been furnished by the United States, consisting principally of foodstuffs, textiles, and construction material. The percentage shows a decrease from 78.06 for the period October–March, 1927-1928, to 69.73 per cent for the same months of 1928-1929. The following are the trade percentages since 1915.

Country	Average first 5 years 1916-1921	Average second 5 years 1921-1926	1925-1926	1926-1927	1927-1928	Average for decade 1916-1926
Imports from:						
United States	87.09	79.37	74.22	76.56	75.30	82.62
France	4.71	5.97	7.27	6.56	6.89	5.47
United Kingdom	5.85	7.30	7.24	5.02	6.69	6.43
All others	2.35	7.36	11.27	11.86		5.48
Exports to:						
United States	52.85	11.02	6.79	7.81	8.18	29.74
France	35.98	62.29	65.13	47.51	49.77	48.99
United Kingdom	1.45	4.40	3.58	5.16	4.50	3.13
All others	9.72	22.29	24.50	39.52		18.14
Total trade:						
United States	72.53	45.63	39.41	42.68	39.85	57.59
France	18.39	33.83	37.25	26.84	29.54	26.18
United Kingdom	4.03	5.85	5.35	5.08	5.53	4.95
All others	5.05	14.69	17.99	25.40		11.28

Textiles comprised the largest importations, 23 per cent of all imports, $23,281,222; wheat flour was second in value, $14,229,-947; rice third, $7,996,509; fish fourth, $4,546,563; and iron, steel, and their manufactures fifth, $4,338,776. Of Haitian exports the United States normally took about 5 per cent before 1915 against 8.18 per cent in 1927-1928, dropping to 6.81 in March, 1929. In 1927-1928 the principal exports were coffee, 79.04 per cent, valued at $17,916,464; raw cotton, 8.83 per cent, $2,001,520; logwood, 3.12 per cent, $706,968; raw sugar, 2.87, $650,242; cacao, 1.97, $445,544. The major portion of the coffee exported goes to Havre which serves as the distributing center for Europe. The market price of logwood fluctuates and exportation will decrease as the supply becomes less accessible and no attempt is made at replanting.

The total value of imports for 1927-1928 amounted to $20,-248,257, of exports, $22,667,246, giving an excess of exports of $2,418,989. The increase of imports over the previous fiscal year was 28.55 per cent and of exports 48.16 per cent.

As Haiti possesses no merchant marine all freight payments go to other countries. In 1927-1928, American vessels carried 53.24 per cent of the total value of import tonnage, Dutch were second, with 30.23, French third, with 6.12, and German fourth, with 3.37. Of the total value of exports, Dutch ships carried 41.04 per cent, American 12.47, German 14.49, French 17.03, and British 11.16. Of total tonnage, Dutch increased 23 per cent, and American 6 per cent over 1926-1927.

Agricultural Resources. The resources of Haiti, almost solely agricultural, remain undeveloped for several reasons. The *élite* who hold large tracts of land, grants to their fathers "for services rendered to the state," lack the capital and constructive energy to develop them, and for the most part live in the larger towns and find little attraction in agriculture as a means of livelihood. The peasant mass, ignorant and long-suffering, had, prior to the intervention, endured a century of misrule and oppression under an urban minority; even those among them who owned small plots of land were afraid to work them or to transport the products of their ineffectively cultivated "gardens" to market. Now they are free to cultivate their little gardens, transport their products, and enjoy the fruit of their labor undeterred by fear of petty graft or abuses of governmental authority, but they have no marketing system through which their crops might be profitably exported. Moreover crops grown in such areas as the Artibonite valley under the present inefficient and desultory methods of cultivation have in the aggregate less than a tenth of their potential value under modern irrigation methods. Occupying this land either as small owners, leasers, or squatters the peasants cannot adopt irrigation or cultivation methods essential to the success of any practical irrigation project. They lack money to prepare the land, knowledge of modern farm tools and farming methods, and few are sufficiently secure in their titles to warrant capital investment if the money were available.

The land question is always the heart of the problems raised by an era of transition. What economic system will produce the greatest amount of social happiness and political education? One official believes that

in the long run a system of small landholdings yield far better economic as well as political and social results than do large plantations, often owned and managed by foreigners and employing large gangs of native labor at low wages.[12]

Another considers that, in Haiti, at least, large-scale agriculture offers the only avenue of escape from universal poverty, overpopulation, and primitive agricultural methods.

A reliance on small farming presupposes an intelligence and an incentive on the part of the peasant which he does not now possess. In the second place, small farms and gardens under individual management are not adapted to the production of tropical exports. Individualistic small farming precludes the use of capital, of irrigation, of skilled management, and of efficient marketing.[13]

Relief can be had by means of large-scale agricultural undertakings in appropriate regions, but such undertakings require capi-

12 W. W. Cumberland, *Economic and Financial Survey of Nicaragua*, p. 11.
13 A. C. Millspaugh, "Our Hatian Problem," *Foreign Affairs*, Vol. VII, No. 4, p. 561.

tal, and investors have been discouraged in Haiti by three factors: instability and disorder, the ban on foreign ownership of land, and the chaotic condition of land titles and the uncertainty of boundaries.

The establishment of order in 1915 eliminated the first obstacle. The second was removed by the 1918 Constitution. From the time of Dessalines until the adoption of the 1918 Constitution, the many constitutions had all forbidden foreign ownership of real property. To this law, maintained among American states by Haiti alone, one may partly trace both the country's lack of capitalistic development and the fact that the Republic has remained a country of peasants virtually without a proletariat.

According to an interpretative decree made by the Council of State in 1925, constitutional provisions permit ownership of real property by foreigners residing in Haiti or foreign corporations authorized by the president to transact business in Haiti and domiciled there for agricultural, residential, commercial, industrial, or educational purposes. Corporations "formed in Haiti under Haitian laws having their main place of business in the country, shall enjoy without restriction all the rights attached to Haitian citizenship with respect to the ownership of real property."[14] If the foreigner is absent for five years he may no longer claim ownership and the property may be sold by the State and the proceeds paid to him. Some small areas in Haiti have now come under American sugar, sisal, and pineapple plantations. This acreage is a trifling fraction of the total area of the country, and much of it is land previously uncultivated, and, largely because of defective titles, more is held by long-term lease than by purchase.

Haitian law does not recognize squatters' rights against the State. An unknown number of peasants have either been squatting on state or private land or holding land on obviously illegal papers, or, in the disorders of the past or the divisions of land by inheritance (which are informal and complicated), have lost their papers and have no means of proving that they are not squatters. They may thus be dispossessed in favor of the State. To safeguard

14 Quoted by H. P. Davis, *Black Democracy*, p. 329.

their rights and at the same time afford opportunity for foreign investors involves serious legislative difficulties. A cadastral bill which would meet this third obstacle to large-scale agricultural development is now under consideration.

The assumption made by many Haitians that the United States will retain permanent control in order to provide stable and efficient government gives rise to fear and a resultant antagonism which are detrimental to the spirit of coöperation essential to any constructive program. It was to allay this fear as well as to give assurances to the rest of Latin America that Mr. Hughes said at the Havana Conference of 1928:

It is our desire to encourage stability in the interest of independence. . . . We would leave Haiti at any time that we had reasonable expectations of stability, and could be assured that the withdrawal would not be the occasion for a recurrence of bloodshed. Meanwhile we are endeavoring in every important direction to assist in the establishment of conditions for stability and prosperity, not that we may stay in Haiti, but that we may get out at the earliest opportunity.

Three courses are possible for the United States. The first of these, annexation or permanent control, might have the form of civilian administration but would be based on military force. It has no considerable support in American opinion.

The second possible program would be for the United States, within the remaining period of treaty occupation, viz., before 1936, to plan and to carry out all the engineering, technical, and administrative reforms possible, and then withdraw, although withdrawal could not be complete until all bonds had matured. But without securing Haitian coöperation these purely material betterments would leave Haitian political tendencies at the time of withdrawal virtually as they were during the first fifteen years of the nineteenth century.

The third course is to undertake the comprehensive process of preparing Haitians for the control of their own national existence by training and extensive education, and to carry it on steadily until the civic sense of the Haitians and the administrative ability of a class of leaders have been trained to such a point that there would be "reasonable expectations of stability" to follow a gradual or a total withdrawal by the United States. On the administrative side, although the United States' services have not prepared Haitians to take over the more important directive work of the higher posts, they have nevertheless trained Haitians for subordinate positions. In 1928 the Dean of the Haitian Medical School was called to take part in the work of the sanitary engineering department, and every effort has been made to enlist the coöperation of Haitian physicians in the medical service and to train Haitians who will replace the American commission personnel within the next few years. The Technical Service has already made marked advances in this direction, the percentage of Haitians employed increasing from 74 per cent in 1923 to 89.4 in 1928, and in the Public Works Department five additional Haitian engineers were commissioned during 1928. Improvements on these lines cannot be established promptly and by the methods of the efficiency engineer. There is required a fundamental study by experts of all the elements in the situation, the preparation of a program and submission of it to the highest authorities in the various technical fields.

The adoption of a comprehensive program to carry out this third course is difficult because it might be taken as an announcement that the occupation will continue beyond the present treaty period. As such forces work only gradually and their effectiveness in such a population as the Haitian would be only a matter of speculation, no term could be set for the continuance of American control. The more sound and the more fundamental the measures adopted, the more it might seem as if the American Government intended to remain indefinitely.

In a study of the relations between a controlling patron and a state in tutelage—Great Britain and Egypt, the United States and Haiti—it would be ingenuous to expect that a survey of the facts and a balancing of considerations would produce a general judgment as to the wisdom of any particular course of action. The argument of the school of political *laissez faire* is that civil administration by marines does not make a citizenry capable of self-government; they believe that experience, guided by the principle of trial and error, will teach any people the art of self-government and will alone indoctrinate it thoroughly in their lives. But it may be that a people in an early and arrested stage of self-government, accustomed to financial and political disorder, administrative incapacity, and corruption, are unable to lift their political life above selfish and transitory considerations, spinning as it were on a dead center. John Stuart Mill himself acknowledged that

the early difficulties in the way of spontaneous progress are so great that there is seldom any choice of means for overcoming them; and a ruler full of the spirit of improvement is warranted in the use of any expedients that will attain an end, perhaps otherwise unattainable. . . . Liberty, as a principle, has no application to any state of things anterior to the time when mankind have become capable of being improved by free and equal discussions.[15]

The task of administering the government of an undeveloped people and at the same time of training them to take over their own affairs is one of utmost difficulty. A considerable experience with easy communications, better hygiene, more education, and life on a higher economic level may produce in the Haitian people an effective desire for a mode of living which cannot be had in the interstices of anarchy or the alternations of frequent revolution.

[15] Mill on *Liberty,* introductory chapter.

THE REPUBLICS OF CENTRAL AMERICA

SEVERAL developments in the recent history of Central America are notable. The influence exerted by the United States upon its political destiny has vastly increased; domestic disorders within the several republics and conflicts among them have become less frequent; and serious efforts have been made to achieve, if not federation, at least a closer union among the states between the Isthmus and Yucatan. These second and third tendencies in Central American politics are closely allied to the first. That incessant internal commotions and mutual interference in one another's private concerns, which filled their history in the nineteenth century, have virtually ceased, is owing chiefly to the influence, political, social, and economic, of the United States.

The close relation of the United States with Nicaragua, because of the potential canal through its territory and the peculiar historical and geographical conditions which have made it subject to internal dissensions, have given the United States a greater anxiety for its affairs than for those of other Central American republics. Successively advancing and retiring the policy has culminated in a more positive and direct activity in the affairs of Nicaragua than in those of any other country.[1]

Central America until 1821 constituted one of the major political divisions of the Spanish American empire, the Captaincy General of Guatemala. When it secured political independence many circumstances made difficult the creation and maintenance of stable government. Predominantly an agricultural area, the bulk of its people were Indian or mestizo, and communications between centers of population were scant and primitive. The ruling caste of Spanish descent was essentially conservative, and political enlightenment was meager. Under Spanish colonial rule there had been virtually no self-government.

Republican institutions were incomprehensible to the illiterate

[1] Because of recent events the chapter which deals with Nicaragua is more detailed as to financial and commercial relations than in the case of the other Central American countries. The economic interests of the other Central American republics are treated in Chapter 10.

Indian masses, and were scarcely understood by their well-meaning but doctrinaire and unpractical superiors.

The evil traditions of corruption and favoritism inherited from the colonial régime made it difficult to inculcate respect for law or honesty in administration. The holding of real elections proved to be utterly impossible, for the result of the voting could always be determined in favor of the Government by corruption, official pressure, and fraud. The party in power maintained itself by force and could be displaced only by the same means. Political changes were thus almost invariably accompanied by disorder.

Some of these conditions have existed in several of the . . . countries down to the present day, and recurrent civil wars, with the economic and political demoralization which has accompanied them, have inevitably involved the Governments of these countries in difficulties with foreign Powers. Foreign property has been destroyed; foreign investors have been exposed to extortion at the hands of irresponsible military leaders; and foreign lives have sometimes been sacrificed. Furthermore, Government loans have been contracted abroad, and foreign interests have been besought in some cases and encouraged in others to construct railroads and develop mines and plantations. Because of the risks involved, and sometimes because of the inexperience or venality of local officials many of these investments were made under concessions granting privileges which later proved distasteful and burdensome, and subsequent Administrations, coming into power by revolution, have sought to evade or repudiate the obligations assumed by their predecessors, or have found that disturbed conditions made compliance impossible.[2]

The combined area of the five republics is about 208,000 square miles, and their aggregate population perhaps five million. Their industry and wealth are concentrated upon a fertile, volcanic plateau of moderate height on the western side of the Isthmus. Its highest and steepest escarpment is toward the Pacific; in the direction of the Caribbean it slopes away in long, irregular inclines. Subterranean igneous forces are active throughout the entire region, over thirty active or quiescent volcanoes have been recorded, and earthquakes are frequent, sometimes of a disastrous character. In this volcanic zone occurs a remarkable de-

[2] Dana G. Munro, *Current History,* September, 1927, p. 857.

pression flooded by two lakes, Managua and Nicaragua, in the
Republic of Nicaragua. Lake Nicaragua, called by Nelson the
"inland Gibraltar of Spanish America," is the largest sheet of
fresh water between Michigan and Lake Titicaca in Bolivia,
ninety miles long, with a mean breadth of forty miles and a depth
in some places of two hundred feet. Its overflow goes to the Caribbean through the San Juan River; this is the route of the projected Nicaragua canal.

Much of the eastern seaboard is coralline and alluvial and
fringed with mangrove swamps. Parallel with the shore is a nearly
continuous frieze of coral reefs and islands covered with cocoanut
groves and inclosing spacious lagoons. These waters were the common retreat of the seventeenth-century buccaneers, affording convenient points from which to harry the Spanish Main and the
great treasure fleets. Here they fraternized with the Carib natives,
and furnished the origin for the British protectorate over the so-
called Mosquito Indians which endured till near the close of the
nineteenth century.

A map of the rainfall of Central America is of the first importance in understanding the layout of the cultivated lands, the
situation of the denser populations, and the sites of the capital
cities of Central America. The eastern border of the country is
drenched; the western relatively dry. It is not an accident that
Panama City is on the south side of the isthmus and that the port
of Colon is on the north side. All of the reasons of trade apart from
climate would reverse the position of these cities, the one so large,
the other so small. It is on the east side that one has the dense
jungle, the heavy forest, the uncertain foothold, the swamps, the
bad approach. West of the main axis of the country the land becomes drier, the vegetation is locally park-like. Grazing can flour-
ish and grazing was the main sustenance of the first settlers. This
is a conquerable land. The consequence is that while mere distance
from Europe would have tempted the settlers to stay on the east
coast, they located themselves and flourished on the western side
even though this imposed servitudes of the heaviest kind in getting
their products to market. The economic conditions have been long
sustained and would have completely altered the distribution of

the people if it were not for the fundamental effects of climate and vegetation upon a folk who found these elements composed in the most favorable manner to suit their way of life on the western, or Pacific, watershed rather than the Atlantic. This is a matter of great importance to them in connection with the Canal, for only a canal could give the Central American countries a proper outlet for their goods. This conclusion remains notwithstanding the great development of the tropical fruit plantations on the east. The latter represent a quite special economy developed through American capital to satisfy a specific need. It has had an effect upon the Central Americans, a very great effect, but it does not alter the distribution of the population by more than a small fraction.

CHAPTER FOUR

NICARAGUA

THE center around which revolves Nicaragua's turbulent history is its geography. Its situation in relation to the Panama Canal and the proposed canal through its territory bring it within the sphere of United States interest; lack of communication between the east and west coasts, which are, geographically, commercially, and racially distinct, leads to factionalism and local prejudices, and interferes with the quelling of the resultant uprisings. Credit for the construction of highways and for a railroad to the Atlantic Coast, which would relieve the isolation, is difficult to obtain because of political instability and the danger of earthquakes.

Early in the sixteenth century the Spanish settled western Nicaragua and partly explored the eastern part. The native Indian tribes varied widely from the primitive, savage tribes in the east to those in the west whose relics show a considerable degree of culture; the tribes were so divided that they offered little resistance to the settlers. More than two-thirds of the present population is of Indian stock, one-sixth of European origin, and about one-tenth West Indian negroes; oriental immigration is prohibited. Spanish is the language most commonly used and Spanish traditions and customs prevail.

In the early days, the natural interoceanic route through Lake Nicaragua and the San Juan River was used for transportation. But after the construction of the Panama Railroad and of the first transcontinental railroad, the carrying trade through the isthmus declined. About 1900 an earthquake made the river difficult of navigation, and freight had to be transshipped. For a time most European freight was transferred at Panama to American vessels, but now several lines give direct service between Europe and Corinto, the western port of Nicaragua. Halfway *via* the Panama Canal route from New York to San Francisco, Corinto has the best protected harbor between Panama and San Diego. The two largest cities, Leon and Managua, are connected with it and with

each other by the Pacific Railroad which continues on to Granada, the third city in size.

The plateaus and rolling hills appropriate to agriculture make the western territory largely self-supporting. Since, in addition, a few articles are manufactured, the large population concentrated here absorbs no more than two-thirds of the import trade. The climate is tropical, relatively healthful, with a wet and dry season and an average annual rainfall of 61.5 inches. In the colonial period the west coast developed a profitable trade with Peru and Mexico in cacao, grapes, and olives; this was eventually ruined by raids and by prohibitive Spanish measures, and grapes and olives have never since been cultivated.

The eastern part, with its dense woods, coastal swamps, and mountains, presents a different aspect. Here, with an average annual rainfall of 194.9 inches the climate is humid; during the rainy season almost all transportation is by boat. The Caribbean littoral, with only 7 per cent of the population, takes 33 per cent of the imports. Importation of such common articles of daily diet as beans and rice makes the cost of living high. Bluefields, the chief town, is three days' sailing distance from the Gulf coast of the United States, twenty-four hours from the Panama Canal, and only 180 miles distant from Managua as the crow flies; but with no railroad, five days are needed for the journey to the capital under the best conditions, and a week or ten days if one goes by launch *via* the San Juan River or by muleback *via* Rama.

Agriculture.

The section which has its outlet on the Caribbean has been the source of export mahogany for over a century, but owing to wasteful methods of cutting and lax enforcement of the replanting law, the supply bordering the rivers is depleted; near the headwaters some mahogany, cedar, valuable hardwood, and a turpentine pine belt remain. Bananas, some grown on small farms and bought up by the transportation companies which own the majority of the large plantations, are the chief east coast export, valued at $1,442,383 in 1927, finding their principal market in the United States; constituting from 16 to 19 per cent of the country's exports they rank with cabinet woods, which make up 19 per cent, next to coffee in value. Nicaragua, like Haiti, is largely dependent upon coffee for its revenues and suffers from the dangers inherent in one-crop production. Fluctuation of the average price per pound from 25 to 9 cents between 1910 and 1927 indicates the wide margin of difference in revenues derived from coffee; in years when a low price coincides with a small or poor crop, the effects are serious. The 1927 crop was only two-thirds of the average in quantity for the past six years but averaged 18 cents in price.

Coffee is not native to Nicaragua but the plant was introduced in early days and is now cultivated in well-managed plantations; the best are south of Managua and at Matagalpa, and largely in Nicaraguan, German, and American hands. Because of inadequate preparation, Nicaraguan coffee does not compare in quality with that grown in Costa Rica, Guatemala, and Salvador. In 1927 coffee constituted 45 per cent of the value of exports. Before the War half of the coffee exported went to France and a large part to Germany. During the War Nicaragua developed a market for its coffee in the United States, which in 1926 equaled France in taking approximately a fourth of the total annual export. But in 1927 the United States took only an eighth, France regained its lead with a fourth, Germany was second, advancing a step in its steady progress since 1923 of taking more each year, and Great Britain was third. Gold, 7 per cent, and sugar, of which almost the entire export crop, constituting 5 per cent of total exports, comes to the United States, are the other principal exports.

Diversification of agricultural products is imperative; cattle raising is also a potentially lucrative enterprise which would utilize land at present waste, constituting approximately a third of the estimated total land area of thirty million acres. A million acres, probably 5 per cent of the arable total, are in crops; perhaps ten million acres in merchantable timber, and about six hundred thousand used for grazing. Land is cheap and abundant and can be obtained from the State, which owns about half the total land area, by the simple process of "denouncement."

The backwardness of agriculture may be partially attributed

to the lack of responsibility which the upper classes exhibit toward the peasant. Half of the population is estimated as illiterate and schools are few and inadequate. Inefficient, low-paid labor results in scanty, inferior output and meager purchasing power, and the Government and people are alike impoverished. Not only in agriculture is the Republic undeveloped; roads are few, and thick with dust or incumbered with muddy ruts, trails are overgrown and inundated during the rainy reason, streets unpaved, with the exception of some recent surfacing in Managua; bridges in disrepair are hindrances rather than aids to travel, sewers and other sanitary facilities are practically non-existent, pure water is difficult to obtain—in short, the material apparatus of civilization is lacking.

Disease is an important factor in keeping the peasant at the bare subsistence level at which he lives. The Rockefeller Foundation has done excellent remedial work, but the percentage of children affected with hookworm is large, and syphilis and malaria each represents between 20 and 25 per cent of the death-roll. The Foundation maintains a public health officer who, though holding no official position with the Nicaraguan Government, supervises its public health work.

Without the aid of foreign capital, material progress will be slow. At present foreign investment in Nicaragua is smaller than in any other Latin-American country; the estimated total of $15,000,000 is divided as follows:

$3,000,000 in banana plantations.
2,000,000 in lumbering operations.
2,000,000 in railroads and their equipment.
1,000,000 in mines.
2,000,000 in miscellaneous activities, particularly coffee and commercial establishments.
5,000,000 in foreign holdings of public debt.

Of this total Dr. Cumberland estimates two-thirds as representing United States commitments.[1]

[1] *Financial and Economic Survey of Nicaragua*, p. 15. Department of Commerce figures for the total American investment are $17,000,000.

Trade.

From 1917 to 1927 customs receipts averaged 49.2 per cent of total government income. Per capita imports of $16.07 in 1926 show both the large dependency of Nicaragua on foreign commodities, and the high price which imported goods always command. In view of the fluctuation of imports and exports, this dependence upon revenue from duties on imported commodities, on some of which high rates are levied, makes for fiscal instability. The other chief sources of revenue are the tax on the manufacture and sale of alcoholic beverages, which averaged 39.4 per cent of total internal revenues from 1920 through 1926, and that on tobacco, 17.5 per cent. A tax of one-half of one per cent on the appraised value of properties of $3,000 or more, plus one-half per mill assessed for educational purposes, brought in an average of 10.5 per cent of the internal revenues in the period 1920-26.[2]

The balance of trade usually favors Nicaragua. In four years only, since 1900, has it been unfavorable. The slightly unfavorable balance in 1927, during which imports amounted to C$10,208,242 against exports of C$9,025,676 is accounted for by the large importations of supplies by the Quartermaster's department of the United States marines in Nicaragua whose number ranged from 1,500 to 3,500 and was offset by their large local purchases.[3] Importations of iron and steel decreased from the norm of 7 per cent; cotton goods retained their norm of 29 per cent.

Of the total imports entering Nicaragua, the United States has fallen off from 80 per cent, the highest average attained during the War years, to 66 per cent in 1927. Great Britain furnished an average of 20 per cent from 1911 to 1915, and now averages about 11 per cent. Germany is gradually approaching its 1912 proportion of 12 per cent, furnishing 4 per cent in 1924, 6 in 1925, and 7 in 1926 and 1927, respectively.

In the period 1911-15, exports from Nicaragua to the United States averaged 40 per cent; to France, 25; Germany, 17; and to Great Britain, 10. The effects of the War and of the subsequent economic crisis gave the advantage in buying power to the United

[2] See *Financial and Economic Survey of Nicaragua*, p. 85.
[3] *Report of Collector-General*, 1927, p. 15.

States. In 1924 the United States took 57 per cent of Nicaraguan exports; 1925, 65 per cent; 1926, 53 per cent, and 1927, 55 per cent. For the same years, France imported 16, 14, 23, and 13 per cent respectively of Nicaraguan goods; The Netherlands, 6, 3, 4, and 6 per cent; Spain, 5, 3, 5, 2; Great Britain, 3, 4, 2, and 7; and Germany, 3, 4, 5, and 9 per cent.

Beginnings of Political Strife.

The two political parties, whose strife reminds one of the Guelph-Ghibelline conflicts, originated in the rivalry between Leon and Granada in the early nineteenth century when Granada subscribed to the Central American Federation and Leon demanded Nicaraguan independence. The Conservative Party centered about Granada where lived the aristocracy, a component part of the Catholic Church. Here also were the homes of the cattle ranchers and leading commercial families, for Granada, as the chief town of a rich cacao, cattle, and sugar-producing district, had a flourishing history. The Liberals' stronghold was Leon with its mercantile, professional, and laboring classes, surrounded by a region of small farmers.

Echoing with the triumphs of the American, French, and Mexican revolutions, Nicaragua was torn by internal strife between the Conservatives who wished to join the Central American Federation and the Liberals who were inspired to demand its own declaration of independence. For a time it was a member of the Central American Union but in 1838 it declared its independence with Leon as capital and decreed a new constitution. Chaos marked the next twenty years. There were successive revolutions, bloody and destructive. There was friction with England which, in order to control transisthmian traffic, wished to establish a protectorate over the Mosquito tribes, and in 1841 succeeded in taking San Juan, and wars with Salvador and Honduras over the establishment of the Central American Union. Appeals to the United States by the Nicaraguan Minister of Foreign Relations brought no response, but made an impression which was intensified by the California gold rush in 1849. The attention of the United States thus directed to Nicaragua helped to bring about the Clayton-Bulwer Treaty.[4] The concessions were mainly on the British side: prospects of a canal were dim; Great Britain considered its cotton trade with the United States of greater value than its Central American trade, and thought that even in the event of the construction of a canal its commerce would develop more advantageously if the canal were under a joint Anglo-American neutralization than under Nicaraguan sovereignty. British sentiment then showed a trend toward recognition of closer interest on the part of the United States in Central America and assumed practical form in a series of treaties by which Great Britain withdrew its claims from this field: one with Guatemala, April 30, 1859, fixing the boundaries of Belize as they existed before 1850; another with Honduras on November 28, 1859, recognizing the Bay Islands which it had seized in 1839, and the Mosquito territory within its frontiers as belonging to Honduras; and a third with Nicaragua, January 28, 1860, admitting Nicaraguan sovereignty over the Mosquito territory within its boundaries. The Indians were recognized as citizens of the respective countries in which they resided.

By 1855 Granada had become the capital. The Walker episode[5] united the two parties and a compromise capital was established at Managua. The next "thirty years," 1863-1893, ushered in by President Tomas Martinez, and continuing under a succession of four-year presidents, was a prosperous period of Conservative control. In 1867 a treaty of commerce and navigation was ratified with the United States.

Zelaya and the 1909 Revolution.

In 1893 a Liberal, Zelaya, through a split in the Conservative Party, was able to seize power. He retained it for sixteen years, term after term going through the form of having himself reelected. He had ability, strong executive qualities, force of character, and courage, and during the first part of his dictatorship was a good administrator, building a railroad, making harbor improvements, encouraging industries, keeping order, and even building schools. Later he became tyrannical and ambitious, and

---

[4] See *Survey*, 1928, pp. 45-46.   [5] See *infra*, p. 220.

in his desire to extend his power over Central America, embroiled Guatemala, Honduras, and Salvador in warfare. They appealed to Washington for a settlement which would establish order, and Secretary Root in 1906, responding to their appeal, conceived the idea of a treaty of permanent peace, and to that end suggested that President Diaz of Mexico join with the United States in inviting the Central American states to a conference in Washington. As Zelaya continued to disregard the provisions of the Treaty of Peace and Amity,[6] drawn up at the ensuing conference, the United States was urged by the Central American states to take action. Finally in October, 1909, annoyed by the granting of monopolistic concessions which were stifling all enterprise, foreign merchants of Bluefields and the east coast financed a revolt against Zelaya of which Adolfo Diaz was treasurer, and Emiliano Chamorro, military commander. General Estrada, Liberal governor under Zelaya on the east coast, was proclaimed provisional president in order to win over his province.

Thomas P. Moffatt, United States consul at Bluefields, had previously informed the State Department that a revolution would start on October 8, and on the 12th he reported that the provisional government established was friendly to United States interests. Following the brutal execution by Zelaya of two American adventurers, who were serving the rebel interests, Secretary Knox dismissed the Nicaraguan Minister to Washington; this forced the resignation of President Zelaya. Another Liberal leader, José Madriz, was inaugurated on December 21, 1909, but as Secretary Knox had included the Zelaya *régime* in his indictment, no member of his party could hope for recognition. The revolution continued another six months and was successful largely because the commander of a United States warship at Bluefields refused to allow a government blockade of the port to interfere with American ships or ships carrying American goods, and prevented the bombardment of the city, which was held by the revolutionists, by declaring it a neutral zone. The Madriz government, being deprived of the military advantage inherent in the occupation of Blue-

[6] For provisions of the treaty, see *infra*, p. 264.

fields, and of the customs revenues, consequently fell. When President Madriz protested to President Taft, Secretary Knox replied that "The United States took only the customary step of prohibiting bombardment or fighting by either faction within the unfortified and ungarrisoned commercial city of Bluefields, thus protecting the preponderating American and other foreign interests."[7]

Before according recognition to General Estrada, the State Department sent the United States Minister at Panama, Thomas C. Dawson, to Nicaragua to guide the new government's policy. Mr. Dawson secured the signature of Adolfo Diaz, Luis Mena, Emiliano Chamorro, and Juan J. Estrada, the four revolutionary leaders, to his "agreements," which provided for (1) the election of a constituent assembly which would make Estrada temporary president and Diaz vice-president, and adopt a constitution which would provide for an election of permanent officials and abolish Zelaya's monopolies; (2) the establishment of a mixed claims commission; (3) the punishment of the executioners of the two Americans; (4) the solicitation of a loan in the United States; (5) the debarring of the Zelayist element from the administration.

On December 31 the constituent assembly chose Estrada president for two years and Diaz vice-president; this government was immediately recognized by the United States. Mr. Northcott, the new Minister, reported, soon after his arrival in January, 1911, that "Estrada has given a great deal of thought to the situation and has decided that the only hope for Nicaragua is close alliance with the United States." President Estrada had suggested that the United States should guarantee free elections in Nicaragua and disband the armies of the five Central American republics, substituting a United States police force. Mr. Northcott said that Central American opposition to this policy was already apparent and that "the natural sentiment of an overwhelming majority of Nicaraguans is antagonistic to the United States," adding that some members of Estrada's cabinet had "a decided suspicion, if not distrust of our motives."[8] In conclusion Mr. Northcott urged

[7] *For. Rel.*, 1910, p. 753. [8] *For. Rel.*, 1911, p. 655.

the hastening of a loan. On March 27 he reported that many revolutionary plots were current and that Estrada was "being sustained solely by the moral effect of our support and the belief that he would unquestionably have that support in case of trouble."

Emiliano Chamorro, the Conservative leader who controlled the constituent assembly, tried to put through a constitution which would make that body superior to the president, whereupon President Estrada dissolved the assembly and Chamorro left the country. General Mena, who as Minister of War controlled the army, stacked a new constituent assembly with his supporters. In May President Estrada, at the instigation of General Moncada, minister of *gobernacion*, tried to remove Mena from office. As the situation soon got out of hand, President Estrada and General Moncada resigned, and Vice-President Diaz became president. Divided between two leaders, Chamorro and Mena, the Conservative Party was in constant friction within its own ranks. In view of the continuous plots and disturbances United States war vessels were sent to patrol both coasts.

Financial Plan of 1911.

A succession of weak administrations had cumulatively inflated the currency, and increased the public debt and the claims against the Government. Following the report of the United States financial expert, sent down in accordance with the Dawson agreements, the Knox-Castrillo Convention was negotiated in order that a contract might be concluded between the Nicaraguan Government and "some competent and reliable American banking group." It provided that the proposed loan should be secured upon the Nicaraguan customs, which were to be collected, for its duration, by a fiscal agent approved by the United States president; no "charges affecting the entry, exit or transit of goods" were to be altered without the agreement of the United States; the United States Government was in turn to "afford such protection as it may find requisite." The Convention was ratified by Nicaragua, but was thrice rejected by the United States Senate. Pending ratification, tenders on the $15,000,000 bond issue included in the treaty were invited. Brown Brothers & Company and J. and W. Seligman & Company of New York were the highest bidders, but as the treaty failed to pass the Senate, no bonds were issued. Nevertheless, while the treaty was pending in the Senate, the State Department, to relieve the pressing financial situation, urged these bankers to interest themselves in straightening out some of the most pressing financial complications in Nicaragua, and to make the necessary cash advances.

According to the contract of September 1, 1911, which the bankers signed with the Nicaraguan Government "in anticipation of the favorable resolution of the Senate," they agreed to buy an issue of short-term treasury bills to the amount of $1,500,000, secured by customs receipts which were to be collected by a Collector-General of Customs appointed by the Nicaraguan Government on the nomination of the bankers and with the approval of the Secretary of State. The bankers reserved the right "to petition the United States for protection against the violation of this agreement or aid in imposing its fulfilment." Colonel Clifford D. Ham was appointed Collector-General of Customs and remained in office until his resignation in June, 1928. In addition to his duties as Collector-General he administered lighthouses, wharves at all ports (although the Corinto wharf was under private ownership), harbors and ports including buoys and aids to navigation, revenue cutters, warehousing and sanitation at Corinto, and foreign mail in part.

The bankers also appointed a commission, paid by Nicaragua, to study monetary conditions. The representative of the Republic in the negotiations with the bankers had reported that the circulation of paper currency amounted to 30,902,630 pesos; a statement furnished by the Minister of Finance as of December 18, 1911, however, gave the outstanding circulation of paper currency at that date as 48,307,603 pesos, the Diaz government having issued 16,000,000 additional pesos to pay certain preferred claims. This great increase in the paper money outstanding added considerably to the difficulties of the financial experts in determining the rate at which the currency should be stabilized. The Commission therefore suggested that the Government borrow $550,000 to buy and retire enough paper pesos to reduce circulation to a point where it could be converted into new gold currency, and as a part of this financial operation the bankers also contracted to lend the Government $255,000 for current monthly expenses. The Commission finally determined on a rate of 12.50 pesos to the córdoba, the new unit to be created, which is equivalent to the United States dollar. The rate in January, 1912, was 18 pesos to the dollar, and not until January 13, 1913, was the eventual rate of 12.50 established. The actual conversion of the outstanding currency into the new córdobas began on March 23. This is the only monetary system of Latin America which went through the slump of 1921-22 without depreciation, and one of the few in the Western Hemisphere, beside that of the United States, to remain substantially on a gold basis during the World War.

As part of the new financial plan, a National Bank was incorporated in the United States under a Connecticut charter, and opened on August 9, 1912, under the management of the New York bankers. The bankers subscribed half the capital, retaining 51 per cent of the stock, and furnished the Government's share by way of a loan. A ninety-nine year concession was given and an option on the remaining bank stock, on any loans to be negotiated, and on the railroad stock. Arrangements were made that disputes should be settled by two arbitrators, or if they could not agree, by a third to be appointed by the Secretary of State. Six directors were appointed by the bankers, one by the Secretary of State, and two by the Nicaraguan Government. The National Bank was to be the sole depositary of the Republic with power to issue legal tender notes and coin money with or without guaranties. On October 8, 1913, the capital was increased from the $100,000 with which the Bank began operations in 1912, to $300,000, the present capital.

Meanwhile the Mixed Claims Commission began its work. The total of the 7,908 claims, $13,808,161, was scaled down to $1,840,-432, the smaller awards being paid out of customs revenues. The European governments prevented some of their nationals from accepting the awards, objecting to a Commission composed of two Americans, one appointed by the State Department and one by Nicaragua on the recommendation of the State Department, and one Nicaraguan. The claims were later taken up by the Public Credit Commission.

The bankers, as agents of the Republic, were successful in arranging a new contract with the Corporation of Foreign Bondholders, London, May 25, 1912, by which the interest on the Ethelburga sterling loan, made by Zelaya in 1909, was reduced from 6 to 5 per cent and the bonds were placed under the Collector-General for payment, interest and amortization constituting a first lien on customs receipts. On February 28, 1929, outstanding bonds of this loan, payable in gold, amounted to £663,720 maturing in 1944, callable at par on six months' notice. The office of the Collector-General is to continue until both the Sterling Bonds of 1909 and the Guaranteed Customs Bonds of 1918 have been retired. The bankers also undertook to refund the foreign debt, service charges on which were then in default.

Revolution of 1912.

Meanwhile, Mena had become more hostile to Diaz and in the revolution which started late in July, 1912, sought openly to overthrow him. This the United States could not countenance in view of its sponsorship of the 1907 Peace and Amity Treaty and the Dawson agreements. When asked by the United States Minister to protect American life and property President Diaz confessed his incapacity and requested United States aid. The next day a detachment of troops arrived in Managua. Eight United States warships were sent during the next two months, and on September 25, General Mena surrendered to the commander of the United States forces, who then ordered the evacuation of a fort overlooking Masaya, because, he said, in hostile hands it threatened the railroad which the United States must keep open at all costs. As the Liberal commander refused to evacuate, American troops seized the fort, and with the subsequent surrender of Leon to another American officer the revolt was crushed.

In the election which was then due Diaz controlled the machinery and was successful in having himself reëlected. Although this self-succession disregarded a provision of the Nicaraguan Constitution, the United States recognized Diaz. Emiliano Chamorro, who had been the Conservatives' real choice for president, was given the post of Minister to Washington. After the election all United States marines were withdrawn except a so-called legation guard of 101 enlisted men and four Marine Corps officers. Stationed in one of the forts of the capital as a sort of fire brigade, they were successful during the next thirteen years of Conservative control in preventing smoldering Liberal aspirations from breaking into flame. Mena was deported to Panama.

This revolt cost the Government $2,000,000, set back financial reforms, and added several millions to the claims. Funds were insufficient for salaries and other current needs, and the bankers were forced to give assistance by making another million dollar loan, October 8, 1913, and by exercising their option of buying 51 per cent of Pacific Railroad stock, reselling to the Government in 1920 at a small advance when it was in a stronger financial position. The contracts to cover these financial transactions were first submitted to the State Department and had its approval. Management by the J. G. White Management Corporation has transformed the railroad from a "streak of rust" into a transportation system which earns a yearly profit for the Government. In 1912 the railroad was incorporated under State of Maine laws and given a ninety-nine year concession with exemption from all Nicaraguan taxes and import duties for thirty years; the Government receives a rebate of one-half the regular rates on its own shipments.

With a view to stabilizing conditions and securing funds, negotiations were begun in December, 1912, to give the United States an option on a canal route through Nicaragua. In the following February a convention was signed providing for the payment by the United States to Nicaragua of $3,000,000 in return for exclusive canal rights, and the cession of naval bases in the Caribbean and on the Pacific. The Wilson administration offered terms by which

Nicaragua agreed not to declare war without the consent of the United States, or to enter into treaties with foreign governments affecting her independence or territorial integrity, or to contract public debts beyond her ability to pay, and by which she recognized the right of the United States to intervene in her affairs when necessary to preserve her independence or to protect life and property in her domain.[9]

This provision, modeled on the Cuban "Platt Amendment," the United States Senate refused to accept, and it was omitted in the treaty signed on August 5, 1914. For a payment of $3,000,000, to be expended under its direction, the United States received the exclusive right to build and operate a transisthmian canal anywhere through the republic, a ninety-nine year lease of the Great Corn and Little Corn Islands off the Nicaraguan coast in the Caribbean, and for a like period the right to establish a naval base on Nicaraguan territory in the Gulf of Fonseca.

Because of Senate opposition to the protectorate clause, the payment did not become available until November, 1917, and was distributed with the approval of the Secretary of State as follows:

Bonds of 1909, interest to Jan. 1, 1917 and 6 per cent interest thereon	$ 622,779.77
Bonds of 1909, sinking fund to Jan. 1, 1917	138,906.31
Bonds of 1909, 25 per cent of interest due July 1, 1917	36,773.09
Treasury Bills of 1913, one-half of principal	530,000.00
Treasury Bills of 1913, interest to November 1, 1917	211,181.14
Emery Claim—Protocol with United States, September 18, 1909	485,000.00
National Bank of Nicaragua—Loans and Interest	111,404.83
Internal and floating debts and claims	334,840.83
Expenses, fees, commissions, etc.	26,512.66
Government of Nicaragua, back salaries and expenses	500,000.00
Expense of Exchange, etc.	2,601.37
	$3,000,000.00

In a letter of January 7, 1915, which Senator Borah read to the Senate twelve years later, Elihu Root made the following comments upon the Bryan-Chamorro Treaty:

I am . . . troubled about the question whether the Nicaraguan Government which has made the treaty is really representative of the people of Nicaragua and whether it will be regarded in Nicaragua and

9 Dana G. Munro, *The Five Republics of Central America*, p. 252.

in Central America as having been a free agent in making the treaty. I have been looking over the report of the commanding officer of our marines in Nicaragua, and I find there the following: "The present government is not in power by the will of the people; the elections of the House of Congress were mostly fraudulent."

And a further statement that the Liberals, that is to say, the opposition, "constitute three-fourths of the country." It is apparent from this report and from other information which in a casual way comes to me from various sources that the present government with which we are making this treaty is really maintained in office by the presence of the United States marines in Nicaragua.

*   *   *   *   *

Can we afford to make a treaty so serious for Nicaragua, granting us perpetual rights in that country, with a president who we have reason to believe does not represent more than a quarter of the people of the country, and who is maintained in office by our military force, and to whom we would, as a result of the treaty, pay a large sum of money to be disposed of by him as President?[10]

Financial Plan of 1917.

The 1916 election resulted in the triumph of the candidate supported by the United States Minister. The Liberals, who were in the majority, had desired the withdrawal of the United States marines so that they would have a chance of winning the election, but security of American interests demanded the continuance in power of the Conservative Party; and when the Liberals nominated Irías, Zelaya's minister, as their candidate, they were warned that no one who had been associated with the Zelaya *régime* would receive United States recognition.

The World War increased financial difficulties, and Emiliano Chamorro, who became president January 1, 1917. was presented with an empty treasury; moreover, in consequence of a suspension in interest payments, the bankers had enforced their lien on all customs revenues, and the British Government had served notice that certain claims totaling approximately $100,000, which it had adjudicated with Nicaragua, should have prior payment. President Chamorro publicly charged the customs service with

[10] *Cong. Rec.*, January 13, 1927, p. 1557.

misappropriation of funds, and threatened to recover the custom-houses by force, but the State Department made it clear that the money was in the Bank, and warned him that a seizure of customs would be a breach of faith. Financial aid thus became imperative, and the plan of 1911 had to be revised.

The failure of the 1911 loan had left the Nicaraguan Government without funds to pay the claims awarded by the Mixed Claims Commission, and other claims had in the meantime accumulated. To settle all, a Public Credit Commission was created February 14, 1917. The claims, amounting to $13,578,314.35, were adjudicated at $5,304,386.21, of which $1,427,336.79 was paid in cash and $3,744,150 in guaranteed customs bonds of 1918, bearing interest at 5 per cent and redeemable out of an amortization fund consisting of the balance of pledged revenues after payment of interest. But the bond awards were accepted unwillingly by those who needed to convert them at once, for the bonds declined more than 50 per cent in value; those who were able to await amortization drawings received full value. The bonds are callable at par without notice and secured by a surcharge of 12½ per cent on import duties, collected by the Collector-General and deposited in the National Bank to the order of the High Commission, which uses all funds deposited to its account to defray (1) its operation expenses, (2) interest payments, (3) semiannual drawings of bonds at par. Other revenues assigned as security for these bonds —a tax on capital and on the transfer of property, 50 per cent of receipts from the sale of public domain lands, and a contingent charge against the surplus revenues—are collected under the direction of the Ministry of Finance. Service has been met regularly and the bonds outstanding reduced to $2,047,000, February 28, 1929. They are not listed on the New York Stock Exchange; on May 24, 1929, the market "over the counter" was 80 bid, 85 asked.

By the financial plan drawn up in 1917 the Public Debt Commission was converted into the High Commission and made permanent. It was composed of two Americans designated by the State Department (since 1928, the Collector-General has been one of the members), and one Nicaraguan appointed by his Government, who in practice has been the Minister of Finance. This was a compromise arrangement in place of the financial adviser desired by the creditors and strongly opposed in Nicaragua. The High Commission assists in forming the budget, acts as fiscal agent, and, in addition, as arbitrator in cases of disagreement between the Collector-General and the Government.

Responding to the slightest encouragement Nicaragua recuperates quickly; notwithstanding its revolutions, governmental straits, the World War, and the low price of coffee, commerce in the decade 1910-19 doubled over that of the previous decade. Customs revenues slumped in the two years of crisis, 1921 and 1922, but recovered and in 1928 were treble those of 1911.

By 1919 the treasury bills, given the bankers in 1917 to cover half of their loan, and other arrears were paid. As the country was out of debt to the bankers the proposal to build a railroad to the east coast was revived; but criticism of the presence of United States commissioners in Nicaragua was everywhere rife, the crisis of 1921 came on while negotiations for a loan to build the railroad were under way, and the bankers finally declined to exercise their option to buy the bonds for the new railroad. As no other bankers were found to make the loan, plans for the railroad were dropped, and in 1924 Brown Brothers withdrew.

In 1920 the Financial Plan of 1917 was revised, stipulating an annual budget of C$1,260,000. In addition C$319,992 may be authorized, with the approval of the High Commission, for added requirements. If and when the general revenues for any four successive fiscal years exceed the general revenues for the fiscal year ending June 30, 1920, the budget may be increased by an amount proportionate to the average increase in the general revenues. In fact, the general revenues, that is, all revenues, both internal and those from customs duties, after a reduction of payment for debt service, have never for the necessary four fiscal years exceeded those for 1920, but by agreement of the High Commission and the bankers, the budget has been increased three times: the last time to C$125,000 monthly. The Plan provides also that if the internal revenues fall below C$200,000 in any three months, their collection shall be taken over by the Collector-General of Customs.

Chamorro's coup d'état.

Diego Chamorro succeeded his nephew, Emiliano, as president in 1920; on his death, October 12, 1923, Vice-President Bartolomé Martinez became president, but his hopes for election in 1924 for the next full term were dashed by the State Department on the ground that the Nicaraguan Constitution forbade self-succession on the part of a president. Consequently Martinez rejected the proposal that United States observers should supervise the election, although H. W. Dodds, who had prepared the Nicaraguan election law of 1923, and fourteen assistants, had already been engaged. They were dismissed, and Martinez also declined a later offer of the State Department to have legation guard marines act as observers.

Carlos Solorzano, a Conservative, was declared by congress as a canvassing body elected president, and Juan B. Sacasa, a Liberal, vice-president, Martinez seating enough Coalitionists to secure a majority in Congress. Because of "patent election frauds"[11] the State Department hesitated to recognize Solorzano until a day or so before his inauguration. In a note of November 14, 1923, the United States legation at Managua had notified Nicaragua that its Government wished to withdraw the legation guard "as soon as practicable." But nothing was done toward that end until January, 1925, when the State Department announced withdrawal within three weeks. Protests from the American interests on the east coast were immediate and vigorous, and in compliance with Solorzano's request that a constabulary be organized under United States officers the Department postponed withdrawal. The next summer the organization of a constabulary was initiated and the marines were withdrawn August 3, 1925.

On October 25, 1925, General Chamorro seized La Loma Fort. Diaz, his associate, forced President Solorzano to advance $10,000 for the expenses of Chamorro, to make him General-in-Chief of the Army, and to agree to the expulsion, on the ground that they were fraudulently elected, of the eighteen Coalitionists seated by Martinez. The ousted Conservatives were substituted, and the congress, thus purged, elected Chamorro president after Solorzano

[11] *Relations between the United States and Nicaragua,* Government Printing Office, Washington, 1928, p. 26.

had resigned. Adopting the principles of the General Treaty of Peace and Amity,[12] signed February 7, 1923, "as its policy in the future recognition of Central American Governments as it feels that by so doing it can best show its friendly disposition towards and its desire to be helpful to the Republics of Central America," the Department of State refused to recognize Chamorro.

Upon his assumption of the presidency on January 17, 1926, General Chamorro, having complete control over congress, proceeded to administer the government as a dictator. His *régime* was probably neither more nor less harsh than the exigencies of his situation required. He was greatly aided by a full treasury, efficient revenue collection by the American Collector-General, conditions of general prosperity, rising revenues, and large surpluses each half year, January and June, 1926, after the service of the foreign debt and the budget appropriations had been deducted.

On May 2, General Sandoval, a Liberal leader, led a movement which captured the port of Bluefields in the name of the Liberal vice-president, Dr. Sacasa, who had asserted his title to the presidency. Sandoval's men seized some $160,000 from the Bluefields Branch of the National Bank. General Chamorro at once outfitted an expedition which restored the Government's control at Bluefields and on the Atlantic coast, within a month after the success of Sandoval's sporadic raid.

From the first of June until the first week in August General Chamorro enjoyed a calm which was broken by the arrival of the Mexican vessel *Tropical* near Coseguina on the Bay of Fonseca. A band of Liberal sympathizers who had a rendezvous with this expeditionary force on the coast near Leon, sallied forth to the appointed place where the expedition was to supply them with arms and leaders to launch the revolution. As the expedition was delayed, it landed at Coseguina, where it was joined by some two or three hundred Liberals hurriedly advised of the new plan. In the meantime the Government got wind of the mobilization near Leon and fell upon the assembled Liberals and dispersed them with ease. It then dispatched a force to Coseguina where the small band of Liberals was routed completely. After making a long stay

12 See p. 267.

in Salvadorean waters, the *Tropical* then returned to Mexico. Had the *Tropical* expedition been on time and met the Liberals near Leon, a formidable and possibly successful movement might have been launched.

Some two weeks later, the vessel *Foam* landed a well-armed expedition, headed by General Moncada, at Bragman Bluff on the east coast. Another vessel and numerous small coast boats brought other Liberal forces. The plan was to have the *Tropical* start a movement on the west coast near Managua where the Government was strongest and at the same time to have the *Foam* and other vessels launch the main offensive on the east coast, whose inaccessibility to the government forces would give the Liberal expedition time to form and gather volume.

As the west coast expedition plan miscarried, the Liberal movement concentrated on the east coast, the first objective being Bluefields, which General Moncada besieged in late August. The revolutionists' handicap was increased by the United States declaration of an embargo on the exportation of arms and munitions to Nicaragua which was notified to Costa Rica, Honduras, Guatemala, El Salvador, and Mexico. All agreed to coöperate, except Mexico, which declined on the ground that there was so little manufacture of that kind in Mexico that it was unnecessary. The circumstantial evidence, however, all points to the conclusion that these expeditions were fitted out in Mexico, largely with Mexican Government arms and stores, and that the funds were also obtained in Mexico.

Dr. Sacasa, after Chamorro's assumption of the presidency, fled the country as a measure of personal safety. He went first to Washington, told the State Department the tale of the *coup d'état*, and explained the present plight of the Liberals. The State Department, deploring the illegality of Chamorro's proceedings and existing dictatorship, told Sacasa that the United States would withhold recognition from Chamorro and not extend it until a constitutional government was set up; but the State Department could neither assist Sacasa materially to oust Chamorro nor view with approval any violent measures he might take to this end. The Department had no suggestion as to how a constitutional government might be set up in the face of Chamorro's attitude, and added the wish that both parties would come to a "constitutional settlement by friendly agreement." This was not helpful to Sacasa or his friends, who no doubt remembered how Porfirio Diaz in Mexico, Estrada Cabrera in Guatemala, Zelaya in Nicaragua, Gomez in Venezuela, and many other dictators had remained in power after their *coups d'état*.

Dr. Sacasa then went to Mexico and laid his story before the Calles government, which disapproved strongly of the Chamorro government. The result was the expeditions which eventually forced the series of events culminating in Chamorro's withdrawal, Diaz's designation, Colonel Stimson's settlement, and Moncada's election, with a continuance of American intervention.

The Mexican attitude toward Nicaragua seems to have been the determining factor in American policy. Had Dr. Sacasa and the Liberals been able, unaided by Mexico or unaided visibly by Mexico, to carry on a revolution against Chamorro no occasion for the United States to intervene would have arisen and the State Department could have viewed the movement with neutrality and with satisfaction at the effectiveness of its non-recognition policy. When it became apparent, however, that Dr. Sacasa's movement owed its effectiveness to the Mexican contributions, Washington was forced to look for an issue from the situation which would put an end to Mexican participation in the affair. It could not recognize Chamorro, after all that had passed, not even to circumvent the Mexican-aided revolution; on the other hand it had no convincing pretext for checking the Sacasa movement.

The State Department therefore promoted the Corinto conference, which was a last endeavor by Washington to work out a solution. The conference failed, as Chamorro was unwilling to make enough concessions to satisfy the Liberals and as they rightly felt sure of winning out against Chamorro. Generally when a revolution is not promptly suffocated, it wins in the long run; the government slowly weakens in the struggle, while time is all on the side of the revolutionists. At this stage the State Department was not prepared to go so far as to present an ultimatum of disarmament such as that later delivered by Colonel Stimson to General Moncada at Tipitapa, and thereby to dominate the situation so as to guarantee fair play.

Following the Corinto conference, it was not difficult for the American *chargé d'affaires* to persuade most of Chamorro's supporters that Chamorro could not hold out against the Mexican-aided revolution without an aid which the United States would not give him. The obvious solution for two out of the three parties to the complication was the withdrawal of Chamorro and the making of Diaz president through some procedure which Washington might qualify as constitutional. The Conservatives could gain no advantage by changing horses in the middle of the stream if not thereby to secure American support against the Mexican-aided revolution. The choice of Diaz was obviously indicated since in two past presidential terms he had earned the reputation of being always willing to carry out the desires of Washington. President Chamorro resigned on October 30, 1926, "depositing" the presidency with Uriza, the second designate, but the State Department refused to recognize Uriza on the ground that he was not "constitutional," because the congress had not been reconstituted on the basis of its composition as elected in 1924. Uriza summoned congress in special session, November 10, 1926, recalling the former eighteen coalitionist members expelled by Chamorro in December, 1925. Only half of them appeared or sent alternates, but the anti-Chamorristas had a majority and on November 11, Diaz was elected. Although Diaz had participated in a *coup d'état*, American recognition was given in advance for informal delivery on the date of his inauguration. In his message to Congress, January 10, 1927, President Coolidge stated that the Nicaraguan congress had "substantially the same membership as when first convened following the election of 1924." Since President Solorzano had resigned and Vice-President Sacasa had been out of the country for a year, Mr. Coolidge believed that the designation of Diaz "was perfectly legal and in accordance with the constitution"; but if the contention of Dr. Sacasa, now Nicaraguan Minister in Washington, is valid that Chamorro persecuted him, "employing violence to the point of obliging him to leave the country," it can hardly be said that a case of "constitutional" absence existed; the congress was not, nor could it have been, reconstituted for no one knows who were the rightful members.

Immediately after his inauguration, on November 15, President Diaz appealed to the United States for help in preserving order, stating that his inability to protect life and property was due solely to Mexican support of the Liberals. In December, 1926, he anticipated the January, 1927, revenue payments by borrowing $300,000 from the National Bank; and in March, 1927, he negotiated a $1,000,000 credit with the New York bankers. The original bankers had sold their interest in the Nicaraguan National Bank to the Mercantile Bank of America and in 1924-25 the Nicaraguan Government paid off the treasury bills, thus regaining control of the National Bank. Through the connection of the Guaranty Trust Company of New York with the Mercantile Bank of the Americas, the Trust Company now joined J. and W. Seligman and Company as bankers for Nicaragua. The New York loan was at 6 per cent, plus one per cent commission, secured by and payable from liens on:

New Customs taxes:
    a. Additional 12½ per cent general import duties.
    b. Additional 50 per cent liquor and tobacco duties.
    c. Surtax on export coffee duties.
50 per cent of surplus general revenues.
Dividends of the Pacific Railroad and National Bank.
Further security of all the stock of the Railroad and Bank and
    an option for all loans made by the Government for a period
    of five years.

Expenditure was intrusted to a board of three, one being the resident High Commissioner. Of the loan, $650,000 was eventually used to pay off the Liberal and Conservative forces when they were later demobilized. The new customs duties were so productive and the surplus revenues so large that the loan was repaid by April 21, 1928.

On the ground that it was inconsistent to recognize President Diaz and yet deny him arms when his opponents were securing them from Mexico, the arms embargo was lifted in January, 1927. All the Central American republics were asked to recognize Diaz;

Salvador and Honduras complied, and Salvador immediately sold him some arms. Shortly afterward the Diaz government was recognized by Great Britain, France, Germany, Italy, Spain, and Colombia. Great Britain, Italy, and Belgium, on January 5, 1927, asked the United States Government to protect their nationals; this was commented on from State Department sources as recognizing a special sphere of United States influence in Nicaragua.

But the Liberals were wholly dissatisfied with the outcome, and with Moncada at their head went on with the revolution against the Conservative government. The American naval forces thereupon gave up the appearance of neutrality and aided the Diaz government as far as they could without defending it with their arms, declaring neutral zones as fast as they could detail the necessary detachments to maintain them. This had the double effect of depriving the Liberals of opportunity of capturing and holding a strategic point and of releasing Diaz troops from its defense for service elsewhere. Still this was not enough; Moncada avoided the neutral zones and pushed on toward Managua.

American fruit and lumber companies sent daily protests to the State Department, although they were suffering no losses except for interference with production as an inevitable consequence of any disorder; American lives and property were respected by both sides until after the Tipitapa agreement. On January 8 marines were ordered to the west to protect the railroad and to constitute the Fort Loma garrison. Although called a "legation guard," this meant personal protection to the Government as Fort Loma commands the Nicaraguan capital.

Reasons for Intervention.

In the special message to Congress, January 10, President Coolidge gave as the reasons for intervention: (1) protection of life and property; (2) enforcement of the Central American Treaty of 1923—although not a party to the treaty the United States "has felt a moral obligation" to apply the treaty principles; (3) protection of the rights of the United States in the Panama and proposed Nicaraguan canals; (4) jeopardy of American interests by outside influences or by any foreign power.

all Liberals, insisted upon the resignation of President Diaz, offering to resign himself if Diaz would; but President Diaz refused and also rejected all suggestions of arbitration, offering the United States instead an offensive and defensive treaty, with United States supervision of certain Nicaraguan governmental affairs, a constabulary officered by Americans, the right of the United States to pass upon foreign loans and to intervene for the prevention of internal disorders. The State Department declined the categorical offers, but in practice United States supervision of Nicaraguan affairs became effective.

In this conjuncture, it was plainly a case of arresting the revolution or having an American-recognized president, the constitutionality of whose designation was challenged, ousted by the constitutional vice-president of the Solorzano *régime* aided by Mexico.

The Stimson Mission.

In April President Coolidge therefore sent Colonel Henry L. Stimson as his special representative to settle the difficulties in Nicaragua. After conferences with Diaz and Moncada, Colonel Stimson concluded that the "evil of government domination of elections lies, and has always lain, at the root of the Nicaraguan problem." At Tipitapa on May 4, which has become a national holiday, the Sacasa delegates and all of Moncada's generals except Sandino accepted Colonel Stimson's terms: supervision by the United States of the 1928 elections; retention of Diaz in office; general disarmament—$10 and some clothing were to be given for each gun surrendered and those unwilling to give up their arms would be forcibly disarmed; appointment of Liberal *Jefes Politicos* (governors) in six of the thirteen Departments; a constabulary organized under United States officers, and a temporary continuance of the marines in Nicaragua. General Moncada ended his capitulation with these phrases:

I am not inhuman. For a noble and generous cause I would put myself at the front of the constitutional forces, but I cannot advise the nation to shed all its patriotic blood for our liberty, because in spite of this new sacrifice, this liberty would succumb before infinitely greater forces and the country would sink more deeply within the claws of the North American eagle.

Before I end I desire the country to know that both the delegates of Dr. Sacasa and I showed Mr. Stimson that from this moment henceforth, the responsibility for all that might happen in the present or in the future in Nicaragua, will rest absolutely upon the Government of the United States, and in no wise on the Liberal Party, the conqueror in the contest.

The 1928 elections, supervised, in accordance with the Stimson agreement, by United States commissioners, for which legal authority was given by an executive decree promulgated by President Diaz after the Nicaraguan congress had refused to sanction it, brought out a vote of 90 per cent of the registrants and were hailed by both factions as fair. Under Brigadier General Frank R. McCoy, 45 army and navy officers acted as chairmen of the national and departmental electoral boards, with 432 privates or non-commissioned officers as chairmen of the precinct boards; the other members of these boards were Nicaraguans, one from each party. Marines presided over all polling places, penetrating remote fastnesses where heavy rains made communication impossible after their arrival except by airplane. As 70 per cent of the adults in Nicaragua are illiterate, ballots were designed so that the voter had only to mark the party he preferred. General Moncada was elected president by a majority of 19,689 out of 133,633 votes. As of January 1, 1929, the Chamber of Deputies, which contains forty-three members, has a Conservative majority of three; the Senate is composed of eleven Conservatives and thirteen Liberals. At the time of Moncada's inauguration an exchange of amenities took place to a degree unprecedented in Nicaraguan politics.

The disarmament permitted a reduction of marines in July from a brigade to a regiment of fifteen hundred. But after Sandino, with a small body of followers, took to the northern jungle, reinforcements were sent in December to run him down; in January, 1928, an additional fifteen hundred were sent, making a total of five thousand marines. For a time many Nicaraguans considered Sandino a patriot, but the pressure of the United States forces against him was too strong; he could not hold his local support and after several months had to flee the country. After the November election and Moncada's inauguration, the number of marines was reduced to thirty-five hundred.

On June 15, 1927, a third Claims Commission, created by law of December 3, 1926, composed of two Nicaraguans, one from each political party, and the resident United States High Commissioner, was appointed to pass on claims arising out of the revolution from its outbreak, October 25, 1925, to December 31, 1927, although peace had not yet been universally established. When suspended, March 31, 1928, for lack of funds to pay adjudicated claims, the Commission reported a total of 17,551 claims filed amounting to $17,278,808.59. In addition to the amount that may be allowed on these claims, the Nicaraguan Government owes the following debts arising out of the revolution which are not subject to adjudication and are not discountable:

United States Government for arms and ammunition	$256,000
El Salvador Government for arms and ammunition	65,000
Loan from New Orleans Banks	95,000
Sundry loans from foreigners	84,000
	$500,000

On December 22, 1927, the United States agreed to organize a non-partisan constabulary to fulfil military and police functions. The agreement has not been approved by the Nicaraguan legislature but is nevertheless being carried out by executive decree.

In view of the possibility of loan assistance and the coöperation of the United States in financial and other matters, the State Department had a survey made by Dr. W. W. Cumberland. That survey contains recommendations which would extend supervision by the United States further and more permanently than the United States has thus far gone in any Caribbean republic, but the State Department, in publishing the report, declares that the recommendations are the personal views of the author.

CHAPTER FIVE

PANAMA

UNTIL 1903 the Isthmus of Panama constituted a state or department of the Republic of Colombia, and was therefore not commonly counted as a part of Central America. Its political destinies were associated with those of the southern continent. Independent statehood divorced it from the south, and geographical position, topography, and association with United States strategic interests have identified it with the Central American group. It is with this sixth and youngest of the republics that relations of the United States have been of greatest significance since the opening of the present century.

The Captaincy General of Panama, by a bloodless revolution in 1821, had declared its union with Colombia at the same time as its independence from Spain. A separatist movement in 1830, however, was successful for a few months; another in 1840-41, proclaiming the Free State of the Isthmus, survived thirteen months. Numerous insurrections occurred during the next sixty years, most of which were identified with the strife in Colombia between conservatives and federalists. The assertion that Panama tried many times to secede, or that before 1903 it was ever a truly independent state is scarcely accurate; on the other hand, the distance of the Isthmus from Bogotá, and its isolation—because of the forests and mountains in the way of overland travel, communications were possible only by sea—made for the persistence of a strong feeling of local independence.

The project of cutting an interoceanic canal through the central part of America first drew the attention of the United States to Panama. The story is long and merely a part of it is germane to our subject. Only after surveys, occasioned by the gold rush to California, were made in 1849-50 by American engineers, was a real knowledge of the engineering difficulties obtained. A railway was projected across the isthmus from Colon to Panama City, and a canal through Nicaragua, but the railway alone was built, in 1852-55.

Treaties with New Granada and Great Britain.

Meantime two treaties had been concluded by the United States which were to have an important bearing upon subsequent relations with that part of the world. On December 12, 1846, a treaty of amity and commerce was signed with the Republic of New Granada, as Colombia was then called, which in one of its articles guaranteed "to the Government of the United States that the right of way or transit across the Isthmus of Panama upon any modes of communication that now exist, or that may be hereafter constructed, shall be open and free to the Government and citizens of the United States" upon the same terms enjoyed by citizens of New Granada. In return the United States guaranteed to New Granada

in order to secure to themselves the tranquil and constant enjoyment of these advantages . . . the perfect neutrality of the before-mentioned isthmus, with the view that the free transit from the one to the other sea may not be interrupted or embarrassed in any future time while this treaty exists; and, in consequence, the United States also guarantee, in the same manner, the rights of sovereignty and property which New Granada has and possesses over the said territory.[1]

The treaty was ratified by both governments in 1848.

On numerous occasions of revolutionary activities in Panama

United States sailors and marines have policed the railroad, its terminal cities, and its harbors—sometimes by Colombia's request and sometimes without it—prohibiting action sometimes by forces of the party in power and sometimes by the forces of the party out of power, but always enforcing peace upon the line of transit.[2]

But the Washington Government also more than once stated its position, as expressed by Secretary Seward in 1865, that

the purpose of the stipulation was to guarantee the Isthmus against seizure and invasion by a foreign power only. It could not have been contemplated that we were to become a party to any civil war in that country by defending the Isthmus against another party.

---

[1] W. N. Malloy, *Treaties, Conventions . . . between the United States of America and other Powers*, Washington, 1910, I, 312.

[2] Elihu Root, *Addresses on International Subjects*, p. 184-185.

In 1850 the Clayton-Bulwer Treaty, occasioned by American desire to construct a canal through Nicaragua, was concluded with Great Britain, which claimed dominion over the Mosquito Coast and in the Bay of Honduras. Its stipulations were made to apply "to any other practicable communication, whether by canal or railway, across the isthmus . . . and especially to the interoceanic communications . . . proposed to be established by the way of Tehuantepec or Panama." The treaty was based upon the principle of the freedom of international waterways, and provided that neither contracting party should "ever obtain or maintain for itself any exclusive control" over the proposed Nicaragua canal, or erect or maintain any fortifications commanding or near it, "or occupy, or fortify, or colonize, or assume or exercise any dominion over Nicaragua, Costa Rica, the Mosquito Coast, or any part of Central America." The parties agreed to protect the canal, when built, from "interruption, seizure or unjust confiscation," to guarantee its neutrality so that it might "forever be open and free," and to invite other nations to enter into similar stipulations.[3]

The long and tortuous international discussions occasioned by this treaty do not concern us. It stood in the way of the construction of a canal under exclusively United States auspices which, with the acquisition of California and the steadily increasing importance of the Pacific states, American policy demanded. The obstacle was finally removed by the Hay-Pauncefote Treaty, signed in its second and amended form in Washington on November 18, 1901, which while nominally retaining the general principle of neutralization, abrogated the Clayton-Bulwer Treaty of 1850, and permitted the United States to construct, own, and operate a transisthmian canal, and by implication to fortify it. Neutralization could now mean little more than assurance of commercial use of the canal on equal terms.

The Panama Canal.

Meantime, after the successful completion and operation of the Suez Canal (1869), French capital had directed its attention to

[3] Malloy, *op. cit.*, pp. 659 ff.

the Isthmus of Panama. A concession obtained from the Colombian Government by a French engineer, Lieutenant Wyse, was purchased by the Universal Oceanic Canal Company organized in 1879 by Ferdinand de Lesseps, and construction was begun upon a sea-level canal which consumed two milliards of French capital and sacrificed thousands of lives. Bankrupt in 1889, the company was reorganized in 1894, but financing was discouraged by the entry of the United States Government into the field as a probable competitor in canal building. The route always favored by the United States was through Nicaragua; surveys made by American engineers between 1870 and 1875 had resulted in a report recommending this route, and several treaties had been negotiated in Nicaragua, all but one of which had failed of ratification by the United States Senate.

The prospect of a canal constructed under French control roused all the susceptibilities of the United States Government, and President Hayes in a special message to Congress, March 8, 1890, recommended a canal under exclusive American control. In 1889, when the French Government proposed to come to the aid of the French Panama company by guaranteeing its bonds, the United States Senate passed a resolution

That the Government of the United States will look with serious concern and disapproval upon any connection of any European government with the construction or control of any ship canal across the Isthmus of Darien or across Central America, and must regard any such connection or control as injurious to the just rights and interests of the United States and as a menace to their welfare.[4]

An American corporation, the Maritime Canal Company, organized in 1886, and with concessions obtained later from Nicaragua and Costa Rica, began digging at Greytown, but was driven into bankruptcy by the financial panic of 1893. Further examinations and reports were made by commissions of engineers authorized by Congress in 1895, in 1897, and again in 1899 at the close of the Spanish-American War, when Congress appropriated $1,000,000 for an exhaustive survey of all available routes. Mean-

[4] *Cong. Record,* Fiftieth Congress, Second Session, 1888-1889, p. 567.

time active lobbies were maintained in Washington by both French and American canal companies, each trying to influence Congress in favor of its particular project.

On November 16, 1901, the Isthmian Canal Commission reported that after considering all the facts, including the terms offered by the new Panama company, it recommended the route through Nicaragua. Exactly one month later the ratification of the Hay-Pauncefote Treaty cleared the way for a canal under exclusively American auspices, and on January 9, 1902, the Hepburn Bill authorizing the construction of a Nicaragua canal passed the House of Representatives by almost unanimous vote.

The terms offered by the French canal company for its rights and property had been $109,141,500. But its concession terminated nominally in November, 1904, an extension to 1910 might be abrogated by Colombia, and in any case the company could not hope to continue operation in competition with another canal under construction by the United States Government. On January 4, 1902, therefore, it definitely offered to sell out for $40,000,000, the sum estimated by the Canal Commission as the value to the United States of the equipment and work done. A fortnight later the Commission reversed its recommendation and urged the adoption of the Panama route; to conform to this change the Canal Bill in Congress was amended, the Nicaragua route to remain an alternative only if satisfactory arrangements could not be concluded within a reasonable time with the French company and with the Republic of Colombia. In this form it was passed by Congress, and signed on June 28, 1902.

Negotiations with Colombia.

Apparently the only remaining formality was to acquire a right of way from Colombia, and negotiations were at once undertaken by Secretary of State Hay. But

Colombia seemed disposed to drive a very stiff bargain. So unsatisfactory were the Colombian replies that Mr. Hay finally called the attention of the Colombian minister to the fact that if a satisfactory treaty could not be arranged with Colombia the President was authorized to proceed with the construction of a canal by another route.[5]

The Hay-Herran Treaty, finally signed on January 23, 1903, and approved by the United States Senate in the following March, authorized the French company to transfer its properties and concessions to the United States; it gave the United States exclusive right to construct and operate the canal for one hundred years, with full option of renewal for similar periods, and full control over a strip of land three miles wide on each side of the canal, not including the terminal cities of Colon and Panama. Colombia was to retain its sovereignty over the territory and to have the right to transport its vessels, troops, and munitions of war through the canal without charge. In return for these concessions, the United States promised to pay Colombia $10,000,000 in cash and an annuity of $250,000.

The treaty, however, was not ratified by the Colombian Senate. Immediately a strong tide of public opinion against it developed in Bogotá, and the newspaper press was bitterly hostile. In order to undermine the Government, enemies of the administration united in an onslaught upon an unpopular measure. Colombians professed to believe that only the Panama route would ever be adopted by the United States, and that the alternative of Nicaragua was merely a maneuver to force an advantageous bargain with Colombia; hence negotiations might safely be prolonged and better financial terms exacted. Whatever its original intentions, the Government was perhaps now taken by surprise and therefore hesitated to press the issue. As early as the beginning of May it was rumored in Bogotá that the price was inadequate and could be greatly augmented. In June the representative of the French company in Bogotá was officially notified by the Colombian Government that if the company would pay the Government $10,000,000 ratification could be secured. In July General Rafael Reyes asked the United States Minister to inform Secretary Hay that the treaty could be ratified at once with two amendments, one providing for the above-mentioned sum from the canal company for the

[5] Graham H. Stuart, *Latin America and the United States*, p. 76.

privilege of transferring its rights and property, the other for an increase of the cash payment from the United States to $15,000,-000. At the end of September a project was broached by certain senators to annul the extension of the canal company's franchise beyond 1904, by returning with interest the 5,000,000 francs paid for it by the company; Colombia, then in possession of all the company's rights and property, could arrange to receive from the United States the $40,000,000 offered to the company. In October a Senate committee, without making such a proposal, intimated the benefits to be derived by Colombia from such action.

Meantime Secretary Hay had taken a strong stand against amendment of the treaty. In a telegram to the United States Minister on June 9, he stated:

The Colombian Government apparently does not appreciate the gravity of the situation. The canal negotiations were initiated by Colombia, and were energetically pressed upon this Government for several years. The propositions presented by Colombia, with slight modifications, were finally accepted by us. In virtue of this agreement our Congress reversed its previous judgment and decided upon the Panama route. If Colombia should now reject the treaty or unduly delay its ratification, the friendly understanding between the two countries would be so seriously compromised that action might be taken by the Congress next winter which every friend of Colombia would regret.[6]

This admonition was followed by another on July 31:

This Government has no right or competence to covenant with Colombia to impose new financial obligations upon the canal company and the President would not submit to our Senate any amendment in that sense, but would treat it as voiding the negotiation and bringing about a failure to conclude a satisfactory treaty with Colombia. No additional payment by the United States can hope for approval by the United States Senate, while any amendment whatever requiring reconsideration by that body would most certainly imperil its consummation.[7]

These warnings had no appreciable effect upon the situation in

6 *For. Rel.*, 1903, p. 146.   7 *Ibid.*, p. 168.

Bogotá. The sessions of the Colombian Congress closed on October 31 and the treaty died by limitation rather than by legal enactment, although a vote of disapproval had been passed on August 12.

The ethics of General Reyes' proposal to extract $10,000,000 from the French company may be reproached, and the advances in price for which the Colombian Government were haggling were trifling when measured by the subject matter of the negotiation, but such behavior, whether shabby or not, is the prerogative of an independent state, and Colombia was under no legal obligation to accept the treaty.

The issue of the canal route was settled, however, not in Bogotá but on the Isthmus. Three days after the adjournment of the Congress at Bogotá, a group of conspirators at Panama, with general popular concurrence, declared the Isthmus an independent republic, and within another three days the United States passively recognized the new state by instructing its consul to enter into relations with it as the responsible government of the country.

Revolt of Panama.

During this period rumors had been current that the people of Panama would revolt if the treaty were not ratified. As early as the previous July, members of the Colombian Congress arriving at Bogotá from Panama had stated that the isthmus territory would revolt if the treaty were not accepted. Senator Obaldia, newly appointed governor of Panama, was reported to have said to the President, in accepting the post, that if Panama had to declare its independence in order to secure the Canal he would stand by Panama, and it is abundantly clear from the evidence that the Colombian Government anticipated a movement of this sort. United States newspapers in September and October were filled with rumors of an expected rising, and the State and Navy Departments could not fail to be aware of them. In view of the circumstances the United States took the usual step of having naval vessels present to keep the transit open and protect its citizens and their property. The cruiser *Nashville*, sailing from Kingston under sealed orders on October 31, arrived at Colon on the evening of November 2. On the same day a telegram from Washington instructed the commander to

maintain free and uninterrupted transit. If interruption threatened by armed force, occupy the line of railroad. Prevent the landing of any armed force with hostile intent, either government or insurgent, either at Colon, Porto Bello, or other point.

Similar instructions were at the same time dispatched to the cruiser *Dixie* at Kingston, and to the *Marblehead* and *Boston* on the Pacific coast, which were ordered to proceed with all speed to the Isthmus. On the following day orders were sent to prevent Colombian troops at Colon from proceeding to Panama. Before the receipt of the above telegram, about 450 Colombian troops from Cartagena were landed at Colon. After the revolution began, these troops were forbidden by the commander of the *Nashville* to cross by the railway to Panama. And when the Colombians threatened reprisals against United States citizens in Colon, marines were landed to prevent bloodshed. Panaman troops were likewise forbidden to cross to attack the Colombians at Colon. The success of the secessionist movement was thus assured, and on November 5 the Colombians returned to Cartagena on a British steamer.

The following day General Reyes, official candidate for the presidency and close to the administration in Bogotá, informed the United States Minister that if his Government, upon request, would land troops to preserve Colombian sovereignty and the transit, the Colombian Government would declare martial law, and by virtue of the authority vested in it constitutionally for application during disturbances, would by decree approve the ratification of the treaty as signed. Senator Caro, leader of the Opposition, now proposed that the Government call a convention to amend the constitution so that the treaty might immediately be ratified. Nothing resulted from either of these offers, for they came too late.

Recognition of Panama.

The rôle which the United States played in the Panama Revolution has been much criticized, but there is no evidence to refute the statement of President Roosevelt in his message to Congress, January 4, 1904:

that no one connected with this Government had any part in the preparing, inciting, or encouraging the late revolution on the Isthmus of Panama, and that save from the reports of our military and naval officers . . . no one connected with this Government had any previous knowledge of the revolution except such as was accessible to any person of ordinary intelligence who read the newspapers and kept up a current acquaintance with public affairs.

Mr. Root has argued in *The Ethics of the Panama Question*[8] that the fission of the State of Panama from the federated United States of Colombia was due to the constant desire of the Panamans to become independent; the revolt of 1903 had unanimous local support. The United States, Mr. Root contended, was not bound for the fourth time to put down an insurrection in Panama in the interest of Colombia. The success of the insurrection was due to no action of American troops but to the fact that the Colombian troops "found themselves alone among a hostile and unanimous people with an overwhelming insurgent force in arms against them which left no alternative but capture or retreat." When, therefore, the United States made the treaty it was with the true owner of the territory.

The fact remains, however, that the United States Government, by ordering the commander of the *Nashville* to forbid the Colombian troops to cross the Isthmus prevented a state with which it was on friendly relations from attempting to suppress an outbreak of revolution within its territory.

Less would have been said about it if Roosevelt had not so emphatically declared that he "took the canal." Roosevelt justified his action on the broad ground that the Canal was essential to meet a world need, and that strict respect for the title of a state would have kept the boon indefinitely from accruing to civilization.

"If ever a government could be said to have received a mandate from civilization to effect an object the accomplishment of which was in the interest of mankind," he wrote, "the United States holds

[8] *Op. cit.*

that position with regard to the interoceanic route."[9] Ten years later he thought that to "have acted otherwise than I did would have been on my part . . . recreancy to the interests of the world at large."[10]

The Roosevelt philosophy is not limited to the Big Stick school. At the opposite pole of political thought, Bertrand Russell agrees that the rights of small nations must not be allowed to impede world intercourse: "the rights of a nation as against humanity are no more absolute than the rights of an individual as against the community." Although he saw no reason why the Panama Canal should belong to the United States, "it would be absurd" for it "to belong absolutely" to the people who live near it.[11] The sum of the situation may lie in the aphorism that "there are certain moments in the lives of men when the only course of action morally possible lies along immoral lines."

On November 13, 1903, President Roosevelt formally recognized the independence of the Panama Republic by receiving a minister from the new government, and on the 18th the Hay-Bunau-Varilla Treaty was signed in Washington. The treaty was ratified by Panama in the following December, and by the United States in February, 1904. By its terms, the Republic of Panama ceded in perpetuity to the United States "the use, occupation and control" of a zone ten miles wide extending across the isthmus, and certain adjacent islands, for the construction, maintenance, operation, sanitation, and protection of a canal; and provision was made for the use and occupation of any other lands and waters outside the zone that might be needed for these purposes. The United States was granted authority to enforce, if necessary, its sanitary regulations in the cities of Colon and Panama, and to maintain public order in these cities and adjacent territories and harbors in case the Republic of Panama should be unable to do so. The Canal was to be permanently neutralized, and Panama was to have the right to transport through the Canal at all times and without charge its vessels, troops, and munitions of war. In return the United States guaranteed the independence of

9 Moore, *Digest of International Law*, III, 75.   10 *Autobiography*, p. 566.
11 *The Prospects of Industrial Civilization*, p. 97.

the Republic, and agreed to pay $10,000,000 in gold on exchange of ratification, and an annual rental of $250,000 beginning nine years after the treaty went into effect.[12]

Repercussions of United States Action.

The intervention of the United States in the Panama revolution roused strong resentment in all parts of Latin America. Colombia, of course, was especially bitter, and sent General Reyes to Washington to seek redress. As no diplomatic adjustment seemed possible, Colombia later proposed that the matter be submitted to arbitration by the Hague Tribunal. Secretary Root refused on the score that this would involve the question of the independence of the Panama Republic, which the United States and most other countries had already definitely recognized. Subsequent attempts were made by negotiation to assuage Colombia's embittered feelings, but considerable difficulty was encountered in satisfying its demands. After several settlements had been rejected, a convention was concluded in 1914 whereby the United States agreed to pay Colombia $25,000,000, and to permit its Government and citizens to use the Canal on the same basis as the Government and citizens of the United States; in addition sincere regret was expressed "that anything should have occurred to interrupt or to mar the relations of cordial friendship that had so long subsisted between the two nations." A treaty without this apology was finally approved by both governments in 1921, and ratifications were exchanged in the following year. On May 15, 1924, Colombia formally recognized the independence of Panama.

The constitution of Panama, which dates from February, 1904, states that in return for the guarantee of Panama's sovereignty and independence the "Government of the United States of America may intervene in any part of the Republic of Panama to reëstablish public peace and constitutional order in the event of their being disturbed." (Article 136.) A close fiscal supervision is maintained, and the expenditure of government loans placed in the United States has been restricted. The United States has also

---

[12] *Treaties, Conventions,* etc., II, 1349.

objected to certain railway concessions on the ground that they would interfere with the defense of the Canal; and more than once, when domestic disturbances seemed imminent, the United States has sent in military forces from the Canal Zone to supervise elections or to assume police powers in the cities of Panama and Colon. When General Huertas, commander of the Republic's army of two hundred men, as early as November, 1904, threatened a *coup d'état* against the government of President Amador, prompt warning by the United States *chargé d'affaires*, and the prospect of intervention by marines from the Canal Zone, saved the situation; General Huertas' resignation was demanded and received, and the army was disbanded. Before or after virtually every national election in Panama one party or another has appealed to the United States to intervene in order to insure a fair contest, and United States commissions have supervised elections twice, in 1908, and in 1912, at the request of the Panama Government.

Relations with Panama.

From the beginning the United States and Panama disagreed as to the exact nature of the rights which the former acquired in the Canal Zone. While conceding to the United States the exercise of certain sovereign rights, Panama has always insisted that it retains actual sovereignty. Article III of the Canal Treaty of 1903 states:

The Republic of Panama grants to the United States all the rights, power and authority within the zone mentioned and described in Article II of this agreement and within the limits of all auxiliary lands and waters mentioned and described in said Article II which the United States would possess and exercise if it were sovereign of the territory within which said lands and waters are located to the entire exclusion of the exercise by the Republic of Panama of any such sovereign rights, power or authority.[13]

On December 3, 1904, a working agreement covering certain details was negotiated by Mr. Taft as Secretary of War.[14] It permitted the importation into the Canal Zone of goods to be sold

---

[13] *For. Rel.*, 1904, p. 544.   [14] *Treaties, Conventions*, III, 2758.

only by the Isthmian Canal Commission to employees of the Zone, except upon payment of the proper duties to the Panama Republic. It provided for the free importation of goods and the free passage of persons between Panama and the Zone, and for the reciprocal use of harbors, and it regulated the postal service between the two areas. This agreement, in reality a series of executive orders issued by the President of the United States and approved by the Panama Government, was ratified by the United States Congress in the Panama Canal Act of August 24, 1912. The dispute in regard to sovereignty, however, was not settled then or later, and was recently brought into prominence again in connection with the negotiation of the treaty of July 28, 1926.[15]

In 1921 a boundary dispute between Panama and Costa Rica threatened to cause war and strained relations between the United States and Panama to the breaking point. The dispute dated from long before the Revolution of 1903, when Panama was still a part of the Republic of Colombia. Efforts to determine the frontier by treaties of 1825, 1856, 1865, and 1876 with Costa Rica had failed. By conventions of December 25, 1880, and January 20, 1886, the question had been submitted to the arbitration of the King of Spain, but the treaty lapsed before the "cases" were presented. By another agreement of April 4, 1896, the matter was referred for decision to the President of France, and on September 11, 1900, an award was made public by President Loubet. The Loubet line on the Pacific side of the cordillera was satisfactory to both parties, but on the Atlantic side it was objected to by Costa Rica as vague and indefinite. An attempt in 1905 to define the award by treaty between Panama, the heir to Colombia's rights, and Costa Rica, failed of ratification; and in 1907 Costa Rica appealed to the United States to lend its good offices to the end that the interpretation of the award might be submitted to the Chief Justice of the United States Supreme Court. Panama was finally prevailed upon to accede, and a convention to this effect

15 The completion of the Canal in August, 1914, and the vital need of protecting it in war-time were the occasion for an arrangement (August 29, 1914) granting to the United States permanent control of all wireless telegraphic stations in Panama, and of a more extended treaty (September 2, 1914) which redefined and somewhat modified the boundaries of the Canal Zone. *Ibid.*, 2768-2777.

was signed by the two parties at Washington, March 17, 1910, both countries agreeing to abide by the result.

Chief Justice White announced his decision on September 12, 1914. Each side gained and lost, but the Panama Government, carried along by a wave of popular disapproval largely compounded of local politics, rejected the award on the ground that the arbitrator had exceeded his powers. During the World War nothing was done to carry out any part of the award. On February 21, 1921, Costa Rica occupied the Coto district on the Pacific side of the Isthmus given it by the original Loubet award and conceded by Panama; the latter sent a constabulary force which disarmed the Costa Ricans and reoccupied the territory, whereupon Costa Rican soldiers crossed the Sixaola River into Panama's territory on the Atlantic side, and both countries threatened war. Feeling in Panama was at fever heat. President Porras was reported as saying in an interview that a war over valueless territory was an absurdity; a committee waited upon him on February 28 and demanded his resignation. Upon his refusal, the crowd broke into the palace, but was dispersed, with several casualties, by the guard. As a result two hundred United States soldiers from the Canal Zone appeared in the city to maintain order.

Secretary Colby on February 28 warned the two governments against the use of force in settling their controversy. Replies were received on March 5, the day after Mr. Hughes entered upon his duties as Secretary of State; Mr. Hughes immediately dispatched identic notes to Costa Rica and Panama, upholding the decision of Chief Justice White, and calling for a cessation of hostilities. The next day, President Porras again disavowed the White award, but declared his willingness to submit the dispute to an arbitral tribunal. An armistice was obtained on the 7th, in response to Secretary Hughes's demands, and the armed forces on both sides retired behind their former lines.

While preparations for war continued further notes were exchanged in March and April, and the United States served notice on Panama that its attitude would not be changed. President Porras was inclined to be conciliatory, but the National Assembly of

Panama on April 7 issued what was virtually a defiance of the United States Government. On April 29 and May 2 the latter demanded action, stating that if, upon the expiration of a reasonable time, the territory in dispute had not been surrendered, the United States would "find itself compelled to proceed in a manner which may be requisite in order that it may assure itself that the exercise of jurisdiction may be appropriately transferred." The Government of Panama, however, still delayed action; instead it sent a special mission to Washington, and proposed various alternatives, such as a plebiscite in each of the two areas in dispute, or the submission of the quarrel to the Permanent Tribunal at The Hague. It also tried to stir up sentiment in its favor in South America, and unsuccessfully invited the mediation of the Argentine Government. Finally on August 18 Secretary Hughes served notice that there was no reason for further delay in Costa Rican occupation of the Coto region, and that the United States would not allow a resumption of hostilities by reason thereof. At the same time the battleship *Pennsylvania*, sailing south to join the Pacific fleet, took on four hundred marines for the Isthmus, presumably to keep the peace and if necessary enforce the award. On August 23 the Government of Panama, under protest, ordered its civilian officials to abandon the disputed area. It was formally occupied by Costa Rica on September 9. In accordance with the convention of 1910, a mixed commission of engineers prepared to delimit the boundary, but Panama refused to coöperate, and the line was eventually determined without its aid. Diplomatic relations between Panama and Costa Rica were not resumed until October, 1928.

On August 24, 1921, the President and Cabinet at Panama signed a manifesto in which protest was lodged "before the world" against the forcible deprivation of its territory. On the same day the Secretary of Foreign Relations of Panama addressed a note to Secretary Hughes, referring to the refusal of the United States Government to support Panama's suggestion of arbitration; he declared that the United States had taken upon itself the rôle of sole judge and executive between other sovereign states, and that the procedure it followed "would sow the seed of an inexhaustible hate between the two bordering countries . . . that as long as Panaman hearts beat in the world she would keep open the deep wound inflicted to her dignity and pride."

The Government of the United States had indeed required the acceptance of an arbitral award in a case, the decision of which had twice been submitted by common consent to an impartial tribunal and twice rejected by Panama. The value of the territory involved was insignificant compared with the annoyance and ill-feeling aroused. Moreover the parties had agreed in the treaty of 1910 that

the award, whatever it be, shall be held as a perfect and compulsory treaty between the high contracting parties. Both high contracting parties bind themselves to the faithful execution of the award and waive all claims against it. The boundary line between the two Republics as finally fixed by the arbitrator shall be deemed the true line, and his determination of the same shall be final, conclusive and without appeal.

Whether Panama had any just basis for its demand for a third arbitration or not, there is no question that had the United States supported its contention, Latin American critics would have accused the United States of upholding the territorial claim of a protectorate in which it had special interests against the rights of a weak and defenseless neighboring republic.

Panama and the League.

The dispute aroused an interesting repercussion in the League of Nations. On February 28 Sir Eric Drummond, Secretary General of the League, instructed the political advisers of the League Council to investigate the differences between Panama and Costa Rica, as both countries were members of the League; on March 4 the Council sent a cable to the foreign ministers of the two countries reminding them of their obligations as members, and a few hours later an appeal was received from the Panama Government giving a history of the incident and asking the League to intervene. The Council was called together again, and in another cable replied that it was "happy to know that the United States Government has offered its good offices, and that these have been accepted by the Government of Panama. The Council would be glad to be kept informed of the development of the situation." A few days later both governments assured the League that the conflict was "virtually terminated," and that they were willing to leave the settlement in the hands of the United States. Dr. Gastao da Cunha, President of the Council, stated that the Council took the position that the United States had always exercised a good influence in Central American affairs, and that in the present case the Council could only give the United States an opportunity to do something before the Council should take any action.[16] The Congresses of Salvador, Honduras, and Guatemala sent messages of sympathy and adhesion to the Congress of Costa Rica supporting the White award.

The ill feeling aroused in Panama by this episode has probably contributed to the present opposition to the treaty of July 28, 1926, between Panama and the United States. The conviction that the existing arrangements between the two republics were intended to operate only during the construction of the Canal, and no longer provided "an adequate basis for adjustment of questions arising out of the relations between the Canal Zone authorities and the Government of Panama, and . . . that the agreement should be replaced by a more permanent arrangement,"[17] led President Harding on September 5, 1922, to recommend to Congress the abrogation of the executive orders known as the Taft Agreement, and the negotiation of a new treaty "which is desired on the part of both the Government of the United States and the Government of Panama." A joint Congressional resolution, approved on February 12, 1922, authorized the President to proceed in this sense, and on May 28 President Coolidge, by an executive order to take effect on June 1, 1924, declared the Agreement at an end.

The subsequent negotiation involved the supersession not only of the Taft Agreement but also of the Hay-Bunau-Varilla Treaty of 1903. One of the provisions of the treaty which Panama desired to have modified referred to the valuation of lands expropriated

[16] *New York Times,* March 8, 1921.
[17] Letter of Acting Secretary Phillips to President Harding, September 1, 1922. (Sixty-seventh Congress, Second Session, Senate Document 249.)

for uses connected with the Canal. Another was that relating to the right of the United States Government to intervene in behalf of peace and order in the Panama Republic. A third point referred to the relations between the Government of Panama and the Canal authorities, in connection with which misunderstandings had frequently arisen; Panama wished to have the status of the Canal Zone administration more exactly defined. Still another matter was the question of the right of United States commissary stores in the Canal Zone to sell to persons outside the Zone, to which Panama objected on the ground that it seriously interfered with the business of Panaman merchants. The United States Government, on its part, desired complete control over Panama's military activities in any case where the safety of the Canal was involved.

In a speech before the League of Nations Assembly in September, 1927, Dr. Eusebio Morales, delegate of Panama, and the commissioner who negotiated the new treaty of 1926, stated that his Government contended that the United States had no authority by unilateral action to abrogate the Taft Agreement of 1904. The United States, however, maintained that the Agreement was constituted in reality by a series of United States executive orders, approved by the Government of Panama, which, as between the United States and Panama, had no legal and conventional binding character. On the other hand, referring to the discussions preceding the treaty, Dr. Morales declared:

During the discussion of this Convention Panama enjoyed full liberty of action, and despite the fact that the negotiations took place between one of the most powerful and one of the weakest countries in the world there was not the slightest tendency to impose onerous or humiliating conditions upon Panama. On the contrary, these negotiations were marked throughout by a spirit of mutual consideration and respect, a fact which, in itself, is deserving of mention.

The issues in regard to land valuations and United States commissary stores were adjusted in the treaty by concessions to Panama's position. Arrangement was made for the exchange of commodities between the two countries, and for the passage of persons between the Zone and Panama. Panama promised to construct roads beneficial alike to Panama and the United States, and secured a promise from the United States of reasonable appropriations for such construction. The Canal Zone, at Colon and other important points, was extended for the adequate protection of the Canal in the event of war, and for better sanitation. The most important article of the new treaty is Article XI:

The Republic of Panama agrees to coöperate in all possible ways with the United States in the protection and defense of the Panama Canal. Consequently the Republic of Panama will consider herself in a state of war in case of any war in which the United States should be a belligerent; and in order to render more effective the defense of the Canal will, if necessary in the opinion of the United States Government, turn over to the United States in all the territory of the Republic of Panama, during the period of actual or threatened hostilities, the control and operation of wireless and radio communication, aircraft, aviation centers, and aerial navigation.

The civil and military authorities of the Republic of Panama shall impose and enforce all ordinances and decrees required for the maintenance of public order and for the safety and defense of the territory of the Republic of Panama during such actual or threatened hostilities, and the United States shall have the direction and control of all military operations in any part of the territory of the Republic of Panama.

For the purpose of the efficient protection of the Canal, the Republic of Panama also agrees that in time of peace the armed forces of the United States shall have free transit throughout the Republic for manoeuvres, or other military purposes, provided, however, that due notice will be given to the Government of the Republic of Panama every time armed troops should enter her territory. It is understood that this provision for notification does not apply to military or naval aircraft of the United States.

Another clause provides for the transfer from Panama to the Zone jurisdiction of a portion of Colon on which Canal Zone employees' quarters and recreation buildings are now being constructed.

In Panama, the treaty, although defended by spokesmen for the Government, roused considerable popular opposition. The municipal council of Colon passed a resolution condemning the treaty as depriving Panama of liberty and independence, and requested the National Assembly to reject it, calling upon other municipalities to coöperate to this end. A month later (January, 1927) the National Assembly, in response to this sentiment, resolved to postpone indefinitely further consideration of the agreement. Apart from the exigencies of local politics, the question uppermost was probably a more specific recognition of Panama's absolute sovereignty;[18] for it is a common observation that the younger generation in Panama would be glad to ignore the conditions under which Panama's independence was secured and maintained. After failure to obtain ratification, President Chiari announced that he would try to negotiate a convention more favorable to Panama's interests. No action has since been taken, and the last statement of the Panaman standpoint was made by Foreign Secretary Arosemena, who said "By acquiescing Colon virtually would be hemmed in on two sides by the Zone. It would mean the beginning of the end of our second largest city."[19]

League of Nations officials and other circles in Europe were somewhat ruffled by the announcement of the treaty, on the score that it violated Panama's obligations as a League member. Under the article cited above, Panama agrees that whenever the United States goes to war it will instantly be at war also, although, under Article XII of the Covenant, Panama had agreed to submit to arbitration or to inquiry by the League Council all disputes which might lead to a rupture, and in no case to resort to war until three months after a decision had been reached. The treaty also conflicted with Panama's engagements under Articles XVI and XX of the Covenant.

There is no doubt of the contradiction; and although there was also no doubt in the mind of any League member that, in the event of international difficulties, Panama in any case would do exactly

[18] Dr. Mendez Pereira, Secretary of Education, in defending the treaty in a speech at the National Institute, said that the absolute sovereignty of nations no longer existed, owing to the limitations imposed by the Locarno treaties and similar compacts, and added that nations were developing into the conditions of citizens with reciprocal rights which must be respected. *New York Times,* January 1, 1927.

[19] *New York Times,* May 24, 1929.

what the United States dictated, putting the situation on paper
was regarded as useless and embarrassing. No evidence has been
adduced, however, to show that the Department of State wished to
flout the League. Panama occupies a special position as part-cus-
todian of the Canal which the United States has built, fortified,
and will hold against all comers. It stands in much the same relation to the United States as Egypt, by reason of the Suez Canal,
does to Great Britain, and the latter has allowed no latitude to
Egypt in its League relationships which may impair the security
of Suez. On December 4, 1924, the British Goverment announced
to the League that it would insist upon maintaining "the special
relations between Egypt and itself long recognized by other countries," and would resent "any attempt at interference in the affairs of Egypt."

It is inconceivable "that, in the event of a war, in which a protecting power was engaged, the protected country would remain
free to declare neutrality, or to put obstacles in the way of movements of troops made by the former to insure that very protection."[20] The treaty effected no changes in the realities of the situation, and the possibilities of war in the world or even in the western
hemisphere were in no wise increased.

[20] Philippe Bunau-Varilla in *Figaro*, Paris, January 23, 1927.

CHAPTER SIX

COSTA RICA

OF all the Central American republics, Costa Rica has been the most tranquil and progressive. Its constitution, dating from 1871, is the oldest of those current in the Isthmus, and the government is the most stable and democratic. Popular elections, although sometimes corrupted, represent in the main the desires of the people; judicial courts seem to have escaped executive influence, and are far above the average in these countries; opinion finds free expression in the public press, and graft and bribery are less common than in some neighboring states. The population is predominantly white, the number of small agricultural proprietors is unusually large, and the Republic prides itself "on spending more money on her schools than on her army, and on having more school teachers than soldiers."

Costa Rica took a leading part in the war to expel the American filibuster and would-be dictator, William Walker, from Nicaragua. In 1855 the Liberal faction in Nicaragua invited Walker and his band of fellow adventurers to help it against its Conservative rivals; within a year Walker made himself president of the Republic. Central America promptly united against the foreign intruder, and armies gathered from all the neighboring states; instigated by Cornelius Vanderbilt, whose Accessory Transit Company had been deprived of its concession by Walker, and encouraged by Great Britain, Costa Rica struck the decisive blow. One of its forces cut Walker's communication, *via* the San Juan River, with New York, and on May 1, 1857, he abandoned Nicaragua. Hoping to control the route of the proposed interoceanic canal, Costa Rica then declined to evacuate the territory on the south bank of the San Juan River; hostilities between the two republics were averted only by the news of Walker's sudden reappearance. On April 15, 1858, Costa Rica and Nicaragua signed a boundary convention, the Canas-Jerez Treaty, Article VIII of which bound Nicaragua to make no concession for canal purposes without first asking the opinion of Costa Rica.

Interest in Nicaraguan Canal.

Thereafter the canal question was invariably associated with the question of the Costa Rica-Nicaragua frontier. Although the Costa Rican Government generally appeared desirous that the United States should take up the construction of a canal through Nicaragua, it interposed its interests when canal concessions were discussed and demanded a hearing. On December 24, 1886, a convention was signed by the two neighboring republics, through the mediation of Guatemala, to submit to the President of the United States the question of the validity of the 1858 treaty. The convention was ratified in 1887, and the decision of President Cleveland, confirming the validity of the treaty, and interpreting certain of its provisions, was delivered on March 22, 1888.[1] In another convention, concluded for the delimitation of the boundary line, the President of the United States was requested to name an engineer to coöperate with a commissioner appointed by each of the signatory states. The boundary line delimited in this fashion was announced as completed on September 30, 1897, and was promptly accepted by both Nicaragua and Costa Rica.

The question of the rights of Costa Rica along its Nicaragua frontier came into prominence when the Bryan-Chamorro Treaty was under negotiation. Soon after the conclusion of the original convention of February, 1913, vigorous protests were made by Costa Rica and Salvador that it infringed their respective rights on the San Juan River and in the Gulf of Fonseca. In April the Costa Rican Minister at Washington informed Secretary Bryan that the proposed convention violated the treaty of April 15, 1858, as well as the Cleveland award. Articles X and XI of the latter stated:

X. The Republic of Nicaragua remains bound not to make any grants for canal purposes across her territory without first asking the opinion of the Republic of Costa Rica, as provided in Article VIII of the Treaty of Limits of the 15th day of April, one thousand eight hundred and fifty-eight. . . .

XI. The Treaty of Limits of the 15th day of April, one thousand eight hundred and fifty-eight, does not give to the Republic of Costa

[1] *For. Rel.*, 1888, Part I, p. 456.

Rica the right to be a party to grants which Nicaragua may make for inter-oceanic canals; though in cases where the construction of the canal will involve an injury to the natural rights of Costa Rica, her opinion or advice, as mentioned in Article VIII of the treaty, should be more than "advisory" or "consultative." It would seem in such cases that her consent is necessary, and that she may thereupon demand compensation for the concessions she is asked to make; but she is not entitled as a right to share in the profits that the Republic of Nicaragua may reserve for herself as a compensation for such favors and privileges as she, in her turn, may concede.

Later in the year the Salvador Government proposed a meeting of delegates of Salvador, Costa Rica, Honduras, and Guatemala to take a common stand against acquisition by the United States of rights in Fonseca Gulf. In July, 1914, Costa Rica also entered formal protest at Washington against the protectorate plan in the new treaty as injurious to its autonomy and as nullifying the purpose of the 1907 Washington treaties.[2] Secretary Bryan in July and August gave Costa Rica repeated assurances that none of its rights would be disregarded, and suggested that the United States was ready to purchase an option on its part of the canal route, and to lease a naval base near the southern extremity of the Republic. He denied that the action of the United States violated the terms of the 1858 treaty, and called attention to the fact that in December, 1900, Costa Rica and Nicaragua had executed separate protocols of agreement with the United States "whereby each separately engaged to enter into negotiations with the United States to settle details of agreements found necessary to accomplish the ownership and control" of an interoceanic canal.[3] In the ultimate analysis the significant point of international law raised by the dispute was "the right of a state in its sovereign capacity to negotiate as a free agent with another sovereign state concerning matters of vital interest to other neighboring states."

The opposition of Nicaragua's neighbors led the United States Senate to add a clause declaring that nothing in the convention was intended to infringe any existing rights of Costa Rica, Salvador, or Honduras. This conciliatory gesture had little effect,

2 See *infra*, p. 264.　　　　　　　3 *For. Rel.*, 1916, p. 820.

and the offers of the State Department to make similar agreements with them to safeguard their rights and to indemnify them with pecuniary compensations, proved unavailing. On March 27, 1916, after the Nicaraguan treaty had been ratified by the United States Senate, but before its promulgation, the Costa Rican Government notified the State Department that it, as a co-riparian state on the San Juan River, had brought suit against the Republic of Nicaragua before the Central American Court of Justice, to enjoin Nicaragua from carrying out the treaty provisions.

The United States Government took the position that when the Central American Court of Justice was established in 1907 its jurisdiction in cases concerning diplomatic relations between the signatory powers and the United States had not been contemplated. The Costa Rican view was that, since in signing the treaty Nicaragua had invaded the rights of Costa Rica, the case was logically one for the tribunal to decide. Nicaragua also refused to recognize the competence of the Court, on the ground that it could not adjudicate concerning questions arising prior to its establishment; nevertheless the Court took jurisdiction of the case.

The Court handed down its decision on September 30, 1916, Judge Navas, the representative of Nicaragua, dissenting. It declared that Nicaragua had violated the boundary treaty of 1858, the Cleveland award of 1888, and the Treaty of Peace and Amity of December 20, 1907. The Court refused to accept the Nicaraguan claim that the treaty granted the United States merely an option, holding that the treaty "contracted a perfect alienation, a transfer in consideration of a fixed price of the property rights necessary and suitable for the canal route, of which the Republic of the United States is made owner in perpetuity and without any limitation."

The Court pointed out that the Senate proviso "was ineffective as regards the legal relations between the nations at variance, inasmuch as the injury inflicted upon the rights of Costa Rica was consummated and the amendment does not produce the effect of restoring matters to the legal status" which the boundary treaty had created. However, since it had no jurisdiction over the United States, it declined to make any statement concerning Costa Rica's assertion that the convention was void. The decision created an embarrassing situation. The United States was in the position of having become party to a contract made in apparent violation of the rights of Costa Rica as defined by President Cleveland in 1888.

There can be no doubt that the Court had jurisdiction over the question at issue, under the terms of the Washington conventions, or that the other Central American countries, and particularly Costa Rica, had strong cases against the convention, based not only upon international law and treaty provisions, but also upon the necessity for protecting their vital national interests. . . . It may well be doubted whether even the great military value of the proposed naval base, or the theoretical value of an option on another canal route, (was) worth the permanent alienation of Central American public opinion and the abandonment of the considerations of justice and good will which (had) hitherto governed our relations with the five republics.[4]

In June, 1921, at San José, the signature of a protocol, preliminary to a treaty, was announced by which Costa Rica would cede to the United States rights along the San Juan River; the treaty has not as yet materialized.

The Tinoco Revolt.

Even Costa Rica, stable and relatively progressive as it is, has in recent times passed through the throes of revolution. On January 27, 1917, its president, Alfredo Gonzalez, was deposed by a military *coup d'état*. Joaquin Tinoco, brother of the Minister of War, seized control of the barracks, thus gaining military control of the Republic; the President sought the protection of the United States legation and soon after left the country for New York. The Minister of War, Federico Tinoco, had quietly replaced officers of the army with his own partisans, and took possession of the capital without disorder or bloodshed. Tinoco announced a cabinet composed of men of high repute representing all factions, and issued a decree calling for an election of deputies by popular vote on April 1 for the purpose of devising a new constitution and electing a president.

[4] Munro, *op. cit.*, p. 257.

The excuse for the revolt was that, contrary to constitutional precepts, President Gonzalez was planning to secure reëlection. The underlying reasons were the unpopularity of his fiscal policy, especially his land and income tax measures which excited the hostility of the powerful privileged classes, and probably the intrigues of certain foreign interests and concession seekers, British and American. The business element, preferring to any further trouble the peace which Tinoco's ascendancy assured, accepted the revolution as a *fait accompli.*

The United States refused to recognize the revolutionary *régime* on the score that the subversion of the established government by violence was "a menace to the peace and unity of Central America." To Tinoco's inquiry whether the United States would accord recognition if he were elected by a free vote, Secretary Lansing replied, addressing the United States Minister in San José: "By authorization of the President you are instructed to inform Tinoco that even if he is elected he will not be given recognition by the United States."[5] The Washington Government also issued a public statement that it would not support the claims of any who gave financial assistance to or had business relations with those who overturned the Costa Rican Government.

No effective opposition developed against Tinoco and early in April he was elected by popular vote. A new constitution, drawn up by a hand-picked assembly, was promulgated in June, whereupon Tinoco asserted that this constitutional reorganization had been accomplished by the "free and manifest will" of the nation expressed in the April elections, and that Washington's opposition constituted an unwarranted intervention in Costa Rica's domestic concerns. On April 9, after the United States declaration of war upon Germany, the Washington agent of the Tinoco government, in a note to the Secretary of State, gave assurance of Costa Rica's sympathy, offering to the United States Navy the use of Costa Rican ports and waters. But this brought Tinoco no nearer to recognition by the United States, which continued to accept Señor Castro Quesada, minister in Washington of the defunct Gonzalez *régime,* as the diplomatic agent of the country, inform-

[5] *For. Rel.,* 1917, p. 308.

ing the other Central American governments in September that it would not regard their recognition of Tinoco "as evidence of a friendly feeling toward the United States."[6] Honduras had already recognized the Tinoco *régime* on June 11, and in spite of the warning from Washington, Salvador and Guatemala eventually followed suit.

The State Department was meanwhile careful to discountenance any revolutionary movement in the personal interests of former president Gonzalez or his supporters. When in December, 1917, Alfredo Volio, through the United States Minister at Panama, sought to secure the Department's approval of an invasion of Costa Rica from Nicaragua to overthrow Tinoco and hold a free election, the Government of Panama was warned not to permit armed forces to leave its territory to operate in either Nicaragua or Costa Rica. "You may inform Volio," Secretary Lansing wrote to the United States Minister, "that the Government of the United States will not countenance armed activities such as he contemplates, inasmuch as this Government feels that only by moral force can a constitutional and duly legalized government be set up in Costa Rica."[7]

In May, 1918, Costa Rica declared war on Germany, but even this was of no avail. The Allied governments of Europe followed the lead of the United States, and Costa Rica was the only one of the belligerent-enemies of Germany not invited to sign the Treaty of Peace. Tinoco had consistently refused to withdraw "at the intimation of a foreign power," while his government, without funds and in the face of increasing popular unrest, slowly drifted toward a military dictatorship. The issue of large amounts of paper money caused dissatisfaction among the laboring and merchant classes; the Government was crippled by the war-time reduction of steamship service, and it faced the prospect of losing the export tax on coffee, already partially discounted, and of a further reduction of its receipts from import duties. After two years Tinoco found his position no longer tenable. Early in May, 1919, revolutionists crossed the border from Nicaragua, issued a proclamation naming Julio Acosta provisional president of Costa

6 *For. Rel.*, 1917, p. 343.   7 *Ibid.*, p. 349.

Rica, and requested the recognition of the other Central American republics. Guatemala, Honduras, and Nicaragua recognized the belligerency of the revolutionists a month later, and at about the same time United States marines were landed at Punta Arenas on the Pacific, and at Puerto Limón on the Caribbean, to protect foreign property interests. In August, President Tinoco fled the country, and in September the revolutionists obtained possession of the government. On August 20 Costa Rica had been informed that the United States would recognize no government unless it were elected by the people in accordance with the Costa Rican constitution; and after a short provisional *régime* under Señor Barquero, the old constitution was restored. In December, Julio Acosta was elected president in constitutional fashion; he was installed in May, 1920, and on August 2 his government was recognized by the United States.

In the following year an attempt of the new government to repudiate public engagements made by President Tinoco occasioned a diplomatic difficulty with Great Britain. In August, 1920, the Congress passed a law invalidating all contracts between the executive power and private persons during the Tinoco period. It also repudiated legislative decrees of June 28 and July 8, 1919, authorizing respectively the issue of 15,000,000 colones in currency notes, and the circulation of notes of the denomination of 1,000 colones; it annulled all transactions in such notes. This legislation affected the interests of the Central Costa Rica Petroleum Company, a British corporation, owning the Amory exploration concession granted by the Tinoco government in 1918. It also involved the Royal Bank of Canada, whose branch in San José had accepted from the former government a deposit of 1,000,000 colones in 1,000 colones notes. Of this deposit Federico Tinoco had withdrawn 50 per cent just before his flight, half for himself "for expense of representation of the Chief of State in his approaching trip abroad," the other half for his brother, José Joaquin Tinoco, whom he appointed minister to Italy, for salary and legation expenses for four years.

The British Government delivered an ultimatum to Costa Rica in February, 1921, demanding recognition of the Amory concession and the Royal Bank claim, but on January 12, 1922, agreed to submit the controversy to the arbitration of Chief Justice Taft of the United States Supreme Court. Mr. Taft's award, rendered in October, 1923, was in favor of Costa Rica. The Amory oil concession was invalid under the Tinoco constitution of 1917, and therefore the legislation annulling it worked no injury. The claim of the Royal Bank was without merit inasmuch as the Bank, when it honored the checks, knew that Tinoco was misappropriating government funds for the personal benefit of himself and his brother. However, on the theory that the Government could not be paid twice, the Bank was allowed the benefit of a mortgage for $100,000 given to the new government of Costa Rica by the widow of José Joaquin Tinoco.

United States intervention in Nicaragua during the troublous years 1926-27 aroused popular hostility in Costa Rica against the United States, evidenced by student demonstrations, press articles, and speeches in the National Congress. In general, however, relations between the United States and Costa Rica have recently been without incident.

CHAPTER SEVEN

SALVADOR

IN area the smallest of the Central American republics, Salvador is the most densely populated, and one of the most prosperous. Climate and soil are excellent, the people are more Spanish in blood than in the other states except Costa Rica, and most of the wealth is in the hands of citizens rather than of foreigners. Interference in its affairs by the factional leaders of Guatemala and Nicaragua—which was a source of constant domestic unrest in the nineteenth century—has ceased, and the administration of public affairs has tended to become more and more stable, controlled by an intelligent oligarchy of the wealthy and landed classes who reveal a sense of political sobriety and responsibility and a spirit of progress. More money is spent upon schools than in most of the neighboring states; the legislature and the supreme court seem to be freer from presidential dictation; and peace and order are maintained by a well-organized and efficient army. Salvador was the only one of the Central American states not to enter the World War on the Allied side. In foreign matters Salvador has displayed an initiative and an independence of judgment that in recent years have made it in a sense the spokesman for the Central American republics.

Relations with Salvador.

In the nineteenth century diplomatic relations with Salvador were not unlike those with its neighbors, ranging over the not unusual matters of asylum for political refugees, recognition of revolutionary governments, mediation between warring factions, protection of United States commercial rights, adjustment of claims of United States citizens, and not infrequently good offices in adjusting claims of the nationals of other countries.

The leaders of the government turned out of office by revolt were inclined to seek the hospitality of the United States legation or of a United States warship or commercial steamer, and if their lives were in danger generally received asylum. Frequently the next problem was to obtain assurances from the victorious party that their lives would not be forfeited, and that they would be given a fair trial. In August, 1891, for instance, Salvadorean officials demanded the surrender of General Letona who was aboard the Pacific Mail steamship *City of Panama*, then loading in La Union harbor, informing the captain that Letona was a political criminal. The latter had boarded the ship at Corinto, Nicaragua, and was bound for San José de Guatemala. The captain refused to recognize the order as legal or to give up Letona, and when the port authority denied him clearance papers he sailed without them. Upon the arrival of the *City of Panama* at La Libertad, Salvador, the captain was notified that his ship had been declared confiscated for having left La Union without the necessary license. Again ignoring the port officials, the steamer sailed for San José. The United States Government defended the principle of asylum aboard ship for political prisoners, protested against any arbitrary action by the Government of Salvador with respect to the steamer, and obtained assurances that upon its return to Salvadorean ports it would not be detained.

Again in 1894, when Vice-President Ezeta of Salvador and several associates took refuge on the U.S.S. *Bennington* and were carried to San Francisco, the new provisional government of Salvador demanded their surrender under the terms of the extradition treaty of 1874. They were examined before a United States judge in San Francisco, and Ezeta was discharged; whereupon the Salvadorean Government gave notice of its desire to terminate the extradition treaty. The United States Government, however, declared that it saw no need of this step, and a new extradition treaty was not negotiated until 1911.[1]

The ambition of President Rufino Barrios of Guatemala, which led him, on the one hand, to attempt to force the other states into a Central American union under his auspices, and, on the other, to threaten war against Mexico in defense of a disputed frontier, called into play all the diplomatic resources of the State Department. For some years the United States Government had been

[1] For similar episodes during this decade see pp. 242, 243, 256.

consistently advocating a confederation of the five republics, and had encouraged President Barrios in his plans for union; when Barrios, however, in alliance with Honduras, in 1885, attempted to coerce Salvador, the United States had to make clear its neutrality, and use its good offices to prevent a conflict. The situation was complicated by the fact that all the Central American states, including Salvador, made use of the Pacific Mail steamers, an American company operating between San Francisco and Pacific ports of Central America, for the transportation of munitions of war. The death of President Barrios in battle with the Salvadorean army in April, 1885, cleared the atmosphere, but not before a revolution in Salvador had eliminated its president and put General Francisco Menendez in power.

A few years later, in July, 1890, on the occasion of another war between Salvador and Guatemala growing out of a revolutionary movement in the former country, the United States again tendered its good offices. They were refused by the revolutionary government of Salvador, as well as by Guatemala; but when, in a two days' battle in the city of San Salvador, the United States consulate was seized by troops, the United States flag hauled down, and the property and archives of the consul destroyed or carried away, the United States assumed a much firmer tone. The case was aggravated by the fact that the consul was refused a pass to leave the country, and prevented from communicating by telegraph with his government. Salvador, however, at once responded with a written apology, fired a salute of twenty-one guns, and promised an indemnity for damages inflicted; a few days later both governments accepted the proffered mediation, and peace was arranged between them on September 24.[2] A threatened attack by Guatemala and Honduras upon Salvador in February of the following year again called forth the friendly activity of the United States. In these episodes, as in others, the United States minister was specifically warned by his government "to use his good offices and proffer earnest counsel, without dictation and with conspicuous impartiality."

---

2 *For. Rel.*, 1890, pp. 28-144; 1892, pp. 20-37, 44-49. In 1893 the Government of Salvador paid to the United States an indemnity of $2,500. *Ibid.*, 1893, pp. 174-184.

Mediation and Arbitration.

One of the most interesting and significant cases touching claims of United States citizens was that of the Salvador Commercial Company. In the latter part of 1894 it had received from Salvador a concession to develop a new port on the Pacific coast in the Bay of Jiquilisco, the present port of El Triumfo. For a period of twenty-five years it was given the exclusive right of steam navigation in this bay, to transship passengers and cargo to any steamer calling there, to carry on a coasting trade with neighboring ports, and to establish a line of steamers to connect with other Pacific states from Colombia to California. In return the company was required to provide within six months such facilities as were needed to handle the next coffee crop; and within the year to build and furnish an appropriate customhouse and a steel pier which were to be the property of the Government of Salvador, and to furnish the buoys, steam tugs, etc., which the traffic might demand. The majority of the stock in the enterprise, 53 per cent, was held by United States citizens. The terms of the franchise had apparently been complied with by the end of March, 1896, and, with a much larger volume of traffic than had been anticipated, financial success was assured. Thereupon in 1898 the vice-president and the secretary of the company, both citizens of Salvador, called a directors' meeting in the absence of the president, ousted the American management, and had a Salvadorean receiver in bankruptcy appointed, with the purpose of appropriating the concession and the investment of American shareholders for the benefit of the conspirators. When representatives of the majority shareholders endeavored to have these illegal acts vacated and to install a representative directorate, the President of Salvador issued an edict closing the port of El Triumfo to all importations; later he granted to a group of Salvadorean citizens a concession of everything covered by the original franchise of 1894. No attention was paid to the protests of the American shareholders, and they appealed to the United States Government for protection and redress.

Attempts to adjust the claim amicably failed, and the Government of Salvador, in October, 1901, suggested resort to an international tribunal of arbitration; a protocol to this effect was signed on December 19. The arbitral board, consisting of the Chief Justice of Canada, Señor José Rosa Pacas representing Salvador, and Judge Don M. Dickinson representing the United States, on May 8, 1902, gave a majority opinion that the company was entitled to compensation, and fixed the damages at $523,178.64.[3] The Salvadorean representative refused to sign.

As the Government of Salvador seemed disinclined to honor the award, the plaintiffs, with the approval of the State Department, in August, 1903, entered into an agreement with the Salvadorean minister at Washington to accept in payment 6 per cent national bonds equivalent to 67½ per cent of the award, and secured by 10 per cent of the Salvadorean customs. This arrangement the Congress of Salvador ratified on September 22, but it did not guarantee the bonds with 10 per cent of the customs, and it made mere delivery of the bonds the payment of the claim. Thereupon, in February, 1904, the United States Government informed Salvador that failure to conform to the agreement would constrain it to demand payment of the full amount of the award of May, 1902. A month later Salvador acceded to the American request by passing legislation correcting the deficiency of the earlier enactment.

Marblehead Convention.

The outbreak of another war between Salvador and Guatemala in 1906, into which Honduras was soon drawn on the side of Salvador, was the occasion of a friendly mediation by the United States and Mexico which was to have far-reaching consequences for the future. The mobilization of troops along the Salvador-Guatemala frontier in the beginning of June, and reports of minor conflicts, led the United States ministers in the two countries to urge self-restraint in vigorous terms,[4] and to try to secure pledges

[3] *For. Rel.*, 1902, pp. 836-873. The Gelbtrunk claim for $22,654.43, pending against the Salvadorean Government, for seizure of merchandise by revolutionary troops in 1898, was, at the suggestion of Secretary Hay, submitted to the same arbitrators, and was unanimously disallowed. *Ibid.*, 1902, pp. 873-881.

[4] *Ibid.*, 1904, p. 538.

from each side to withdraw and disband troops pending negotiations. Meantime the cruiser *Marblehead* was ordered to the Salvador coast, and President Roosevelt sought the coöperation and moral support of the Mexican Government in preserving peace. Minister Thompson in Mexico City was directed to say to President Diaz that "the President, earnestly wishing to help in avoiding war in Central America, desires to rely largely on the advice of President Diaz." Parallel or coöperative action by the United States and Mexico had been suggested by the latter in August, 1895, during the earlier war between Salvador and Guatemala. In 1906, President Diaz responded whole-heartedly to the suggestions from Washington, and the mediation thereafter was joint.

On July 13, 1906, President Roosevelt dispatched an appeal to the presidents of Salvador and of Guatemala urging arbitration or direct negotiation. The President of Salvador at once accepted his offer of the *Marblehead* deck as a neutral meeting-place, and suggested that the United States ministers to Salvador and Guatemala and the Mexican minister to Central America take part in the conference. As the President of Guatemala accepted in the same spirit, an armistice was arranged for July 18, and the conference took place the following day. Meantime, the Costa Rica Government, conjointly with the United States, extended its good offices in favor of peace, either by delegating authority to the United States minister in Salvador or by sending a representative to confer and act with him; and the Government of Honduras, which was in alliance with Salvador, also indicated its desire to join in negotiating the same terms with Guatemala. When the report came that the Nicaraguan Government had likewise appointed a representative to the conference, the State Department was constrained to make clear that "this is not a general conference of Central American states, but a negotiation for peace between the belligerents." It also reiterated that the representatives of the United States and Mexico were to be present simply in a friendly and advisory capacity, on the understanding that the belligerents purposed direct negotiations.

The peace which was signed on July 30, 1906, included an agreement to negotiate a treaty of friendship and commerce within two months, and to submit any difficulties over the treaty and all future concrete complaints between the three countries to the arbitration of the United States and Mexican Presidents.[5]

The treaty stated that it was made with the moral sanction, not only of the mediating powers, but also of Costa Rica and Nicaragua, whose representatives assisted in a complementary capacity; in the following month Costa Rica invited delegates of the other republics to meet at San José on September 15, the anniversary of Central American independence, to draw up a treaty of amity and commerce. President Zelaya, however, declined on the ground that Nicaragua had not been a party to the *Marblehead* convention. On September 24 and 25 the four states represented signed three treaties, one providing for the establishment of a Central American International Bureau, along the lines of the present Pan-American Union in Washington, another for the creation of a Central American Pedagogical Institute in Costa Rica; and the third, a general treaty of friendship, arbitration, and commerce. Thereafter disputes between the signatories were to be settled by mediation or arbitration by the sister republics, or by appeal to the United States and Mexico.[6]

Trouble broke out afresh early in 1907, this time between Nicaragua and Honduras. President Zelaya was supporting revolutionary activities against the government of President Manuel Bonilla of Honduras, and the latter was now aided by its ally, Salvador. As Nicaragua was not a signatory of the general treaty of arbitration, attempts to settle the dispute locally by the means it provided were unsuccessful, and in February the Presidents of the United States and Mexico again intervened to propose arbitration, which the belligerents accepted; but the Nicaraguans continued fighting, and only after Tegucigalpa had been occupied and the port of Amapala invested, did President Zelaya agree to a peace conference. As Honduras after its defeat was without a recognized government, the conference at Amapala was between

[5] *For. Rel.*, 1906, pp. 850-851.
[6] In August, 1907, the State Department communicated with the Mexican ambassador before recognizing the provisional government of Honduras, and the Mexican Government again acted in conjunction with the United States.

the foreign ministers of Nicaragua and Salvador, and resulted
in a treaty of peace signed on board the U.S.S. *Chicago* on April
23, 1907. This treaty, like that of July 20, 1906, also provided
that subsequent disputes between the parties concerned should be
submitted to the arbitration of the United States and Mexico.
Within a few months, however, another conflict threatened between Guatemala and the truculent President of Nicaragua, and
Presidents Roosevelt and Diaz in September, 1907, induced the
five Central American states to send delegates to a general peace
conference in December at Washington. There, with the friendly
assistance of representatives of Mexico and the United States,
were signed the 1907 Washington Conventions.[7]

Salvador's Case against the Bryan-Chamorro Treaty.

The negotiations for the Bryan-Chamorro Treaty caused as
unfriendly a reaction in Salvador as in Costa Rica; Costa Rica was
concerned about its co-riparian rights along the San Juan River,
Salvador about the establishment of a United States naval base
on the Gulf of Fonseca within a few miles of its own shores and in
close proximity to one of its important seaports.

Salvador had always shown a friendly interest in the proposed
Nicaragua canal. By some officials it was considered of more vital
importance to Salvador than to any other Central American republic; for Salvador is the only one which does not possess an
Atlantic as well as a Pacific seacoast, and a canal would provide an
Atlantic outlet and therefore considerable commercial advantage.
In fact the Salvadorean Government took steps to obtain a "manifestation" on the part of all the Central American republics in
favor of the Nicaragua project. It preferred that the canal be
constructed under American auspices, and that it be owned and
controlled by the United States.[8]

In July, 1913, however, considerable popular excitement was
reported in Salvador against the proposed acquisition of the
naval base on the Fonseca Gulf. And in September, the Government invited Guatemala, Honduras, and Costa Rica to a con-

[7] See *infra*, p. 264.   [8] *For. Rel.*, 1883, pp. 57-58.

ference to discuss not only this, but also the proposed protectorate over Nicaragua involved in the clause nicknamed the "Platt Amendment." Nicaragua, however, protested against the conference, and the invitation was not well received by the governments to which it was sent. This was followed in October by a lengthy and well-conceived protest by Salvador to the Government at Washington against the contemplated lease of the naval station. Minister Duenas stated that the geographical and juridical situation of the Gulf of Fonseca was such that the lease of any one of its parts must necessarily affect the others. From the days of the Spanish conquests, he maintained, the Gulf had belonged to the three riparian countries, Salvador, Honduras, and Nicaragua, under whose sovereignty and jurisdiction it still remained. During the early days of federation, indeed, the Gulf had been claimed by the United Provinces of Central America, but after the Union was dissolved, it became the joint property of the three republics, whose previous advice and consent to the lease was necessary.

Salvador, when later presenting its case to the Central American Court of Justice, maintained that:

It must be patent to every one, that the establishment, by a powerful state, of a naval base in the immediate vicinity of the Republic of El Salvador would constitute a serious menace—not merely imaginary, but real and apparent—to the freedom of life and the autonomy of that Republic. And that positive menace would exist, not solely by reason of the influence that the United States, as an essential to the adequate development of the ends determined upon for the efficiency and security of the proposed naval base, would naturally need to exercise and enjoy at all times in connection with incidents of the highest importance in the national life of the small neighboring states, but would be also, and especially, vital because in the future, in any armed conflict that might arise between the United States and one or more military powers, the territories bounded by the Gulf of Fonseca would be converted, to an extent incalculable in view of the offensive power and range of modern armaments, into belligerent camps wherein would be decided the fate of the proposed naval establishment—a decision that would inevitably involve the sacrifice of the independence and sovereignty of the weaker Central American

States, as has been the case with the smaller nations in the present European struggle under conditions more or less similar.[9]

Salvador also asserted that the treaty was detrimental to general Central American interests. The constitutions of the several republics had

consecrated the principle that the said republics are segregated parts of the former Central American Federation and hence recognize it as their positive duty to contribute to the restoration of the Central American nationality. This . . . incapacitates them . . . from impairing the integrity of Central American territory without the concurrence of the others and more especially at points and in parts where two or more states have common rights and interests.

United States Efforts at Conciliation.

Secretary Bryan replied in February, 1914, that the grounds of the claim of "undivided and joint ownership" were not evident, nor did they appear to be admitted by Nicaragua and Honduras.[10] The Secretary of State also denied that the establishment of a naval base on the Gulf of Fonseca would alter the political situation and jeopardize the interests of Honduras and Salvador; he maintained rather that it would safeguard Central American interests and sovereignty and stated his willingness to consider a concession from either Salvador or Honduras, or both, similar to that granted by Nicaragua. The treaty with the latter, he added, would give to the United States no further interests than those already possessed in Central American political affairs, and would not prove an obstacle to Central American union. To the suggestion of a concession to the United States by Salvador, the Government of the latter replied that its constitution forbade the consideration of treaties or conventions which in any way impaired its territorial integrity or its sovereignty. And in July, 1914, it lodged a further protest against the contemplated establishment

[9] The United States has itself denied the sovereign right of another state to dispose of its territory in such a way as to menace American interests, as in the Senate Resolution of July, 1912, with regard to Magdalena Bay.

[10] As a matter of fact, the three republics had divided all the islands of the Gulf among them, and each in practice exercised jurisdiction over a portion of it.

by the treaty of a protectorate over Nicaragua, on the ground
that the loss or partial destruction of Nicaragua's autonomy would
seriously affect the autonomy of Salvador, in view of the ties which
had always bound together the Central American states, and asserted that this was a violation of the 1907 Conventions, which had
been concluded for the purpose of strengthening the special relations of the Central American states; later, stress was laid upon the
"violation" of the permanent neutralization of Honduras which
had been provided for by the treaties of 1907, and upon the control by the United States of the expenditure of the $3,000,000
paid to Nicaragua under the treaty which was described as a limitation of Nicaragua's sovereignty.

On January 28, 1915, Secretary Bryan communicated to the
Salvador Government word of the Senate's amendment to the
Nicaragua treaty to the effect that nothing therein should be
construed to impair any rights that Costa Rica might have. He
expressed his willingness to have Salvador "or any other country"
included within the terms of the amendment, and he repeated his
offer to lease a naval base from Salvador or from Honduras if they
so desired "in order to show our impartiality and our desire to
treat all nations alike." But the Salvador Government manifested
no interest in any such arrangement. In fact, in the presidential
campaign recently concluded in Salvador, the protests against the
Nicaragua treaty had played a large rôle, and the internal political effect had been to consolidate opinion in the republic against
the making of any concession to the United States.

In March and April, 1915, indeed, the new administration in
Salvador seemed disposed to join in some arrangement or "alliance" with the United States, provided that all the Central
American republics were included, and that the compensation
offered were other than a money payment. Among the "compensations" suggested were: American capital for the establishment of
a large bank and for the reorganization of the financial system,
the creation of a university along American lines for young men
from all the republics, a rapid and regular steamer communication along the Central American coast, modern lighthouse service
and wireless stations. President Wilson was disposed to consider

the proposal favorably, especially the suggestion of an American university, but the matter dropped out of sight.

When the ratification by the United States Senate of the Bryan-Chamorro Treaty was announced to the Salvador Government, the latter formally declined to recognize its validity, and appealed in September, as had Costa Rica, to the Central American Court of Justice; on February 2, 1917, the Court handed down a decision in every respect similar to that arrived at in the case of Costa Rica in the previous September.

Salvador and the League of Nations.

The adhesion of Salvador to the League of Nations in March, 1920, was the occasion of an interesting diplomatic interchange with the Government at Washington. Before taking this step, in January, 1920, it addressed to the State Department a request for a new interpretation of the Monroe Doctrine in the light of Article XXI of the League Covenant. The State Department's reply, on March 1, quoted President Wilson's address before the Pan-American Scientific Congress at Washington and intimated that no further definition was necessary. In that well-known statement[11] President Wilson declared that "the Monroe Doctrine was proclaimed by the United States on her own authority"; that "it has always been maintained, and always will be maintained, on her own responsibility"; that it "demanded merely that European governments should not attempt to extend their political systems to this side of the Atlantic"; adding, however, that "it did not disclose the use which the United States intended to make of her power on this side of the Atlantic." Doubts and suspicions on this last point had arisen, and must be removed. And among the means he suggested were that the states of America unite "in guaranteeing to each other absolute political independence and territorial integrity," and in "agreeing that all disputes among themselves . . . will be handled by patient, impartial investigation and settled by arbitration." The State Department's reply was evidently satisfactory to the Salvadorean Congress, for it approved the decree of adhesion to the League a few days later.

[11] *Survey,* 1928, pp. 52-56.

In the loan concluded in October, 1923, between the Government of Salvador and the banking house of F. J. Lisman of New York, the State Department became party to the arrangements for guaranteeing the interests of the bondholders. The issue was for $6,000,000 of gold bonds, which were to be a first lien on 70 per cent of the total customs revenues of the Republic, the latter to be collected in United States gold by a representative in Salvador of the Metropolitan Trust Company. In an interchange of diplomatic notes, Salvador gave assurances that it would coöperate with the United States Government and with the bankers in carrying out the terms of the loan contract; the United States took cognizance of the terms of the contract, and under certain contingencies the Secretary of State was to carry out certain of its stipulations. One of these was that

any agreement, question, or difference of any nature whatever regarding the interpretation or performance of the loan shall be referred to the Chief Justice of the Supreme Court of the United States, through the Secretary of State of the United States, for decision, and his decision shall be final and binding.

Today the customs service is thus supervised by an American named by the bankers and accepted by the Salvadorean Government. The interest and sinking fund requirements of the loan are only $744,000, and the average customs receipts are over three millions, so that the customs guarantee is much more than sufficient to cover the service of the debt. The presence of an American supervisor of customs not only has protected the interests of the bondholders, but has considerably increased the income of the Salvador Government from that source; the entire transaction may be accepted as evidence of mutual confidence between the governments of Salvador and the United States.

CHAPTER EIGHT

HONDURAS

HONDURAS, the largest of the Central American republics, lies outside the volcanic zone, and, in consequence of the ruggedness of its terrain, is less fertile and poorer in means of communication than its neighbors. Tegucigalpa, the capital, has no railway connection with the coast, and the provincial towns are isolated, economically and socially. As a result, the native intelligence and aptitudes of a people naturally keen, who are mostly mestizo or mulatto, have remained undeveloped. With the rapid growth of the banana industry, the interior cities, formerly the centers of political life, are being outstripped in economic importance by the newer towns which foreign enterprise is creating on the north coast.

The government has always been a military despotism. Political power and the emoluments of office are the private possession of a few families or of cliques which struggle for the presidency. The great majority of the people have little to lose in a civil war, and possibly something to gain by way of plunder or relief from everyday monotony. Money and arms are secured from foreign concession seekers, and the organization of revolution is therefore easy. The upper classes, rather than engage either in large scale agricultural or commercial enterprise, or in the learned professions, which afford no secure income, devote themselves to politics, and are ready to enter into any intrigue which offers a living at the public expense. In short, the economic backwardness of the Republic is not only an effect of recurrent civil war; it is also one of its causes.

Neutrality Questions.

Honduran quarrels in the nineteenth century raised many questions relating to neutrality. In 1893 the Pacific Mail steamer *Costa Rica* was fired on at Amapala because, after clearance, it refused to surrender to the port authorities the person of the Honduran revolutionist, Policarpo Bonilla, *en route* from Nicaragua to a port in Guatemala. Disavowal and apology were immediately demanded of, and received from the Honduran Government, on the ground that the attempted arrest had been by force and without proper judicial process; nevertheless, Secretary Gresham took occasion to state that the doctrine of asylum had no recognized application to merchant vessels in port, and that the master of a ship had no authority to determine whether or not the offense was one justifying the surrender of the passenger or passengers demanded.[1] The next year the Secretary of State expressed the general opinion that although the United States could not uphold any right on the part of Americans to engage in revolutionary activity, it was morally bound to protect any of its participating citizens from exceptional or unduly harsh treatment.[2]

The Honduras Interoceanic Railway, constructed by British capital, gave rise to another neutrality dispute. A treaty was concluded between the United States and Honduras in 1864; by Article XIV the United States guaranteed the neutrality of the railway, then in course of construction, and recognized the property and sovereign rights of Honduras over it. When war broke out with Salvador in 1871, Honduras sought to take full advantage of this guarantee, and, trusting to United States protection, left the capital defenseless. The United States took the position that the obligation to maintain neutrality did not attach until the railway was completed; the obligations implied by the treaty, moreover, did not impose upon the United States the duty of forcible intervention in quarrels between Honduras and its neighbors.

This constant warfare was partly conditioned by Honduran haplessness *vis-à-vis* its neighbors. Because of its central position among the Central American republics which forced it willy-nilly to take part in nearly all their quarrels, the country was exposed to constant intervention. The Washington conventions of 1907,[3]

[1] This opinion was somewhat at variance with that expressed by Secretary Blaine in the parallel case of General J. M. Barrundia, a Guatemalan political refugee arrested on board the Pacific Mail steamer *Acapulco* in the port of San José de Guatemala in August, 1890, and killed in resisting arrest. *For. Rel.,* 1890, pp. 82 ff.; and *infra.* p. 256.

[2] A similar situation in Nicaragua in 1909 was the occasion for the withdrawal of recognition from President Zelaya, resulting in his expulsion.

[3] See *infra,* p. 264.

signed by the United States and the Central American republics, recognized this state of affairs. Article II of the additional convention to the general Treaty of Peace and Amity provided that "no government of Central America shall in case of civil war intervene in favor of or against the government of the country where the struggle takes place." Article III of the General Treaty provided for the neutralization of Honduras.

Tranquillity, however, was not so easily assured. Within six months of the accord, revolutionists invaded Honduras from Salvador and Guatemala. President Zelaya of Nicaragua practically controlled Honduras through President Davila, and the natural inference was that Zelaya's principal enemies, the Presidents of Guatemala and Salvador, were aiding the revolutionists with a view to striking at him through the Government of Honduras. Zelaya prepared for war, but at the suggestion of Costa Rica, supported by pressure from the United States and Mexico, the Presidents of the three republics agreed to submit their differences to the arbitral action of the newly established Central American Court, meantime reducing their forces to a peace basis. The decision of the Court, handed down on December 19, 1908, brought the incident to a close.

No sooner had this trouble quieted down than President Davila, testifying to his intimacy with the Nicaraguan President, aided him in the revolution of 1909. But the assistance was fruitless, and Zelaya was eliminated; this naturally presaged the fall of the Davila government, and trouble quickly broke out in Honduras, where former President Manuel Bonilla received the support of General Lee Christmas, a picturesque American soldier of fortune. When in August the port of Amapala was seized by the rebels, President Davila requested the United States to give its "decisive coöperation . . . as a service to the foreign residents of the port, and at the same time to end the difficult situation created by the rebel commander and establish legitimate authority."[4] In December Bonilla and Lee Christmas chartered the steamer *Hornet* in New Orleans for a filibustering expedition against Honduras by way of Livingston, Guatemala, and in January, 1911, captured

[4] *For. Rel.*, 1911, p. 292.

the port of Trujillo. President Davila again appealed for United States intervention on the ground that this was necessary for the successful conclusion of a loan convention then being negotiated with United States bankers. Davila offered to deliver the presidency to any competent person to be agreed upon by all parties and approved by the United States Government. The offer of the good offices of the United States was accepted by both parties and at a peace conference, held on board the U.S.S. *Tacoma* at Puerto Cortes in February under the auspices of Thomas C. Dawson, special commissioner of the United States, an agreement was drawn up. This guaranteed the support of all political factions to a provisional president, the division of cabinet posts between revolutionists and the government party, the holding of a free election in October, 1911, the disarming of both the government and insurrectionary forces, a general amnesty, pensions for the disabled, and recognition and payment of debts incurred and losses suffered on both sides. Acting at the request of both delegations, Commissioner Dawson designated Dr. Francisco Bertrand, of the six candidates proposed, as the most desirable for the provisional presidency, and on March 7 Dr. Bertrand was formally elected by the Honduran Congress as "first designate" upon the resignation of the president and vice-president. With the coöperation of all political factions, the new president peacefully assumed office on March 25. At the end of October General Manuel Bonilla was regularly elected constitutional president.

Knox-Paredes Convention.

Until recently one of the most pressing and difficult problems in Honduras has been that of public finance. The external debt of the Republic, amounting to $27,000,000, consisted of the principal and arrears of interest on four loans contracted in Europe between 1867 and 1870 for the construction of a short railway. For the most part the proceeds had been diverted into private hands, no interest had been paid since 1873, and only a few miles of railway gave evidence of the obligations incurred. In 1908 the Council of Foreign Bondholders in London reported that on paper the debt had reached a total of $110,000,000.

Since efforts by British and American syndicates to consolidate the debt proved unavailing, the United States Government, after the signing of the Washington Conventions of 1907, lent its influence to secure a reasonable adjustment. One of the most important provisions of the Washington treaties was that for the maintenance of Honduran neutrality, which, it was felt, would contribute more than any other factor to Central American peace and progress. But to maintain neutrality the Government of Honduras needed the strength and stability that derives from financial sustenance. The State Department was therefore inclined to encourage any responsible American syndicate which

would come forward prepared to carry out a plan which should be of such undoubted merit and fairness as to justify its diplomatic support by the Government of the United States and the assumption by this Government of such relations to the arrangement as would supply the lenders with a proper degree of security.[5]

In 1908 the Council of Foreign Bondholders drew up a contract for the refunding of the debt, and was supported diplomatically by the British Government. The agreement, it was reported, provided for the mortgaging of nearly everything in Honduras, including the railway and wharves of which Americans were the lessees; accordingly, the United States Minister advised the Government of Honduras not to ratify it, and in this stand he was supported by Washington, whose objections to the British bondholders' plan had been the subject of conversations between the State Department and the British Embassy. Feeling that it must present an alternative plan, if its opposition to the British scheme were to be upheld, the State Department initiated discussions between the Honduran Government and representatives of New York banking houses. In 1909, J. P. Morgan and Company came to an agreement with the Council of Foreign Bondholders, and was in a position to make a definite proposal to Honduras, which in September sent two commissioners to New York to undertake negotiations.

[5] *For. Rel.*, 1912, p. 549. Memorandum of the Department of State, undated.

The agreement called for an issue by Honduras of $10,-000,000 in 5 per cent bonds, of which $6,354,000 was to be taken at once by the bankers in exchange for old bonds of a face value of about $19,750,000, and $2,100,000 in cash which was to be applied to the adjustment of certain internal claims, and to the acquisition and extension of the Interoceanic Railway and its appurtenances. Of the remaining $3,646,000 of bonds, $1,146,000 was to be held for the redemption of old bonds still outstanding, and the balance of $2,500,000 was to be reserved until issued for future public improvements. By this arrangement Honduras would be enabled to settle its foreign obligations on the basis of about 15 per cent of their face value without accrued interest.

The United States syndicate[6] required that the loan be guaranteed by a convention between Honduras and the United States similar to the arrangement of 1907 with the Dominican Republic; such an agreement (the Knox-Paredes Convention), signed at Washington on January 10, 1911, during the Bonilla revolution, provided that the two governments would join in securing the faithful execution of a contract to be negotiated with a competent and reliable American banking group. The loan was to be secured on the Honduran customs, the administration of which was to be entrusted to a collector-general appointed by the Honduran Government from a list of names presented by the agent of the loan and approved by the President of the United States; Honduras promised to give to this official full protection in the exercise of his functions, and the "Government of the United States will in turn afford such protection as it may find requisite."[7] Honduras also agreed that it would not alter the customs duties during the existence of the loan without consultation and agreement with the United States, and that a report of the operations of the contract would be submitted to the Honduran minister of finance and to the State Department at least once a year. The transference, in this fashion, of revenue collection from local control was expected to

[6] It included, besides J. P. Morgan & Company, Kuhn, Loeb & Company, the National City Bank, and the First National Bank of New York.

[7] Article IV, *For. Rel.*, 1912, pp. 560-562. This arrangement, which differed somewhat from that made with the Dominican Republic, was imitated in the fiscal contract with Salvador in 1923.

increase the sums available to the Honduran Government and at the same time remove one of the main incentives to rebellion.

On the ground that the treaty assailed the sovereignty and independence of the Republic, and implied that it was unable to administer its own revenues,[8] the Honduran Congress promptly rejected the treaty by a vote of thirty-three to five. However, the loan contract with the bankers was signed by the Honduran commissioners on February 15; five days later the Honduran Congress forbade the conclusion of any such agreement until the matter could be investigated by its committee.

In the United States Senate also strong opposition developed to the loan convention because it involved interference in the domestic concerns of Honduras. Secretary Knox took the position that the United States had in the past been compelled to interfere in the internal affairs of Central American countries without being invited to do so, and that in this case Honduras was requesting its good offices under agreed conditions. It was clear enough, however, that the request had not come from the Honduran Congress, and as the time specified for fulfilling certain of the convenants had expired the Morgan syndicate withdrew.

Nevertheless the Department of State continued to press the loan convention before the Senate Committee on Foreign Relations, as well as the project of a loan contract with American bankers. On May 3 Secretary Knox, in a letter to certain members of the Committee, thus phrased what he considered to be the fundamental principle involved:

Shall the Government of the United States make American capital an instrumentality to secure financial stability, and hence prosperity and peace, to the more backward republics in the neighborhood of the Panama Canal; and in order to give that measure of security which alone would induce capital to be such instrumentality, without imposing too great a burden upon the countries concerned, shall this Government assume toward the customs collections a relationship

---

[8] On February 14 most of the deputies of the National Congress signed a manifesto to the Honduran people explaining their action: the convention was not approved because it entrusted to a foreign power and to foreign officials functions which, by the constitution of Honduras, could not be taken away from the officials of the government.

only great enough for this purpose, a relationship, however, the moral effect and potentialities of which result in preventing the customs revenues of such republics from being seized as the means of carrying on devastating and unprincipled revolutions?[9]

Later in the same month, before the Foreign Relations Committee, he further stated:

From past experience of the United States in Central America it is manifest that either with or without a convention we must to some extent exert influence for peace and order. With the convention as it stands any intervention that may occur will be by virtue of a treaty right. Without the convention any intervention there may be must be of an armed and forcible character. Without the convention we must, when unfortunately necessary, intervene. With the convention intervention will probably be rendered unnecessary.

Whether rightfully or wrongfully, we are in the eyes of the world and because of the Monroe doctrine, held responsible for the order of Central America, and its proximity to the Canal Zone makes the preservation of peace in that neighborhood particularly necessary.

Aside from the purely altruistic motives which have been pointed out above, it must be borne in mind that there is another and a selfish motive which counsels the adoption of the present convention. The development and peace of all Central America must result in a direct and very substantial benefit to the southern ports of the United States—Galveston, New Orleans, Mobile, etc.—as they will all have more frequent intercourse and be able to cultivate a more extensive market for their products, while the Central American Republics, with their production increased, will find a ready market in these gateways of the United States. Railways leading to them must carry this freight for distribution throughout the Southern States.

. . . if this proposition fails how can the United States prevent Honduras from making a similar or some other arrangement with her foreign creditors without such an interference in her affairs and the affairs of the nationals of other governments of a nature far more serious in its possibilities than the contemplated supervision of her customs collections by her invitation? Moreover, what steps will the United States take to prevent the seizure of Honduran customhouses if she makes no settlement with her creditors?[10]

[9] *For. Rel.*, 1912, p. 581.   [10] *Ibid.*, pp. 588, 592, 593.

The refunding schemes of 1911 had failed, partly because of the uncertainties of politics in Honduras, partly because of lack of confidence in the disinterested good faith of the United States. Yet most of the political leaders admitted that a settlement of the old foreign debt was essential, that for this purpose a new loan was necessary, and that an adequate loan could not be secured except under cover of a convention similar to the Knox-Paredes agreement. In 1920 the Government of Honduras called in an American economic expert to draw up a program of financial rehabilitation. The principal features of the plan he presented were: a refunding loan of $5,000,000; a special commission to dispose of outstanding claims; a reduction of national administrative expenditures; an annual budget with a maximum of $2,100,000, including interest on the funded debt; a gold standard of value, with a new gold coin worth one-half the United States dollar; a national bank to issue notes secured by a reserve, and to receive all government deposits; a reform of the customs service; and the development of railways and other public utilities.

In May, 1923, Honduras was reported to have settled its bonded debt with Great Britain on very advantageous terms. Instead of the original debt, £5,500,000 and accrued interest, it promised to pay £1,200,000, spread over a period of thirty years.

Elaboration of Policy.

Within the past decade the United States has taken the responsibility of sending cruisers and marines to persuade politicians to such a state of mind as might bring about free elections in Honduras. In the national elections of 1923, when the Liberals were divided and a violent struggle for the presidency among the three candidates seemed imminent, the State Department gave warning that:

The attitude of the Government of the United States with respect to the recognition of new governments in the five Central American Republics whose representatives signed at Washington on February 7, 1923, a General Treaty of Peace and Amity, to which the United States was not a party, but with the provisions of which it is in the most hearty accord, will be consonant with the provisions of Article

II thereof. The limited period during which the usurper Tinoco was able to hold power in Costa Rica after President Wilson refused to recognize his *régime* shows the beneficial influence of this policy of non-recognition. In such cases it is better to endure the temporary disadvantages of non-recognition than to have an illegitimate government aided in disregarding the peoples' rights through the endorsement of the Government of the United States.[11]

No candidate received the requisite majority, and when Congress undertook to choose a president, none of the three candidates could command a majority of the forty-six congressional votes; this gave President Gutierrez, who was completing a term of five years, an excuse for staying in power after February, 1924, the constitutional date for retirement. General Carias, the Conservative candidate, therefore began a revolution, and a three-cornered struggle ensued. The failure of the political factions to restore constitutional government by peaceful means caused the United States to sever diplomatic relations on February 13, and during the following month marines were landed at various points on both coasts for the protection of foreign property. During hostilities at La Ceiba on February 29, the United States consulate was fired upon, and a United States citizen was killed and another wounded. On March 22 President Coolidge issued a proclamation prohibiting the export of arms and munitions to Honduras.

Fighting for the possession of Tegucigalpa, the rival armies succeeded only in dividing the city into three separate divisions, and conditions became anarchic. Drunken soldiers shot down noncombatants, fired into the United States legation and consulate, and looted the homes and stores of American, British, and Chinese merchants to an amount of some $400,000. At the request of the United States Minister, 167 marines from the U.S. SS. *Milwaukee* were rushed from Amapala to the capital on March 19; they were fired upon by government troops, and the *de facto* authorities demanded their withdrawal, but the United States Minister refused, and a neutral zone patrolled by marines was established in areas near the legation and consulate until order was restored.

By the beginning of April the entire country, with the excep-

[11] *American Journal of International Law*, XIX, 164-166.

tion of the capital, was apparently in the hands of the revolutionists. A State Department representative, Sumner Welles, was sent to Honduras to bring the factions together; on April 24 he arranged a peace conference at Amapala to which the Governments of Costa Rica, Salvador, Nicaragua, and Guatemala accepted invitations. A convention was signed and peace officially restored on May 5; General Vicente Tosta was recognized as provisional president pending new elections. On notification that the United States Government would not recognize any Honduran administration headed by a revolutionary leader, General Carias protested that revolution had been necessary to overthrow a dictator holding office without constitutional justification; but the State Department refused to change its attitude, and General Carias withdrew his candidacy.

Elections for a constituent assembly were held in relative peace at the end of June, 1924; the Conservatives were victorious, and presidential elections were announced for October. But in August the Liberal general, Ferrera, a full-blooded Indian, raised the standard of revolt, and the country was again put under martial law. Again an offer by the United States Government to aid in settling the strife was apparently accepted by both parties; but since fighting continued United States marines were landed at La Ceiba. Not until the end of October were the Ferrera forces routed and scattered. National elections were finally held on December 28-30, and Dr. Miguel Paz Barahona, to whom General Carias had thrown his support, was elected by an overwhelming majority. The irrepressible Ferrera was on the warpath again in February, 1925, and kept the country stirred up until August; this occasioned a request, approved by the State Department, from the new president to the United States Government to purchase 3,000 military rifles, 2,000,000 rounds of small arms ammunition, and 20 machine guns.

In the elections of October, 1928, General Carias once more presented himself as the Conservative leader, and against him the two Liberal factions combined in support of a coalition candidate, Dr. Vicente Mejia Colindres. It was generally predicted that General Carias, who was credited with the support of three-fourths of the government employees, including the governors of departments, would secure an easy victory. But President Paz Barahona had guaranteed absolute freedom and impartiality at the polls, and the Liberal civilian candidate won an unexpected victory by a comfortable majority. This was the first national election in the history of Honduras held without disorder and bloodshed. As an augury of a new era in Honduran politics, President Mejia Colindres gave a banquet in April, 1929, to the members of Congress and of the Supreme Court, most of whom belonged to the opposition party, and secured their pledges of coöperation in the work of reconstruction.

Boundary Questions.

Honduras has boundary disputes with both Guatemala and Nicaragua, neither of which has advanced far toward solution, though in both cases the United States has been called in to arbitrate or to lend its friendly offices. In 1918, and again in 1925, Honduras signed a treaty with Nicaragua agreeing to submit the controversy between them to the arbitration of the United States Government, but so far nothing practical has been accomplished.

A more sustained effort has been made to settle the dispute with Guatemala, though as yet without definitive results. The dispute is more important because the area in question has a considerable population, important transportation lines, and rich agricultural resources now undergoing rapid development. Boundary treaties were negotiated in 1845, 1895, and 1914, the last providing that in case the disputants were unable to arrive at an agreement the question should be submitted to the President of the United States for arbitration. The issue was complicated by the fact that in 1916-17 the Cuyamel Fruit Company, an American banana concern operating under concessions from the Honduran Government, was extending its railway into the disputed territory under the armed protection of Honduras, while on the other side the Government of Guatemala, which sent troops to interfere with the railway construction, had the support of the United Fruit Company.

Both Honduras and Guatemala requested the good offices of

the United States under the treaty, and in April, 1918, commissions from the two countries met with the Secretary of State in Washington. In order to obtain more precise information about the disputed region upon which to base a compromise proposal, an economic survey under the auspices of the State Department was agreed to by both governments. This survey was carried out in 1919. At the closing session of the Central American Conference at Washington in February, 1923, announcement was again made that the boundary question would be submitted to presidential arbitration, but the agreement expired before the question reached the arbitrator.

In March, 1928, Guatemala and Honduras once more requested the United States to assist them in arriving at a settlement; Roy T. Davis, United States Minister to Costa Rica, was appointed to represent the State Department on a mixed commission, which was to study the situation on the ground and if possible lay out a tentative boundary. The commission held a series of meetings in March and April, but nothing was accomplished because the instructions of both delegations were of such a nature as to make any compromise, even of a tentative nature, impossible. Thereupon the State Department in June suggested that the matter be submitted for arbitration to the International Central American Tribunal established by the treaties of 1923. Guatemala accepted the proposal, but Honduras refused, proposing instead to submit the matter to the President of the United States or to the Chief Justice of the United States Supreme Court. Since the State Department shows no inclination to consider this alternative, the dispute is still open, with little prospect of immediate further action.

CHAPTER NINE

GUATEMALA

A FERTILE soil, cheap contract labor, and stability have attracted foreign capital to Guatemala for the development of plantations and ranches. The fact that order was maintained by a military despotism which oppressed the illiterate Indians, descendants of the original proprietors who had a high degree of culture, did not concern the controlling business and landowning interests. Two of the president-dictators, Rafael Carrera and Manuel Estrada Cabrera, each succeeded in holding power for twenty years. But a sentiment against presidential self-succession gradually grew, crystallizing when President Orellana died in office in 1926. The next year the Constituent Assembly succeeded in so recasting the constitution that the executive is shorn of many powers, and when his term of six years ends, he cannot be president again for twelve years. Other decreases in centralization have not undermined stability, and Guatemala retains its lead, among Central American states, in foreign commerce. Its inhabitants, 90 per cent of whom are Indian, constitute approximately 40 per cent of the entire Isthmian population.

Guatemala, like Nicaragua, has with difficulty resisted the temptation to interfere with, or to dominate, the politics of its immediate neighbors. The consequent frequent conflicts, involving rights of asylum and attempts of filibusters to disregard neutrality laws, have been marked by efforts of the United States to restore or maintain the peace. Guatemala borders Mexico, whose southernmost state, Chiapas, was once part of the Spanish Captaincy General in Central America, and has been claimed, at least in part, by Guatemala. As early as 1874 Guatemala sought the friendly offices of United States ministers to assist in bringing about an adjustment of the boundary question. The matter did not reach an acute stage until 1881, and an agreement was reached the next year by the Mexican Minister to Washington and President Barrios. In 1895, when serious difficulties again threatened between the two countries over the delimitation of the frontier, the United States assisted in bringing about agreement on a treaty.

The war of 1890 between Guatemala and Salvador, referred to in an earlier connection, was the cause of diplomatic difficulties between the United States and Guatemala, owing to the seizure at San José de Guatemala of the Pacific Mail steamer, *Colima*, carrying arms for Salvador. Through the intervention of the United States Minister, the steamship company engaged to convey the arms to a neutral port, and at the peremptory demand of the State Department the vessel was released. However, when the arms were being unshipped, they were seized by the Government of Guatemala and temporarily converted to its own use. The United States maintained that it was entitled to an apology or reparation, because of the wrongful seizure of the arms, and because of the indignity and threat toward a United States ship. The Guatemalan Government had returned the arms to the Pacific Mail steamer, *San Blas*, but had not done so "ceremonially," as was expected. The apology, when made, was offered not direct to the United States, but to the steamship company in the person of the captain of the ship *City of New York*, in San José harbor.

Relations were likewise strained by an episode aboard the Pacific Mail steamer *Acapulco* in the same port of San José in August, 1890, when officers attempted without a warrant to arrest General Barrundia, a Guatemalan exile who had tried to invade Guatemala with a revolutionary band from across the Mexican border, and was *en route* from Mexico to Salvador. In resisting arrest Barrundia was killed, and the lives of other passengers were put in jeopardy. The United States Minister had formally consented to the arrest and advised the captain to give up Barrundia, and for this he was abruptly dismissed from his post.

Financial Difficulties.

Like its sister republics, Guatemala has been involved in perennial difficulties with its creditors. After refunding its share of the Central American Federation indebtedness in 1856, it borrowed £500,000 in 1869 from a London banking house. Both loans, totaling £600,000, went into default in 1876, but were refunded in 1889 by a bond issue of £922,700 bearing interest at 4 per cent. Another issue was made at the same time to consolidate its internal debt, but in 1894 the Republic again failed to make payments, and its creditors were forced to accept a further reduction of their claims. In the following year Guatemala's entire indebtedness was refunded by a new issue of £1,600,000, at 4 per cent, secured by a special tax of $1.50 gold on each bag of coffee exported. The Government violated its agreement by reducing the coffee export tax in 1898 and 1899, and by using the proceeds for purposes other than the service of the loan. Payments of interest after 1898 were suspended, and in September, 1901, the Governments of Belgium, England, France, Germany, and Italy, through their respective representatives in Guatemala, jointly requested that the Government live up to its obligations. The United States could not fail to be concerned in the implications of these joint representations to Guatemala. Accordingly, the next April, the German Ambassador to Washington submitted a memorandum to the State Department stating that the Council of Foreign Bondholders of London, in drawing up a new contract in respect of the Guatemalan foreign debt, sought to have it acknowledged by Germany, the United States, and Great Britain, the powers most interested, in order that the Government of Guatemala might be persuaded to keep its engagements. The German ambassador asked whether the United States would be inclined to join in any such proceeding. Secretary Hay replied that

while the Government of the United States is indisposed to join in any collective act which might bear the aspect of coercive pressure upon Guatemala, this Government would reserve for its citizens equal benefits with those which might be obtained for creditors of any other nationality in the adjustment of the Guatemalan foreign debt.[1]

He also advised the Guatemalan Government to the same effect, and received assurances that United States claims would have early consideration.

The ultimatum to Guatemala was delivered at about the time that Germany gave notice to the United States that it was con-

[1] *For. Rel.*, 1902, p. 426.

sidering coercive action against Venezuela, and the memorandum concerning Guatemala was sent to the Secretary of State when joint intervention with Great Britain in Venezuela was being discussed by the two powers. The creditor states did not press matters against Guatemala, either because they chose to accept as satisfactory the promises of the dictator, Manuel Estrada Cabrera, or because their attention was diverted by the larger interests involved in the approaching armed intervention in Venezuela. Interest payments were not renewed until 1913.

In 1912, when the State Department, under Secretary Knox, was displaying lively concern about the rehabilitation of Central American finances, attention was again focused upon Guatemala. Great Britain was once more assuming a stiffer attitude toward the settlement of its bondholders' claims. Secretary Knox used this circumstance to press upon Estrada Cabrera the need of putting his financial house in order. Several United States banking groups had submitted proposals which included the refunding of the foreign debt; and in May, 1912, the Guatemalan Government promised to come to an arrangement within sixty days. At the end of that period the British Government, which had been pressing for an immediate restitution of the coffee revenues pledged in 1895, demanded the settlement of the British claims by arbitration, requesting the diplomatic assistance of Washington. Guatemala also appealed to Washington to procure additional delay until a financial contract with American bankers could be concluded. On September 17 the United States secured a stay of twenty days, but gave warning that

if the Government of Guatemala shall not have completed an arrangement as hereinbefore outlined at the expiration of that delay, the Government of the United States will be obliged to believe that the Government of Guatemala does not really intend to comply with its repeated promises, and under the circumstances will regret to find itself absolutely unwilling to intervene further.[2]

The period of grace elapsed without action. Requesting a further respite, the State Department stated that the delinquent govern-

2 *For. Rel.*, 1912, p. 502.

ment was on the point of concluding the American loan negotiations, adding:

We have to deal with a general situation involving to a great extent the policy of this Government toward a portion of the world where the influence of the United States must naturally be preëminent.[3]

The note urged the British Foreign Office to expedite an agreement between the Council of Foreign Bondholders and the American bankers regarding the terms to be accorded the holders of the old bonds. In this direction, however, Secretary Knox could make no progress. The Council informed the bankers that it had placed the matter in the hands of the Foreign Office and could entertain no outside proposals. At the same time, the Foreign Secretary, Sir Edward Grey, told Washington that the question of conversion was one entirely apart from that with which the Foreign Office was dealing, and was a matter for the private consideration of the bondholders.

At the end of the year an agreement on the terms of a loan contract had apparently been reached with a group consisting of James Speyer & Company, and J. and W. Seligman & Company. It offered to the European bondholders new 4 per cent bonds to an amount equal to the principal of the old debt, these new bonds to be part of a larger issue for financing the economic rehabilitation of the Republic. They were to be secured by all the customs revenues, which would be administered by an agent named by the bankers.[4] The British Government, convinced of the bad faith of the President of Guatemala, refused to consider the conversion proposal, and insisted upon a solution of the difficulty by arbitration, with a covert threat of the alternative of armed intervention. For this Secretary Knox in January, 1913, declined his support, adding that

the attitude of Great Britain in demanding one and only one solution of the difficulty, especially when the solution is one likely to block the

[3] *Ibid.*, 1912, p. 508.
[4] Article XIV of the agreement authorized the Customs Agency "to invoke and obtain from the national government of the bankers such further protection and aid as circumstances may render requisite." *For. Rel.*, 1913, p. 561.

development of a well-recognized policy of the United States in a sphere in which this Government is preëminently interested, would not appear consistent with even an ordinary regard for the broad interests and policies of the United States.[5]

When it became apparent that the Guatemalan Government was again hedging upon the terms of the loan agreement, the State Department decided to take no further action in the matter.

President Estrada Cabrera, in the face of renewed British representation, still temporized, and on the evening of May 10, 1913, the British Minister, Sir Lionel Carden, presented an ultimatum to the effect that unless the coffee revenues were restored to the bondholders within five days diplomatic relations would be severed, and a British warship would immediately be sent to compel the collection of the coffee tax for the benefit of the creditors. An agreement, accepting the British terms, was signed on the same night by the Guatemalan Minister of Foreign Affairs.

CENTRAL AMERICAN UNITY

In colonial times Guatemala, city and province, was the social, political, and ecclesiastical head of the Spanish Captaincy General. There resided the Royal Audiencia or supreme court of appeals, and there was located the University which dated from the seventeenth century. It has never lost this position as the focal center in Central American politics. The independence movement started in Guatemala in 1821; twenty years later, owing to the opposition of its aristocratic, landowning class, the Central American Federation was disrupted; and recently the question of the revival of the federal union has revolved around Guatemala.

In response to news from Mexico of the Conservative revolution led by Agustin Iturbide, an assembly of notables gathered in Guatemala City in 1821 under the presidency of the Spanish Captain General, and declared the independence of Central America. Two parties appeared, one for union with Mexico under a monarchy, the other for an independent republic. The latter was

5 *For. Rel.*, 1913, p. 559.

in the minority, but was particularly strong in Salvador and Costa
Rica. In January, 1822, the Captain General, after consultation
with some of the municipalities, declared Central America annexed to the Mexican Empire, and General Vicente Filosola, with
a force of six thousand men, was sent from Mexico by Iturbide.
The Mexican connection was not popular, however, and after
Iturbide's abdication, Filosola, concluding that the tie could not
be permanently maintained, convoked a National Constituent
Assembly, which on July 1, 1823, proclaimed the independent
United Provinces of Central America, and in 1924 issued a republican and federal constitution.

Political difficulties soon set in—conflicts between the president
and the national congress, between the federal and state executives, and among local factions within the five "sovereign" states.
From 1826 to 1829 the Isthmus was torn by a confused and bitter
war, out of which a leader emerged in Dr. Francisco Morazan, a
native of Honduras, who was liberal, anticlerical, and unionist.
Efforts to repress disorder, however, were unavailing, and the conservatives or anti-unionists gradually regained control of several
state governments. The last federal congress, which adjourned
in 1838, declared that until the federal union was reformed, the
states were free to govern themselves as they saw fit. Within a
year Nicaragua, Honduras, Costa Rica, and Guatemala had declared their independence. Only in Salvador was Morazan's authority recognized, but in 1840 he was driven into exile by an army
from Guatemala. Meantime in Guatemala a mestizo guerrilla
leader appeared on the scene, a semi-bandit named Rafael Carrera. Carrera, at the head of several thousand Indian followers, became the tool of the clericals of Guatemala (who were also sepa-
ratists) against the liberal and unionist party, and for a generation he was the most powerful figure of Central America.[6]

The three middle republics, Salvador, Nicaragua, and Honduras, for a time refused to accept the dissolution of the federation
as a final settlement; congresses frequently met to discuss reunion,

6 In 1843 Morazan, with recruits from Peru and Colombia, seized Costa Rica
as a base from which to reconquer Central America (for the liberals), but the
Costa Ricans, unwilling to be so used, seized and shot him in September, 1843.

and in 1842 and again in 1849, a limited federal organization representing the three states was established, only to be shattered by local jealousies and mutual distrust. In 1871, however, the liberals recovered control as the result of a concerted movement in Guatemala, Honduras, and Salvador, and two years later the great liberal president of Guatemala, José Rufino Barrios, came to power. Barrios undertook to bring the heads of all the states together to compose their differences as a preliminary to federation, and appealed for support to the United States Minister, who lent his active assistance. Among the measures proposed were free trade, uniform currency and postal systems, common diplomatic representation abroad, and agreement not to harbor revolutionists from neighboring states. Negotiations were carried on intermittently for several years, but the other governments, fearful of Barrios' personal ambition, declined to enter into a definite treaty.

The failure of every effort to restore the former union convinced President Barrios that it could be realized only by force. In February, 1885, on the basis of an understanding with the Presidents of Honduras and Salvador, he proclaimed the Federation of Central America, of which he assumed chief military command. He invited the other states to recognize the new government and to send delegates for a constituent assembly to meet in Guatemala City. Honduras accepted unreservedly, but the President of Salvador, in the face of popular opposition, prepared for resistance, and Nicaragua and Costa Rica flatly rejected the proposal. They also appealed to Washington against the designs of General Barrios. The United States Government had sympathized with the plans for union, but it discountenanced coercion by any one state, and began to use its influence for peace. Nevertheless war broke out between Salvador and Guatemala, and in a battle on April 2 General Barrios was killed. Through the mediation of the diplomatic corps a general truce was arranged, and Central America was again at peace.

In June, 1895, the three middle republics renewed the union movement, and entered into a treaty establishing a "Diet," composed of one member from each state selected by the respective congresses, to which was entrusted the conduct of foreign relations. The new organization, called the "Greater Republic of Central America," was recognized by the United States in December, 1896, with the understanding that the responsibility of each of the component members to the United States should remain wholly unaffected. In August, 1898, a constitution was drawn up, and in November an Executive Council, with far broader powers than the old Diet, was installed at Amapala. Costa Rica and Guatemala were also invited to join. The Council had scarcely assembled, however, when the opponents of federation in Salvador overthrew the government; and since neither Honduras nor Nicaragua was willing to make war upon them, the union dissolved.

Washington Conventions of 1907.

The last attempt to unite the five republics by force was also the occasion for calling the Washington Conference of 1907. In that year President Zelaya of Nicaragua overthrew the government in Honduras and imposed another, practically controlled by himself. With the same end in view he prepared to attack Salvador, and aroused the apprehensions of Guatemala. A general Central American war might have ensued had not Presidents Roosevelt and Diaz jointly interposed, urging that the republics send delegates to Washington to discuss their differences. On September 17 a protocol providing for a general conference in November was signed at Washington. The mediating governments were also requested to appoint representatives "to lend their good and impartial offices in a purely friendly way toward the realization of the objects of the Conference."

At the Washington Conference, which met a few months later, the delegates of Honduras, supported by those of Nicaragua, formally proposed that a treaty of union be signed, and stated that the presidents of those countries were ready to lay down their offices if that were necessary to make the execution of the treaty possible. This motion nearly caused the disruption of the conference, for the delegates from Guatemala opposed it, and those from Costa Rica objected even to its being discussed. The representatives from Salvador, who were at first inclined to favor the plan, voted against it as inopportune after receiving instructions to do so from their government, and the matter was finally dropped.[7]

Still a number of important conventions were agreed upon, designed to define and regulate Central American relations, and prepare the way for ultimate union. The five republics pledged themselves not to

recognize any other government which may come into power in any of the five Republics as a consequence of a *coup d'état*, or of a revolution against a recognized government, so long as the freely elected representatives of the people thereof have not constitutionally reorganized the country.

They promised that they would not "in case of civil war intervene in favor of or against the Government of the country where the struggle takes place."[8] They agreed to restrain political refugees from disturbing frontiers; not to allow their territory to be used as a base for revolutionary movements against their neighbors; and permanently to neutralize Honduras. A Central American Court of Justice was created, to be located at Cartago in Costa Rica. It was to consist of one judge from each state elected by its legislature, and was to have cognizance of all controversies among the five republics which could not be adjusted through ordinary diplomatic channels, as well as over other cases of an international character. Provision was made for an international institute for the training of Central American teachers, directed by the Government of Costa Rica but supported by all the others; and for a Central American Bureau in Guatemala City, which was to serve as an office of record, maintain an organ of publicity, and promote social, intellectual, and economic coöperation among the five nations.[9] Future conferences were also provided for to discuss and agree upon uniform legislation in financial, commercial, legal, sanitary, and educational matters.

Many of the provisions of these treaties were immediately put into effect. On May 25, 1908, at Cartago, in a temple constructed

[7] Munro, *op. cit.*, p. 173.

[8] Articles I and II of the Additional Convention to the General Treaty.

[9] These institutions had first been outlined in the San José Conventions of 1906. See *supra*, pp. 234 ff.

by Andrew Carnegie, the Central American Court of Justice was installed in the presence of a high commissioner representing the President of the United States. On September 15 the Central American Bureau was inaugurated in Guatemala City.

In general, however, the program for the political and economic regeneration of the Isthmus was too ambitious to be effected at once. Evils arising from deep-rooted habits and fundamental social conditions could not be done away with by mere international agreement, however sincere the contracting parties might be in their desire for peace and for realization of a closer union. No one could reasonably expect that the five governments would turn at once from their attitude of mutual suspicion and hostility to a harmonious coöperation in undertakings for their common welfare. Nicaragua, in particular, showed little inclination to carry out its obligations until the United States authorized its naval commanders in Central American waters to prevent by force the launching of filibustering expeditions from Nicaraguan ports. After the elimination of President Zelaya, however, conditions began to improve, and since then no international war has occurred in Central America.

The Central American conferences met annually for five years, but the conventions they drew up were not given practical effect by the various governments, and the meetings were finally discontinued. The most serious blow to the Washington conventions developed out of the Bryan-Chamorro Treaty of 1914, when in the suits brought by Costa Rica and Salvador against Nicaragua in the Central American Court of Justice, Nicaragua refused to appear as a party to the case and rejected the Court's decision. The prestige of the tribunal was seriously compromised, and as its ten-year term ended in 1918 it was allowed quietly to go out of existence.

Recent Plans of Federation.

The overthrow in 1920 of the dictator of Guatemala, Estrada Cabrera, who had ruled for twenty-two years, and who had consistently opposed the idea of Central American union, paved the way for a revival of federation plans. Early in 1920 an active propaganda was inaugurated in Guatemala ostensibly in favor of union but covertly directed against the Cabrera *régime*. This ultimate objective was reflected in a decree passed by the National Assembly in March authorizing the President to negotiate plans for union with the other states. Cabrera saw the significance of the movement, and took active measures to suppress it, but without success, for on April 7 the Assembly impeached the President, to all intents and purposes, by declaring him no longer capable of performing the duties of his office, and named a prominent and wealthy sugar-planter, Carlos Herrera, as his successor until national elections could be held. For seven days Cabrera shelled Guatemala City intermittently from the forts; then he resigned and was thrown into prison. In the presidential elections which followed, Herrera was chosen constitutional head of Guatemala, and contrary to the precedent of the Tinoco case,[10] was recognized by the United States Government.

President Herrera and his party had given the signal for a revival of the unionist cause, but it was chiefly through the initiative of Salvador that a conference of delegates from the five republics again met in San José de Costa Rica to discuss the plan. On January 19, 1921, all the republics except Nicaragua signed a treaty providing for a "Federation of Central America," to be effective after ratification by three states. The Treaty of Union laid down the bases of a federation constitution, which called for a plural executive like that of Switzerland, a bicameral legislature on the lines of the United States Congress, and a system of federal courts. Each state was to retain such powers as were not granted to the federal government, and thereafter no states were to contract foreign loans without the sanction of the federal congress.

The pact was quickly ratified by Guatemala, Honduras, and Salvador. The Congress of Costa Rica rejected it by a narrow margin, and Nicaragua refused to enter the federation largely from fear of endangering its rights under the Bryan-Chamorro Treaty. In June, 1921, a provisional government was established at Tegucigalpa, the proposed federal capital, and a constituent assembly, consisting of fifteen delegates from each of the three co-

---

10 *Supra*, p. 225.

operating states, framed a constitution in accordance with the
terms of the San José treaty. The constitution was promulgated
on September 9, elections were held in October, and everything
was in readiness for the installation of a permanent government
in the following January, when a military *coup d'état* in Guatemala City on December 5, 1921, and the deposition of President
Herrera, withdrew Guatemala from the union. General J. M.
Orellana, who headed the new Guatemalan administration, made
overtures to the Federal Council which were repulsed on the
ground that his Government was illegal and unconstitutional; and
when the Council later offered to recognize his Government, he
rejected the offer and repudiated Guatemala's adhesion to the
federal pact. At the time of the revolution a special mission was
in Washington negotiating with the State Department for a formal recognition of the new union. Orellana was chosen President of
Guatemala by an election in February, 1922, in which the unionist
party refused to participate; and, again contrary to other practice, on April 15 he was recognized by the United States Government.

Washington Treaties of 1923.

The most recent step toward the ultimate union of Central
America was taken in 1923. Some of the conventions of 1907
had automatically expired in 1918, and had not been formally renewed; others had never been seriously observed. The possibility
that all might pass into complete desuetude fired the ambitions
of the hungry political "outs," and there was increasing unrest in the Isthmus. After a series of revolutionary efforts on
the part of Nicaraguan malcontents operating from Honduras
and Salvador, a meeting of the Presidents of the three republics,
with their cabinets, was held on board the American cruiser
Tacoma in Fonseca Bay on August 20, 1922. Here they agreed
to renew and extend the General Convention of Peace and Amity
of December, 1907, until a conference of plenipotentiaries could
be held to make new treaties. Costa Rica and Guatemala were invited to adhere, but declined. As a result of the *Tacoma* convention, and at the suggestion of the Central American governments,

the United States on October 21 issued invitations to the five republics to attend a Conference on Central American Affairs in
Washington, December 4, 1922. The Secretary of State, Charles
E. Hughes, and Sumner Welles were appointed United States
delegates, and Mr. Hughes was unanimously selected president of
the conference. After two months of deliberation the delegates
signed twelve treaties and three protocols for the settlement of
their national and international problems. They cover in a general way the same ground as the conventions of 1907.

The former Central American Court was reëstablished as the
"International Central American Tribunal," with a somewhat
more limited jurisdiction and a personnel chosen for each special
case from a permanent list of thirty arbiters nominated by the five
republics. Provision was made for international commissions of
inquiry, along the lines of the Bryan arbitration treaties of 1913,
to investigate and publish the facts in the event of disputes between any of the signatory states. To this treaty the United States
became a party. For a period of five years the republics also agreed
to limit their armaments in accordance with a schedule fixed by
the convention. As in 1907 they engaged not to recognize governments set up by force, and agreed in addition that even if governments originating in revolutions established constitutional order
through popular elections, they would not recognize as president,
vice-president, or designate anyone who had been a leader in the
revolution, or his parents, brothers, or descendants.

CHAPTER TEN

ECONOMIC INTERESTS

CENTRAL AMERICA, once the richest and most prosperous
agricultural region of the Spanish colonial empire, is of economic interest to the United States because it is the source of so
many import requirements in tropical foodstuffs and raw materials. A combination of circumstances makes Central America productive of many tropical crops. The decomposition of the ashes
and scoriae ejected by numerous volcanoes over great distances
forms thick layers of extremely fertile soil; consequently, under
the stimulation of a tropical sun and tropical rains, vegetation is
luxuriant. A wide diversity of climatic conditions between plateaus and lowlands, and in rainfall, permits a variety of products,
of which the chief are coffee, bananas, sugar, tobacco, cotton,
cacao, and maize. The moist low regions contain magnificent
forests of mahogany, cedar, dyewoods, and other trees. The
savannahs and higher plains afford an excellent pasturage for
cattle.

Coffee, bananas, tobacco, and cacao are the chief exports. Minor
to them, but also marketable in the United States, are henequen
fiber and balsam from Salvador; coconuts, ivory nuts, cabinet
woods, mother-of-pearl shells from Panama; cabinet woods and
minerals from Honduras; minerals from Costa Rica. The percentage of the United States' share in Central American trade,
according to the last available Department of Commerce figures,
may be tabulated as follows:

	United States imports from	United States exports to
Costa Rica (1927)	32.9	50.3
Guatemala (1927)	42.6	55.9
Honduras (1926-1927)	76.9	79.4
Nicaragua (1927)	55.6	66.4
Panama (1925)	88.0	67.6
Salvador (1927)	10.0	49.0

Of exports, coffee is the barometer of prosperity in three of the
five republics, being the chief export of Salvador, 75 per cent,

Guatemala, 66 per cent, and Costa Rica, 60 per cent. Except in Costa Rica, where the majority of the plantations are owned by citizens, most of the coffee is raised by foreigners. Guatemalan coffee, unexcelled in the opinion of connoisseurs, is grown principally on the lower slopes of the volcanic range facing the Pacific, a region remarkable for its splendid scenery and relatively dry and pleasant climate. Many foreigners, especially Germans, have settled there, and have invested heavily in coffee plantations; these cover over a fifth of Guatemala's cultivated area.

Bananas, the Ready-Money Crop.

Coffee is the best known of Central American products in world markets. Its popularity in certain European markets, particularly German, is a considerable element in Central American buying power. But, being governed by a highly fluctuating world price, its returns are unsure. To a certain extent bananas have mitigated Central American economic dependence on the vagaries of coffee prices, for bananas are a ready-money crop, bringing in a constant flow of income. Owing to the seemingly unlimited United States market which American enterprise has built up, the banana now constitutes 72 per cent of Panaman and 66 per cent of Honduran exports, and is second only to coffee in the economic calculations of Guatemala and of Costa Rica. Costa Rica holds first place for production of bananas, although they make up only 35 per cent of its exports.

The belt of banana cultivation encircles the earth fifteen hundred miles on each side of the equator. Authorities differ as to whether the fruit is indigenous to America; in spite of world-wide growth the banana is rarely found in a wild state, for it is seedless and propagated by shoots. Cultivation is not difficult, and its rate of growth is rapid.

Fifty years ago the banana was as little known in the United States as the avocado or "alligator pear" is today. Captain Baker of Cape Cod brought a few bunches from Jamaica in 1870; though not the first consignment, these were the beginnings of a trade now worth $65,000,000. Its growth is mainly the achievement of another American, Minor C. Keith, who was in Costa Rica engaged in railway building when the banana was beginning to rise in American esteem. Two years after the Baker experiment Keith consigned two hundred bunches from Panama which were taken up so eagerly that he began immediately to lay out the first banana plantation along the Costa Rica railway. This served also to provide freight for the railway. He found both climate and soil ideally suited to the plant, and gradually extended cultivation over his concession of eight hundred thousand acres. By 1898 he was the most important banana grower in Central America, and had acquired a fleet of steamers to transport the fruit to the American market. In 1897 Keith, with Andrew W. Preston, organized the United Fruit Company, receiving three-fifths of the company's capital for his interests. The vast estates of this company are strung along the Caribbean coast line, with Puerto Barrios as the principal port. A few years ago it was still considered impossible to grow bananas successfully on the Pacific coast; the Atlantic regions which receive more rain were favored. But with the shrinkage of producing areas, owing to the extension of the so-called "Panama disease," the big fruit companies have begun to utilize land on the Pacific.

The capital necessary for handling bananas is so great as to preclude any but large-scale enterprise. Machinery for loading and unloading the fruit, and vessels specially constructed to prevent wastage can be profitably used only when a continuous supply is assured. Foreign corporations have therefore made large investments, affording the countries a considerable revenue in taxes, and employing large numbers of native inhabitants; but no foreign concern approaches the United Fruit Company in its influence upon Central America. Its annual report for 1928 shows assets of $225,000,000, of which $111,000,000 are listed as tropical fixed assets. The assets include 495,000 acres, owned and leased, of improved lands in bananas, sugar, cacao, coconuts, pastures, and building sites; just under 2,000,000 acres of unimproved lands owned and leased; over 1,600 miles of railway owned and operated; and 72 vessels of its own in operation (40 in the American and 32 in the European service), aggregating 335,000 tons, besides 25 more smaller vessels under charter. The pay roll for its tropical divisions alone amounted in 1928 to $24,774,900. It bought $13,205,300 worth of fruit from private growers. The idea of modern corporations that "service helps business" is of especially far-reaching effect in the Caribbean, where practically everything in the way of equipment for convenience of living has been furnished by United States occupation officials or by large business enterprise. The United Fruit Company, for example,

has installed and maintains for their [employees'] well-being, bakeries, ice plants, electric light plants, water works, and sewerage-systems. It also has provided churches, schools, baseball grounds, tennis courts, golf courses, and swimming pools, and has contributed toward the national schools maintained in the vicinity of its plants. . . .

In addition to establishing agricultural schools and aiding students to come to the United States for study, it has

in the last twenty-seven years spent on hospitals and sanitation $13,091,424 . . . and has built and maintains eight modern hospitals, with outlying field dispensaries for the benefit of its employees and the peoples of the countries where it operates. Including employees, about 150,000 people depend upon medical and surgical service from the Medical Department of the United Fruit Company. . . .[1]

Investment in Railways.

The history of United States railroad construction in Central America dates from 1866, when a concession to construct a line from Port Limón on the Caribbean to the Gulf of Nicoya on the Pacific was given by Costa Rica to an American financial group headed by General John C. Fremont. The concession lapsed before construction began, and in 1871 another contract was made with the distinguished railway engineer, Henry Meiggs. The railway, passing through the important towns of Cartago, San José, and Heredia, was to be constructed within three years, and the cost, £1,600,000, was to be covered by government loans placed in London. About 110 miles were built, in three unconnected sections, Atlantic, Central, and Pacific, leaving about 80 miles still

[1] Statement of V. M. Cutter, President, United Fruit Company, to stockholders at annual meeting, February 15, 1928.

to be constructed. The debt, on which in 1874 interest was suspended, amounted in 1883 to approximately $18,000,000, including principal and interest. Most of the advances never reached the object intended. Accordingly on March 30, 1883, a new contract was concluded with Meiggs' nephew, Minor C. Keith, which provided not only for the continued operation and construction of the railway, but also for a refunding of the foreign debt. Keith undertook to arrange with the foreign creditors for a reduction of the interest rate to 2½ per cent, which, after ten years, was to be raised to 3½ per cent, and the Costa Rican Government pledged the customs revenues for the service of the debt. In return Keith, or the company he would organize for the purpose, was conceded the operation of the railway for ninety-nine years, and the title to eight hundred thousand acres of public lands. He was required to build thirty miles of railway to connect the Atlantic and Central divisions, while the Government was to receive one-third of the ordinary paid-up shares of the company, and have the right to one-half of the net proceeds of operation. Keith accomplished his task in the face of unparalleled difficulties, having to conquer miasmic swamp and dense jungle.

Keith then extended his attention to Guatemala and Salvador. In 1904 his group acquired from the Guatemalan Government a 130-mile stretch of railway from Puerto Barrios to El Ranco. The line was carried through the intervening swamp land to Guatemala City and eventually this and the Salvador system came to be operated by the company which in 1912 was established as the International Railways of Central America. The company took a few straggling, poorly constructed, and unprofitable lines and integrated them into a system with an operating ratio comparing favorably with those of the best American roads. In Salvador its line runs from San Salvador to Santa Ana, and a thirty-four mile stretch, which at present separates it from the Guatemala system, is under construction. The International Railways of Central America will then be the largest foreign system operated by United States interests, with 800 miles of road and an investment of $80,000,000.

Hitherto the distance in both time and actual mileage from Santa Ana to United States Gulf ports has been nearly as great as from Liverpool to Santa Ana; the transport time approximated eighteen days, for merchandise from New Orleans had to pass through the Panama Canal and along the Pacific coast to Acajutla, and thence go on to Santa Ana by rail. The new line will enable shipments to be made in less than half this time; the modern port of Guatemala at Puerto Barrios, on the Atlantic side, will be the port of call, and goods may then be consigned direct to Salvador. This should give the coffee plantations of the Pacific slope of Salvador direct access by rail to the Atlantic, with a return carriage of American goods from the Gulf ports and the Atlantic seaboard.

In addition to fruit properties and railways, United States nationals own a considerable proportion of the bonded indebtedness of the Central American republics, as well as lesser interests in mining (particularly in Honduras), public utilities, banking, and merchandising. The Department of Commerce estimate of aggregate holdings is:

Costa Rica		$40,000,000
Fruit and public utilities,	$25,000,000	
Government bonds,	12,000,000	
Miscellaneous,	3,000,000	
Guatemala		$60,000,000
Railroads,	$42,000,000	
Fruit, merchandising, banking, government bonds, and miscellaneous,	18,000,000	
Honduras		$55,000,000
Fruit,	$40,000,000	
Mining,	10,000,000	
Miscellaneous,	5,000,000	
Nicaragua		$17,000,000
Government bonds,	$ 8,000,000	
Fruit,	3,000,000	
Miscellaneous,	6,000,000	
Panama		$40,000,000
Government bonds,	$17,000,000	
Fruit,	12,000,000	
Public utilities,	5,000,000	
Miscellaneous,	6,000,000	
Salvador		$30,000,000
Government bonds,	$16,000,000	
Railroads,	8,000,000	
Mining, banking, and miscellaneous,	6,000,000	
Total[2]		$242,000,000

[2] The new railway developments mentioned above would add about $20,000,000 to these estimates.

CHAPTER ELEVEN

CARIBBEAN POLICY AND ACTIVITIES

Beginnings of Policy.

SPAIN annexed the islands of the Caribbean and the adjacent territory on the mainland in the avid expectation of easily-won wealth. But a land is only the soil of opportunity for man to cultivate, and the English colonial domain outstripped the enterprise of Spain in the Caribbean, which subsequently fell into a state of relative stagnation.

Until the latter part of the nineteenth century the United States took but slight interest in the Caribbean, although far-seeing statesmen were not wanting who protested against this indifference. On this subject as on others Jefferson showed his prescience:

With respect to the Isthmus of Panama I am assured by Burgoyne . . . that a survey was made, that a canal appeared very practicable, and that the idea was suppressed for political reasons altogether. . . . This report is to me a vast desideratum for reasons political and philosophical. I cannot help suspecting the Spanish squadron to be gone to South America and that some disturbances have been excited there by the British. The Court of Madrid may suppose we would not see this with an unwilling eye. This may be true to the uninformed part of our people; but those who look into futurity farther than the present moment or age, and who combine well what is, with what is to be, must see that our interests, well understood, and our wishes are that Spain shall (not forever, but) very long retain her possessions in that quarter. And that her views and ours must in a good degree, and for a long time concur.[1]

Recognizing their strategic possibilities, John Quincy Adams in 1823 spoke of Cuba and Porto Rico as "natural appendages to the North American continent." In the same year Jefferson wrote his celebrated letter approving Monroe's proposed doctrine and

[1] *Works of Thomas Jefferson,* Federal Edition, V, 403-404. Letter dated June 3, 1788.

referring to Cuba as "the most interesting addition which could ever be made to our system of states."

American statesmen were concerned over the possibility of acquisition by European powers of islands in the Caribbean, especially Cuba and Porto Rico, which France or Great Britain might decide to take over in one fashion or another from an enfeebled government. By carving territories into estates and monopolies for the purpose of stimulating trade, the colonial system of the European powers had provided a standing incentive to war in the American hemisphere; consequently, though the islands were not thought particularly desirable for the United States, isolated proposals were bruited to annex territory and lease naval bases in the Caribbean in order to prevent their falling into other powerful hands. But the shadow of American economic power had not spread over the Caribbean, the isthmian canal was a paper plan, the United States as yet had no possessions in the Pacific to guard, and its navy, with a limited industrial plant behind it, was not yet a factor in world politics.

Strategic Expansion.

The overland progression of the American pioneers was regular and compact. In the second quarter of the nineteenth century some parties went all the way to Oregon and California, but most of them were moving out toward the western edge of the humid belt of the central plains and settling down. The caravan movement was so slow that the condition of emptiness in the western half of the country continued until the great railway lines were built, and then settlement began to seek out the better places and rapidly to fill up the plains.

Meantime, in the forties the gold rush to California leaped the space intervening between the Mississippi and the Pacific, and for the gold seekers transportation by sea became a matter of importance, much more after the Mexican War and the acquisition of California than before. This demand was satisfied by sea carriage to and from the Isthmus at Panama, and by the Panama Railway; there was no pressing economic demand for anything more.

But some minds ranged beyond present needs, and the stream

of voyagers and of goods to Colon and across the Isthmus brought Central America nearer, established a connection between its destiny and that of the United States and brought the possibility of a canal through the Isthmus within the vision of practical men.

This Caribbean-consciousness intensified the maneuvers between the United States and Great Britain[2] concerning British possessions and influence in the approaches to a possible canal. These plans began as far back as Polk's time; the United States could not, said Rives to Palmerston, "consent to see so important a communication fall under exclusive control of any other great commercial power." Control of the canal and of the waters neighboring both the canal and the United States was one of the terms of security against attack, and after the recovery from the Civil War led simultaneously to naval expansion and the formulation of a Caribbean policy. There was also an apprehension that the French concession for construction of a canal through Panama and the work of De Lesseps begun in 1879 might expand European interests and influences in the affairs of the American continent. The expansion of the navy in Garfield's administration was energetically carried forward under William C. Whitney, Cleveland's Secretary of the Navy, and trials of the first ship were completed in 1889. In 1891 President Harrison emphasized the importance of a Nicaraguan canal, as a saving of naval operation costs to the Government and of freight costs to commerce. The sixty-six day voyage of the *Oregon* around Cape Horn to join the Atlantic battle fleet off Florida in the Spanish American War dramatized for public opinion the need of rapid sea communication between the eastern and western coasts.

Toward the close of the century Admiral Mahan made his pronouncements on Caribbean strategy. From the commonplace that no other nation had the same interest in an isthmian canal as did the United States, he proceeded to show that no dependence upon a canal was as vital to any nation. The isthmus which severed the two oceans would one day unite them, and

entrance to the Caribbean and transit across the Caribbean to the

2 See *Survey*, 1928, pp. 45-46.

isthmus are two prime essentials to the enjoyment of the advantages of the latter. Therefore, in case of war, control of these two things becomes a material object not second to the isthmus itself, access to which depends on them.[3]

The war with Spain was swift and fortunate, a summer's drama with "a happy ending" played out before the people of the United States, the easiest of victories, the least costly in lives and in expenditure; the remains of the Spanish colonial empire had vanished before men were conscious of the shape of events. The romance that always attends sea operations, the success of all plans for coördination because there was no strength to interfere with them, and the completeness of the results achieved by victory, gave the American people a renewed sense of their relation to the sea, of the way in which it could be made to serve their destiny and of the strength they could bring to bear upon it.

No sooner were hostilities at an end than definite steps were taken to fulfil a policy resting upon the twin supports of national defense and expanding commerce. Addressing himself to this mood President McKinley, in December, 1898, called for the construction of an isthmian canal which, he said, was "indispensable to that intimate and ready communication between our eastern and western seaboards demanded by the annexation of the Hawaiian Islands and the prospective extension of our influence and commerce in the Pacific."

In 1899 the Isthmian Canal Commission, headed by Admiral Walker, and directed to report upon the practicability of an interoceanic canal, accepted Admiral Mahan's view. They thought that United States military strength would be best served if a canal were neutral, were operated and controlled by United States citizens, and were accompanied by a great expansion of naval resources. In fact if these conditions were not fulfilled its value to the United States would be highly doubtful, for the canal was but

one link in a chain of communications, of which adjacent links are the Caribbean Sea on the east and the waters of the Pacific, nearer

[3] A. T. Mahan, *The Interest of America in Sea Power, Present and Future,* 1897, p. 299.

the canal entrance, on the west. Unless the integrity of all the links can be maintained, the chain will be broken. The power holding any one of these links can prevent the enemy from using the communication but can itself use it only when it holds them all.[4]

Before constructing a canal, even before acquiring a route and the right of construction, United States interests required an abrogation of the equality established by the Clayton-Bulwer Treaty of 1850 which was a deterrent to its exclusive acquisition of a route and to its building, maintaining, and fortifying a canal. This once accomplished by the Hay-Pauncefote Treaty of 1902,[5] the canal route itself was obtained through the revolt of the state of Panama against Colombia and through the treaty negotiated immediately thereafter between Panama and the United States.[6]

Control over more than the canal was necessary, both for the security of the canal itself and for completing the mastery over the region of which the canal is the life-artery. This next step, achieved by acquiring islands and naval bases in the Caribbean, made the United States supreme in the region; change in war implements may alter in detail the strategic value of control over the Caribbean, but in the main it will remain much the same. As a part of the "manifest destiny" which presented the Philippine Islands to the United States, the treaty of December 10, 1898, with Spain brought Porto Rico and the adjacent Vieques and Culebra Islands. In 1903, although the United States had disclaimed any intention of itself exercising control over Cuba,[7] continued intervention had led to the additions to the Cuban Constitution pursuant to which Cuba leased the land necessary for a naval base at Guantánamo. On November 18 of the same year the Canal Zone was established.[8] During the World War the Virgin Islands (St. Thomas, with the finest harbor in the West Indies, St. John, St. Croix and the adjacent islands and rocks) were purchased from Denmark on August 4, 1916, for $25,000,000. A negative control over Mole St. Nicho-

[4] *Report* of the Isthmian Canal Commission, 1899, pp. 252-254.
[5] See the *Survey*, 1928, p. 46.
[6] These events are described in Chapter 5 of this section.
[7] Teller Amendment to the Joint Resolution of April 20, 1898.
[8] See pp. 210, 217.

las, now dominated by the Guantánamo naval station, is secured
by a treaty in which Haiti agrees not to surrender any of its territory to any foreign power.[9]

Meanwhile construction of the Canal was started. After three
years of preliminary preparation in which, at enormous cost and
great sacrifice on the part of physicians, yellow fever was stamped
out and the Canal Zone was made habitable for white people,
Culebra Cut, which the French company had left unfinished in
1889, when it had gone into bankruptcy, was completed. The engineering problems involved were intricate and unprecedented in
scale, but after seven years the entire forty-two miles was built at
a cost of $336,650,000.[10] The course of American policy to the
opening of the Canal on July 12, 1920, was steady and deliberate;
motivated by strategic considerations, it went along with economic
expansion.

Growth of Economic Ties with the Caribbean.

The sharp contrast in the nature of the commodities exchanged
between the United States and the Caribbean well exemplifies the
definition of trade as the satisfaction of mutual requirements.
United States machine-made products are exchanged for sugar
from Cuba, bananas from Honduras and Costa Rica, nuts from
Panama, cacao from Santo Domingo. Prior to 1895 United States
trade with the Caribbean countries was so small that the figures
for the five Central American countries were published as one
item; Haiti and Santo Domingo were regarded as one trade area;
and Panama was then a part of Colombia. The following table
shows the latest available statistics as to the proportion of Caribbean foreign trade enjoyed by the United States:

[9] See pp. 131 ff.
[10] An account of the building of the canal is given in W. L. Sibert and J. W.
Stevens, *The Construction of the Panama Canal.* Its operation is described in J. B.
Bishop, *The Panama Gateway,* 1913, rev. ed. 1915; G. W. Goethals, *Government of
The Canal Zone,* 1915; and in the Annual Reports of the Governor of the Panama
Canal.

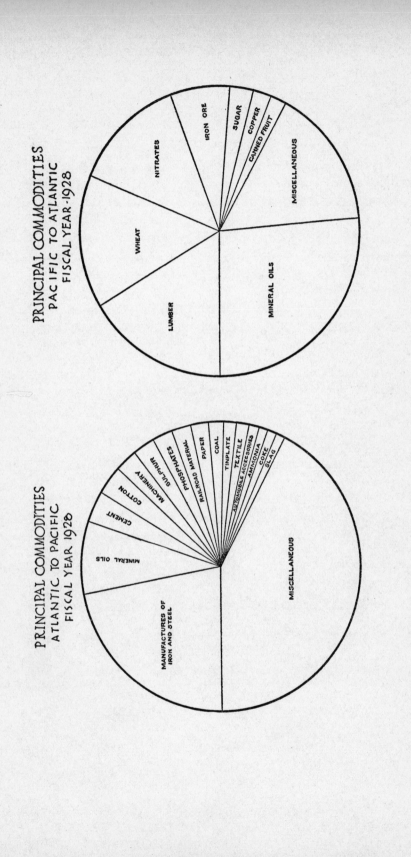

PRINCIPAL COMMODITIES
PACIFIC TO ATLANTIC
FISCAL YEAR · 1928

IRON ORE
SUGAR
COPPER
CANNED FRUIT
NITRATES
MISCELLANEOUS
WHEAT
LUMBER
MINERAL OILS

PRINCIPAL COMMODITIES
ATLANTIC TO PACIFIC
FISCAL YEAR 1928

MINERAL OILS
CEMENT
COTTON
SULPHUR
MACHINERY
PHOSPHATES
RAILROAD MATERIAL
PAPER
COAL
TINPLATE
TEXTILE
AUTOMOBILE ACCESSORIES
AMMONIA
COKE
SLAG
MANUFACTURES OF
IRON AND STEEL
MISCELLANEOUS

TABLE I

PERCENTAGE OF UNITED STATES SHARE OF THE FOREIGN TRADE OF CARIBBEAN COUNTRIES[11]

Country	Percentage of total
Cuba	71 (1927)
Haiti	43 (1926-1927)
Santo Domingo	48 (1927)
Costa Rica	41 (1927)
Guatemala	47 (1927)
Honduras	77 (1926-1927)
Nicaragua	61 (1927)
Salvador	34 (1927)
Panama	71 (1925)

In cutting a continent the Canal united two oceans complementary in their economic functions—the Atlantic, the source of machine-made goods, and the Pacific, a source of foodstuffs and raw materials.[12] It became the gateway to a new commercial world, formerly remote and difficult of access. For the major part of its history the United States had been accustomed to exchange foodstuffs and raw materials for the manufactured products of the industrial European countries; but when the canal rights were secured the United States was feeling its way into the front rank of industrial powers; the character of its foreign trade changed with the growth of its manufacturing activity, and the construction of the Panama Canal helped to direct machine-made products to new markets. The recent commodity movement from the Atlantic to the Pacific has consisted chiefly in iron and steel manufactures and mineral oils, followed in order of about equal tonnage by cement, cotton, machinery, sulphur, and phosphates; from the Pacific to the Atlantic mineral oils constitute the chief tonnage, with lumber, wheat, nitrates, and iron ore next in amounts. For the fiscal year ending June 30, 1928, the eastward flow of tonnage was about two and one-half times as large as that westward.

As in former years, either the east or west coast of North America is the origin or destination of the larger portion of cargo passing

[11] From 1926 and 1927 returns of these countries supplied by the Bureau of Foreign and Domestic Commerce, United States Department of Commerce.

[12] See graphs from Report of Governor of the Panama Canal, 1928, p. 128.

through the canal. . . . In the Atlantic-to-Pacific traffic approximately 66 per cent of the total cargo through the canal during the year originated on the east coast of North America and about 43.5 per cent was destined to the west coast of North America. In the Pacific-to-Atlantic traffic the percentages are a little greater, as about 66 per cent of the total cargo originated on the west coast of North America and approximately 56 per cent was destined to the east coast.

In the following table the volume of cargo tonnage moving over ten of the principal trade routes is shown. Approximately 84 per cent of the total cargo routed through the canal during the past year passed over these routes.[13]

CARGO SHIPMENTS THROUGH THE PANAMA CANAL DURING THE FISCAL YEAR 1928, SEGREGATED BY PRINCIPAL TRADE ROUTES

Trade routes	Tons of cargo 1928
United States, intercoastal:	
Atlantic to Pacific	2,401,872
Pacific to Atlantic	7,665,520
Total	10,067,392
Europe to west coast Canada:	
Atlantic to Pacific	574,969
Pacific to Atlantic	3,093,937
Total	3,668,906
East coast United States to west coast South America:	
Atlantic to Pacific	377,968
Pacific to Atlantic	2,840,510
Total	3,218,478
Europe to west coast South America:	
Atlantic to Pacific	787,214
Pacific to Atlantic	2,118,251
Total	2,905,465
Europe to west coast United States:	
Atlantic to Pacific	256,404
Pacific to Atlantic	2,087,682
Total	2,344,086

13 *Report* of Governor of the Panama Canal, 1928, pp. 15-16.

Trade routes	Tons of cargo 1928
East coast United States to Far East:	
Atlantic to Pacific	1,562,112
Pacific to Atlantic	504,163
Total	2,066,275
Europe to Australasia:	
Atlantic to Pacific	595,985
Pacific to Atlantic	554,678
Total	1,150,663
East coast United States to west coast Canada:	
Atlantic to Pacific	216,943
Pacific to Atlantic	514,233
Total	731,176
United States to Australasia:	
Atlantic to Pacific	580,883
Pacific to Atlantic	57,927
Total	638,810
Cristobal to west coast United States:	
Atlantic to Pacific	34,836
Pacific to Atlantic	314,217
Total	349,053
Miscellaneous routes and sailings:	
Atlantic to Pacific	920,948
Pacific to Atlantic	1,569,457
Total	2,490,405
Total traffic, all routes:	
Atlantic to Pacific	8,310,134
Pacific to Atlantic	21,320,575
Total	29,630,709

As an agent of transportation equaled only by the Suez Canal the Panama Canal has benefited the commerce of the entire world, and particularly that of the United States. Not only has it provided a short cut to markets, giving New York a 2,400 mile advantage over London in the shipping distances to the west coast of South America, but also the opening of the Canal coincided in time with the emergence of the United States as an important industrial exporter, and with the depressing effects on European commerce of the World War. The following table shows the progress since 1910-14:

TABLE II[14]

SHOWING INCREASE IN UNITED STATES TRADE WITH
THE CARIBBEAN SINCE 1910-1914

Country	Annual average	1928	Percentage of increase
Cuba	$ 185,100,000	$ 330,600,000	79
Haiti	6,700,000	14,300,000	113
Santo Domingo	8,000,000	26,200,000	227
Costa Rica	7,200,000	13,700,000	90
Guatemala	5,600,000	22,900,000	309
Honduras	5,600,000	22,000,000	293
Nicaragua	3,800,000	12,900,000	239
Salvador	3,400,000	10,800,000	218
Panama	26,300,000	40,700,000	55
Total	251,700,000	494,100,000	96
South America	121,000,000	1,050,300,000	768
Total foreign trade of the United States	$3,855,000,000	$9,220,000,000	139

Supplementing the Canal.

The growth of Panama Canal traffic has exceeded all expectations. In their supplementary report of 1901 the Isthmian Canal Commission estimated that the traffic of the proposed canal would be 11,375,000 tons in 1924; the figure was 24,411,760 tons, exclusive of 1,205,000 tons of naval traffic. Traffic has risen from 6,217,054 tons, in the calendar year 1917, to 29,458,634 tons in the fiscal year ended June 30, 1928; the figure is considered to be about 50 per cent of what the Canal can handle with its present facilities,[15] or 50,000,000 tons. But the rate of growth achieved in the first decade of operation can hardly continue; much of that traffic came from the uptake of trade from other routes. "A condition more likely to prevail over a long period of future growth," says Hans Kramer,[16] "is that the present annual increment will remain constant, on the assumption that the rate has probably reached its maximum during the past few years." On this basis Mr. Kramer controverts those who set 1940 or thereabouts as the date when the maximum capacity of present facilities will be

[14] Figures taken from *Commerce Year Book*, 1928.
[15] Annual Report of the Governor of the Panama Canal, 1928.
[16] *Proceedings of the American Society of Civil Engineers*, August, 1928, Part I, pp. 1694 ff.

reached, and by a theoretical prognosis of Panama Canal traffic, Suez Canal traffic, and world commerce finds that "the probable prospective earliest date" of such a contingency is 1970. Nevertheless the apprehension that the Panama Canal may prove inadequate for the expected increase of traffic has led to a renewed discussion of a canal route through Nicaragua. This route has

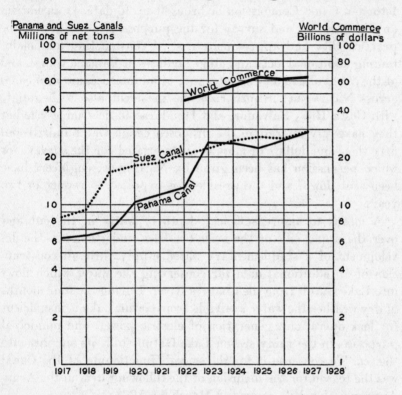

been on the carpet since 1825, and the United States secured an option in 1914.[17] The advocates of this route who think that the demand on the Panama Canal will soon outstrip its facilities also argue the advantages of possessing an alternative route and of affording certain important classes of trade a shorter haul to markets. But political rather than economic considerations keep the project alive; they are concerned mainly with giving the

[17] See pp. 181 ff.

special interest of the United States in the Caribbean two strings to its strategic bow.

From time to time the feasibility of taking advantage of the Nicaraguan option has been brought up for discussion; on March 2, 1929, President Coolidge signed a Joint Resolution dealing with canal questions, which in effect directs that the report of the Isthmian Canal Commission be brought up to date. It authorizes an investigation and survey for the purpose of ascertaining the practicability and approximate cost of constructing and maintaining additional locks and other facilities at Panama Canal, and of the construction and maintenance of an interoceanic ship canal across Nicaragua; it authorizes the president also to negotiate with Costa Rica, Salvador, and Honduras to determine whether they have any interest in the proposed canal. One hundred and fifty thousand dollars or more is appropriated for the survey, for which permission has been given by Nicaragua; engineers have been sent down, and the president is expected to report in two years.

A means to assure sufficient depth of water in the cut and over the upper sills of the locks has been undertaken in the development of a supplementary water supply through construction of an additional dam for conserving the water which flows into Lake Gatun from the Chagres River. During the four months of dry weather the water available from Gatun Lake is insufficient for lock operations, generation of electric power, and municipal purposes. In the rainy season Lake Gatun spills its surplus into the sea. To conserve it for the smooth functioning of the Canal was the reason for the inclusion of the following item in the Army Appropriation Bill, approved March 23, 1928:

$250,000 for commencing the construction of a dam across the Chagres River at Alhajuela for the storage of water for use in the maintenance and operation of the Panama Canal, together with a hydro-electric plant, roadways, and such other work as in the judgment of the Governor of the Panama Canal may be necessary, the cost in the aggregate not to exceed $12,000,000.

In addition to the development of a supplementary water supply, a plan is under discussion to construct a third flight of locks paralleling the present twin flights. Both projects, it is estimated, would increase the present capacity of the Canal by about 70 per cent.[18] The present volume of service does not justify a twenty-four hour service, nor would it be adopted except under great pressure because of the greater difficulty of lock and channel maintenance and the hazards of fog which falls about midnight and is dissipated by eight o'clock in the morning.

Caribbean Purchasing Power.

One factor in the purchasing power of Caribbean countries which makes Caribbean trade uncertain is their limited crop economy. Sugar and coffee are by far the dominant export crops but since these two crops are governed by a world price, productivity in them is not the truest index of Caribbean purchasing power. In 1920, when sugar was selling at 22 cents a pound, the national wealth of Cuba was rated at eight billion dollars; low sugar prices today would reduce this wealth to between three and four billion dollars. Under these circumstances United States commerce must base its export calculations on the variations in the world price of these commodities; for example, the decrease in United States export to southern North America in 1928 was chiefly owing to a $28,000,000 decline in Cuban takings. Good coffee and sugar prices mean an augmentation of Caribbean purchasing power, which might be translated into added sales of American automobiles, radio equipment, phonographs, electric refrigerators, and the like.

Another factor is the lack of good internal communication. Of all the Caribbean countries Cuba alone has over ten miles of highway per thousand inhabitants; only Honduras has over ten miles of railway per thousand inhabitants.[19] Producers of foodstuffs and of raw materials for manufacture, these subtropical areas must of course send their products to the great centers of consumption, manufacture, and distribution, and all of these products, with the

[18] Annual Report of the Governor of the Panama Canal, 1928.
[19] By comparison, the United States has two hundred miles of highway, and over twenty miles of railway for every thousand inhabitants.

return cargoes of manufactured goods, must be carried by sea. A considerable building of lateral railways or of motor highways is needed between the producing areas of the interior and the coast ports, especially in Nicaragua.

Transport facilities are in course of development longitudinally in Central America. Geographically contiguous, the small republics have communicated and traded with each other mostly by sea since the time when Europeans established themselves on the Isthmus and chose the sites of their capital cities in the habitable western region. Few railways and fewer motor roads connect one country with another because of the handicaps of trackless forest, dense jungle, a mountainous terrain, and torrential rains. A new air mail route which brings New York within nine days of Santiago, Chile, is an important step in bringing the Caribbean countries in closer contact with world markets. The United States is also interested in Panaman air development, inasmuch as aircraft flying to and from Panama City must cross the Canal Zone or use the terminals of the Canal. This contingency was not provided for in the agreements between the United States and Panama, and recent exchanges on this subject have still to lead to understanding. In 1926 the Kellogg-Alfara commercial treaty was negotiated, providing for the control and operation of aircraft and radio communication, but was summarily rejected by the national assembly of Panama with a rider requesting further negotiations. No action has yet been taken on this request, but on February 18, 1929, an executive order was issued establishing regulations for foreign aircraft flying over the Zone. The first foreign commercial airplane to enter the Zone under these regulations was a Scadta mono-amphibian which on March 25, 1929, flew the 480 miles from Barranquilla to Cristobal in six hours and thirty minutes; its arrival marks the termination of more than two years' petitioning by Scadta for permission to land in the Canal Zone. An extended service to Colon depends upon the outcome of the negotiations between Panama and Washington.

A third factor is the low standard of living. Of all the Caribbean countries, the scale of living is probably the lowest in Haiti, where field labor is paid from 20 cents to 30 cents a day. In the last twenty-five years the scale has risen about 300 per cent in the Caribbean countries, the greatest increase being in Cuba and Porto Rico, where foreign investments are largest. In Haiti foreign investments are comparatively small, labor is inefficient, and opportunity for work is scarce. The scale of day wages of field laborers is about as follows: Cuba, $3.00, Porto Rico, $1.50, Nicaragua, 50 cents (70 cents on the Atlantic coast), Santo Domingo, 60 cents, and Costa Rica, 50 cents.

Spread of Capital.

Selling more commodities to Santo Domingo, Haiti, Salvador, Nicaragua, Panama, and Costa Rica than those countries pay for in kind, the United States enjoys a so-called favorable balance of trade. Payment may be made by tourists' expenditures, notably in Cuba, or through triangular settlements; in paying for its surplus imports from the United States, Santo Domingo may export sugar to Germany, and Germany may export potash to the United States, thereby creating the dollar exchange wherewith the Dominicans may pay the United States.

From the two tables of trade[20] and investments[21] may be gathered the ratio of both activities to the total world trade and investment of the United States. The trade represents but 5 per cent of the total foreign trade of the United States whereas the loans represent 12 per cent of the volume of total foreign investments. The export industries of these republics include many American as well as native concerns. For many years the United States has been engaged in exporting industries as well as goods; in no other region is this so evident as in Cuba, where Americans control two-thirds of the sugar exportations.

To a substantial extent Caribbean trade has prospered because of development schemes initiated by United States investment enterprise. A considerable part of the exports to Central America is made up of merchandise shipped by United States mining, petroleum, meat-packing, or fruit companies to their foreign establishments; not truly indicative of the buying power of the Dominicans themselves, for example, is the importation of sugar

[20] See p. 284.   [21] See p. 291.

machinery by the Dominican sugar plantations, for 85 per cent of the Dominican sugar output is controlled by foreign capital. Yet the operations of concerns like the United Fruit Company are opening up territory, providing steamship and railroad facilities, increasing government revenues and the buying power of native labor; and such enterprises, entailing a considerable investment in machinery and in special transportation equipment for the production of profits on capital employed, are steadily adding to Central American buying power. The result is that a tariff on tropical foodstuffs which aims at protecting American agricultural production at home is bound to damage considerably other American industries located abroad.

The tariff policy of the United States also makes for trade uncertainty. Of recent years a protective tariff has hampered the development of reciprocal Caribbean trade. Cuban exports to the United States enjoy a preferential tariff, which, however, works out at over 100 per cent on an *ad valorem* basis under the Tariff Act of 1922. Formerly the United States took the greater part of the Dominican and Haitian sugar output which in 1920 made up 14 per cent of United States sugar consumption; in 1928 the proportion had dropped to 1 per cent. Dominican and Haitian sugar is finding new markets in Europe and the exportation is involving a return flow of European manufactures to Santo Domingo and Haiti.

On this point an experienced observer says:

The United States protective tariff has constituted necessarily a material obstacle to the effective development of the natural resources of many of the American Republics. . . . This obstacle is the chief and greatest hindrance to the rapid development of real prosperity in the smaller republics of the continent, and the removal of this obstacle would do infinitely more to promote the creation of stable government in those republics where the United States has frequently felt itself called upon to exercise its police power, than all the myriad discourses which have been declaimed by American statesmen emphasizing the benefits conferred upon those nations by the Monroe Doctrine.[22]

[22] Sumner Welles, *Naboth's Vineyard,* p. 930.

An estimate of 1912 investments indicates that from that time to the present there has been a sixfold increase in United States capital invested in the Caribbean, exclusive of the indebtedness of governments. The huge advance of United States trade with Latin America has synchronized with an equally huge advance in loans. But the investment figures for the Caribbean countries are not so impressive as those for South America, though the rate of increase since the pre-war period is larger than that of total United States foreign investments. The figures of the United States Department of Commerce show that United States Caribbean investments in 1928 were:

TABLE III

Country	United States investments
Cuba	$1,435,000,000
Haiti	25,000,000
Santo Domingo	35,000,000
Costa Rica	40,000,000
Guatemala	60,000,000
Honduras	55,000,000
Nicaragua	17,000,000
Salvador	30,000,000
Panama	40,000,000
Total	$1,737,000,000

Many people in the Caribbean feel toward United States capital somewhat as the spokesmen for the farming and debtor class in the United States itself purported to feel toward the British bondholders a generation after industrial enterprises and state legislatures had done all they could to attract British capital; economic invitation was followed by political denunciation.[23] The inequality of the relationship, the overwhelming economic dominance of the United States, produces a debtor-patriot complex in the Carib-

[23] In the Caribbean this attitude has more of a basis than has the normal discontent of a large debtor class, for the early development of resources in the Caribbean, like most early investments in undeveloped countries, was largely on a basis of special concessions and privileges to foreign capital by governments which promised protection, or by insurgents who offered better terms on condition of support for revolution; the aid thus afforded to partisanship made foreign capital suspect. Foreign capital has latterly shown a tendency to hold aloof from factional strife, depending rather upon its inherent strength *vis-à-vis* local governments.

bean which is intensified by its helplessness; the decline of European capital available for export, the enormous increase of United States wealth, the proximity of the United States, and to some extent the pressure of its policies, combine to endow it with the functions of sole money lender and general guardian of the peace. From one unequal to another this

importation of capital . . . sets up all sorts of complex reactions. It affects the social life, it arouses jealousies and fears, it invokes the idea of aggression and deep laid territorial designs, it lends itself to real exploitation and the sense of wrong that follows exploitation even among primitive people.[24]

All countries in their economic youth turn to foreign capital for the initial stages of their development. Eventually, given good fortune, they may develop the resources and the qualities which will enable them to win back the foreign-owned enterprises. But the parallelism with the United States in its pioneer phase is incomplete. For the most part British capital was loaned to the states of the United States or to enterprises in the South and Middle West; the British were not stockholders absorbing profits; they took only interest, and their debts could be paid. In the Caribbean United States nationals own the equities in banana, sugar, and tobacco properties; they are stockholders *in perpetuum* and consequently cannot be paid off. Trained executives from the United States furnish practically all the management, and engineers and other technicians fill the superior positions. Except with their own consent there is no way of putting an end to their presence in the countries whose natural resources they develop and whose inhabitants furnish them with labor. Although the enterprises are economically beneficial to the natives as well as to the foreign enterprisers, settlers who would become citizens would do more to establish the country economically, socially, and politically; the United States itself, the Argentine, Uruguay, Chile, and southern Brazil have illustrated the benefits of European settlement.

This tidal flow of capital across national boundaries is the inter-

---

[24] Isaiah Bowman, *The New World,* 4th ed., p. 716.

national phase of a universal phenomenon. Wherever capital on a substantial scale comes in from outside, it introduces a new industrial order which destroys the old adjustment between man and work. Its regional effect may be observed in the United States itself, in those parts of northern New England, for example, where water-power control has passed to absentee owners, and where "chain-stores" are displacing the country merchant. The new element in the modern era is the enormous expansion of capital across national boundaries and the international consequences of that process. All parts of the globe are being drawn into the ambit of an industrialized and internationally organized society.

In the case of an undeveloped country contact with an industrial society has complicated effects. Imported manufactures are cheaper and often more serviceable than handmade goods, and native crafts languish and disappear. The foreign trader or storekeeper knows how to create new wants which he brings goods to satisfy. As the subsistence basis of the society slowly passes to a cash crop economy, the foreigner sees the weakness, economically speaking, in small-scale peasant proprietorship, and the possibility of increasing productiveness through the use of machinery, technical improvements, large-scale production, irrigation, expert management and experienced methods of marketing, and capital comes in to further these economic gains. In the new processes the natives play a passive share; the small local group of social and political *élite* seldom have the capacity or training for management, and the native share is mainly that of unskilled labor. The self-contained community, with its own *mores* and its own social hierarchy, gradually merges into a larger world economy which controls its destinies. The Sandwich Islands of yesterday, the Kenya in the making, may serve as examples.

"Dollar Diplomacy."

Since the days when the Caribbean entered into strategic calculation, United States policy has been motivated by a desire to establish the internal stability of the Caribbean states; at the same time the giving of counsel or assistance to this end naturally created an expectation that the assisted state would bring its policy into harmony with that of the benefactor. The growth of a direct and permanent economic interest by United States nationals in the domestic affairs of the Caribbean republics intensified the feeling that to protect that interest, without annexation, United States finance must build new bridges of stability and relationship.

The State Department declared in 1909 that it had for some years sought to interest United States capital in the refunding of the Honduran debt, "but with the rich opportunities of domestic investment there had never seemed to be much hope that American capital would flow into this channel."[25] The year of this memorandum began the era of so-called Dollar Diplomacy ushered in by Secretary Knox. Loans were needed primarily to relieve the Caribbean from its financial bonds to Europe, and these were made, for example, to Cuba, Nicaragua, Haiti, Santo Domingo, and Honduras by American bankers, on the initiative, and in some cases, at the direct request, of the State Department. In some instances the temporary suspension or limitation of a specified sovereign right was involved, most conspicuously in the operation of customs services during the life of a contract or debt. President Taft rationalized the development of this policy as follows:

The diplomacy of the present administration has sought to respond to modern ideas of commercial intercourse. This policy has been characterized as substituting dollars for bullets. It is one that appeals alike to idealistic humanitarian sentiments, to the dictates of sound policy and strategy, and to legitimate commercial aims. It is an effort frankly directed to the increase of American trade upon the axiomatic principle that the Government of the United States shall extend all proper support to every legitimate and beneficial American enterprise abroad.[26]

This exportation of capital has been helped by United States supervision in the interests of political and fiscal stability. In Salvador, for example, customs are collected by an American appointed by an American banking house with State Department approval, and in the case of Cuba capital is safeguarded by the

25 *For. Rel.*, 1912, p. 551.
26 Annual Message to Congress, December 3, 1912.

debt-control clause of the "Platt Amendment." Such guarantees have reduced the interest rates for Central American credit in some cases by 50 per cent.

The inception of Dollar Diplomacy aroused criticism that banking assistance to governments was part of a program to exploit the needy Caribbean republics in the interest of United States capitalists. The charge was misdirected, for the bankers' profits have not been usurious, and it ignores the beneficial effect of such bankers' loans upon the finances of the borrowing state; in fact, the supervision of customs, insisted upon as a condition of many loans, has enormously increased the receipts, and the improved credit, often accompanied by a more honest and productive expenditure has come increasingly to be associated with political stability and Caribbean peace. It is obvious, nevertheless, that Dollar Diplomacy strengthens the influence of the dominant country in which political and financial control are thus unified.

Aspects of Intervention.

The use of armed forces by the United States in the Caribbean, the ultimate form of control of local destiny by a superior power, has had a number of phases.

Under an earlier interpretation of the United States Constitution armed forces could not be employed on an expeditionary scale without legislative sanction. In 1857 Secretary of State Cass said, referring to a proposal for a marine expedition to China:

Our naval officers have the right—it is their duty, indeed—to employ the forces under their command . . . for the protection of the persons and property of our citizens when exposed to acts of lawless outrage, and this they have done both in China and elsewhere. But military expeditions into Chinese territory cannot be undertaken without the authority of the National Legislature.[27]

This view no longer obtains. In the exigencies of the new era in the Caribbean and the Pacific, and under the vigorous leadership of President Roosevelt as commander-in-chief, the extent to which armed forces shall be used has become a matter of executive policy.

[27] Moore, *Digest of International Law*, VII, 164.

This question of extent is of prime consequence in international law and international relations. The controversy over the use of armed force in the Caribbean generally employs question-begging words for attack or defense of policy. Hostile critics will call an act an "intervention," because, in the special sense, that word connotes acts of interference in the affairs of another state which violate its independence or disregard its sovereignty. Defenders of administration policy will call the same act an "interposition" in order to establish it as an act of protection against an emergency (such as a local riot) which manifests no intention to disregard the sovereignty of the local government. The verbal aspect of the controversy arises over an attempt to identify international law with the moral code appropriate to varying situations, but there is in fact no such identity.

"The difference between intervention and interposition is most clearly drawn in the principles which have governed and the practice which has been followed by this country," said the solicitor of the State Department in 1912 in a memorandum,

for while it has been the studied policy most rigidly adhered to . . . to refrain from interfering in purely political affairs of other countries . . . yet no nation, it would seem has with more frequency than this government used its military forces for the purpose of occupying temporarily parts of foreign countries in order to secure adequate safety and protection for its citizens and their property.[28]

Prior to 1898 the United States landed armed forces on soil of what are now Caribbean republics on sixteen or more occasions to protect its citizens and their property.[29] In the early days these activities were mainly reprisals against pirates who interfered with shipping; but with the new emphasis on canal strategy and with the modification in American economic direction in the closing years of the nineteenth century, the conception of United States interests broadened, and the conditions inviting the use of armed forces in the Caribbean became kaleidoscopic in variety.

[28] Reuben Clark, *Right to Protect Citizens in Foreign Countries by Landing Forces*, Rev. Ed., 1912, p. 30.
[29] These instances exclude landings in Mexico, or skirmishes with pirates on the water which led to chase on land.

Since the Spanish War, which may be regarded as the prototype of all later interventions, the reports of the Secretary of the Navy record twenty-three instances in which armed United States forces, varying in size from a squad to five or six thousand marines and bluejackets, have been landed in various Caribbean countries.

While various reasons have been offered in support of these interventions, the aim in each case, as shown by the course of events, has been the reëstablishment of law and order, and the organization of a stable government. To supplement the use of marines as landing forces, a naval squadron, known as the Caribbean Squadron, was assigned in 1908 to permanent service in the Caribbean with headquarters at Panama. In 1921 this squadron was reorganized into the Special Service Squadron "the special mission of which," according to the Secretary of the Navy, "is . . . to promote friendly relations and to contribute to the growth of a better understanding in all respects between the United States and the other Republics of the Western Hemisphere."[30] Under this eirenic formula the squadron, by producing what is commonly called "a moral effect," combines the functions of a general guardian of the peace with those of a watchman looking after the security of invested capital.

In some instances of "preventive intervention" forces have been landed before any fighting has taken place, or before United States citizens have suffered or even been seriously threatened with injury. In a few cases armed forces have been used to aid United States officials in the collection of the customs revenues of various Caribbean republics or in the supervision of their finances; strategic interests have influenced a number of interventions, and possibly some cases of interposition. In some of the longer interventions, all since the acquisition of the Panama Canal Zone, there has been an interplay of various factors in combination with a general interest in orderly and efficient government and economic development.

No matter how well intentioned, however, an alien self-appointed guardian cannot escape suspicion and misunderstanding, and critics of United States policy in the Caribbean center their

[30] *Report* of the Secretary of the Navy, 1921, p. 8.

attack on the use of armed force. During the 1928 Pan American Conference at Havana the question was precipitated by a resolution offered by Salvador in the plenary session of February 18: "no State has the right to intervene in the internal affairs of another." This resolution came as a result of the recommendation of a subcommittee, to which the question of intervention had been referred, that its consideration be deferred to the next conference. In the committee thirteen states favored the principle of complete non-intervention. The Argentine representative stated the opinion of those who favored immediate action on the question of intervention:

Intervention—diplomatic or armed, permanent or temporary—is an attempt against the independence of nations, and cannot be justified on the plea of duty of protecting the interests of citizens. For the weaker nations cannot exercise such a right when their citizens suffer damage during convulsions in strong states.[31]

The delegate from Salvador expressed the general desire of the Latin American states for some joint, legal means of deciding questions of intervention.

The right of intervention is the right of might. It is the strong who intervene in the internal affairs of a small country. Legal means should first be established of ascertaining the facts; a decision should then be given, after which the weak nation should be made to execute its duty.[32]

In reply Mr. Hughes unequivocally asserted the right of the United States to decide for itself when the internal affairs of the small republics become sufficiently disturbed to warrant intervention. "The difficulty," he said,

if there is any, in any one of the American Republics is not of any external aggression. It is an internal difficulty. . . . I am speaking of the occasions where government itself is unable to function for a time because of difficulties which confront it and which it is impossible for it to surmount. It is the principle of international law that in such a

[31] *Foreign Policy Association Information Service*, Vol. IV, Apr. 27, 1928, p. 68.
[32] *Ibid.*, p. 70.

case a government is fully justified in taking action . . . for the purpose of protecting the lives and property of its nationals.[33]

The conference postponed consideration of intervention to the seventh conference which is scheduled to meet in 1932.

Instances of emergency use of force in the Caribbean to protect lives or property of United States or other nationals have occurred; entry is sometimes to be supported on that score. But the development of United States Caribbean policy has not rested upon international law; continued occupation in order to civilize a people, to stabilize their governments and make their outbreaks of violence less likely in the future, in short, the making of a Pax Americana for the region, has to do with expedient statecraft rather than with law. A tutelage, which for the time being suspends or diminishes the independence of a sovereign state in order to educate it to a greater sense of its political responsibilities, is based upon policy and not upon technical legal right.[34] The overwhelming economic difference between the United States (not as a political entity, but as an aggregate of economic power and energy) and the small republics into which Americans have poured some of their surplus of capital and of managerial enterprise puts a tremendous strain upon the theory of the political equality of states on which so many of the principles of international law are based. United States citizens, corporations, and capital are gaining an essential position in the economic life of those countries, and the United States feels a waxing interest in the political stability of countries whose standards are not identical with its own.

The Monroe Doctrine.

The instances of the more forcible exercise of United States Caribbean policy are not infrequently referred to the Monroe Doctrine. On this support for the major lines of Caribbean activity, apprehension is created in the minds of all Latin Americans that the Doctrine, being applicable to the whole western hemi-

[33] From the text of the final revised form given out by the Department of State; original speech in *New York Times*, Feb. 19, 1928.

[34] A note is attached to this chapter whose purpose is to outline the principles of international law relating to intervention.

sphere, warrants the United States in taking similar action throughout the continent. If the Monroe Doctrine extends to all the Americas, how can the syllogistic conclusion be avoided that the Caribbean activities can be extended to any South American country? Latin Americans, logically minded, inevitably ask the question.

The Monroe Doctrine, it is true, can be invoked to withdraw these republics from the field of contention or ambition of other great powers, and the Doctrine has been used to protect them also when European powers have pressed claims, governmental and individual, against them. The corollary of this has been that when the claim of a European country has had a reasonable basis, the United States, in denying that country its international right to exercise pressure for the satisfaction of its claim, has felt obliged itself to take action that will produce an equivalent effect. As a result, Europe, while deferring to the privileged position of the United States, looks to it for action whenever protection of European interests is desired. This consequence of the Monroe Doctrine falls in with the Caribbean policy of the United States, but the steps taken under special conditions in consequence of the adoption of a doctrine do not necessarily form part of the doctrine itself. Mr. Hughes has emphatically presented this idea:

Confusion has been caused by what appears to be a prevalent notion that the Monroe Doctrine is the justification or excuse for every action that we take in relation to Latin America. We have other policies; they should be explained, criticized or defended upon their merits; they should neither gain nor lose by confounding them with the Monroe Doctrine. For example, we have a definite policy of protecting the Panama Canal. We deem it to be essential to our national safety to hold the control of the Canal and we could not yield to any foreign power the maintaining of any position which would interfere with our right adequately to protect the Canal or would menace its approaches or the freedom of our communications. This applies just as well to American powers as to non-American powers. We have the right to protect American lives and property when endangered in circumstances and areas where governments have ceased properly to function, and this principle is applied although there may be no prospect of non-American interference and no occasion for applying the Monroe Doctrine. We recognize that other States have a similar right. It is true that our interposition in such cases may have the actual and intended effect of avoiding the interposition of non-American powers and the consequent activities and developments at which the Monroe Doctrine was aimed, but our own right to protect our nationals is quite distinct from the Monroe Doctrine.[35]

Specific Instruments of General Policy.

Recognition. Diplomatic recognition has been used by the United States in its twentieth-century dealings with the Caribbean nations as an instrument to discourage revolutions, and to coerce governments to fulfil their obligations to the United States or its citizens; experience has shown that recognition by the United States is essential to the continued existence of a government in the Caribbean region.

The traditional United States policy in the matter of recognition was expressed by Henry Clay in 1818: "Whatever form of government any society of people adopts, whomever they acknowledge as their sovereign, we consider that government . . . as the one to be recognized . . . so far as we are concerned the sovereign *de facto* is the sovereign *de jure*."[36]

The first break in this *de facto* policy came under Secretary Seward in 1861 when a reconciliation of that policy with the anti-secession principle would have been awkward: Seward adopted a policy similar to the one now in operation in respect of the Caribbean. "The policy of the United States," he said, "is settled upon the principle that revolutions in republican states ought not to be accepted until the people have adopted them by organic law."[37]

The *de facto* policy, readopted after the Civil War, lasted until Spanish-American War acquisitions made the United States acutely conscious of the problems arising from Caribbean "revolutions." Frequently recurring revolutions, which ordinarily involved a shift of dictators but not a change in principles thereafter were viewed in the light of the growing conservatism of

---

[35] Charles E. Hughes, *Our Relations to the Nations of the Western Hemisphere*, pp. 18-19.
[36] *Annals of Cong.*, Fifteenth Cong., First Sess., II, 1468.
[37] *For. Rel.*, 1866, II, 630.

modern intricate and highly organized economy. The basis for the new principle of recognition was phrased by President Coolidge in these terms:

Toward the government of countries which we have recognized this side of the Panama Canal, we feel a moral responsibility that does not attach to other nations. We wish them to feel that our recognition is of real value to them and that they can count on such support as we can lawfully give them when they are beset with difficulties. We have undertaken to discourage revolutions within that area and to encourage settlement of political differences by the peaceful methods of elections.[38]

The principle of this recognition policy was first explicitly accepted by the Latin Americans themselves in the following provision included in the Additional Convention to the General Treaty of Peace and Amity signed at the 1907 Central American Conference in Washington:

The Governments of the High Contracting Parties shall not recognize any other Government which may come into power in any of the five Republics as a consequence of a *coup d'état* or of a revolution against the recognized government, so long as the freely elected representatives of the people thereof, have not constitutionally reorganized the country.

In a new convention signed at the second Central American Conference at Washington in 1923, this resolution was repeated and the following clause added:

And even in such a case they obligate themselves not to acknowledge the recognition if any of the persons elected as President, Vice-President or Chief of State designate should fall under any of the following heads:

1. If he should be the leader or one of the leaders of a *coup d'état* or revolution, or through blood relationship or marriage, be an ascendant or descendant or brother of such leader or leaders.
2. If he should have been a Secretary of State or should have held some high military command during the accomplishment of the

38 *New York Times*, April 26, 1927, p. 10.

coup d'état, the revolution, or while the election was being carried on, or if he should have held this office or command within the six months preceding the *coup d'état*, revolution, or the election.

Furthermore, no man disqualified by the constitution of the state for these offices was to be "recognized." The treaty was intended to put a quietus on revolution by robbing the leaders of the fruits of victory. The United States was a party to neither of these conventions, but it fostered both conferences and approved the treaties adopted; in practice it has, with a certain degree of opportunism, adhered to the policy set down in these conventions and insisted on compliance with them.

Before extending recognition, one government may exact promises or concessions from another, and the United States has sometimes adopted this policy in the Caribbean. As early as 1904 it refused to recognize General Morales as president of Santo Domingo until his government had pledged itself to recognize all engagements entered into with the "present or preceding administrations," and similarly in Haiti. In Nicaragua in 1923 General Emiliano Chamorro was persuaded to step aside on the ground that he had commanded an army in a revolution, and in 1926 he was refused recognition because he had engineered a *coup d'état*. In recognizing the Government of Honduras in January, 1925, the State Department expressed its gratification that a constitutional government had been established which could be recognized in harmony with the treaty of 1923.

A local government may invoke the help of the United States, thinking that its assistance is necessary for political and social security, or for a loan essential to the improvement of finances or for a debt-refunding which will avert the pressure of maturing obligations; its petition may, on the contrary, have no motive except the desire of the faction in control to obtain aid against rebellious forces that more nearly represent popular wishes. The opposition, on the other hand, despairing of a free election, is prone to the device of abstention from the polls, "declining responsibility" for the consequences; in the resulting revolutionary movement it may try to provoke United States intervention by destroying a sufficient amount of foreign-owned property in the hope that a supervised election will follow which will afford a chance of defeating the party in power.

The policy of recognition on the basis of constitutionality is criticized on the ground that it puts the United States, when called upon to decide which candidates are eligible for election, in the position of interpreting the constitution of the state. In answering requests of leaders as to their eligibility, the State Department may, in a critical instance, virtually have to determine who the president of a republic shall be; this gives the appearance of favoring a faction, and embroils the United States in local politics. So also when customs are controlled, the granting or withholding of revenue to the local administration is an effective means of supporting it or of contributing to its overthrow by another political element. It is charged that the State Department cannot give sufficient consideration to the ability of the government to establish a stable *régime;* when faced with the dilemma, on the one hand instability and on the other unconstitutional disorder, the rule obliges the Department to recognize a weak administration, or to step in and itself establish a government.

It is further said that the policy puts the United States in the anomalous position of helping to keep oppressive governments in power; by discouraging revolution the present recognition policy gives greater security of tenure to corruption and forbids the friends of reform to hope, for the difficulty of having free and fair elections in the Caribbean makes revolution almost the only effective way of changing administrations. The charge is made that the United States prefers its own interest in stable government to the relief of Nicaraguans or Dominicans from oppression by process of revolution. A final ground of opposition to the policy is that by suppressing discontent it renders revolutions more violent when they do occur, and then robs them of their effectiveness by disqualifying the real leaders of the people for high office.

These are formidable criticisms, but there are countervailing arguments. The Central American countries themselves adopted the policy in a sincere effort to replace disorder and revolution by orderly processes of government. Revolution, though an apparent necessity, meant too frequently, instead of an improvement in government, only a change in dictators with a new bitterness of feuds, and an accompanying increase of debts involving danger of direct foreign intervention. The decision to build the Canal rendered it imperative, in the eyes of the State Department, that in the areas adjoining the Canal Zone there should be sufficient security for life and property to avoid the possibility of European intervention. The withholding of recognition from revolutionary governments appeared to offer a means by which the United States could aid in the establishment of stability; this was preferable to intermittent intervention, which seemed the only alternative. If law and order could not be established by some such means as this, permanent operation of governmental functions in these republics by the United States seemed inevitable. To the contention that the United States is inconsistent in not applying the same rule of recognition to governments outside the Americas, the answer is that this is a regional policy adopted by the countries interested, that a uniform policy would be appropriate only to a uniform world, and that a principle of foreign policy must be adapted to the varying complications of international life.

The argument is that the Caribbean peoples can master the processes of democratic government only under conditions of peace and prosperity. Two factors are noted as having retarded the growth of republicanism. First, since native governments were too early heirs to a republican form of government copied from politically more advanced nations, their traditional concept of governmental positions as lucrative spoils, a concept to which the payment of inadequate salaries has contributed, has deprived them of sound administration. It may be said that politics and spoils are inseparable, and that in the United States ways have not thus far been found of fostering the one without promoting the other; yet in such matters differences in degree are of the utmost importance. As John Selden said in the seventeenth century: " 'Tis not juggling that is to be blamed, but much juggling, for the world cannot be governed without it." Second, constant civil war for control of the central power has undermined a foundation upon which to construct stable governments. The centralization which existed under Spanish rule, and still obtains, has not allowed opportunity for the local experience essential to the effective ordering and conduct of democratic machinery.

Orderly government can be attained in two very different situations. An oligarchy provides stable government under one set of conditions, a democracy under another. Oligarchy is strong and assured when it rules over a people rendered docile by ignorance, superstition, poverty, and the consequent traditions and habits of subservience to or reverence for authority, and when the number of persons who aspire to govern is so small that the governing organization can absorb them all; few governments are more stable than that of superstition-ridden, poverty-stricken Thibet. Oligarchy comes to an end when general education, economic opportunity, and the consciousness of national unity become so widespread that the people in the rising but imperfect consciousness of their common interests, assert the right to control their own political destinies. The conditions that are fatal to the old type of oligarchy are precisely those which are requisite for the stability of democracy.

There is an intervening period when the numbers of the ambitious and politically energetic are too great for government to absorb; their rival groups contend for mastery, and the struggle is intermitted only during an occasional dictatorship. The slow transition to a more truly democratic system takes place under the influence of rising standards of living, the spread of education, and frequent experience with the benefits of better government. In time there develops an articulate public opinion which in the reflection of national interests will rise superior to personal ambitions and factional bickerings.

The history of the Caribbean has moved along a diagonal resulting from the pull of two opposing forces. The internal urge for autonomy, accompanied by turbulence and distraction in the undisciplined uprisings that release ambitions in the name of liberty and turn the spirit of adventure into destructive channels, has been met by the insistence of foreign capital on security and order with the inevitable concomitant of dominance. Liberty and order have always been hard to reconcile save in the slow school of experience; their opposition has been peculiarly strong in the Caribbean, where the demand for order has been in the local opinion mainly associated with an alien economic control, offering its good and evil of greater comfort and economic progress together with the danger of domination and exploitation.

Embargoes. In turbulent times the manipulation of munition supplies has been frequently resorted to by the United States in the hope of restoring and maintaining local order and efficient government. As supplies of arms are more easily obtainable in the United States than in Latin America or Europe, an embargo on the shipment of arms from the United States damages the hope of revolutionary success; the hope may be irretrievably lost when the United States takes the positive step of selling government supplies to the administration combating revolution. On the other hand, a lifting of the embargo permits revolutionary forces to buy munitions freely in the United States, and is a sign of favor. A standing joint congressional resolution of March 14, 1912, authorizes the president to impose an embargo upon the shipment of war material to any country where domestic violence prevails.

By virtue of this authority the president imposed an embargo on the shipment of arms to Santo Domingo in 1905, to Mexico in 1912, 1915, 1919, and 1924, to Cuba in 1924, and to Nicaragua in 1926. When President Wilson desired the overthrow of the Huerta government, he lifted the arms embargo. In 1917 the United States sold arms to the Cuban Government threatened with revolution, to the Obregon government in Mexico during the Huerta revolt of 1924, to the Diaz government in Nicaragua during the Sacasa revolt in 1927, and to the Gil government in Mexico in 1929. The coöperation of other American states in the application of this policy makes for international harmony and domestic order; during the Nicaraguan revolution of 1926-27 the State Department gained the agreement of Costa Rica, Honduras, Salvador, and Guatemala to a general arms embargo against Nicaragua.

The difficulty of decision in these cases is inescapable, and each must be judged on its own merits. As Mr. Hughes has said:[39]

[39] C. E. Hughes, *Our Relations to the Nations of the Western Hemisphere*, 1928, p. 35.

"These questions are delicate, and their determination involves the choices which all, even governments, must make between good and evil in a world of moral decisions."

Conciliation, Mediation, and Arbitration.

In promoting stability and tranquillity the susceptibilities of Latin American countries can be conciliated by using the collaboration of other neighbor-states. In 1906, when Guatemala was at war with Honduras and Salvador, and all Central America seemed likely to become embroiled, President Roosevelt, taking the advice of President Diaz of Mexico, arranged, on board the cruiser *Marblehead*, a successful peace conference which was expanded the next year into a general Central American Conference under their joint auspices. This precedent was followed in South America in 1910 when Ecuador and Peru were on the brink of war over a boundary dispute; President Taft and Secretary Knox invoked the coöperation of the Argentine Republic and Brazil in a "tripartite offer of mediation."

This collaboration with other Latin American states has at times saved the United States from the imputation of pursuing a selfish policy. Besides giving to a decision the appearance of a mandate from the American states, it affords reasonable assurance of the employment of the principles upon which Mr. Root has laid stress:

The great state ought to be especially considerate in the assertion and maintenance of its position; ought always to base its acts not upon a superiority of force but upon reason and law; and ought to exert no rights against a smaller state because of its weakness which it would not exert against a great state notwithstanding its power.[40]

The policy does not have to be confirmed by an anticipatory engagement to coöperate; it can be developed experimentally and pragmatically.

Arbitration treaties for the settlement of government disputes, as distinguished from arbitration of individual claims, have been approved in principle by all the American republics. The first

[40] *For. Rel.*, 1915, p. 694.

general treaty of this nature was signed at the First Pan American Conference in 1890, but died for want of ratification. In 1908-1909 Mr. Root negotiated arbitration treaties with Costa Rica, Haiti, and Salvador; by 1928 all but the treaty with Haiti had lapsed. These treaties excepted from arbitration all questions involving "vital interests, the independence, or the honor of the two contracting states." Bryan conciliation treaties were negotiated with Costa Rica, Guatemala, and Honduras in 1913-1914 providing that all questions "of every nature whatsoever" should be submitted to a permanent Commission of Inquiry. All were in force in 1928, but the permanent commissions are nonexistent; this type of treaty is valueless unless the commissions are kept *in esse*.

A conciliation convention, known as the Gondra Convention, was signed at the Fifth Pan American Conference in 1923; of the countries concerned in this chapter the United States, Cuba, Guatemala, and Haiti ratified it. Covering all kinds of disputes it provided for the submission to an inquiry commission of all controversies which could not be settled through diplomatic channels or submitted to arbitration. Two permanent commissions, consisting of the three American diplomatic agents longest accredited at Washington and Montevideo respectively, were set up to look after the machinery for the appointment of an inquiry commission. The Gondra Convention has since been supplemented and strengthened by a new conciliation convention signed at the International Conference of American States on Conciliation and Arbitration held at Washington in 1928-1929. Much wider in scope than the previous Convention, it gives the two diplomatic committees, the one at Washington and the other at Montevideo, power to convene commissions of conciliation when the nations concerned refuse to act, thus making the conciliation procedure compulsory. This convention was ratified by the United States March 29, 1929, and on July 15, 1929, by Venezuela.

A general arbitration treaty, signed at this conference, also marked an advance over all previous treaties signed by the United States. It makes compulsory the arbitration of justiciable disputes, and defines their scope. Two exceptions to the treaty are disputes of a domestic nature, "not controlled by international law," and those involving the interests of third parties. This treaty includes the broadest arbitral commitments ever made by the United States, which signed without reservation; thirteen of the Latin American republics affixed reservations before signing. Up to July 1, 1929, only the legislatures of Guatemala and Santo Domingo had approved the treaty; it is pending in the United States Senate. The other notable effort in the interest of arbitration was the organization of the Central American Court of Justice.[41]

The arbitration of pecuniary claims is relatively simple, and the United States has been foremost in its advocacy and practice. The claims of injured foreigners, especially of United States nationals, against the revolution-ridden countries of the Caribbean have been numerous and large. The Second Pan American Conference took up this question and a convention was signed providing that "the High Contracting Parties agree to submit to arbitration all claims for pecuniary loss or damage . . . which cannot be adjusted through diplomatic channels." This convention was extended to 1912 at the Third Conference, and in 1910 a new convention with similar provisions was drawn up to remain in force indefinitely. The United States has ratified all these conventions. Another indication of its attitude toward the arbitration of debts, as well as of pecuniary claims, is furnished by the adoption at the Second Hague Conference, largely upon United States initiative, of the Porter Convention Limiting the Employment of Force in the Recovery of Contract Debts. This Convention substituted arbitration for forcible collection save in cases where the debtor state blocks arbitration processes.

The chief defect of the present system is that the settlement in each case must be taken care of by a claims commission which can be organized only upon the negotiation of a special agreement. As a result of tendencies to procrastinate, such commissions are organized only every twenty or thirty years; meanwhile accumulating claims serve as a constant source of irritation in the relations of governments because of the claimants' pressure for ag-

41 See p. 264.

gressive action. Interest charges pile up until they exceed the original claim; and then if the interest has to be disallowed because the burden is too heavy the result is unfair to honest claimants.

A study of the awards allowed by these claims commissions demonstrates their usefulness, and points to the importance of having such claims submitted to judicial scrutiny. Some kind of a permanent claims commission, to which such claims could be submitted for settlement as they arose, would expedite justice to individuals and promote harmony in Caribbean relations.

Caribbean governments have usually found it necessary to borrow money for the payment of such awards. Since 1904 the United States has exercised varying degrees of control over loans of this kind. In practically all cases it has insisted as a prerequisite to its approval of the loan that the proceeds be applied first to the liquidation of outstanding debts and claims. In the Bryan-Chamorro treaty, for example, Nicaragua was required to promise not to pay out any of the $3,000,000 it was to receive for the canal rights except on approval of the United States Secretary of State; in fact, $2,163,821.86 was paid by the United States direct to Nicaraguan creditors. The approval of a $17,000,000 loan to Santo Domingo in 1907 and of a $30,000,000 loan to Haiti in 1916 was conditioned upon a promise to pay all categories of outstanding indebtedness before any of the proceeds could be devoted to public improvements.

Problems of Administration.

For the most part, United States official activity in the Caribbean has been motivated by canal strategy; for the rest, its interventions have been a consequence of the economic enterprise of American citizens as well as of other foreigners rather than hunger for more territory to people or to govern. Each intervention has had an emergency as its basis, and has been embarked upon with the double intention of restoring order and of assisting the natives to set up an efficient government on democratic principles. That these are disparate aims and might require wholly different methods, and that rule by electoral majority is a form of government in which many of the Caribbean countries are as yet inexperienced, have not been clearly taken into account in the United States.

Each occupation, except perhaps that of Haiti, has been expected to be of short duration. In view of official insistence on the temporary nature of United States interventions, neither Congress nor the executive has felt charged to organize a system of administration that would provide unified policy and administrative technique, and bring the advantage of controlled experiment and coördinated and analyzed experiences. Opportunism must therefore bear the blame for such ineptitudes of administration as there have been, for the inexpertness and want of finesse of some of the men first sent out, their ignorance of French or Spanish, of local traditions and customs, and of the tempo and philosophy of Hispanic American life. If a continuing overlordship is to be exercised in the Caribbean, not only efficiency in the plan of action but a policy conducive to lasting quality requires the organization of an administrative department, the recruiting of a personnel in sufficient force to meet all requirements, a careful and discriminating choice of the qualities essential in administrators, with emphasis on civilian training for posts of civil administration, a considerable permanency of tenure of office and of service, and promotion dependent on achievement. Such a department would have its own civil service school with practice in French and Spanish, and, *mutatis mutandis*, the other features of British training for colonial administration.[42]

Because intervention has been in each instance an emergency undertaking, and because in some cases it was entered on during the World War when attention was concentrated on Europe, administrative responsibility has been distributed among different departments or bureaus at Washington. Since the Panama Canal was constructed by army engineers, the administration of the

[42] Candidates selected for colonial appointments "are required to undergo a course of instruction covering an academic year at either Oxford or Cambridge and about a month in London before taking up their appointments. The subjects comprise tropical hygiene, accounting, criminal law—evidence and procedure, tropical economic products, surveying, international law, Mohammedan law, and ethnology." *The Dominions Office and Colonial Office List*, 1929, p. 585.

Canal Zone was left with the War Department, not in connection with the Bureau of Insular Affairs, but in a bureau by itself. When the Virgin Islands were acquired from Denmark, the Navy Department took control because of the plan for a naval station on St. Thomas.[43] The supervision of the Dominican customs administration is confided to the Bureau of Insular Affairs. The High Commissioner in Haiti, with jurisdiction over the financial adviser, customs administration, supervisor of public works, sanitary adviser, and police officials, is an official under the State Department. The Nicaraguan customs administration is in the hands of the State Department.

In attempting to govern any of the Latin American peoples, United States representatives meet with difficulties, deeper rooted than those of administration. Those representatives come from a country with a unique background of colonial individualism. The inheritance of the town-meeting, of representative and parliamentary government, the independence of the judiciary, the pragmatic development of the common law, the tolerant habit of trial and error, the practice of self-help, and the instinct for organization and for collective action—all of these have gone into the structure of American political and social life. The United States Constitution established a system of checks and balances to protect the interests of the majority, and has also adopted a bill of rights and expanded it by constitutional usages on the theory that it is a higher function of government to protect the rights of the minority than to assert and enforce the will of the majority. At the same time the people of the United States display an extraordinary passion for unity in their political life: they have the Anglo-Saxon reluctance to think and to engage in theoretical discussion, the tendency to prefer skill and energy in action to ideas.

There is a sharp contrast between these social and political folkways and those of the Caribbean republics, where, in the days of Spanish supremacy and ever since, government has connoted the prescriptions of a central authority, where political struggles have consisted in large part of efforts to dominate by military force and of the attempts of the executive to appoint and so control the

---

[43] The Virgin Islanders are "stateless," Congress having taken no measures to define their status.

legislature and the judiciary, where collective action without government initiative, management, and payment of cost is rare, and where law is codified and prescribed by central authority. Among them social and political leadership is in the hands of small groups who derive their culture from Europe and have been educated at Paris or Madrid, who usually prefer the enjoyment of sophisticated ease to the spur of action, and who in their political activities are ideological and accustomed to an uncompromising clash of ideas or of interests rather than to settlement by accommodation. Phenomenal advances in invention and in the organization of industry have trained the people of the United States in a technique of mechanization which is spreading irresistibly, but whose very efficiency goes counter to many Latin American susceptibilities. The work of the American, as one Haitian critic expressed it, is too apt to appeal to the eye and too little to the heart of the Latin American.

One special difference in collective psychology attracts little attention in the United States. Puritan morality referred itself to the authority of the Scriptures and expressed itself in the terms of Old Testament theology. However much the type of morality may have altered, tradition and phraseology survive changes of practice, and it is a convention of Americans in public life to express decisions of the *haute politique* or of commercial energy in terms of religious duty, to invoke the blessings of Providence upon their practical enterprises and their political projects. Catholics, as all Latin Americans are, have no such habit and no such phraseology, and the combination of missionary and commercial interests is strange to their more realistic ways of thinking. The moral purpose of Americans in these endeavors is genuine, but their statements of high moral purpose are expressed in such association with less altruistic interests as to create in the people patronized a suspicion of hypocrisy.

When the question of war with Spain was under debate in Congress in March, 1898, Senator Thurston of Nebraska said he was not a jingo. Jingoism was dead. He believed in the doctrine of Christ. Force meant war. War meant blood. But it would be God's force, for it was humanity and liberty. It had other virtues:

War with Spain would increase the business and the earnings of every American railroad, it would increase the output of every American factory, it would stimulate every branch of industry and domestic commerce, it would greatly increase the demand for American labor, and in the end every certificate that represented a share in an American business enterprise would be worth more money than it is today.[44]

To President McKinley, in prayer as to the right disposition of the Philippines, it came "that there was nothing left for us to do but to take them all, and to educate the Filipinos, and uplift and civilize and Christianize them, and by God's grace do the very best we could by them as our fellow men for whom Christ also died."[45] The commercial interest was not mentioned in this speech to the Methodist ministers, but it was present on another occasion when he spoke of "the commercial opportunity to which American statesmanship cannot be indifferent. It is just to use every legitimate means for the enlargement of American trade."[46]

Mr. Coolidge in his inaugural address of March 4, 1925, used such conventional expressions. The legions, he said,

which she (America) sends forth are armed not with the sword but with the cross. The higher state to which she seeks the allegiance of all mankind is not of human but of divine origin. She cherishes no purpose save to merit the favors of Almighty God. . . . We extended our domain over distant islands in order to safeguard our own interests and accepted the consequent obligation to bestow opportunity and liberty upon less favored people.

There have been many such invocations; they are taken lightly at home, but their impact upon the consciousness of the peoples whose destinies they affect can scarcely be measured and has enduring psychological consequences.

Latin American inability to understand the ideas thus expressed relates to something more substantial than phraseology. The essential relation of religion to worldly prosperity was a cardinal doctrine of the Geneva Calvin. "Convinced that character is all and circumstances nothing, he (the Calvinist) sees in riches, not an

[44] *Cong. Rec.*, XXXI, 3165, March 24, 1898.
[45] C. S. Olcott, *Life of William McKinley*, 1916, p. 111.
[46] Quoted by Charles and Mary Beard, *The Rise of American Civilization*, II, 376.

object of suspicion, though like other gifts they may be abused, but the blessing which rewards the triumph of energy and will."[47] Latin Americans, although perhaps not less acquisitive or less thrifty, yet have not been trained in the association of the two motives, which as ideas they find antipathetic. The strength of their economic egotism, their appetite for gain, may be as powerful as those of Puritan and Quaker descendants; such impulses are commonplaces of every age and need no emphasis, for Anglo-Saxons, Latin Americans, and Continental Europeans possess them in full measure. The "moral" advantage of the Anglo-Saxon which the Latin does not share is "the change of standards which converts natural frailty into a resounding virtue."[48]

Critics at home and abroad have seen in the Caribbean activities of the United States the working out of a program of political imperialism. The charge cannot be refuted *in toto*, for Senator Lodge and his following carried into the twentieth century the "manifest destiny" tradition of the nineteenth, and the annexations of the Hawaiian and Philippine islands are recent events in the long pageant of history. And when a great power has weak and sometimes disorderly neighbors, the concern which it will inevitably manifest in their affairs because of the consequences to itself, the insistence that they shall conform to certain standards of behavior of its own imposition—*droit de voisinage*, the French call it—is obviously the index of an unequal relationship, even though the label "imperialism" be inappropriate. In the course of administration, moreover, it is difficult to control at all times and at all points the zeal of administrators and to keep them from adopting a proconsular attitude in the discharge of their tasks. But the spiritual and political forces set in motion by the War— the downfall of articulate imperialism, the grant of self-government to the "succession states," the adoption of the mandate principle, all approved by the political conscience of the American people though it took no part in the fulfilment of them—have frustrated any movement in the United States in the direction of political imperialism. So far as public opinion can express itself on

[47] R. H. Tawney, *Religion and the Rise of Capitalism*, p. 230.
[48] *Ibid.*, p. 247.

policy—representatively in Congress and sporadically in some direct form—it is opposed both to annexation and to direct political control of the Caribbean republics when they show even a modicum of ability to govern themselves; the State Department recognizes this attitude and executes it as the continuous policy of the United States. In each case where occupation has been undertaken, whether the management of events that culminated in occupation was sagacious or not, it was announced that occupation was to be as brief as was essential for the accomplishment of a limited purpose, and the successive withdrawals from Cuba, Nicaragua, and Santo Domingo are as much expressions of deliberate policy as are the interventions. If *Divide et Impera* is a sound motto for political expansionists, then the effort the United States makes to establish stable government in the Caribbean republic is the contrary of a tendency toward political imperialism.

Expansion there is of course, but its impulsion is economic and comes from the civilization in which we all exist; capital furnishes the resources without which no change in economic levels is possible, the producing and merchandising technique, the skill and apparatus of the industrial era. To the capitalist, indeed, as well as to the inventor civilization owes the advances in mechanized production and comfort which are the distinguishing marks of modern life. All inventive as well as economic gain needs an accumulated force to set it working; "that store must always take the shape of money, and money not hoarded but in motion."[49] The operations of capital extend over the globe, and no way has been found to protect the traditional culture or the independent economy of remote and undeveloped countries from its encounter, whether in the Sudan, or in the Mosul region or in China. In regions where the mountaineers have a confident independence or where there are ancient cultural traditions, there may be resistance to the coming of the *régime* of capital. But this is not true in the Caribbean republics; settled from Europe (save Haiti) they have always been acquainted with the uses and consequences of capital and exhibit every desire for its coming. Possessing resources in fertile lands and essential raw materials but being unable to use

[49] Brooks Adams, *Civilization and Decay*, p. 314.

them, they offer concessions for their exploitation as a means of
raising themselves to higher economic levels. The complications
in the situation arise from the fact that once alien capital has been
attracted to the work of exploitation, it demands changes in the
political and social structures for its own security, upon which the
whole new order of things—foreign and native interests alike—
has come to depend. The local right to maintain poor government, which may at times degenerate into something less than government, is incompatible with the willingness of foreign capital to
make government loans or private investments; capital could be
warned not to invest or to do so at its own risk, but the consequence would be a return to usurious loans, and to the waste and
destruction of recurrent revolutions, and that in turn would result in more usurious loans, state bankruptcy, economic disorder,
and human misery.

This is a new instance of an old process, picturesque individualism giving way to routine and the conformity required by organization. Since the beginning of the commercial era no period has
been exempt from the process. The railway displaces the stage-
coach; cottage crafts yield to the loom and the spinning jenny; the
arts of the skilled carver of cathedrals, the tapestry-weaver and the
village smith are forgotten, and even the reflective cobbler is no
more. In all such transitions some types of human beings must go
to the wall; one writer pictures Caribbean natives toiling on
wharves and selling curios to tourists instead of tilling their corn
patches. Only those types survive which are suited to the new conditions of the incessant warfare for existence.

The problem is characteristic of the spread of capital, intrastate as well as international. When the expansion is intrastate,
local politics and the mobility of population take up the shock.
When the expansion is into foreign countries, national feelings
are aroused, and economic inequality generates difficulties and
antagonisms in the political field. The relation of a great state "to
other states and races, inferior to her in civilization and political
capacity . . . is," as Lord Eustace Percy says, "in the modern
world, the very stuff and crux of foreign policy."[50] Performance

[50] *The Responsibilities of the League,* pp. 71-72.

of the task set for itself by the great state needs to be accompanied by the reflection that a relation in which the self-interested stronger party is trustee for the interests of the weaker contains the seeds of discord, and for its successful discharge requires a choice of coördinated means in administration, an elastic opportunism in procedure, and a frequent and skeptical scrutiny of the results.

NOTE ON DIPLOMATIC PROTECTION
OF LIFE AND PROPERTY

COERCIVE intervention in the Caribbean, involving the use of actual or threatened force, has often been justified by reference to a supposed rule of international law that a state may adopt any measures which it deems necessary to protect the lives and property of its nationals, when in its own judgment the state of their foreign residence fails to give them adequate protection. Indeed, Mr. Coolidge went so far as to state that "the person and property of a nation are part of the general domain of a nation, even when abroad."[1] That there is a rule of international law on the subject, that occasions for its application in the Caribbean have arisen, and that, as with most customary law, the rule undergoes evolution with changing concepts of international duty, can scarcely be questioned. That it authorizes any "preventive protection" by force which the protecting state may consider expedient or that it justifies the statement of Mr. Coolidge is more than doubtful.

As the purpose of this Note is solely an attempt to define a rule of international law, in aid of giving precision to discussion, it is important to observe that international action may be justified on the highest moral grounds without reference to the sanctions of international law. The rules of international law concerning intervention are based upon a theory of the independence of every sovereign state, and no intervention can be legal unless it be directed against a state which is guilty of an international wrong. But the theory of independent equality has no correspondence in the facts, and it is therefore "unlikely that interventions will in practice ever be limited to those for which a legal justification can be pleaded, until it is also possible for the law to restrain some of the anti-social uses which states at present make of their independence."[2] An intervention which may have no support in a principle of international law, may, nevertheless, from the moral point of view, be wholly justifiable.

[1] *New York Times*, April 26, 1927, p. 10. Address before United Press Ass'n Dinner.

[2] See J. L. Brierly, *The Law of Nations*, p. 156, *passim*.

It is a well-known principle of international law that states have exclusive jurisdiction over all persons and property within their territorial limits. When, therefore, an alien enters a state he subjects himself to local law and must abide by its rules, except so far as a definite rule of international law gives him a different status. But the practice of nations, as expressed in the acts of government officials and in the decisions of arbitral tribunals, recognizes that nations have obligations to one another to afford a certain degree of security and just treatment to the aliens and alien property in their respective territories. The measure of this security is the minimum amount of protection that is commonly afforded in practice by civilized states everywhere. The obligation to provide this minimum protection is expressly or impliedly assented to by all states on admission to the family of nations, and is independent of the extent of security actually afforded by a state to its own nationals at any given moment. If an alien is injured in his personal or property rights through the failure of a state to provide this minimum amount of protection, a liability is incurred under international law to afford redress to the state of the injured alien.

A state is of course responsible only for its own acts or omissions, not for every injury committed within its territorial jurisdiction; "the law of nations," says Eagleton, "does not make the state a guarantor of life and property." When an alien sustains an injury at the hands of an individual, the state is ordinarily not internationally liable unless there has been a failure of due diligence on the part of the state officials to prevent the injury, or a denial of justice in the courts. The latter has recently been defined as "a denial, unwarranted delay or obstruction of access to courts, gross deficiency in the administration of judicial or remedial process, failure to provide those guaranties which are generally considered indispensable to the proper administration of justice, or a manifestly unjust judgment."[3] The same principles apply in

---

[3] Article 9, Draft Convention on the Responsibility of States for Damage Done in Their Territory to the Person or Property of Foreigners, prepared by the Advisory Committee on Research in International Law, Harvard Law School, in anticipation of the first conference on the codification of international law, The Hague, 1930. *American Journal of International Law,* XXIII, Special No. (April, 1929), 173.

general to injuries to aliens resulting from mob violence, save that in clashes growing out of ill feeling toward aliens generally, or those of a particular nationality, states are sometimes held to the exercise of a greater degree of diligence to prevent injury.

In the case of injuries to aliens resulting from a wrongful act or omission of officials, a distinction has been commonly drawn between acts of higher authorities, that are in effect acts of the state itself, and acts of subordinate officials or employees. In the former case, international responsibility is generally considered to be direct and to attach immediately. It may, of course, be satisfied by adequate local redress, but in most states the acts of such authorities are not reviewable by other authorities. In the case of subordinate officials, state responsibility does not ordinarily arise unless there has been a denial of justice as described above or unless no local redress is given and the state fails to disavow the act by disciplining the official.

In the case of an injury resulting from the wrongful breach of a contractual obligation owed by a government to an alien, international responsibility does not ordinarily arise until the local remedies, if any, have been exhausted. In cases of this character, states usually confine themselves in the first instance to the exercise of "good offices" to obtain redress. Where this is unsuccessful, states are at liberty to interpose diplomatically as in the case of any other breaches of international law. States are, however, more reluctant to invoke any coercive measures to obtain redress in claims of contractual origin than in other types. In the case of claims for the recovery of contract debt, the Hague Convention of 1907 prohibits the resort to forceful measures for the settlement of such claims unless the defaulting state refuses to arbitrate.

As a general rule a state does not ordinarily incur international responsibility to make reparation until the local remedies available to an injured alien have been exhausted.[4] Until this is done, the state of the injured alien cannot usually be said to have suffered any wrong for which it can claim redress through diplomatic channels. Of course where local remedies are defective or nonexistent this rule does not apply. Likewise, if, in exhausting local reme-

[4] See Article 6 of the draft convention referred to above.

dies, the alien suffers a denial of justice as described above, an international responsibility toward the alien's state arises directly. The Latin American states have sought to strengthen the rule of exhaustion of local remedies by inserting it in their constitutions and laws in various forms. In so far as these stipulations seek to modify or enlarge the international rule, they have, of course, no validity as international law; such a modification can be achieved only through treaty agreements. Some states have agreed by treaty stipulation to limit the exercise of diplomatic protection to cases in which the local remedies have been exhausted and a denial of justice has occurred, but the United States generally refuses to enter into such treaty stipulations whenever it lacks confidence in a local judicial system.

*   *   *   *   *   *   *

Whenever an international liability has been incurred, the usual procedural methods are open to the injured state for securing redress for a violation of international law. These procedural methods may, writes Professor Borchard, be amicable or non-amicable, ranging from "diplomatic negotiations, the use of good offices, mediation, arbitration, suspension of diplomatic relations, a display of force, retorsion, reprisals, or armed intervention, to war in the full sense of the word."[5] He adds that "the methods of diplomacy are in international law as truly legal a form of procedure as any of the forms of judicial procedure known to municipal law." The great majority of international claims arising out of injuries to aliens are settled by diplomatic negotiation. Failing this, such claims are usually allowed to accumulate until there is a sufficient number to warrant the expense of establishing an arbitral tribunal.

In the case of countries which habitually maintain effective government, says Professor Borchard,

the protective function of the national government of the resident alien is usually limited to calling the attention of the local government to the performance of its international duty. The right, however, is always reserved, and in the case of less stable and well-ordered gov-

[5] Edwin M. Borchard, *The Diplomatic Protection of Citizens Abroad*, p. 439.

ernments frequently exercised, of taking more effective measures to secure to their citizens abroad a measure of fair treatment conforming to the international standard of justice.[6]

If, when a state is internationally liable, it fails to make redress and refuses to discuss or arbitrate the question, the method and extent of protection exercised by the injured state is ordinarily a question of policy and is conditioned ultimately by the relative power of the two states.

Strong states have sometimes taken the stand that extended and continued failure to afford protection gives the aggrieved nation the right under international law to extend its own protection by force within the domain of the offending state. Whatever the advisability of such a step in terms of policy, no rule of diplomatic protection in international law permits a state to violate the territorial integrity of another, where government is carrying on its functions, until the duty to make reparation has arisen and has not been discharged. In some countries of the Caribbean area unstable governmental and commercial conditions have made it irksome to apply the rules of international law *strictissimi juris*. Injuries are committed for which the local state does not provide prompt redress, and apprehensions are easily entertained that more injuries to foreigners are likely to happen. Continued periods of disorder and the relative weakness of these states thus invite the intervention of a strong neighboring state. In defending its intervention policy, spokesmen for the United States have distinguished sharply between political intervention and non-political intervention or interposition, and have officially declared that the United States is committed to a policy of non-intervention. A study of the facts of each case is necessary, however, in order to decide whether the use of coercive measures has been *legally* justified or not. Pradier-Fodéré defines intervention as follows:[7]

As to the form of the exercise of protection, it is necessary to take also into consideration, and not to confound intervention with the means of obtaining reparation for an injury and for an offense. The

[6] *Ibid.,* p. 27.

[7] *Traité de Droit International Public,* I, Sec. 406, p. 625, quoted by Offutt, *op. cit.,* p. 4.

observations, the demands for explanations, the complaints, the offers of friendly settlement and arrangement, mediation, arbitration, demands for satisfaction, retorsion of law, war—all this is not intervention. He alone intervenes who—imposing his authority on a state weaker and incapable of escaping through fear of the consequences of its resistance—is a burden upon the sovereignty of that country, suppresses its laws, acts contrary to its institutions, meddles in the administration of its justice, orders the measures which it is to take, suppresses measures taken, substitutes, in a word, his will for the effaced will of the government of that state; he intervenes also especially who does not limit himself to directing, to requiring, but who attempts by invasion, by military occupation, to impose upon the will of a country, to interfere in its internal affairs, to direct its conduct in determined ways.

Professor Borchard lists from Reuben Clark's *Memorandum on the Right to Protect Citizens in Foreign Countries by Landing Forces* the following purposes for which United States troops or marines have been landed in foreign countries:

1. For the simple protection of American citizens in disturbed localities, the activity of the troops being in the nature of police duty;
2. For the punishment of natives for the murder or injury of American citizens in semi-civilized or backward countries;
3. For the suppression of local riots, and the restoration and preservation of order;
4. For the collection of indemnities, either with or without the delivery of a previous ultimatum;
5. For the seizure of customhouses, as security for the payment of claims, and for purposes such as the maintenance of a state government, the destruction of pirates infesting certain areas, and other objects. At times the punitive operations undertaken for the protection of nationals and their interests have bordered close upon belligerent action in the full sense and would have been so considered had they been directed against stronger states.[8]

The official justification given for American intervention in Nicaragua in 1927-28 was the necessity of protecting the lives

8 Borchard, *op. cit.,* pp. 449-450.

and property of resident United States citizens and also of establishing and maintaining order in a relatively backward state. Marines were used against Sandino in order to render the country stable, and to guarantee a fair election, in order that a good government might be elected to protect American life and property. At the end of the revolution, it was said that both parties requested United States supervision of elections. What was at first an entry *in invitum* was converted by a later consent into a presence by request *ab initio*.

The chief difficulty in the matter of diplomatic protection has hitherto lain in determining exactly when an international obligation to make reparation for injury has come into being. Such phrases as "denial of justice," "minimum standard of justice," "due diligence," and "manifest injustice," are relative terms, requiring interpretation for each new case that arises. This difficulty is of course present in all systems of customary law; for example, in the application of the phrase "due process of law" in this country. The difficulty is greater in international law because of the absence of permanent judicial machinery for the interpretation of these variable terms in each case, and the fact that the parties must themselves usually act as judges of the extent of their own rights.

This difficulty has often been overcome by the signing of conventions in which the parties agree to create permanent or *ad hoc* commissions of inquiry to determine the fact of international liability when charged but not admitted. The reports of commissions of inquiry are not binding on the parties but provide an excellent means for determining the facts and delaying the use of force. An example of this type of treaty, though it has not been used, is the Gondra Treaty of 1923, concluded at the Fifth Pan-American Conference. Treaties of this nature can be useful in preparing the way for an impartial and sometimes conclusive determination of the existence of international liability in a disputed case.

More frequently states have agreed to arbitrate the question of responsibility, and sometimes have also consented in advance to abide by the impartial decision of a permanent or *ad hoc* judicial body. In the General Treaty of Inter-American Arbitration signed at Washington on January 3, 1929, the parties bind themselves (Article I) to submit to arbitration all differences of an international character (except domestic questions which "are not controlled by international Law" and questions affecting states not signatory to the treaty) arising between them "by virtue of a claim of right made by one against the other under Treaty or otherwise, which it has not been possible to adjust by diplomacy" and which involves, among other things, "(c) the existence of any fact which if established would constitute a breach of an international obligation" or "(d) the nature and extent of the reparation to be made for the breach of an international obligation." The same clauses appear in the Statute of the Permanent Court of International Justice (Article 36) and constitute for those states which have signed the "Optional Clause" a legal obligation to submit to judicial settlement all disputes involving the determination of the existence of the fact of international responsibility and the nature or extent of the reparation to be made.

The General Treaty of Inter-American Arbitration was signed by twenty American States, but thirteen countries signed with reservations and none of the signatories up to May 1, 1929, had ratified the treaty. In any difference of an international character which may arise over the fact of a breach of international duty or over the nature and extent of redress, and which cannot be diplomatically adjusted, the injured state has in this treaty voluntarily agreed not to use coercive measures and has agreed instead to abide by the decision of the arbitral tribunal.

Because of the reservations of the thirteen states, disputes may still arise over their international obligations arising out of the decisions of their judicial tribunals. Costa Rica, for example, refuses to obligate itself to arbitrate any case which has been decided by its courts. This is not only an insistence upon the conclusiveness of local redress, but is at the same time practically a refusal to admit that any denial of justice can have taken place in any case which the local courts have decided. If Costa Rica should refuse to arbitrate the question whether or not it is internationally responsible for decisions of its courts which to another state seem to constitute a denial of justice, the situation as regards Costa Rica will remain the same as if no treaty existed.

The other states making reservations are willing to arbitrate cases of denial of justice, but are insistent upon the customary rule of international law that local remedies must be exhausted before there shall be any resort to international arbitration. "Mexico makes the reservation that differences which fall within the jurisdiction of the courts shall not be the subject of the procedure established by the convention, except in the case of denial of justice, and until the decision handed down by the appropriate national authority has entered into the category of a decided question."

The Venezuelan reservation likewise insists upon the rule of local redress, admitting that a denial of justice may arise even after the local courts have taken jurisdiction.

The questions which in conformity with the Constitution and the laws of Venezuela come within the jurisdiction of its courts; and especially those relative to pecuniary claims of foreigners, are excluded from this Treaty. In these cases Arbitration will not be undertaken until, the claimant having exhausted legal resources, it appears that there has been a denial of justice.

The same insistence upon the rule of local redress with regard at least to pecuniary claims and the same conception of denial of justice appear in the Colombian, the Uruguayan, and the Ecuadorian reservations.

The Dominican Republic impliedly leaves the definition of the rule of local redress and denial of justice to international determination:

The Dominican Republic, when signing the General Treaty of Inter-American Arbitration does so in the understanding that controversies relative to questions which fall within the jurisdiction of its courts shall not be referred to arbitral jurisdiction except in accordance with the principles of international law.

The Salvadorean reservation insists upon the rule of local redress in all pecuniary claims except when there is "denial of justice or abnormal delay in its application," and international arbitration shall be resorted to only in these two cases which are "provided for by the Salvadorean Constitution and laws."

Chile refuses to accept obligatory arbitration for questions "which, falling within the exclusive national jurisdiction, the interested parties desire to withdraw from the cognizance of the established judicial authorities, except when said authorities refuse to decide with respect to any action or exception which any natural or juridic foreign person may present to them in the manner established by the laws of the country." According to Chile, then, denial of justice would be only a refusal of access to local judicial remedies.

In Article 2 of the Pact of Paris the signatory states have obligated themselves never to seek the settlement or solution of disputes or conflicts of an international character except by pacific means. The suggestion has been made that since coercive measures can hardly be described as "pacific means," the Caribbean policy of the United States must be brought within the four corners of the Pact of Paris. This suggestion leaves several factors out of consideration that would make Article 2 inapplicable to the Caribbean interventions of recent years. Those interventions, it is suggested, have not been for the sake of enforcing claims or disputes of United States nationals against the government of the territory entered. Such claims the United States has shown its willingness to settle by a mixed claims commission or by similar pacific means, given the existence of effective government in the offending state. But in case government does not function in the offending state what then? This is the situation on which intervention has frequently been based. Reference of such an action to the pacific means of settlement provided by arbitration or by the procedure of a conciliation commission under the terms of the Conciliation Conventions of 1929 could yield no result, for the reason that, *ex hypothesi*, the other side would lack an effective government to express its case.

II.

INTERNATIONAL ORGANIZATION

CHAPTER ONE

THE WORLD COURT

THE practice of the United States Government for a long
time after the Jay Treaty with Great Britain of 1793 con-
formed to the public opinion which had been developing during
the nineteenth century in favor of the settlement of international
disputes by arbitration. Experience with arbitration persuaded
the Government that this means of settling disputes between nations was more to be relied upon than force; and therefore, bearing
in mind also the practice of the Supreme Court as a tribunal before which the states of the union could submit their differences,
the United States took the lead at the Conference of The Hague
in 1899 in urging the setting up of a Permanent Court of International Justice which "would express the desires and aspirations
of this nation."[1] The members of the conference, particularly the
representatives of the great European Powers, were not ready to
follow the lead of the United States; one of the objections was
that there would be no cases before the Court. The spectacle of
an international court with no litigants would, it was believed,
harm rather than help the increasing practice of arbitration.

The conference, however, did take a step toward institutionaliz-
ing arbitration.[2] In its convention for the pacific settlement of international disputes it included a permanent court of arbitration,
which, however, fell far below the standard aimed at by the American delegation. The Court was a panel of four appointees of each
signatory Power who were competent and willing to act as arbitrators in any dispute which might be laid before them. The
signatory Powers could select from this panel the arbitrators to
sit in a particular case. Thus there were no permanent judges
and the old difficulty of selecting members for courts of arbitration, one of the serious hindrances in the way of the more general
use of the procedure, was not met. A degree of permanence was
given to the Court by the establishment of an international bureau

[1] Instructions to the International Peace Conference at The Hague, 1899, Scott,
The Hague Peace Conferences, II, 8.
[2] *Ibid.*, p. 55.

at The Hague through which communications relative to the Court and submission of arbitrations could pass and which would serve as a record office for the Court. Furthermore, the treaty contained rules for arbitral procedure which avoided a second difficulty in arbitral process, the determination in each instance of rules of procedure by which the tribunal would be governed. A state submitting a question to the Permanent Court of Arbitration knew in advance the rules of procedure which would be applied.

Mr. Root as Secretary of State urged upon the American delegation at the next Hague Conference of 1907 the creation of a Permanent Court. He declared

there can be no doubt that the principal objection to arbitration rests not upon the unwillingness of nations to submit their controversies to impartial arbitration, but upon an apprehension that the arbitrations to which they submit may not be impartial. . . . If there could be a tribunal which would pass upon questions between nations with the same impartial and impersonal judgment that the Supreme Court of the United States gives to questions arising between citizens of the different States, or between foreign citizens and the citizens of the United States, there can be no doubt that nations would be much more ready to submit their controversies to its decision than they are now to take the chances of arbitration.[3]

The American delegation succeeded in persuading the Powers to take another step forward by the adoption of a resolution approving the creation of a Judicial Arbitration Court, which was to be composed of permanent judges paid an annual salary and devoting full time to their duties. The nations agreed on the desirability of the Court as an organ of international justice, but not on the method of election of the judges. Disputes between the great and small Powers as to the relative weight of their votes prevented the organization of the Court up to the time of the World War. Prior to 1914 the United States had taken the lead in initiating plans for a world court, and it was the European states principally which had doubted the practicability of a per-

[3] Scott, *The Hague Peace Conferences,* II, 191.

manent organ of international justice. Though finally agreeing
in principle to its creation, the nations had not yet attained a sufficient appreciation of the need for the setting up of means other
than war to end disputes between nations.

Then came the World War and its aftermath. Public opinion
in Europe demanded that the governments should take steps to
prevent the recurrence of such a catastrophe, and was ready to
take the risks involved in the closer international organization of
the world for peace to gain security against the greater risks of
war. Governments and peoples agreed to a sentiment which has
never been expressed better than by Mr. Root:

Public opinion, however, cannot make itself affirmatively effective
except by the creation of institutions adapted to give it effect. Mere
verbal expressions of opinion get nowhere. . . . To get things done,
some human agency must be designated to give effect to the general
desire that they be done.[4]

In the field of political and economic action, the League of Nations and its subsidiary organizations had come to fill the need for
a human agency, and through the League a permanent court
was made possible. The negotiators at Paris did not include
the statute of a court in the Covenant, but recognized throughout the Covenant that a permanent court was a necessary part
of the world organization of the future. The Council in Article
14, was required to formulate and submit to the members of the
League for adoption "plans for the establishment of a Permanent
Court of International Justice," and at its second public meeting
on February 13, 1920, proceeded to carry out this duty. It passed
a resolution creating an advisory committee of distinguished
jurists, including Mr. Root, to draw up a plan for a court. The
committee met at The Hague on June 16, 1920, and within six
weeks was able to agree unanimously upon the draft scheme for a
Permanent Court of International Justice. The great difficulty
of devising a plan for the election of judges was solved, through
the suggestions of Mr. Root and Lord Phillimore, by providing
for their election by the Council and Assembly of the League sit-

4 *Foreign Affairs* (N. Y.), April, 1925, p. 351.

ting separately, so that the great Powers with permanent seats on the Council would have a preponderant voice in one branch of the electoral body and yet all Powers, great and small, would have a vote in the popular chamber. The candidates who obtained an absolute majority of votes in Assembly and Council would be elected; provisions were made for a joint conference in case the two bodies could not agree and for the filling of vacancies by the Court itself in the event that the two electoral bodies deadlocked. Another device kept the election of the judges as free from political considerations as possible by using the four appointees of each government to the Permanent Court of Arbitration at The Hague as a nominating body. The machinery of the League was used to solve the difficult problem of election of members and to provide the money necessary to pay the judges and the expenses of the Court.

The advisory committee took a decided position in recommending compulsory submission to the Court of all disputes of a judicial nature. The Council and Assembly adopted in the main the report of the advisory committee; its position in respect of compulsory jurisdiction was too advanced for the governments, but the Statute of the Court as recommended by the first Assembly in December, 1920, contained an optional clause which any nation could sign if it were willing to submit all its disputes of a judicial nature to the Court.

The Statute as recommended by the Assembly was submitted to the members of the League, and also to the states mentioned in the Annex to the Covenant, thus including the United States. It was at once accepted by the members of the League, and the first election of judges was held by the Council and Assembly in September, 1921.[5] The Court promptly met to formulate its rules. A question destined to be of first importance in the operation of the Court and in the matter of the adherence of the United States was dealt with in the rules. The Statute contained no mention of

[5] John Bassett Moore, the foremost international jurist in the United States, was elected one of the nine judges, but he resigned before the expiration of his term in order to devote himself to writing, and on September 8, 1928, Charles Evans Hughes was elected to the vacancy.

advisory opinions, but the Court concluded that the provisions of Article 14 of the Covenant which authorized the Council or Assembly to ask for advisory opinions were incorporated by implication; the Court would determine, however, whether in a particular case it would give such an opinion.

With the adoption of the rules and the first session of the Court under the rules, the "human agency" to effectuate the general desire for judicial settlement of international disputes had come into being. Commenting upon the importance of this event, Mr. Root has said:

The important thing is to get the right kind of an institution started, even though it be in the most rudimentary form. There is one unfailing characteristic of human nature which comes into play when an institution is once started. It is that after an institution is established and is conspicuous and universally known, it enters into the basis of thought of the people who have to do with the subjects to which it relates. People begin to think differently about such subjects. They begin to think that way, and if the institution is so conducted as to command confidence within its original limited scope, it grows naturally and inevitably because the fundamental idea being no longer a novelty and being accepted, enlargements and improvements of the idea are soon readily accepted.[6]

How truly he grasped the importance of the human institution is evident from the history of the Court. From 1922 to April, 1929, it decided thirteen cases and rendered sixteen advisory opinions, thus answering the doubt as to whether the Court would have business enough to keep it occupied. This record is in striking contrast with that of The Hague Court of Arbitration. In the first six years of The Hague Court only four cases were submitted to an arbitral tribunal formed from the panel; from 1907 to 1913 ten cases were so submitted; since the War it has rendered decisions in four cases. The United States was a party in three cases before the War, in two since the War.

In the first six years of the Court's activity the advisory opinion proved to be a helpful factor in settling differences between na-

[6] *Foreign Affairs* (N. Y.). *Loc. cit.*

tions. Many of the questions submitted by the Council—the Assembly has not asked for an advisory opinion—have involved disputes between governments which the governments themselves have not been ready to submit to the Court for decision, but which they have been willing to allow the Council to bring before the Court for its opinion. The opinions were not binding upon the countries concerned, but they were followed in practice as laying down the law, and accords were negotiated in conformity with them. Of this sort was the controversy over the right of British subjects in Morocco to be exempt from French military service. On the ground that the question was one solely of domestic concern, France refused to submit the controversy to the Court in the form of a litigation. In 1923, however, it was willing that the Council should take the advisory opinion of the Court as to whether the question was international or not, and acquiesced in an opinion of the Court adverse to its own contention. The element of internationality having been found, France and England then had no difficulty in resolving the problem.

Under Article 14 of the Covenant the "advisory opinion" might have taken one of several forms. Many of the members of the League were, of course, accustomed to the *avis consultatif* inherited from the Roman law, according to which the *juris consultus* gave confidential advice to the political power, advice which that power was not bound to follow. This for Americans would be analogous to the advice which an Attorney-General gives to the executive in the states of the American Union. There is a second form of "advisory opinion" embedded in the constitutional practice of some states of the United States, under which the legislature is entitled to have the advice of the highest state court as to the constitutionality of a pending bill before its adoption; the practice avoids the social waste, conflicts, and abortive adjustments which follow legislation of doubtful validity. This is an inheritance from the English custom according to which the judges, on the demand of the House of Lords, give consultative opinions to that body, "a survival of the days when the judges were members of the great council of the realm."[7] This form of advisory

---

[7] Cardozo, J., in *Matter of State Industrial Commission*, 224 N. Y. 13 at p. 16.

opinion is a matter of greater solemnity, the judicial department advising a coördinate governmental department; but as the rights of individuals are not brought in question, the element of an adjudication upon a concrete interest is wanting.

The Court followed neither of these usages but adopted a practice which was intended to obviate the objection that the functions of a court and those of a confidential advisor are incompatible. Under the Rules of the Court a request for an advisory opinion has been treated in much the same way as a suit between nations. All governments signatory to the Statute have been informed of the request and given an opportunity to present arguments. In addition, international organizations which the Court thinks able to furnish information on the question are notified and permitted to file statements; in some cases they have even been heard in oral argument. The opinion is pronounced publicly, and only after it has been rendered is it sent to the Secretary General of the League. John Bassett Moore says:

These decisions, by which judicial methods are applied to the rendering of advisory opinions, have been fully carried out. The Court has not thought it feasible to fill a dual rôle, acting at one moment as a judicial body rendering judgments on international differences, and at the next moment as a board of counsellors giving private and *ex parte* advice on such matters. Indeed, an auditor or spectator would detect no difference between a proceeding for a judgment and a proceeding for an advisory opinion.[8]

Judge Moore therefore reached the general conclusion that "the rules adopted by the Court . . . assimilate the process as far as possible to a judicial proceeding, and exclude any supposition that advisory opinions may be rendered in a diplomatic sense and without any publicity."[9]

Furthermore, the Court held that it would not render an advisory opinion involving the interests between two nations, one not a member of the League, unless the non-member consented to appear before the Court. The Council requested the Court to advise it on a treaty between Finland and Russia in respect of the

8 Moore, *International Law and Some Current Illusions*, p. 131.
9 *Ibid.*, p. 115.

territory of Eastern Carelia which remained Russian; notice was sent by the Court to the Soviet Government, which refused categorically to take any part in the proceedings, and the Court therefore refused to comply with the request of the Council, since to do so "would be essentially equivalent to deciding the dispute between the parties." The Court found it "well established in international law that no state can without its consent be compelled to submit its disputes with other states either to mediation or to arbitration, or to any other kind of pacific settlement."[10] The Court, as a court of justice, must be governed by the rules of law even in giving advisory opinions, and cannot indirectly set up over nations not members of the League a compulsory jurisdiction to which they have not consented. Judge Moore writes that the declaration of the Court in this case

should dispel the apprehensions of those who have reiterated that the Court would, as the creation or creature of the League, enforce the League's organic law, the Covenant, above all other law, without regard to the rights under international law of nations not members of the League. The Court has in fact done just the contrary. While expressly holding, on the one hand, that the Covenant does not give rights to the League as against non-member States, because "they are not bound by the Covenant," the Court has upheld the rights of such States under international law.[11]

The case of a non-League state came before the Court again when the Council requested the Court for an opinion on the character of the decision the Council should make under a provision of the Treaty of Lausanne. Great Britain and Turkey had agreed in this Treaty to submit the Mosul boundary dispute to the Council if they could not settle it between themselves. Before the Council Turkey maintained that the Council was to act as a mediator without power to fix the boundary definitely; Great Britain contended that the Treaty bound the parties to accept the line traced by the

---

10 Opinion of the Court quoted in Moore, *op. cit.*, p. 127.

11 Moore, *op. cit.*, p. 129. The decision in the Eastern Carelia case, announcing the Court's independence of a political connection, constitutes an important precedent, but the vote of seven to four shows that a minority in the Court believed in the advantage to be had from the *avis consultatif* and had not been persuaded that advisory opinions must be treated as a judicial function.

Council. Faced with a grave situation on the Iraq-Turkish frontier, the Council submitted its request to the Court. Both governments were notified; Turkey refused to accept the jurisdiction of the Court, but referred to its argument before the Council and subsequently sent an official publication to the judges. Taking into consideration these communications of the Turkish Government, and holding that the question submitted did not go into the merits of the dispute but only into the competence of the Council under the Treaty of Lausanne, the Court complied with the request.

ADHERENCE OF THE UNITED STATES

AFTER the Washington Conference in 1921 negotiations proceeded between the United States and the Powers signatory to the Protocol of the Court looking to the adherence of the United States. All difficulties were overcome, and on February 24, 1923, when President Harding sent a message to Congress urging the adherence to the Protocol with the reservations which the President and Secretary of State had agreed upon, he could say that he had good reason to believe that the conditions he submitted would be acceptable to the signatory Powers. Nothing definite, he thought, could be done until the Senate had recorded its approval, and he therefore urged that "favorable advice and consent . . . be given in the short period which remains of the present session." The President expressed his opinion that, with the reservations suggested, the United States could adhere to the Protocol and "remain wholly free from any legal relation to the League or assumption of obligations under the Covenant of the League."

The President's message and the accompanying letter from Secretary Hughes show that the only difficulty the administration experienced in recommending adherence to the Protocol was that its act might be construed as involving the country with the League of Nations. President Harding had developed a strong anti-League position, and both the Republican party and the country, he felt, were firmly opposed to the assumption of any responsibility under the Covenant. The Secretary of State's letter was an argument to show that the Court was truly a World Court and not an organ of the League, and that with the reservations he suggested there would be no entangling relationship with the League. Mr. Hughes wrote:

The practical advantage of the present system of electing judges by the majority votes of the Council and Assembly of the League acting separately is quite manifest. It was this arrangement which solved the difficulty, theretofore appearing almost insuperable, of providing an electoral system conserving the interests of the powers, both great and small. It would be impracticable, in my judgment, to disturb the essential features of this system.

He observed that the members of the Council and Assembly in electing the judges do not act under the Covenant but under the Statute of the Court, an independent treaty of the signatory nations. He also considered that it would be appropriate to provide "that the Statute should not be amended without the consent of the United States."

Then follow the Hughes reservations:

1. That such adhesion shall not be taken to involve any legal relation on the part of the United States to the League of Nations or the assumption of any obligations by the United States under the Covenant of the League of Nations constituting Part I of the Treaty of Versailles.

2. That the United States shall be permitted to participate through representatives designated for the purpose and upon an equality with the other States members, respectively, of the Council and Assembly of the League of Nations, in any and all proceedings of either the Council or the Assembly for the election of judges or deputy judges of the Permanent Court of International Justice, or for the filling of vacancies.

3. That the United States will pay a fair share of the expenses of the Court as determined and appropriated from time to time by the Congress of the United States.

4. That the Statute for the Permanent Court of International Justice adjoined to the Protocol shall not be amended without the consent of the United States.

The requirement that the United States should have a voice in the election of the judges both in the Council and in the Assembly on equality with the Great Powers was the only material addition to the Statute and was known to be acceptable to the Powers. The fourth reservation merely states the law as it exists; even without it the Statute as a treaty could not be changed without the consent of the United States. The first reservation also states the legal situation and was included more to quiet apprehensions at home than through doubt as to the status of the country in respect of the Covenant.

The situation in the Senate was not favorable to the prompt passage of the resolution. It was referred to the Committee on Foreign Relations from which to secure passage it would normally have to be reported with favorable recommendation. For the Senate to act without a report from the Committee would be contrary to parliamentary practice, a practice based on the important custom of having a thorough consideration in committee of the details of a measure before it may be brought forth for debate on the Senate floor. Usually a committee hostile to a bill or a resolution prevents its coming on the floor of the Senate or House, thereby depriving even a strong majority of an opportunity to pass it.

The chairman of the Committee on Foreign Relations to which the Hughes proposal was referred, Senator Lodge, was a determined enemy of the League of Nations. As chairman of the Committee he had taken the lead in the protracted delay in acting on the Versailles Treaty which had changed a sentiment favorable to the ratification of the Treaty into a sentiment of hostility; he had, therefore, had recent experience in the possibilities of delay in dampening enthusiasm. Next to Senator Lodge on the Republican side of the committee was Senator Borah, an equally determined enemy of the League of Nations and of the Permanent Court as a "League Court." The other Republican members of the Committee were decidedly anti-League, and might be expected to back up their chairman in his opposition to the Court.

At once began a contest between the administration and the

Republican group which was determined to prevent United States adherence to the Protocol. The President and Secretary of State took the lead of the pro-Court forces. They attacked the objection that the Court was subject to the League, stressing the points made in Secretary Hughes's note; Mr. Hughes insisted that the Court was "an independent judicial body of the highest character." Both argued that the Permanent Court was on a sound basis and the only court in prospect, so that if the people of the United States still believed in judicial settlement of international disputes they should adhere to the existing world tribunal.

President Harding relied upon the overwhelming preponderance of public opinion in favor of the plan. He wrote to the Federation of Women's Clubs on May 9, 1923: "Not since I have been President has there been in connection with any great question of public policy so impressive a demonstration of substantially unified opinion." He was still firmly opposed to entering the League, but participation in the Court "will not be an entry into the League by the side door, by the back door, or by the cellar door." He approved the assembly as the electoral body. In his address before the American Society of International Law at Washington, December 27, 1923, Mr. Hughes disposed of the objection that the British Empire would have seven votes in the Assembly when that body acted as part of the electoral machinery of the League by pointing out that the United States would vote in the Council as well as in the Assembly, and in the Council the British Empire had but one vote. He put the issue to the people:

It is not too much to say that there will be no world court if this Court cannot be made one, and whether or not it is to be in the fullest sense a world court depends upon our own action.

Senator Borah, representing the group who advocate a comprehensive system of which the "outlawry of war" is one element, voiced objections that the Court had no compulsory jurisdiction, and that there was no international law for it to apply; there must be a code before there could be a court. The debate went on actively in the country. President Harding made the statement that a judgment of public opinion favoring the Court was being reached "as the result of earnest, deliberate and studious consideration of the subject in all respects."

The irreconcilable group in the Senate would not yield. They persisted in fighting the Hughes plan on the ground that the Court was a League court and that the people of the United States had firmly determined not to enter the League. Their influence was too strong for President Harding. The fight in the party had become bitter, and the President was evidently persuaded that he would have to abandon his position. He started in June on a western trip, during which he was to carry the Court fight to the people. In his first important speech—at St. Louis, June 21, 1923, —he capitulated to Senator Lodge and his friends, declaring that the tribunal must be in form and in substance "beyond the shadow of a doubt a World Court and not a League Court," and that the United States must "occupy a plane of perfect equality with every other Power." To make the Court completely independent of the League he suggested that it be made self-perpetuating, either by empowering the Court itself to fill any vacancy or by continuing the existing authority of the Permanent Court of Arbitration to nominate, thus transferring the power of election from the Council and Assembly of the League to the remaining members of the Court itself. The contributions for expenses could be collected by a commission through the machinery of the Permanent Court of Arbitration; any state might ask an advisory opinion and the "disparity in voting between a unit nation and an aggregated empire" would disappear. Although the President declared that this program involved no change in his position, it was evident that he had surrendered to the irreconcilables and was advocating their project, that is, the divorce of the Court from the League, which by removing the structural base of the Court would destroy the Court itself; he had sacrificed the World Court on the altar of party harmony. The plan he advocated stood no chance of adoption by the Democratic Senators, who could prevent its approval by the Senate, and, even if the Democrats had been willing to accept the proposal, there was small possibility that the League members would join in this attempt to undo the accomplishment of the Committee of Jurists, the Council, and the Assembly, and try again to find some way of reconciling the differences between the great and the small Powers.

The overwhelming popular opinion in favor of the Hughes plan, of which Mr. Harding had been so convinced in May and which he appeared to doubt in July, did not cease to make itself evident after his death. Notably the American Bar Association, the most competent technical body in the United States, on August 21 approved the plan as submitted to the Senate.

The leadership which President Harding had abandoned at St. Louis was taken up by his successor, who returned to the original Hughes plan in his address before Congress on December 6, 1923. President Coolidge said:

As I wish to see a Court established and as the proposal presents the only practical plan upon which many nations have ever agreed, though it may not meet every desire, I therefore commend it to the favorable consideration of the Senate with the proposed reservations, clearly indicating our refusal to adhere to the League of Nations.

The anti-Court forces did not acknowledge defeat; they persisted in trying to fuse both pro-Court and anti-League opinion into a project to divorce the Court from the League and set up an entirely new Court. Senator Lodge, a strenuous advocate in Roosevelt's time of the prerogatives of the executive, introduced a resolution to create a new World Court by amending the Statute so as completely to divorce the Court from the League. He suggested the calling of a Hague Conference to organize a court and to provide for the codification of international law, and directed the President to submit as a statute for the new court a text which was contained in the resolution.

Senator Lodge's resolution raised protests which were voiced at a hearing before the Committee by such organizations as the American Bar Association, the American Federation of Labor, the United States Chamber of Commerce, numerous church bodies, women's organizations, and other groups. The Committee then reported out through Senator Pepper another resolution which accomplished the result aimed at by Senator Lodge in a more tactful way. It recommended adherence to the Court on condition that specified changes in the Statute of the Court be made, principally to provide for the election of the Court judges by a special electoral assembly in which the constituent members of the British Empire would have but one vote, and for administrative purposes substituting the Secretary General of the Permanent Court of Arbitration for the Secretary General of the League.[12] The Pepper resolution, like the Harding St. Louis speech, was a blow to the hope of adherence to the Protocol. Even had it been approved in principle it would have encountered all the difficulty which frustrated the original Hague plan—the dispute over the electoral body. If the governments, and especially the small Powers, had been unable to agree on an electoral body in the years preceding the War, there was little probability that they would agree on a new electoral body in 1924, particularly when that project involved a blow at the prestige of the League of Nations. For the Democratic minority Senator Swanson introduced a resolution at the same time as the Pepper resolution, adopting the Hughes proposals and so warning the Republican opposition that any other plan was hopeless. Senator Lenroot, an administration Republican, joined his Democratic colleagues.

All the maneuvering during the winter and spring had been in preparation for the battle-ground of the national conventions. The action of the Democrats was not in doubt and their World Court plank renewed the party's declaration of confidence "in the ideal of world peace, the League of Nations and the World Court of Justice as together constituting the supreme effort of statesmanship and religious conviction of our time to organize the world for peace."

President Coolidge controlled the Republican convention. In neither the spring nor winter campaign had he been forced, by the stress laid on party harmony, from his position in favor of the Hughes resolutions. His candidacy for the nomination as President was practically uncontested, and his views on the World

[12] Senate Document No. 116, 68th Congress, 1st Session.

Court were incorporated in the platform upon which he was to run. The Republican plank was positive—

The Republican Party reaffirms its stand for agreement among the nations to prevent war and preserve peace. As an immediate step in this direction we indorse the Permanent Court of International Justice and favor the adherence of the United States to this tribunal as recommended by President Coolidge.

The executive had seemingly triumphed in his fight with the irreconcilable Senate leaders, and his overwhelming victory in the election tended to encourage him to press his idea at the coming session of Congress. The anti-Court forces suffered another loss in November through the death of Senator Lodge; the political leadership of the campaign against the Court and against the President fell to Senator Borah, who was equally determined in his opposition but did not have the same influence as the President in the Republican party councils.

In his message to Congress, December 3, 1924, President Coolidge again urged adherence to the Protocol with the Hughes reservations, but he added a condition that the United States should not be bound by an advisory opinion to the giving of which it had not consented. Thus advisory opinions came to the front of the stage, but in a form which was little more than the expression of a rule which would have applied even without the reservation; in law the advisory opinions have no binding force[13] and obviously the United States could not be bound by an opinion given at the request of the Council.

The answer of the Committee on Foreign Relations was again to propose the divorce of Court from League, but no action was taken in the Senate during the short session of Congress which ended on March 4, 1925. The House, however, took a share in the fight and the House Committee on Foreign Affairs, after full hearing, reported out through Mr. Burton of Ohio a resolution expressing its earnest desire that "the United States give early adherence to the protocol establishing the Permanent Court of Inter-

---

[13] Moore, "The Organization of the Permanent Court." *Col. Law Review*, XXII, 497, 507.

national Justice, with the reservations recommended by President Harding and President Coolidge," and declaring its readiness to enact necessary legislation. The sentiment of the more popular branch of the national legislature was expressed by a vote of 301 yeas to 28 nays. Plainly the House shared the opinion of the Republican convention that the people were ready to accept the Court as it stood, with the right to share in the elections.

In his Inaugural Address the President reasserted his leadership in the contest for the Court; the effect of the Republican convention and of the insistence of the executive were plain in the special session which began on March 5. Senator Swanson reintroduced his resolution, adding to it the Coolidge reservation on advisory opinions, and Senator Willis of Ohio, a Republican, introduced a similar resolution. As Senator Pepper did not again bring his resolution before the Senate, the way was clear for action. The opposition was still strong enough to prevent a vote at the special session, but on March 13 the Senate agreed by a vote of 77 yeas and 2 nays that the Swanson resolution be taken up on December 17. The curious spectacle was thus presented of a Republican majority in the Senate, with the encouragement of a Republican administration, taking from a committee controlled by Republicans a measure introduced by a Democrat and forcing it to the floor. The Democratic resolution had been indorsed by all the Democratic members of the committee, and by one Republican, Senator Lenroot; it was the proposition which the Republican President and the Secretary of State had submitted in 1923, and another Republican President had recommended on December 31, 1924. Interparty as well as intraparty politics played an important part in the conflict, but the deciding factor in this intermediate proceeding was the active body of opinion in the country advocating the Court.

Senator Borah, now chairman of the Committee on Foreign Relations, continued his vigorous opposition to the President's policy. In a speech on April 2, he placed himself squarely in opposition to the World Court, and later in his own state he said that he felt so strongly on the matter that "if I had to tender my resignation in the Senate or vote for this Court as it now stands, it wouldn't take me one minute to resign." Still arguing that he wanted a World Court, which it would be safe for us to join and which would help promote the cause of peace, he declared the existing Court to be practically "judicial despotism," since the people did not elect the judges, could not recall them, and could not appeal from their decisions. He also asserted that the Court could not prevent war, since it could not summon an offending nation before it; and, as a capital objection, he urged that the Court had no law to govern it, except that made by itself, and that a code of international law should precede establishment of the Court.[14]

For practical purposes the question of advisory opinions took the center of the stage; it was evident that the President and Senators were both opposed to secret advisory opinions, and they maintained that no opinion should be given unless both sides to a dispute consented. Senator Pepper is said to have made a proposal which would prohibit the Court from rendering advisory opinions.[15] At the base of the objection to advisory opinions lay the fear that the Court would render an opinion affecting the Monroe Doctrine, immigration, or some other issue which the United States would never of its own motion bring before the Court.

The political situation was not favorable to compromises. The Democrats had accepted the reservations urged by Republican presidents and were in no mood to permit the Republican leaders to force them further along the road toward separation of the Court from the League. The Swanson resolution carried out both Republican and Democratic platforms; the Democrats could prevent Senate approval of further reservations, and thus throw upon the Republican majority the onus of refusing the demand for the World Court. The President was reported to be in consultation with Senator Pepper and Senator Borah at various times to try to work out an arrangement which would bring together Republican irreconcilables and not be certain of defeat at the hands of the Democrats, but he came to the session of 1925 without any agreement to modify the Swanson resolution. His annual message contained a long discussion of the proposal to adhere to the Protocol.

14 *New York Times*, July 1, 1925.   15 *Ibid.*, August 3, 1925.

He approved the proposal which had been submitted by President Harding and amended by himself, indorsing the Swanson resolution without mentioning it, and he asserted that the Court appeared independent of the League, and that the method of nominating and electing the judges protected their independence which, in the end, depended on their ability, character, and personality. The space given to advisory opinions evidences the importance of this issue. The President said: "It does not seem that the authority to give advisory opinions interferes with the independence of the Court. Advisory opinions in and of themselves are not harmful, but may be used in such a way as to be very beneficial because they undertake to prevent injury rather than merely afford a remedy after the injury has been done." The message dwelt on the freedom of the Court to give or refuse an advisory opinion and declared that in practice this function had not impaired its independence.

THE DEBATE IN THE SENATE

THE Swanson resolution, Senate Resolution 5, came up for debate at the appointed time. It provided for adherence to the Protocol and statute without accepting the optional clause, subject to the five reservations suggested by Republican presidents:

1. That such adhesion shall not be taken to involve any legal relation on the part of the United States to the League of Nations or the assumption of any obligations by the United States under the Covenant of the League of Nations constituting Part I of the Treaty of Versailles.

2. That the United States shall be permitted to participate through representatives designated for the purpose and upon an equality with the other States, members, respectively, of the Council and Assembly of the League of Nations, in any and all proceedings of either the Council or the Assembly for the election of judges or deputy judges of the Permanent Court of International Justice, or for the filling of vacancies.

3. That the United States will pay a fair share of the expenses of the Court as determined and appropriated from time to time by the Congress of the United States.

4. That the Statute for the Permanent Court of International Justice adjoined to the Protocol shall not be amended without the consent of the United States.

5. That the United States shall be in no manner bound by any advisory opinion of the Permanent Court of International Justice not rendered pursuant to a request in which it, the United States, shall expressly join in accordance with the Statute for the said Court adjoined to the Protocol of signature of the same to which the United States shall become signatory.

The signature of the United States to the said Protocol shall not be affixed until the Powers signatory to such Protocol shall have indicated through an exchange of notes their acceptance of the foregoing reservations and understandings as a part and a condition of adhesion by the United States to the said Protocol.

The resolution was destined to suffer material changes as a result of searching criticism in the Senate debate. The bitter-enders made it plain that they were determined to fight even this qualified acceptance of the Court in spite of the overwhelming indorsement which the resolution had received from the country. An impressive list of petitions from organizations which had indorsed American adherence was presented on the first day of the debate, and was augmented as the debate continued; the petitions against Senate approval were few and not representative of any large section of the people. The popular interest was further attested by the great number of letters and telegrams received by various Senators from constituents and organizations in their districts. But these public expressions intensified, rather than mitigated, the opposition of the bitter-enders to the pro-Court movement, which they asserted was being financed by persons selfishly interested in bringing the United States into closer relations with Europe. Senator Reed of Missouri demanded an inquiry into the source of this alleged propaganda, but his fellow Senators did not share his apprehension.

The American Bar Association, the United States Chamber of Commerce, the American Federation of Labor, the church groups, the women's organizations again sent in their strong indorsements. American leadership for nearly a century in the struggle for judicial settlement of national disputes, the importance of American participation in the plan for the Permanent Court, the value of the Court as a means of assuring peace were stressed; the memorialists clearly did not consider that the United States was in any danger of entanglement in European affairs by doing its share to fulfil at long length the desire for a world court. The declaration for the Court by public opinion came as a result of a long-continued and acrimonious campaign in which the issues were fought over on many platforms and in numerous pamphlets, and seemed to represent a settled conviction in favor of the Court, combined with a belief in reservations to the adherence of the United States such as the Hughes-Coolidge formula satisfied. Clearly the popular pressure to which both parties had responded in their 1924 platforms had not lessened by December, 1925.

The opponents of the Court at first tried to make again the point that the Court was the back door to the League; that the United States, in entering the Court, would be bound by the Covenant and by the Treaty of Versailles. Again it was declared that the Court was a League court, its judges controlled from Geneva, and even that the Statute of the Court could be amended by Council and Assembly. It was asserted that the United States would be compelled to join the League in enforcing the judgments of the Court, and that the country would be involved in foreign wars, so that the cherished isolation and even the sovereignty of the American republic would be sacrificed. In vain did Senators Walsh, Swanson, and Lenroot argue that Covenant and Court statutes were separate treaties, that an American jurist, Mr. Root, had devised the expedient of using the Council and Assembly as electoral bodies, and so had successfully broken the deadlock which rendered futile earlier plans for a world court. Senator Pepper, once strongly in favor of separation of Court and League, now assured his colleagues that the resolution would not imply a backdoor entry into the Court. The debate did not change votes in the Chamber, nor did it affect, apparently, the public sentiment outside the walls of the Capitol.

The opponents of the resolution differed widely among themselves in everything but their hostility to the League. Senator

Borah objected to the Court because it had no compulsory jurisdiction; a real court should be able to compel one state to plead at
the demand of another. This was contrary to the view of Senator
Reed of Missouri, who said that a judge would always be influenced by his national feeling; "only an American tribunal should
decide questions which affect America vitally." Senator Johnson
of California would not submit American questions to foreign
judges. Senator Fernald of Maine denounced adherence to a court
the names of ten of whose judges "could not be pronounced cor-
rectly by any American living in this country," though he admitted that the name of the English judge, Finlay, as well as that
of Moore, was within the possibilities of the American tongue.

The opponents of the resolution objected to entering the Court
because they maintained that the League was bound to enforce
obedience to its judgments. Senator Borah was against any court
whose judgments could be enforced by armed power. He favored
an obligation on the part of all states to appear before the Court,
but he was opposed to obligatory acceptance of Court judgments,
since he believed that world opinion would be sufficient and in any
case a world court which had to depend on force to compel obedience to its decrees would perpetuate the danger of war and would
not be an instrument toward peace. His fellows had no such principle in mind. They were against any American participation in
European affairs; this they asserted would result from the action
of the League to enforce Court decrees. Their policy was frankly
isolationist and logically would have opposed the kind of court
which Senator Borah was advocating as much as the Permanent
Court. It was pointed out that the League was no less bound to
enforce the judgments of The Hague Tribunal of Arbitration
than those of the Permanent Court; but the danger that League
action would involve the United States was in their minds limited
to League action in support of the decrees of the Permanent
Court, since that, they reiterated, was a League court.

Two conflicting notions of the organization of the Court were
developed in the course of the debate. One was based on the notion that the judges were national judges appointed by their
governments, so that their judgments would be affected inevi-

tably by the prevailing opinion in their countries: with the feeling in Europe against the United States, it would be unsafe to trust American questions to a Court; we could not be sure of a just settlement of questions involving the United States, or of reasonable sympathy with American aspirations and opinions. The other theory was that the Court as a creature of the League would be swayed by the will of the Council and particularly of the great Powers which ruled it. The first objection disregarded the method of election of the judges; they were not appointed by their governments, were not even nominated by their governments, and must depend for their election on the suffrages of all the members of the League, and they consequently represented an international interest and not varied national interests. The Mavromattis case, which involved certain Palestine concessions, was cited in answer to the second objection; the Court had decided against the British Government; Greece, a small country, had judgment against a Great Power. In the Eastern Carelia matter the Court had refused to entertain a request for an advisory opinion from the Council, though the great Powers had urged it. Such instances seemed to the supporters of the Court evidence of the Court's freedom from national bias and from the influence of the League or of its most powerful members.

The opinion was presented that the process of submission of cases to the Court involved membership in the Court by the submitting state to the extent of enforcing the Court's decisions; from this it was argued that the United States as a participant in particular decisions would be further obligated in respect of the political issues out of which they arose. The argument appeared again and again that the Court was useless, since it could not be a court of justice without a code of laws upon which its decisions could be based; before the Court could function a code should be adopted, as adherence to the Court Protocol in advance of the drafting of the code would constitute adherence not to a court of law but to an arbitral tribunal which would be influenced by national prejudices and political considerations, and, as a sufficient arbitral tribunal already existed in The Hague Tribunal, why create another, and why put in the hands of a group of men chosen in advance the solution of delicate international problems unaided by law? The answer was made that the nations of the world had been developing customary international law through centuries, had established arbitral tribunals to apply that law and were daily applying it in their relations with one another. A great part of the business of the Court would be the interpretation and application of the terms of treaties, and the judges as trained lawyers could be trusted to apply legal principles to treaty construction. With the rules recognized as the customary law of nations, and with the great and growing volume of treaty regulation of relations between states, there would be no lack of rules for the Court to apply.

The old argument that the British Empire had seven votes in the Assembly, one of the electoral bodies under the Court statute, was pressed from beginning to end of the debate, but it failed in the Senate as it had failed in public discussion to block the conviction that the Root plan for election of members was an effective solution of the most serious problem in the way of the realization of a world court.

The serious debate in the Senate did not center on any of these objections; the foci were advisory opinions, especially in their possible relation to the Monroe Doctrine, and domestic questions. Here the debate caused material amendments in the resolution, amendments which were supported as strongly by the friends of the Court as they were urged by its opponents as essential for the protection of the United States if the step were to be taken at all. The two questions were interrelated. By not signing the optional clause of the Protocol the United States could prevent any question coming before the Court in a suit between itself and another country, as only with its consent could such a suit be entertained; no adjudications could be made affecting the Monroe Doctrine, or questions like immigration, the European debts to the United States, and the repudiated debts of Southern states, unless the United States itself were willing to enter into a special agreement giving authority to the Court to pass upon them. The apprehension that the executive might submit a vital question against America's interest was quieted by an amendment to the resolution which expressly protected the right of the Senate to have its advice and consent made a prerequisite to the submission of any matter to the Court; the Senate thus reserved not only its own power to pass upon all questions to be submitted for adjudication, but also the power of a future minority exceeding one-third to prevent submission of any issue to the Court.

The door was thus locked and double-locked against the possibility of a judicial decision by the Court on any question in respect of which the United States did not desire a determination. Differently, however, lay the land in respect of advisory opinions. Without a seat on the Council the United States would not be able to prevent an advisory opinion being asked of the Court, which might involve one of the very questions which this country would not be willing to submit in a suit, and which in fact it might definitely refuse to submit. An advisory opinion by the Court which, though having no binding force, would have great persuasive force, might define the Monroe Doctrine or proclaim a principle in respect of immigration which would embarrass this country in pursuing its fixed policies. The reservations in the Swanson resolution confirmed this view and made it a definite part of the engagement of the United States. This would not interfere with the action of the Court or the functioning of the League Council; an advisory opinion could be rendered by the Court at the request of the Council or the Assembly, without consideration of this country.

It was argued that in the Eastern Carelia decision the Court itself had established a rule which would prevent an advisory opinion in a dispute in which the United States as a non-member of the League would be concerned. The Court had held that it was not bound in any case to render an opinion at the request of the Council or Assembly, and was free to refuse a request if in its judgment compliance would be incompatible with its character as a Court. It furthermore decided that it would not respond to a request for an advisory opinion involving the rights of a non-League nation which refused to appear in response to notice by the Court. As a result of the Eastern Carelia decision the United States would be protected against the possibility of an advisory opinion being rendered on a matter in which it was directly interested if it did not join in the submission. The point was made, however, that the opinion was that of a majority of the Court only, and that the Court might in the future modify its procedure; furthermore, the Council had shown dissatisfaction with the refusal of the Court to comply with its request. It was argued that the United States was not sufficiently protected by the Eastern Carelia decision and would not be sufficiently protected even if the principle there laid down were included in the rules of the Court, since both decisions and rules of the Court were subject to change by the Court itself; the only safe way would be to incorporate the rule of the case in a reservation to the statute so that it would become part of the statute and therefore beyond the reach of the judges. Senator Pepper suggested an addition that no advisory opinion be given directly affecting the United States without the consent of the United States; he believed, however, that advisory opinions should not be abolished. Another complication of the advisory opinion problem was the fact that only by rule of the Court were the proceedings conducted and opinions delivered in a public session; secret advisory opinions might be reinstated by a majority of the judges, and this should be prevented.

The sponsors of the resolution introduced reservations, remodeled to secure publicity of procedure in advisory opinions and to assure to the United States the right to object to the issue of an advisory opinion in any case in which it "had or claimed" an interest.

The debate had turned largely on the assertion that any great Power sitting in Council and Assembly could stop a request for an opinion and that the United States desired only to put itself in a position of equality with them, but regardless of the question of equality, the Senate was determined to assure to the United States a veto in respect of any advisory opinion to which it objected. Senator Walsh argued for equality, but for him this meant an absolute veto. He said:

Under the Covenant of the League of Nations each of the great nations has a representative upon the Council of the League and any one of them, therefore, because the Council proceeds by unanimity, can prevent the submission to the Court of any request for an advisory opinion which it does not want to have submitted. This gives the United States exactly the same power by denying to the Court the jurisdiction to entertain a request for an advisory opinion with respect to any question concerning which the United States claims an interest.

Senator Lenroot took a different ground averring that

the change in reservation five merely carries out and insures and makes permanent, so far as the United States is concerned, the rule of Court laid down by its decision in the Eastern Carelia Case, so that in no event, at any time, or under any circumstance, can an advisory opinion be rendered, affecting the right or interest of the United States or claimed to affect our rights or interests, without the consent of the United States.

Senator Swanson also maintained that the amended fifth reservation would absolutely prohibit the Court from giving an advisory opinion "where the United States has or claims a right— without its consent. All the United States would have to do under this reservation would be to notify the Court that they claimed an interest and objected to an advisory opinion." None of these Senators limited the power which they intended the United States to possess by a consideration of equality. A point subsequently much discussed—whether under the reservation the Court would have a right to pass upon the protest of the United States and decide whether the United States had an interest in the subject matter, and so any basis for its objection—was not developed in the debate, but the evident purpose of the supporters of the amendment to prevent any advisory opinion on questions like the Monroe Doctrine or immigration which might embarrass the United States indicates that the Senate had no intention of vesting in the Court the power to decide whether or not the United States was justified in its protest.

The argument in respect of the Monroe Doctrine was enlightening on this point. Senator Reed of Missouri, a persistent opponent of adherence to the Protocol, wished a further resolution added that "the Monroe Doctrine be declared as a principle of International Law binding the Court." The Reed amendment would give the Court power to define the doctrine which under the fifth reservation as amended, it could never do without the consent of the United States, and Senator Swanson immediately countered with the statement that "the Monroe Doctrine is not international law. It is a political policy of the United States to assert our ideas of justice and right;[16] . . . It is a policy which has been maintained by the United States as one of our political policies, and we are not willing to have it incorporated into the body of international law." Senator Lenroot agreed that the Monroe Doctrine is not international law, but our own policy.

Senators Reed and Borah even suggested that the Monroe Doctrine might come up in the course of a suit between two states, and Senator Reed expressly wanted protection in such a case against a decision contrary to the Doctrine. During the debate no attempt was made to define the Monroe Doctrine; the two typical cases which Senator Reed and Senator Borah feared might be submitted, by agreement of the parties, involved not the forcible taking of land in the western hemisphere by a foreign Power, but cases in which rights to American territory might be granted by treaty to a foreign government.

The Senate was ready to vote on the resolution and was becoming restive at the opponents' intention to prolong discussion indefinitely, so on January 25, 1926, it voted, 68-26, to close debate after allowing one hour to each Senator desiring to address it. On January 27, the resolution was adopted by a vote of 76-17, in a form materially different from the original Swanson resolution. As adopted the reservations read:

1. That such adherence shall not be taken to involve any legal relation on the part of the United States to the League of Nations or the assumption of any obligations by the United States under the Treaty of Versailles.

2. That the United States shall be permitted to participate through representatives designated for the purpose and upon an

16 See *Survey*, 1928, p. 37.

equality with the other states, members, respectively, of the Council and Assembly of the League of Nations, in any and all proceedings of either the Council or the Assembly for the election of judges or deputy judges of the Permanent Court of International Justice or for the filling of vacancies.

3. That the United States will pay a fair share of the expenses of the Court as determined and appropriated from time to time by the Congress of the United States.

4. That the United States may at any time withdraw its adherence to the said Protocol and that the Statute for the Permanent Court of International Justice adjoined to the Protocol shall not be amended without the consent of the United States.

5. That the Court shall not render any advisory opinion except publicly after due notice to all states adhering to the Court and to all interested states and after public hearing or opportunity for hearing given to any state concerned; nor shall it, without the consent of the United States, entertain any request for an advisory opinion touching any dispute or question in which the United States has or claims an interest.

The signature of the United States to the said Protocol shall not be affixed until the Powers signatory to such Protocol shall have indicated, through an exchange of notes, their acceptance of the foregoing reservations and understandings as a part and a condition of adherence by the United States to the said Protocol.

The resolution contained the following:

Resolved further, As a part of this act of ratification that the United States approve the Protocol and Statute hereinabove mentioned, with the understanding that recourse to the Permanent Court of International Justice for the settlement of differences between the United States and any other state or states can be had only by agreement thereto through general or special treaties concluded between the parties in dispute; and

Resolved further, That adherence to the said Protocol and Statute hereby approved shall not be so construed as to require the United States to depart from its traditional policy of not intruding upon, interfering with, or entangling itself in the political questions of policy or internal administration of any foreign state; nor shall adherence to the said Protocol and Statute be construed to imply a relinquishment by the United States of its traditional attitude toward purely American questions.

The right to withdraw from the Protocol had been added to the reservations and the Senate was guaranteed the right to decide whether a case should go before the Court; the resolution contained the provision protecting the traditional policy of the United States overseas and its traditional policy toward American questions, i.e., the Monroe Doctrine, which had been made a condition of United States adherence to the Permanent Court of Arbitration of 1899.

Most important was the change in the fifth reservation. In its original phrasing the Coolidge reservation in no way interfered with the relations between Court and League; it would have become effective *after* the pronouncement of an advisory opinion and only then in connection with its bearing upon the United States; in its new form the reservation would operate *before* the handing down of an opinion. The debate does not indicate that the Senators recognized this transformation or that it created the necessity for an administrative device to bring the Council and the United States into contact for an interchange of views on a given situation.

Under the new reservation it would be of vital importance to the League members to know how the United States would express its objection, since the Court could not proceed until the United States had spoken. If the President alone could interpose the veto there might be a reasonable hope of getting a sufficiently prompt decision; but if the Senate must consent by a two-thirds majority to the action of the President, and if the Court must delay until the Senate and President should agree not to "claim" an interest in the subject matter of a request by the Council, the consequent delay might extend over a period long enough to destroy the usefulness of advisory opinions.

ACTION OF THE SIGNATORY STATES

THE Secretary of State communicated the action of the Senate to each of the signatories of the Statute and to the Secretary General of the League, and the Secretary General put the matter before the Council at its meeting on March 18, 1926. The Council did not share the theory that a multilateral agreement like the Protocol should be changed by separate agreement of the signatory nations, but, believing that substantial changes in its provisions should be made only after consultation among the nations interested, directed the calling of a conference of the signatory states and the United States to consider the proposed reservations. The Council went to the heart of the fifth reservation from the League point of view: it felt that this was not merely a limitation on the work of the Court, but in practice might be a limitation on the action of the Council and Assembly; explanation in conference was essential to settle not only the meaning of the reservation but also its application.

The Secretary of State declined the invitation to attend the meeting. He considered himself bound by the decision of the Senate in the matter of principle as well as by its decision on the matter of procedure. The "assent of each signatory by direct exchange of notes" having been required by the Senate, the Secretary felt it would be "a matter of regret" if the Council should create the impression that there were "substantial difficulties in the way of such direct communication." The Secretary also differed from the Council on the reservations: he felt that they were "plain and unequivocal," and that they could take effect as amendments to the statute without further action than the approval of the signatory states; he added, however, that the United States had no objection if the states signatory to the statute desired to confer among themselves.[17]

The judges of the Permanent Court of International Justice made a revision of the Rules of the Court at their session in the summer of 1926. The rules assure to governments notice and a right to present memoranda in case of a request for advisory opinion. An important modification expressly assures to members of the League, states entitled to appear before the Court, and

---

[17] Minutes of the Conference of States Signatories of the Protocol of Signature of the Statute of the Permanent Court of International Justice—held at Geneva, Sept. 1-23, 1926, *Publications of the League of Nations*, V, Legal, 1926, V. 26.

international organizations considered by the Court able to furnish information on the point at issue, the right to comment on statements made by other states, members, or organizations. Thus a state would have the right not merely to file a memorandum but also to reply to the memoranda of other governments and be heard. Another important modification, in conformity with the first part of the fifth reservation, required advisory opinions to be read in open court after proper notice to governments. The same object, publicity of the opinions, was secured by adding a new requirement that the number of judges constituting the majority should be mentioned in advisory opinions.

The conference of the signatory states met on September 1, 1926, in the building of the Labor Office at Geneva. Forty states were represented, including Canada, Uruguay, Venezuela, Panama, and the Dominican Republic from the American hemisphere. No difficulty arose over the first three reservations. The fourth caused a lively discussion on the question whether a League member could withdraw from the Statute: even after withdrawal it would still be bound to bear its share of the cost and still be entitled to vote for judges as members of the Council or Assembly. Since the Court would be open to it whether signatory to the Statute or not, it would have all the advantages flowing from the existence of the Court and would still have an organic relation to the election of judges through the provision in the Statute creating the Council and Assembly of the League the electors of the judges. The United States, however, was not a member of the League, and was therefore entitled to insist upon freedom to withdraw whenever in its own interest it felt such a step desirable.

The first part of the fifth reservation, requiring publicity of advisory opinions, was discussed without incident; the principal difficulty came through the second part of this reservation. All of the speakers dwelt on the importance to the League of advisory opinions and the vital part they were called upon to play in the procedure for the settlement of international difficulties. The conference proceeded on the theory deduced from the arguments in the Senate, particularly from the speech of Senator Walsh, that all the United States wanted was equality with the Powers represented on both Council and Assembly in the possession of the same power to stop consideration of advisory opinions by the Court which any other great state enjoyed by virtue of its position in the League. In the course of the discussion the Eastern Carelia case was frequently cited as authority and, except for some doubt expressed by a representative of Finland, the speakers agreed that the decision in that case would be sustained and that the United States need not therefore fear that an advisory opinion would be given without its consent in a case in which it was directly interested or in regard to a dispute to which it was a party. A different question was involved where the United States was not a party to the dispute, but where it "claimed" an interest. Did this mean that the United States might interpose a veto arbitrarily, or could it be construed to mean that the Court could pass on the objection of the United States and determine whether or not an interest existed of such a character as to warrant the American Government's objection?

The United States would in any case have an advantage over the governments represented in the Council and Assembly, since it would not be obliged to sustain its objection in conference with other governments, and since it had none of the responsibilities of a member of the League under the Covenant. None of the speakers was prepared to lay it down that unanimity was necessary in a request for an advisory opinion; it was even maintained by some speakers, notably M. Rolin of Belgium, that unanimity was unnecessary, since a demand for an advisory opinion was a matter of procedure and not a decision on a matter of principle for which unanimity was required. Even if unanimity were required under the Covenant,[18] the decision on the Mosul boundary (Advisory

[18] Article V of the Covenant:

"Except where otherwise expressly provided in this Covenant or by the terms of the present Treaty, decisions at any meeting of the Assembly or of the Council shall require the agreement of all the Members of the League represented at the meeting.

"All matters of procedure at meetings of the Assembly or of the Council, including the appointment of Committees to investigate particular matters, shall be regulated by the Assembly or by the Council and may be decided by a majority of the Members of the League represented at the meeting."

Opinion No. 12) would indicate that the parties at interest should not be permitted to vote in the Council. Clearly the conference had no power to interpret the Covenant, but it was urged that the conference request the Council to ask the Court for an authoritative opinion on this point. Three objections were made to carrying out this procedure: one on the part of Czechoslovakia and Switzerland, that the Assembly and not the Court should interpret the Covenant. The second, more persuasive, was that the League was yet young, and that to allow its jurisprudence to develop slowly, case by case, was better than to put the Covenant in the Procrustean bed of a judicial interpretation before experience showed the difficulties which might arise; it might even appear that some advisory opinions would relate to matters of procedure, whereas others would require unanimity.

The British and French representatives advised that the conference suggest to the United States that its veto before the Court be treated exactly as a vote given in the Council or the Assembly; the United States would therefore gain its desired equality and the development of the procedure of the League would not be hampered. But this met with the third objection, namely, that even if the request to the Court for an advisory opinion required a unanimous vote it might be that a party in interest would not be counted, and equality on that basis would not satisfy the United States, while if a majority sufficed the evident purpose of the Senate would be thwarted, as the United States did not have a veto.

This question of equality was not the only difficulty; the members of the League were uncertain what procedure would be necessary for the expression of its veto by the United States. Sir George Foster, representing Canada, was particularly emphatic on the difficulties which would arise if agreement between the President and Senate were necessary; great delay was possible, and even though the vote of the United States eventually would have only the same weight as the vote of a member of the Council, nevertheless the time consumed in prognosticating that vote might make it difficult to obtain the prompt action which was often important for the functioning of the League.

In summing up the discussion the presiding officer thought that the speakers had agreed that the United States desired equality, but that they were doubtful whether the fifth reservation did not go further than that. They were clearly desirous of protecting the action of the Council; the United States had probably not realized the "constitutional difficulties" which might arise from its reservation; it was hard to prepare a reply to the United States without the help of a representative of that country to explain the doubts which had arisen in respect of the interpretation of the reservations. He complimented the conference for taking in its discussion "an exalted standpoint—a standpoint where the mere jurist had given place as far as possible to the man of action who desired to carry out a good work," that is, for trying to overcome the difficulties which stood in the way of adherence by the United States to the Statute.

The final act of the conference accepted the first, second, and third reservations and the first part of the fourth assuring to the United States the right to withdraw at any time. The first part of the fifth, publicity of hearings and pronouncement of advisory opinions, was dealt with by an express declaration that these opinions should be delivered in public session, but the conference preferred that the procedure should remain within the control of the Court. It stated that the revised rules appeared to give full satisfaction to the wishes of the United States, but refrained from approving their incorporation in the Statute, leaving the Court free to change its rules as to procedure. The second part of the fifth reservation dealt with two situations: the Eastern Carelia decision, it was averred, should satisfy the United States that the Court would not render an advisory opinion on a question in which it was a party without its consent; where the United States was not a party but, according to its own view, "had" or "claimed" an interest, no objective legal fact would be present, and the United States would have an arbitrary veto on the request of the Council. This veto would not concern the Court, but it would concern the functioning of the League. The conferees took the position that they would be willing to assure to the United States the same position which a member of the Council or of the Assembly would have, and would permit the expression of its wish to the Court to have the same effect as if it voted as a member in the Council or Assembly; they were not competent to go further and declare whether a majority or a unanimous vote of Council or Assembly were required for a request.

The conference was not willing to commit itself unreservedly even to this position. It recognized the importance of advisory opinions in the proper functioning of the League. A member of the League, in Council or Assembly, takes its position in full knowledge of the circumstances, after deliberating with its sister nations as to the common benefit to be had from common action, and with a sense of the responsibilities it bears as a member of the League; the United States is outside the League, is not represented at the meetings, and has no such responsibility. In practice, the exercise of the right of the United States is a matter which interests primarily the League and its functioning, not the Court, and the conference declared that "it was desirable that the manner in which the consent provided for in the second part of the fifth reservation will be given should form the object of a supplementary agreement," which, it suggested, should be made between the United States and the Council.

Also, in order to balance the right reserved by the United States to withdraw if it felt that its interests so required, the conference stipulated that "to assure equality of treatment . . . the signatory states, acting together, and by not less than a majority of two thirds, should possess the corresponding right to withdraw their acceptance of the special conditions" of the second part of the fourth and of the fifth reservations.

The conference finally observed that "the application of some of the reservations of the United States would involve the conclusion of an appropriate agreement between the United States and the other States signatories of the Protocol." It therefore suggested a form of agreement which should be subject to "such further exchange of views as the Government of the United States may think useful."[19]

[19] Minutes of the Conference of States Signatories of the Protocol of Signature of the Statute of the Permanent Court of International Justice, *op. cit.*

AFTER THE SENATE VOTE

The counter proposals of the conference were not well received by the administration. The President considered that they were not the same as the fifth reservation, since it might be held hereafter that requests for opinions could go to the Court by a majority vote.

On Armistice Day, 1926, the President publicly declared that he intended to stand by the Senate resolution and not to ask the Senate to "modify its position." "Unless," said he, "the requirements of the Senate are met by the other interested nations, I can see no prospect of this country adhering to the Court." That his speech represented Senate opinion is evidenced by the approval of both pro-Court and anti-Court leaders; Senators Walsh and Swanson joined with Senators Borah and Moses in approving the President's stand.

The Geneva Conference left the door open to final agreement by requesting a conference with the United States in the hope that explanation would make agreement possible. An influential group of Americans petitioned the President in December to open negotiations under the offer of the Geneva conferees, but he replied that no result could be expected from further consultation; the Senate stood by its position and the signatories to the Permanent Court Statute were apparently not willing to accept American terms.

THE ROOT MISSION

THIS was the situation down to the closing months of the Coolidge administration. Little progress had been made toward meeting the American conditions of entry into the World Court. Only seven small states of the forty signatories of the Protocol had by January 1, 1929, accepted them; twenty-four states, including the Great Powers, had answered on the lines of the Geneva Conference.

At the League Assembly of September, 1928, the French delegation submitted a proposal for a revision of the Statute of the Court in the light of the experience of the preceding eight years.

The discussion made it clear that any amendment should relate only to matters of detail in respect of which experience might have revealed the possibility of improvement, and should preclude any possibility of a suspicion that the tendency of the proposed study could in any degree weaken the prestige of the Court or impair the basic principles of its existing constitution. The proposal was unanimously adopted by the Assembly, which considered it advisable that amendments to the Statute should be made before the renewal in 1930 of the terms of office of the members of the Court.

In pursuance of this resolution the Council in December appointed a committee of jurists which included Sir Cecil Hurst, Mr. Politis, and other jurists of international distinction, and pursuant to authority given to them the President of the Council and the rapporteur of the committee asked Mr. Root to become a member of it. The President and Vice-President of the Court, Judges Anzilotti and Huber, were also asked to give their assistance.

At an early stage it was decided that the committee could not interfere in any way with the Rules of the Court: "That is a matter for the Court itself, and as a large number—in fact, practically all—of the Rules relate to procedure, they obviously cannot be affected by any examination of the Statute."

The preliminary committee work synchronized with a proposal of the State Department for a reëxamination of the terms on which the United States might become a member of the Court. On February 19, 1929, the Secretary of State addressed a letter to each signatory of the Court Protocol and to the Secretary General of the League which recalled that at the 1926 conference the recommendation had been made that, in replying to the proposal of the United States, the states members of the Court should adopt a preliminary draft of a protocol, the gist of which was as follows:

Should the United States offer objection to an advisory opinion being given by the Court, at the request of the Council or the Assembly, concerning a dispute to which the United States is not a party or concerning a question other than a dispute between States, the Court will attribute to such objection the same force and effect as attaches to a vote against asking for the opinion given by a member of the League of Nations either in the Assembly or in the Council, and that the manner in which the consent provided for in the second part of the fifth reservation is to be given should be the subject of an understanding to be reached by the Government of the United States with the Council of the League of Nations.

Observing that the Court had already pronounced upon the matter of disputes between a member of the League of Nations and a state not a member, and held in Advisory Opinion No. 5 (the Eastern Carelia case) that it would not pass on such a dispute without the consent of the non-member of the League, Mr. Kellogg's note went on to say that some elements of uncertainty in the bases of these suggestions required further discussion:

The powers of the Council and its modes of procedure depend upon the Covenant of the League of Nations which may be amended at any time. The ruling of the Court in the Eastern Carelia case and the rules of the Court are also subject to change at any time.

For these reasons he feared that the proposed Protocol would not furnish adequate protection to the United States and hoped that its interest might be protected "in some other way or by some other formula." He thought that an informal exchange of views such as had been proposed by the twenty-four conferee states meeting at Geneva in 1926 might lead to agreement upon some provision which would appropriately bring about the result of adherence by the United States to the Court Statute, inasmuch as "there seems to be but little difference regarding the substance of these rights and interests."

It may be well at this point to give an epitome of the proposals for the amendment of the Statute as they were eventually presented by the committee of jurists to the Council. The changes proposed relate to the composition and functions of the Court and have a bearing upon the membership of the United States. As stated in the report, the committee was

in general actuated by the desire to give the States full assurance that the Permanent Court of International Justice established by the League of Nations is a real *judicial* body which is constantly at their disposal for the purpose of hearing and determining their disputes and which possesses alike the necessary juristic competence and experience of international affairs.

Some of the proposals, it was thought, could have effect by means of *voeux* or recommendations. These related to the qualifications of the candidates proposed for the Court by national groups. They are self-explanatory and are as follows:

The Secretary-General, in issuing the invitations provided for in Article 5 of the Statute, will request the national groups to satisfy themselves that the candidates nominated by them possess recognised practical experience in international law and that they are at least able to read both the official languages of the Court and to speak one of them; he will recommend the groups to attach to each nomination a statement of the career of the person nominated showing that he possesses the required qualifications.

As to amendments of the Statute, experience had shown in the first place that in respect of work done and of emoluments no difference should be made between judges and deputy-judges, and accordingly that the latter should be omitted and the roster of judges increased from eleven to fifteen, with no suggestion of increase beyond that number. Provision was made for the procedure in the case of a judge desiring to resign—the resignation would be addressed to the President of the Court for transmission to the Secretary General of the League of Nations and would become effective upon its receipt by the latter official; in order to fill vacancies the Secretary General would be empowered within one month of the occurrence of a vacancy to issue the invitations provided for in Article 5, to be followed at the next session of the Council by fixing the date of the election. The judge elected to fill a vacancy should hold the appointment for the remainder of his predecessor's term.

One important change was suggested in Article 16 relating to activities of the members of the Court, which it is proposed shall read as follows:

The members of the Court may not exercise any political or administrative function, nor engage in any other occupation of a professional nature. Any doubt on this point is settled by the decision of the Court.

The committee considered that the Court was in course of attaining "that permanent character which its title denotes, and which its promoters had contemplated in order to advance the progress of international justice." They recommended therefore doing away with extraordinary sessions, and the establishment of sessions like those of national Courts "for a real international judicial year." The provision, proposed in the form of a redraft of Article 23, is as follows:

The Court shall remain permanently in session except during the judicial vacations, the dates and duration of which shall be fixed by the Court at the end of each year for the following year.

Members of the Court whose homes are situated at more than five days' normal journey from The Hague shall be entitled, apart from the ordinary vacations, to six months' leave every three years.

Members of the Court shall be bound, unless they are on regular leave or prevented from attending by illness or other serious reason duly explained to the President, to hold themselves permanently at the disposal of the Court.

Other provisions related to rotation in sittings, special chambers for labor cases and for transit and communication cases, the salaries of judges, and other minor matters.

Considering advisory opinions, the committee thought that the essential parts of the provisions in the Rules of the Court "should be transferred to the Statute of the Court in order to give them a permanent character, which seems particularly desirable today in view of the special circumstances attending the possible accession of the United States to the Protocol of Signature of the Statute of the Court." Of the provisions in this regard proposed by the committee the following are the most important clauses:

Chapter IV—Advisory Opinions

Article 65

Questions upon which the advisory opinion of the Court is asked shall be laid before the Court by means of a written request, signed either by the President of the Assembly or the President of the Council of the League of Nations, or by the Secretary-General of the League under instructions from the Assembly or the Council.

* * * * *

Article 66

I. The Registrar shall forthwith give notice of the request for an advisory opinion to the Members of the League of Nations, through the Secretary-General of the League, and to any States entitled to appear before the Court.

The Registrar shall also, by means of a special and direct communication, notify any Member of the League or State admitted to appear before the Court considered by the Court (or, should it not be sitting, by the President) as likely to be able to furnish information on the question, that the Court will be prepared to receive, within a time-limit to be affixed by the President, written statements, or to hear, at a public sitting to be held for the purpose, oral statements relating to the question.

* * * * *

Article 67

The Court shall give its advisory opinions in open Court, notice having been given to the Secretary-General of the League of Nations and to the representatives of States and Members of the League immediately concerned.

It was upon these proposals as drafted by two of its members, Messrs. Fromageot and Politis, that the committee was about to begin its work when Mr. Kellogg's communication was received at Geneva. At the first meeting of the Council thereafter Sir Austen Chamberlain, expressing satisfaction at the attitude taken by the United States, proposed that the Council invite the committee of jurists which might be able to furnish valuable assistance toward reaching the agreement contemplated in the Secretary of State's note, to examine the question and offer its advice thereon. This proposal was unanimously and enthusiastically adopted by the Council, all of the members present seizing the opportunity to express their satisfaction with the resumption of negotiations and with the prospect they afforded of adherence to the Court by the

United States, especially in view of Mr. Kellogg's sympathetic statement that "the Government of the United States desires to avoid in so far as may be possible any proposal which would interfere with or embarrass the work of the Council of the League of Nations, doubtless often perplexing and difficult."

Meanwhile Mr. Root, after consultations at Washington with Senate leaders of both parties, had arrived at Geneva bearing with him a proposal in the form of a suggested redraft of Article 4 of the Protocol of 1926. That proposal was in the following terms:

The Court shall not without the consent of the United States render an advisory opinion touching any dispute to which the United States is a party.

The Court shall not without the consent of the United States render an advisory opinion touching any dispute to which the United States is not a party but in which it claims an interest or touching any questions other than a dispute in which the United States claims an interest.

The manner in which shall be made known whether the United States claims an interest and gives or withholds its consent shall be as follows:

Whenever in contemplation of a request for an advisory opinion it seems to them desirable, the Council or Assembly may invite an exchange of views with the United States and such exchange of views shall proceed with all convenient speed.

Whenever a request for an advisory opinion comes to the Court the Registrar shall notify the United States thereof among other States mentioned in the now existing Article 73 of the Rules of Court stating a reasonable time-limit fixed by the President within which a written statement by the United States concerning the request will be received.

In case the United States shall within the time fixed advise the Court in writing that the request touches a dispute or question in which the United States has an interest and that the United States has not consented to the submission of the question, thereupon all proceedings upon the question shall be stayed to admit of an exchange of views between the United States and the proponents of the request and such exchange of views shall proceed with all convenient speed.

If after such an exchange of views either while a question is in contemplation or after a question has gone to the Court, it shall appear (1) that no agreement can be reached as to whether the question does touch an interest of the United States within the true meaning of the second paragraph of this article; and (2) that the submission of the question is still insisted upon after attributing to the objections of the United States the same force and effect as attaches to a vote against asking for the opinion given by a Member of the League of Nations either in the Assembly or in the Council; and if it also appears that the United States has not been able to find the submission of the question so important for the general good as to call upon the United States to forego its objection in that particular instance leaving the request to be acted upon by the Court without in any way binding the United States; then it shall be deemed that owing to a material difference of view regarding the proper scope of the practice of requesting advisory opinions the arrangement now agreed upon is not yielding satisfactory results and that the exercise of the powers of withdrawal provided in Article 7 hereof will follow naturally without any imputation of unfriendliness or of unwillingness to coöperate generally for peace and goodwill.

This proposal asked for no commitment or concession which was not to be found in the Final Act of the 1926 Conference of Signatories. It avoided the two problems which had hitherto been the subject of study and discussion—the question of unanimity in requesting opinions, and the definition of "has or claims an interest."

At the first meeting of the committee of jurists on March 11 Mr. Root explained that

the chief difficulty resulting from the second part of the fifth American reservation was due to the way in which that reservation had been drafted. Its terms were so general that they seemed to afford powers of general interference in the business of the Council and of the Assembly in regard to advisory opinions. What was required in order to reach the agreement proposed in the first paragraph of Article 4 of the preliminary draft of the Protocol? The scope of this possible interference must be limited. The theoretical question raised by the second part of the fifth reservation could be discussed for ever and without any positive result. In his note, he had tried to solve the difficulty in a practical way, and to limit the scope of the American reservation.

The Chairman, M. Scialoja, thought there would be no harm in establishing the rule of unanimity in the case of a request for an advisory opinion. The Court had held that its opinions were binding on the parties who had asked for them, and an act of that kind belonged to the class which under the terms of the Covenant could be effected only by a unanimous vote. Owing to the absence of any rule on the subject, the Council, instead of consulting the Permanent Court, had adopted the custom of consulting groups of jurists, thus remaining free not to follow their opinion if it so wished.

If the Council continued to follow that system in all cases in which it did not wish to be bound by an opinion, and if it consulted the Permanent Court only when it was willing to be bound by such opinion as the Court might put forward, the question would fall to the ground and there would be no obstacle to the adoption of a system which would permit of the accession of the United States.

Notwithstanding this argument, it was thought wiser not to adopt any rule but to handle the question in the particular rather than in the general, the idea prevailing that if the United States should be invited to confer with members of the Council concerning the request for an advisory opinion the likelihood of an agreement upon the course to be taken was so great that the controversy between unanimity and majority requests would never find application.

Under Mr. Root's plan the United States would have no dealings with the Council unless that body should request an exchange of views in advance; normally notice would come from the Registrar of the Court and it was to the Court that any objection was to be made known. This plan was inspired by an "anxiety to avoid interfering in any way with the procedure and work of the Council." Sir Cecil Hurst suggested the more direct and logical course of dealing with the body propounding the request—the Council or Assembly. Since Sir Cecil felt that the Council would prefer it, Mr. Root accepted the proposal willingly.

The essential feature of both plans is the exchange of views. When the final text was prepared it was provided in general terms that whenever "any proposal . . . for obtaining an advisory opinion" is "before" the Council or Assembly, the Secretary General shall inform the United States through any channel which the latter may designate. These words were carefully chosen to preserve a certain elasticity—on the one hand to avoid invoking this procedure over any vague informal suggestion for requesting an opinion, and, on the other hand, to avoid the necessity for waiting till the matter is actually on the agenda or actually discussed by the Council. An exchange of views then proceeds "if desired" by either party. The several possible alternatives in such an exchange of views were set out in Mr. Root's original proposal, but were not repeated in the Hurst redraft. It was the general consensus of opinion that, as Mr. Root said, the exchange of views would in practice result in agreement.

Mr. Root at the second meeting of the committee of jurists said that

the Council might decide to request an advisory opinion without reference to interests of the United States which might in certain cases be involved. This reservation was due to apprehensions in respect of the rights and interests of the United States. He had also in his proposals endeavoured to meet apprehensions of another kind, namely, that the reservation of the United States might be used to interfere with the Council or the Assembly in the discharge of its duties and to embarrass its procedure. There was no intention on the part of the United States to hamper the procedure of requesting advisory opinions upon unreal and unsubstantial grounds. It was difficult in an abstract formula to discriminate between the multitude of possible interests involved and he had endeavoured in his proposals to allay apprehensions on both sides by dealing with the problem in a concrete form. . . . The essential point was that the United States should be promptly informed of the intentions of the Council in dealing with any matter in which they might be interested, and that there should be some kind of informal conference in regard to any concrete case which might arise. Such a solution would make it possible to avoid discussing detailed questions of procedure, such as whether decisions to request an advisory opinion should be taken unanimously or by a majority vote.

He constantly emphasized turning from the abstract to the concrete.

Near the end of this meeting Mr. Root made a pregnant general utterance:

. . . There was a process at present taking place in Europe for the promotion and maintenance of peace which was somewhat novel in diplomacy. A good deal of business was being taken out of the hands of foreign offices and settled by means of informal and friendly conversations between foreign ministers. He thought that this was an admirable method of doing business.

M. Urrutia, the Colombian jurist, saw another consequence flowing from the same situation. The threat or possibility of withdrawal from the Court by the United States was so serious a matter —it was so much to the interest of the Council to retain the participation of the United States in the Court—that the United States under the provision for its withdrawal would in practice have the power of exercising a kind of involuntary pressure on the Council. The privilege of withdrawal would almost certainly be claimed by other states; Russia, for example, "would ask for similar treatment. Whenever the Council desired to ask the Court for an advisory opinion, it would, therefore, be necessary to apply a complicated procedure, and to conduct correspondence with the States which had a right to be consulted. The practical effect of such a system would be a tendency to abolish the whole system of advisory opinions." M. Urrutia said he would not greatly regret their disappearance; M. Scialoja, as already stated, was disposed to abandon them; but the smaller nations were not prepared to take so complete a step, and it became evident that the question of unanimity or majority could not be handled.

On these points the Committee of Jurists in its report to the Council adopted at the Committee session April 11–19, 1929, made the following observations:

The system of asking the Court for an advisory opinion has proved to be of substantial utility in securing a solution of questions which could not conveniently be submitted to the Court in any other form. It has also on occasions enabled parties to a dispute to ask for the submission of their difference to the Court in the form of a request for an advisory opinion when they were for various reasons unwilling to submit it in the form of international litigation.

The Committee has also felt obliged to reject another method by which satisfaction might without difficulty be given to the conditions laid down by the United States. It is that of recommending the adoption of a rule that in all cases a decision on the part of the Council or of the Assembly to ask for an advisory opinion from the Court must be unanimous. As is pointed out in the Final Act of the Special Conference of 1926, it was not then possible to say with certainty whether a decision by a majority was not sufficient. It is equally impossible today. All that is possible is to guarantee to the United States a position of equality in this matter with the States which are represented in the Council or the Assembly of the League.

The Hurst plan contained a further provision to cover the case in which the proposal to request an advisory opinion is not broached till the last moment in a Council meeting. In such a situation it might not be possible to exchange views with the United States in advance. This eventuality was covered by providing that whenever a request came to the Court the Registrar should notify the United States, and if within the time limit fixed by the President of the Court the United States gave notice of a claim, proceedings would be stayed till the exchange of views could take place.

In all stages of requesting an advisory opinion the vote of the United States would have the same effect as that of any member of the Council or Assembly.

If the exchange of views just described still left an irreconcilable divergence of view, the withdrawal of the United States "will follow naturally without any imputation of unfriendliness or unwillingness to coöperate generally for peace and good will." As stated in the original Root draft this deadlock would indicate "that owing to a material difference of view regarding the proper scope of the practice of requesting advisory opinions the arrangement now agreed upon is not yielding satisfactory results."

It is important to read the fifth article of the draft protocol in connection with all the other articles, especially Article 1 which is an acceptance of the five reservations, and Article 4 which is an effective acceptance of the first clause of the fifth reservation. Article 5 opens with the statement "with a view to ensuring that the Court shall not, without the consent of the United States, entertain any request for an advisory opinion, etc." It is to be noted also that under Article 8, United States withdrawal would take effect as soon as notified to the Secretary General, so that with regard to an advisory opinion it could always resume non-member status before an opinion could be rendered; other members, on the other hand, must wait till they have a majority of two-thirds in order to make effective a notification of desire to withdraw from this Protocol and this majority in order to be effective must be secured within one year from the date of receipt of the notification.

The committee has reported to the Council two separate Protocols, one on the amendments to the Statute, and one on United States adherence. At its session in Madrid on June 12, 1929, the Council decided to place the problem of revision of the Court's Statutes on the agenda of the September session of the Assembly. It decided also to convoke a conference at Geneva for all the states which are signatory to the Court Statutes for the purpose of examining the constitutional changes designed to permit United States accession, and instructed the Secretary General to make formal and appropriate reply to Mr. Kellogg's note of February 19, and to transmit the American conditions to all the states which are members of the tribunal. It was recommended in the report of the committee of jurists of March 18, 1929, that

. . . every effort should be made to secure that delegates to the meeting of the Assembly or of the Special Conference, if there should be one, should be authorised to sign the instrument and should actually sign it before they leave Geneva. The signature of representatives of States not Members of the League should be obtained at the same time.

As provided in Article 7 of the draft, the Protocol will come into force as soon as it has been ratified by the States which have ratified the Protocol of December 16th, 1920, and by the United States, and as soon as it has come into force it will be possible for the United

States to take the necessary steps to become a party to the Protocol of December 16th, 1920, and to any further Protocol which may have been concluded for introducing amendments into the Statute of the Court.

The Protocol defining the special terms for adherence to the Court by the United States is as follows:

The States signatories of the Protocol of Signature of the Statute of the Permanent Court of International Justice, dated December 16th, 1920, and the United States of America, through the undersigned duly authorised representatives, have mutually agreed upon the following provisions regarding the adherence of the United States of America to the said Protocol subject to the five reservations formulated by the United States in the Resolution adopted by the Senate on January 27th, 1926.

Article 1

The States signatories of the said Protocol accept the special conditions attached by the United States in the five reservations mentioned above to its adherence to the said Protocol upon the terms and conditions set out in the following articles.

Article 2

The United States shall be admitted to participate, through representatives designated for the purpose and upon an equality with the signatory States members of the League of Nations represented in the Council or in the Assembly, in any and all proceedings of either the Council or the Assembly for the election of judges or deputy-judges of the Permanent Court of International Justice, provided for in the Statute of the Court. The vote of the United States shall be counted in determining the absolute majority of votes required by the Statute.

Article 3

No amendment of the Statute of the Court may be made without the consent of all the contracting States.

Article 4

The Court shall render advisory opinions in public session after notice and opportunity for hearing substantially as provided in the now existing Articles 73 and 74 of the Rules of Court.

Article 5

With a view to ensuring that the Court shall not, without the consent of the United States, entertain any request for an advisory opinion touching any dispute or question in which the United States has or claims an interest, the Secretary-General of the League of Nations shall, through any channel designated for that purpose by the United States, inform the United States of any proposal before the Council or the Assembly of the League for obtaining an advisory opinion from the Court, and thereupon, if desired, an exchange of views as to whether an interest of the United States is affected shall proceed with all convenient speed between the Council or Assembly of the League and the United States.

Whenever a request for an advisory opinion comes to the Court, the Registrar shall notify the United States thereof, among other States mentioned in the now existing Article 73 of the Rules of Court, stating a reasonable time-limit fixed by the President within which a written statement by the United States concerning the request will be received. If for any reason no sufficient opportunity for an exchange of views upon such request should have been afforded and the United States advises the Court that the question upon which the opinion of the Court is asked is one that affects the interests of the United States, proceedings shall be stayed for a period sufficient to enable such an exchange of views between the Council or the Assembly and the United States to take place.

With regard to requesting an advisory opinion of the Court in any case covered by the preceding paragraphs, there shall be attributed to an objection of the United States the same force and effect as attaches to a vote against asking for the opinion given by a Member of the League of Nations in the Council or in the Assembly.

If, after the exchange of views provided for in paragraph 1 and 2 of this Article, it shall appear that no agreement can be reached and the United States is not prepared to forego its objection, the exercise of the powers of withdrawal provided for in Article 8 hereof will follow naturally without any imputation of unfriendliness or unwillingness to co-operate generally for peace and goodwill.

Article 6

Subject to the provisions of Article 8 below, the provisions of the present Protocol shall have the same force and effect as the provisions of the Statute of the Court and any future signature of the Protocol of December 16th, 1920, shall be deemed to be an acceptance of the provisions of the present Protocol.

Article 7

The present Protocol shall be ratified. Each State shall forward the instrument of ratification to the Secretary-General of the League of Nations, who shall inform all the other signatory States. The instruments of ratification shall be deposited in the archives of the Secretariat of the League of Nations.

The present Protocol shall come into force as soon as all States which have ratified the Protocol of December 16th, 1920, and also the United States, have deposited their ratifications.

Article 8

The United States may at any time notify the Secretary-General of the League of Nations that it withdraws its adherence to the Protocol of December 16th, 1920. The Secretary-General shall immediately communicate this notification to all the other States signatories of the Protocol.

In such case, the present Protocol shall cease to be in force as from the receipt by the Secretary-General of the notification by the United States.

On their part, each of the other Contracting States may at any time notify the Secretary-General of the League of Nations that it desires to withdraw its acceptance of the special conditions attached by the United States to its adherence to the Protocol of December 16th, 1920. The Secretary-General shall immediately give communication of this notification to each of the States signatories of the present Protocol. The present Protocol shall be considered as ceasing to be in force if and when, within one year from the date of receipt of the said notification, not less than two-thirds of the Contracting States other than the United States shall have notified the Secretary-General of the League of Nations that they desire to withdraw the above-mentioned acceptance.

The provisions of this Protocol have obvious bases. Article 1 accepts all of the United States reservations, so that only those reservations are repeated for whose application terms and conditions need to be established.

As applied to the Tenth Article of the Statute of the Court, viz.,

those candidates who obtain an absolute majority of votes in the Assembly and the Council shall be considered as elected,

the second reservation of the United States, viz., that it should be permitted to participate equally in any or all proceedings of either the Council or the Assembly for the election of judges, requires the addition of a sentence specifically directing the officials in charge of the receiving and accounting of the vote in the Council and Assembly to count the vote of the United States; this direction is given in Article 2.

Article 3, meeting the Senate's reservation that the Statute should not be amended without the consent of the United States, extends the requirement of consent to all the signatories to the Statute; this makes explicit what would in any case be the rule as to such multilateral engagements.

Article 4, requiring advisory opinions to be rendered in public session after notice of opportunity for hearing substantially as provided in the rules of the Court, makes change of this procedure by an alteration of its rules impossible for the Court.

Article 5 prescribes the practice for giving effect to the fifth reservation of the United States stipulating that the Court shall not render any advisory opinion touching any dispute or question in which the United States "has or claims an interest." Some machinery, of course, is necessary to apprise the United States of a proposal, pending in the Council, to ask the Court for an advisory opinion, and for the United States in turn to inform the Court whether it "has or claims an interest" in the dispute or question, or the contrary. The article, conceding the full effect of the reservation, brings the parties together for an exchange of views and allows the United States the full right at such a conference which it would have if it were a member of the League represented in the Council or in the Assembly; if the conference does not produce a common attitude toward the advisability of having an advisory opinion the United States may end its responsibility by withdrawing from the Court. In the exceptional case of a request for an advisory opinion followed by so early an adjournment of the Council that the objection of the United States could not be delivered to the Council, the United States may file its objection with the Court itself and thereafter the Court may not render its opinion until opportunity has been given for an exchange of views between the Council (or the Assembly) and the United States.

These provisions in effect give the United States a veto power. Neither the enlarged Council, now containing the representatives of many of the smaller nations and showing in this matter an attitude of painstaking conciliation, nor the Assembly, whose business it is to keep the peace of the world, is likely to quarrel with the United States over the importance of having an advisory opinion and so to alienate from the Court's support as well as from their own counsels the nation whose coöperation in juristic organization and in less formal processes for keeping the peace has seemed to justify the exceptional arrangement made in its favor.

The fifth reservation of the United States, adopted January 25, 1926, provided that the signature of the United States should not be affixed to the Protocol of December 16, 1920, "until the powers signatory to such Protocol shall have indicated, through an exchange of notes, their acceptance" of the reservations of the United States. This reservation could not be given effect in the manner prescribed. The Protocol of the Court Statute is an international instrument formally ratified by the governments of the respective signatories, and could not be altered by an exchange of notes emanating from the foreign offices of the respective signatory governments. Undertakings designed to make the Senate reservations internationally binding must find their place in a new Protocol such as that now proposed for submission to the United States and to the states already members of the Court, and for their ratification.

CHAPTER TWO

THE PACT OF PARIS

O N the tenth anniversary of the entry of the United States into the World War, April 6, 1927, Monsieur Briand declared through the Associated Press that as testimony to the common desire for peace of the two great democracies and to furnish an example to other nations, France would be willing to subscribe publicly with the United States to any mutual engagement "outlawing war, to use your way of expressing it." The press failed to grasp the importance of this offer and three weeks passed before public interest was aroused by a letter in the New York *Times*. Discussion then became so keen as to lead Monsieur Briand early in June to inquire of the State Department whether it would welcome a treaty. On receiving a favorable reply, he presented to Ambassador Herrick a draft "engagement" for transmission to the Secretary of State.[1]

Background of the Negotiations.

The significance of this offer lay less in the nature of the proposal than in the fact that it brought the United States, however tentatively, into the movement for organizing world peace. Already in the Covenant League members had pledged themselves not to resort to the free use of war for their selfish designs, and in Articles 11 and 16 had engaged in coöperation against war, Ar-

[1] The full story of the negotiations, with the documents and an illuminating narrative of the accompanying circumstances will be found in *War as an Instrument of National Policy and its Renunciation in the Pact of Paris*, by Dr. James T. Shotwell. With Professor Joseph P. Chamberlain, Dr. Shotwell was the draftsman of a model treaty intended to serve such purposes as those entertained by Monsieur Briand and containing the clauses of the Briand draft; included also was a self-defense clause, such as Mr. Kellogg in effect introduced by interpretation, a clause denying the benefits of the treaty to any signatory breaking it, which was finally incorporated in Mr. Kellogg's preamble, and provisions for conciliation and arbitration which did not appear in any of the diplomatic drafts or in the Pact as signed. That Dr. Shotwell played the leading part in mobilizing American public opinion in favor of the Pact cannot of course be discovered in his book. Mr. David Hunter Miller, who was one of the draftsmen of the League Covenant, has also written an admirable narrative and exegesis of the Pact in *The Peace Pact of Paris*.

ticle 16 in particular providing for the use of an economic boycott as a measure of applying coöperative sanctions against any country resorting to war in disregard of its covenants under Articles 12, 13, or 15.

As resort to war was not expressly prohibited by the Covenant except when there should be a unanimous report of the Council, or in the case of disputes which the parties "recognize to be suitable for submission to arbitration," what came to be known as the "gap" existed in the Covenant; a strong movement to prohibit all war began, therefore, in the League and culminated in the Geneva Protocol submitted to the Assembly of 1924. This Protocol declared war . . . of aggression an international crime, and the signatory states agreed "in no case to resort to war . . . except in resistance to acts of aggression" or in the application of "sanctions"; the Council of the League was to determine when sanctions should be applied. A peaceful method was prescribed for the settlement of all types of international controversies and the aggressor was to be identified as the "state which resorts to war in violation of the undertakings contained in the Covenant or in the present Protocol."

The Geneva Protocol was signed for Great Britain by the Labor government of Ramsay MacDonald. Before ratification could be taken up, a change of government occurred and the new Baldwin government reversed its predecessor's policy, a decision which was communicated to the Council meeting of March 12, 1925, by Sir Austen Chamberlain. Apart from the fact that the new commitment of the British Empire was too ambitious and too vague to please a Conservative government, the possibility of conflict with the United States in the event of the British navy being used to enforce the economic sanction by "pacific blockade" or other means was disturbing. The whole situation "is changed," said Sir Austen, "by the mere existence of powerful economic communities outside the limits of the League." He would prefer to "supplement the Covenant by making special arrangements to meet special needs . . . purely defensive in character . . . framed in the spirit of the Covenant, working in close harmony with the League and under its guidance . . . knitting together the nations most immediately concerned, and whose differences might lead to a renewal of strife." The military experts would advise, of course, that an obligation to apply sanctions could be undertaken much more safely if the field for their employment were to be local rather than universal.

That the British attitude was based on caution and not on obstructiveness was evidenced by "the Locarno treaties" which were initialed in October, 1925. The Treaty of Mutual Guaranty signed by Germany, Belgium, France, Great Britain, and Italy guaranteed the maintenance of the *status quo* in the Rhineland. Reciprocal agreements not to resort to war were entered into between Germany and Belgium, and Germany and France, with the further proviso that if the Council should decide that the guaranty had been violated they would "come to the assistance of the Power against whom the act complained of is directed," or at once if the act of aggression were unprovoked and immediate action should be necessary. The four arbitration treaties provided for efforts at conciliation through a Commission, and, in the event of failure, for submission to an arbitral tribunal or to the Permanent Court of International Justice of disputes over "their respective rights."

The eighth League Assembly in 1927 adopted a Polish resolution denouncing all "wars of aggression," and favoring the employment of "every pacific means to settle disputes" between states; the Pan-American Conference at Havana in 1928 adopted a similar resolution for the countries of the American continent represented, not of course affecting Canada or the possessions of European Powers.

Though the United States was not a partner of the Great Powers in any of the peace enterprises, it was apparent from the expressions of opinion in public bodies and in the movements fostered by private groups and religious and civic organizations that important elements of the American people desired an opportunity for the United States to associate itself with a worldwide movement to reduce the possibility of war.

Preliminary Exchanges.

On December 28, 1927, Mr. Kellogg, besides welcoming Monsieur Briand's proposal of eight months earlier, expressed the opinion that the two governments, instead of being content with "a bilateral declaration . . . might make a more signal contribution to world peace by joining in an effort to obtain the adherence of the Principal Powers to a declaration renouncing war as an instrument of national policy . . . in favor of the pacific settlement of international disputes." Monsieur Briand counter-proposed that France and the United States sign first and then invite other states to adhere, and that the renunciation be concerned with "all wars of aggression." These modifications, taken from the formula and procedure used in League of Nations treaties, were ignored by Mr. Kellogg.

Under Article 20 of the Covenant "the Members of the League . . . solemnly undertake that they will not hereafter enter into any engagements inconsistent with the terms" of the Covenant. The correspondence between Mr. Kellogg and Monsieur Briand developed the understanding that an agreement would infringe neither the Covenant of the League nor the Locarno treaties. In one of the Briand letters "an instrument of national policy" was defined as "a means of carrying out their own spontaneous, independent policy," obviously in order that police-work under the League should not have the stamp of the sort of "war" renounced by the Pact. France in its note of March 30 suggested a universal treaty. Having in mind its dependent friends, Belgium and Poland, it thought that "the treaty contemplated could not operate in respect of one Power which is a party thereto unless the other states exposed to the possibility of grave controversies with that party were also signatories thereof." Mr. Kellogg yielded to this desire, for any question of signatories became unimportant if the parties to the treaty were to be released from all obligation to a Power violating it. The Locarno parties were thus all brought in and the new instrument was made coterminous with the Locarno treaties.

With the consent of the Quai d'Orsay Mr. Kellogg on April 13, 1928, sent a preliminary draft of a treaty with an explanatory note to the foreign offices of Great Britain, Germany, Italy, and Japan. The French a week later submitted a similar treaty, incorporating the points which Mr. Kellogg had asserted were inevitable corollaries of his own draft. The American form was the one accepted in the negotiations.

Germany, replying on April 27, accepted the overture enthusiastically; the points it mentioned were that the proposed treaty would not conflict with the Covenant or with "the Rhine pact of Locarno," that if one state should violate the treaty the other states would be free to take up arms against the breaker of the peace, and that the treaty should be open to all nations.

Sir Austen Chamberlain replied on May 19. He thought it unnecessary to reserve the right of self-defense under the treaty, but in view of the Covenant and of the Locarno treaties it might be well to give expression to the general opinion that a violation of the treaty should release all the signatories from their obligation under the treaty toward the violator.[2] He then proceeded:

The language of Article 1, as to the renunciation of war as an instrument of national policy, renders it desirable that I should remind your Excellency that there are certain regions of the world the welfare and integrity of which constitute a special and vital interest for our peace and safety. His Majesty's Government have been at pains to make it clear in the past that interference with these regions cannot be suffered. Their protection against attack is to the British Empire a measure of self-defence. It must be clearly understood that His Majesty's Government in Great Britain accept the new treaty upon the distinct understanding that it does not prejudice their freedom of action in this respect. The Government of the United States have comparable interests any disregard of which by a foreign Power they have declared that they would regard as an unfriendly act. His Majesty's Government believe, therefore, that in defining their position they are expressing the intention and meaning of the United States Government.[3]

In such a matter, Sir Austen explained, "His Majesty's Government in Great Britain . . . could not undertake to participate

2 This point was taken care of in the third preamble of the treaty.
3 On August 4, 1928, the British Government transmitted to the Secretariat of the League copies of the notes setting forth the British interpretations of the Pact, and requested that they be communicated to "all members of the League"; this was done. These interpretations, however, were not transmitted by the United States with the text of the treaty to those states which the United States invited to adhere.

otherwise than jointly and simultaneously with His Majesty's Governments in the Dominions and the Government of India; fortunately," he concluded, "they are all in cordial agreement with the general principle of the proposed treaty."

Japan replied on May 26, mentioning the right of self-defense, and the obligations under the Covenant and the treaties of Locarno; the Irish Free State also called attention to the obligations of League members; but it was left to Canada to develop more fully the relation of the treaty to the Covenant and to the operations of the League:

The question whether the obligations of the Covenant of the League would conflict in any way with the obligations of the proposed pact has been given careful consideration. His Majesty's Government in Canada regards the League, with all its limitations, as an indispensable and continuing agency of international understanding, and would not desire to enter upon any course which would prejudice its effectiveness. It is, however, convinced that there is no conflict either in the letter or in the spirit between the Covenant and the multilateral pact, or between the obligations assumed under each.

The preëminent value of the League lies in its positive and preventive action. In bringing together periodically the representatives of fifty states, it builds up barriers against war by developing a spirit of conciliation, an acceptance of publicity in international affairs, a habit of coöperation in common ends, and a permanently available machinery for the adjustment of differences. It is true that the Covenant also contemplates the application of sanctions in the event of a member state going to war, if in so doing it has broken the pledges of the Covenant to seek a peaceful solution of disputes. Canada has always opposed any interpretation of the Covenant which would involve the application of these sanctions automatically or by the decision of other states. It was on the initiative of Canada that the Fourth Assembly, with a single negative vote, accepted the interpretative resolution to which the Secretary of State of the United States recently referred, indicating that it is for the constitutional authorities of each state to determine in what degree it is bound to assure the execution of the obligations of this article by employment of its military forces. The question of sanctions has received further consideration by later Assemblies. It is plain that the full realization of the ideal of joint economic or military pressure upon an outlaw

Power, upon which some of the founders of the League set great store, will require either an approach to the universality of the League contemplated when the Covenant was being drawn, or an adjustment of the old rules of neutrality to meet the new conditions of coöperative defence.

In any event, if, as would seem to be the case, the proposed multilateral treaty does not impose any obligation upon a signatory in relation to a state which has not signed the treaty or has broken it, any decision taken to apply sanctions against a member of the League which has made war in violation of its Covenant pledges would not appear to conflict with the obligations of the treaty.

Australia and India accepted without comment. "His Majesty's Government in the Union of South Africa" in accepting "took for granted" the three points generally established as to self-defense, obligation toward a violator, and the harmony between this treaty and the Covenant and Locarno treaties. The replies of Italy and New Zealand raised no questions of importance.

One of the most significant notes came from Czechoslovakia, July 20. Dr. Beneš observed that nothing in the treaty was opposed to the League of Nations Covenant, the Locarno treaties, the neutrality treaties "or, in general, to the obligations contained in existing treaties" of Czechoslovakia. Noting the freedom of the parties from obligation toward any violator of the Pact and making some observations on the right of self-defense, Mr. Beneš related the general aim of the treaty to the special interests of Czechoslovakia in a significant passage:

As thus defined both in the text of the preamble and in the statement of your Excellency's letter, the goal of the new treaty, according to the opinion of the Czechoslovak Republic, is to consolidate and maintain peaceful relations and peaceful and friendly collaboration under the contractual terms in which these have today been established between the interested nations. By their signature, the contracting parties will renounce war as an instrument of their national policy aimed to satisfy their selfish interests.

Mr. Beneš, whose policy it has been, as foreign minister of a "succession state," to maintain the political arrangements established by the Treaty of Versailles, concluded his note with the statement that "the foreign policy of our country sees therein the realisation of the ends which it has pursued for ten years."

As Mr. Miller says:[4]

The policy of Czechoslovakia for the maintenance of the *status quo* could hardly be more plainly indicated; and viewed in this light it is natural that the treaty should be regarded as "an immense benefit for humanity" and hardly less natural that Czechoslovakia "rejoices to see" that the Treaty is to be invested "with as universal a character as possible."

We may note here that Hungary, according to its note of October 6, 1928, adhered to the Treaty "under the supposition that the Government of the United States as well as the governments of the other signatory Powers would seek to find the means of rendering it possible that in the future injustices might be remedied by peaceful means." This is of course feasible under Article 19 of the Covenant which gives the Assembly the right "from time to time to advise the reconsideration by members of the League of treaties which have become inapplicable, and the consideration of international conditions whose continuance might endanger the peace of the world"; Article 11 gives countenance to friendly *démarches* to the same end.

MR. KELLOGG'S INTERPRETATIONS

Fourteen governments other than the United States were invited to become original signatories of the treaty, viz., France, Belgium, Czechoslovakia, Great Britain and other members of the British Commonwealth, Germany, Italy, Japan, and Poland. In his invitation, dated June 23, the Secretary of State mentioned the correspondence which had passed between the United States and France and recalled the chief features of an address he had delivered on April 28, 1928 before the American Society of International Law on the considerations emphasized by France:

(1) *Self-defense.* There is nothing in the American draft of an antiwar treaty which restricts or impairs in any way the right of

[4] *The Peace Pact of Paris,* p. 109.

self-defense. That right is inherent in every sovereign state and is implicit in every treaty. Every nation is free at all times and regardless of treaty provisions to defend its territory from attack or invasion and it alone is competent to decide whether circumstances require recourse to war in self-defense. If it has a good case, the world will applaud and not condemn its action. Express recognition by treaty of this inalienable right, however, gives rise to the same difficulty encountered in any effort to define aggression. It is the identical question approached from the other side. Inasmuch as no treaty provision can add to the natural right of self-defense, it is not in the interest of peace that a treaty should stipulate a juristic conception of self-defense since it is far too easy for the unscrupulous to mold events to accord with an agreed definition.

(2) *The League Covenant.* The Covenant imposes no affirmative primary obligation to go to war. The obligation, if any, is secondary and attaches only when deliberately accepted by a state. Article 10 of the Covenant has, for example, been interpreted by a resolution submitted to the Fourth Assembly but not formally adopted owing to one adverse vote to mean that "it is for the constitutional authorities of each member to decide, in reference to the obligation of preserving the independence and the integrity of the territory of members, in what degree the member is bound to assure the execution of this obligation by employment of its military forces." There is, in my opinion, no necessary inconsistency between the Covenant and the idea of an unqualified renunciation of war. The Covenant can, it is true, be construed as authorizing war in certain circumstances but it is an authorization and not a positive requirement.

(3) *The Treaties of Locarno.* If the parties to the treaties of Locarno are under any positive obligation to go to war,[5] such obligation certainly would not attach until one of the parties "has resorted to war in violation of its solemn pledges thereunder." It is therefore obvious that if all the parties to the Locarno treaties become parties to the multilateral antiwar treaty proposed by the United States, there would be a double assurance that the Locarno treaties would not be violated by recourse to arms. In such event it would follow that resort to war by any state in violation of the Locarno treaties would also be a breach of the multilateral antiwar treaty and the other

---

[5] Many protests are now offered against the confusion of hostilities of two opposing types under the single word "war," i.e., nationalistic war and collective defense or repression of a peace-breaker.

parties to the antiwar treaty would thus as a matter of law be automatically released from their obligations thereunder and free to fulfil their Locarno commitments. The United States is entirely willing that all parties to the Locarno treaties should become parties to its proposed antiwar treaty either through signature in the first instance or by immediate accession to the treaty as soon as it comes into force in the manner provided in Article 3 of the American draft, and it will offer no objection when and if such a suggestion is made.

(4) *Treaties of neutrality*. The United States is not informed as to the precise treaties which France has in mind and cannot therefore discuss their provisions. It is not unreasonable to suppose, however, that the relations between France and the states whose neutrality she has guaranteed are sufficiently close and intimate to make it possible for France to persuade such states to adhere seasonably to the antiwar treaty proposed by the United States. If this were done no party to the antiwar treaty could attack the neutralized states without violating the treaty and thereby automatically freeing France and the other powers in respect of the treaty-breaking state from the obligations of the antiwar treaty. If the neutralized states were attacked by a state not a party to the antiwar treaty, the latter treaty would of course have no bearing and France would be as free to act under the treaties guaranteeing neutrality as if she were not a party to the antiwar treaty. It is difficult to perceive, therefore, how treaties guaranteeing neutrality can be regarded as necessarily preventing the conclusion by France or any other power of a multilateral treaty for the renunciation of war.

(5) *Relations with a treaty-breaking state*. As I have already pointed out, there can be no question as a matter of law that violation of a multilateral antiwar treaty through resort to war by one party thereto would automatically release the other parties from their obligations to the treaty-breaking state. Any express recognition of this principle of law is wholly unnecessary.

(6) *Universality*. From the beginning it has been the hope of the United States that its proposed multilateral antiwar treaty should be world-wide in its application, and appropriate provision therefor was made in the draft submitted to the other governments on April 13. From a practical standpoint it is clearly preferable, however, not to postpone the coming into force of an antiwar treaty until all the nations of the world can agree upon the text of such a treaty and cause it to be ratified. For one reason or another a state so situated

as to be no menace to the peace of the world might obstruct agreement or delay ratification in such manner as to render abortive the efforts of all the other powers. It is highly improbable, moreover, that a form of treaty acceptable to the British, French, German, Italian and Japanese Governments, as well as to the United States, would not be equally acceptable to most, if not all, of the other powers of the world. Even were this not the case, however, the coming into force among the above-named six powers of an effective antiwar treaty and their observance thereof would be a practical guaranty against a second world war. This in itself would be a tremendous service to humanity and the United States is not willing to jeopardize the practical success of the proposal which it has made by conditioning the coming into force of the treaty upon prior universal or almost universal acceptance.

The Secretary stated in this note that he was enclosing a revised draft of the proposed treaty, recognizing in the preamble that all parties to the treaty would be released from obligation to any party resorting to war in violation of it, and providing for signature by all parties to the treaties of Locarno.

THE TREATY

THE fourteen governments to which the note of June 23 was addressed accepted the treaty in its revised form, and on August 27 met with Mr. Kellogg at the Quai d'Orsay and signed the multilateral anti-war treaty. In the eloquent address with which Monsieur Briand ushered in the act of signing, two passages have special significance:

Freed from the old bondage, the nations that have signed the new contract will gradually forsake the habit of associating the idea of national prestige and national interest with the idea of force, and this single psychological fact will not be the least important factor in the evolution that is needed to lead to the regular stabilization of peace.

Oh! But this is not realism, it has been said, and are not sanctions lacking? It might be asked whether true realism consists in excluding from the realm of facts the moral forces, among which is that of public opinion. In effect, a state which would act so as to incur the reprobation of all its partners would run the positive risk of seeing all of them gradually and freely gather against it with formidable consequences that would not be long in ensuing. And where is the country, signatory to this pact, whose leaders would on their own responsibility expose it to such danger?

*   *   *   *   *   *   *

Peace is proclaimed. That is well; that is much; but it still remains necessary to organize it. In the solution of difficulties right and not might must prevail. That is to be the work of tomorrow.

The English text of the treaty is as follows:

The President of the German Reich, the President of the United States of America, His Majesty the King of the Belgians, the President of the French Republic, His Majesty the King of Great Britain, Ireland and the British Dominions beyond the Seas, Emperor of India, His Majesty the King of Italy, His Majesty the Emperor of Japan, the President of the Republic of Poland, the President of the Czechoslovak Republic,

Deeply sensible of their solemn duty to promote the welfare of mankind;

Persuaded that the time has come when a frank renunciation of war as an instrument of national policy should be made to the end that the peaceful and friendly relations now existing between their peoples may be perpetuated;

Convinced that all changes in their relations with one another should be sought only by pacific means and be the result of a peaceful and orderly process, and that any signatory Power which shall hereafter seek to promote its national interests by resort to war should be denied the benefits furnished by this Treaty;

Hopeful that, encouraged by their example, all the other nations of the world will join in this humane endeavor and by adhering to the present Treaty as soon as it comes into force bring their peoples within the scope of its beneficent provisions, thus uniting the civilized nations of the world in a common renunciation of war as an instrument of their national policy;

Have decided to conclude a Treaty. . . .

*   *   *   *   *   *   *

Article I

The High Contracting Parties solemnly declare in the names of their respective peoples that they condemn recourse to war for the solution of international controversies, and renounce it as an instrument of national policy in their relations with one another.

Article II

The High Contracting Parties agree that the settlement or solution of all disputes or conflicts of whatever nature or of whatever origin they may be, which may arise among them, shall never be sought except by pacific means.

Article III

The present Treaty shall be ratified by the High Contracting Parties named in the Preamble in accordance with their respective constitutional requirements, and shall take effect as between them as soon as all their several instruments of ratification shall have been deposited at Washington.

This Treaty shall, when it has come into effect as prescribed in the preceding paragraph, remain open as long as may be necessary for adherence by all the other Powers of the world. Every instrument evidencing the adherence of a Power shall be deposited at Washington and the Treaty shall immediately upon such deposit become effective as between the Power thus adhering and the other Powers parties hereto.

It shall be the duty of the Government of the United States to furnish each Government named in the Preamble and every Government subsequently adhering to this Treaty with a certified copy of the Treaty and of every instrument of ratification or adherence. It shall also be the duty of the Government of the United States telegraphically to notify such Governments immediately upon the deposit with it of each instrument of ratification or adherence.

Plenipotentiaries of Germany, the United States, Belgium, France, Great Britain (signing for all parts of the British Empire which are not members of the League), Canada, Australia, New Zealand, South Africa, Irish Free State, India, Italy, Japan, Poland, and Czechoslovakia signed in order.

By its terms the treaty was to become effective as soon as all parties should have deposited in Washington their several instruments of ratification. This having been completed, the treaty was proclaimed on July 24, 1929. As of that date, thirty-one of the forty-eight nations invited by the Secretary of State to adhere to the treaty had deposited definite instruments of ratification and those of five other states were officially reported to be on their way.

Soviet Observations.

Like envoi to a ballad came a note of the Government of the U.S.S.R. of August 31, 1928, to the French Ambassador at Moscow, accepting the invitation of the French Government to adhere to the Pact. Though addressed to M. Herbette, it was, after the fashion of ballads, intended for "Princes and Lords of every sort." In this note the Soviet Government recited the fact that it had presented at Geneva proposals for complete and for partial disarmament which had been rejected in the Preparatory Commission of the League; and had offered to conclude bilateral compacts forbidding wars of attack, in which only Germany, Turkey, Afghanistan, Persia, and Lithuania had seen fit to join. These circumstances were "irrefutable proof of the fact that the very idea of suspension of wars and armed conflicts as a matter of international policy is a basic idea of Soviet foreign policy"; yet "the initiators of the Pact of Paris" had not invited the Soviet Government to participate in the negotiations or the elaboration of the text of the compact, nor such Powers interested in guaranteeing peace as Turkey, Afghanistan, and China. Nevertheless the Soviet Government, invited by France to join in the compact, could not be deprived of the right to explain its attitude.

First of all the Government regretted the total absence of obligations in the realm of disarmament, which it regarded as indispensable to peace; new international groupings, especially in relation to the renewal of armaments, seemed to underlie this situation. It objected to the vagueness of the treaty, believing that war must be forbidden not only as an instrument of national policy, but also as serving oppressive and reactionary forces. Besides war such military actions as intervention, blockade, and military occupation of foreign territory and foreign ports from which Russia had suffered and China was suffering should also be forbidden.

Among the unpeaceful means for solving international disputes which the Soviet Government considered forbidden by the compact it placed the rupture of normal relations between peoples or the refusal to resume them.

The Soviet note concerned itself with the British statement which reserved the right to make war in case of "interference" with regions not enumerated, and gave Great Britain both freedom of action with regard to the areas it might select as specially under its influence and power to decide what would constitute an unfriendly act of "interference." This the Soviet Government found objectionable because it was arbitrary and because it would lead to similar reservations on the part of other countries until there might be no "place on the terrestrial globe regarding which the compact could be applied." The British statement therefore seemed to the Soviet Government "an attempt to use the compact itself as an instrument of imperialistic policy."

The decision to adhere to the Pact, which was later made effective, was evidently based on grounds of expediency, for it came as a *non sequitur* to the arguments of which the note was composed.

FORCE OF PRE-TREATY UNDERSTANDINGS

CONSTRUED in extreme simplicity, war as an instrument of national policy would mean any war in the assertion or promotion or defense of policy or of interests or of "rights." The result would be to bar any war except one waged in defense of a national domain. This interpretation would bring all the foreign wars of the United States—1812, 1846, 1898, 1917—under the ban, irrespective of the soundness or morality of the policy upon which each was based. Each was a war to support a policy or interest or "right," not a war of territorial defense.[6]

The same interpretation would condemn such wars as the

6 Without considering the desire for expansion, of which, in the era of "manifest destiny," President Polk was the leading exponent, and the popularity of the war in Texas and the Mississippi Valley, the immediate cause of the Mexican War was Polk's act in attempting to solve by force a dispute over a barren tract of land in the Mexican state of Tamaulipas to which the claim of Mexico by occupation and by the exercise of jurisdiction was superior to that of Texas. S. E. Morison, *Oxford History of the United States*, II, 79.

Crimean war, all three of Bismarck's wars for German unity, the war of Cavour and Napoleon III against Austria, and the Russo-Japanese war of 1904. It would bar all the eleven types of war that Great Britain's interests, according to Sir Henry Hamilton Johnston, in his *Common Sense in Foreign Policy*, would justify it in waging. It would also prohibit the United States from using its navy in asserting the Monroe Doctrine.

None of the Great Powers intended such an abandonment of absolute sovereignty, the "free prerogative" of nations in their international relations. Hence Sir Austen's insistence upon a "distinct understanding" that the treaty does not prejudice British freedom of action in protecting from attack those "regions of the world the welfare and integrity of which constitute a special and vital interest for our peace and safety." An attack on an area adjacent to the Suez Canal would mean to Britain a potential severage of the life-line to the Indian Ocean, a cutting off of Australian wheat, mutton and wool, and of the markets of India. Since the mandated countries of Asia Minor, such as Palestine and Iraq, the Anglo-Egyptian Sudan where British sovereignty is uncertain, territories like the Kingdom of the Hedjaz where British influence is potent, are not protected by the multilateral treaty, no government being signatory for them, the British observations are meant to indicate the sort of British guardianship whose fulfilment in protection against attack or "interference" must not be taken as a violation of the treaty by Great Britain.

This assertion of what came to be called the British Monroe Doctrine did not pass unnoticed by sovereign Powers adjacent to the affected areas. In their respective notes to the United States of September 4, and October 4, 1928, Egypt and Persia objected to the British observations and declined to be bound by them by implication in adhering to the treaty. Turkey, in a note of October 31, 1928, considered itself "reciprocally bound by the text of the proposed act exclusive of all the documents which have not been submitted as an integral part of the Pact to the collective signature of the participating states."

The question arises: What is the legal effect of these pre-treaty "understandings"? In the hearings before the Senate Committee on Foreign Relations Mr. Kellogg was subjected to a barrage of questions in order that this point might be elucidated. It was contended that if ambiguities appeared in the language of a contract recourse might be had to the negotiations to determine the meaning. Senator Reed of Missouri felt that in such an event elucidation of ambiguities only was allowable, the inference being that the treaty must be regarded as an integral instrument. Senator Walsh of Montana thought that the rule as given by Senator Reed defied dogmatic statement. He had had occasion "to study it pretty carefully in connection with the treaty of 1909 with Canada, and in the interpretation of that treaty by the International Joint Commission the whole course of negotiation leading up to it was received with a view to determining just exactly what was meant by the treaty." Secretary Kellogg agreed that this rule should apply to the anti-war treaty, but also agreed with Senator Reed that "if there was anything in these notes contrary to the provisions of the treaty, naturally the treaty would control." The Turks, the Egyptians, and the Persians, as has been shown, wished to be certain on this point, since prior "understandings" are binding on governments which ratify a treaty without protesting against them.[7]

THE PRINCIPLE OF SELF-DEFENSE

THE crux of the matter lay in the definition of self-defense. Secretary Kellogg held that it was not necessary to make any definition of "aggressor" or "self-defense." In point of fact, he felt that it could not be done accurately. "They have been trying to do it in Europe for six or eight years, and they never have been able to define accurately 'aggressor' or 'self-defense.' " Hence the word "self-defense" does not occur in the treaty. In the opinion of the Secretary of State, not only is self-defense an inalienable prerogative of sovereignty, but the right to define self-defense is also such a prerogative. For this reason Mr. Kellogg made no objec-

---

[7] For precedents see *For. Rel.*, 1899, p. 147; David Hunter Miller, *Reservations of Treaties, Their Effect and the Procedure in Regard Thereto*, pp. 87-89.

tion to the British observations. He regarded them as superfluous, since his own interpretation, viz., that each nation "may decide whether circumstances require recourse to war in self-defense," was broad enough to include those territories or regions which, like Egypt and the Persian Gulf, the Caribbean Islands and the Central American states, lay within the orbit not of sovereignty but of national policy; he therefore assured the Senate that the Monroe Doctrine was unaffected.

This apparent widening of the field of self-defense has troubled many proponents of the Pact. Yet it is merely the expression of something that had already been understood between governments. For the United States, which has relatively little occasion to consider danger to its territory, the right of self-defense has little practical advantage unless it includes the defense of intangible interests as well as of territory, and Mr. Kellogg's interpretation would classify under the head of self-defense the protection of those "rights," interests and concerns which a nation considers to involve its security or to be essential to its welfare. The treaty guaranty of the independence of Panama is thus an "interest" of the United States, and defense of that interest comes under the theory of "self-defense."

Divorcing the treaty from all the setting of contemporaneous events and tendencies, therefore, jurists conclude that it carries no binding contractual obligations, for Article II, forbidding the settlement or solution of any dispute except by pacific means, is subject as well as Article I to the principle of "self-defense" interpreted as we have indicated.

The preamble establishes an identity between "national interests" and "national policy." If a nation is free to decide for itself that the maintenance of a trade route, or the procurement of a supply of food, e.g., wheat or bananas, or of tropical raw materials essential to its manufactures, e.g., rubber, oil, manganese, is an interest vital to its welfare, and also to decide that the assertion of so vital an interest (i.e., policy) is self-defense, to distinguish between a war waged as an instrument of a particular national policy and a defensive war would become impossible.

The use of the term "right" adds to the confusion, for the support of an interest is called a "right" and invested with an ethical quality. The fact is that in a general war there is never a question of right and wrong, but of right and right according to the point of view. "Evil," says Santayana, "is an inevitable aspect which things put on when they are struggling to preserve themselves in the same habitat, in which there is not room or matter enough for them to prosper equally side by side."

THE MONROE DOCTRINE AND SELF-DEFENSE

To many Americans there are applications of the Monroe Doctrine or of the Caribbean policy which have as vital a meaning as British protection of the zones mentioned in the Chamberlain note has to the British people. It was inevitable that the problem would trouble senatorial minds when they were called upon to assent to the treaty. A twelve-day debate convinced the chairman of the Committee on Foreign Relations, Senator Borah, that in order to obtain ratification he would have to make a concession to the insistent demand for explanation. This he did by introducing into the Senate with the treaty a report of the Committee on Foreign Relations in which the treaty was interpreted as being not incompatible with the Monroe Doctrine. The report pointed out that the Monroe Doctrine is based on the principle of self-defense. Senator Borah emphasized the fact that the report was to be regarded solely as a record of interpretation and not in any sense as "for the purpose or with the design of modifying or changing the treaty or in any way effecting a reservation or reservations to the same." Consent to the treaty, given on January 15, 1929, by a vote of 85 to 1, was accordingly accompanied by no reservations or interpretations for communication to other nations.

In view of what has already been said, one is left in doubt as to the purpose of the Senate in declaring an equivalence between the Monroe Doctrine and the principle of self-defense. Was it, as has been supposed, to declare officially that hereafter the Monroe Doctrine shall cover nothing except the natural and reasonable meaning of self-defense as applied to the situation of the United

States? This would conform to the definition of the Doctrine given by Mr. Hughes[8] as

being opposed (1) to any non-American action encroaching upon the political independence of American states under any guise; and (2) to the acquisition in any manner of the control of additional territory in this hemisphere by any non-American Power. It thus relates to the interests or the action of a non-American state. . . .

Or did the Senate intend to declare that "self-defense," in the interpretation of the anti-war treaty, is to be as broad as any past distortion of the Monroe Doctrine or any future metamorphosis of it, including the complex of Caribbean policies, that the United States feels inclined to insist upon? The doubt covers the whole difference between the doctrine of Monroe and "the Monroe Doctrine," and the delay of the Latin American states in ratifying the Pact bears testimony to this uncertainty.

POPULAR INTEREST IN PEACE

CIVILIZATION, in the sense of the stabilization of society, both domestic and international, proceeds less by the compulsion of contractual obligations than by a figuration of behavior in which many strands of interest and habit are woven; on this account it is of no avail to attempt a quantitative appraisal of the Pact of Paris. The figuration which the League of Nations is weaving results from the pressures exercised in the last resort by public opinion. To some extent it may be said that the peoples of the various states are "willing to change substantially their daily life to prevent the coming of war." The international pressure brought to bear on Italy at the time of the Corfu incident, the peremptory order to Pangalos by collective Europe acting through the Council to retire from Bulgaria, were orders to stop fighting prior to negotiation. The aggressor would have been the one who disregarded the recommendation of the Council. Again in the Bolivia-Paraguay imbroglio, world opinion immediately set itself against recourse to war regardless of whether the Chaco belonged to Bolivia or to Paraguay and of who fired the first shot.

[8] Sherrill Foundation Lecture at Yale University, March 23, 1929.

Is it too much to expect that this process will be cumulative, that each instance will diminish the potential bellicosity of the next fracas? This much is certain, that, though expressed in terms of governmental obligations, the Pact of Paris expresses primarily the deep-felt aspiration of peoples. Sometimes the making of war is the act of governments as political entities; sometimes, on the other hand, it is forced by popular opinion against the desire of a government, whether that opinion be spontaneous or fabricated by powerful interests. Both the negotiating and consenting organs of government have assured the world that nothing in this treaty impairs the liberty of action of the signatory nations; but under governments are the individuals who give their lives, who bear the burden of war taxes and war debts, and who have pressing motives for the restriction of war, and the new treaty has encouraged them in each country to believe that the desire for peace is universal. Such a declaration must be a source of energy and of political force in the struggle to create coöperative habits and technique in world organization. It may indeed give a new direction to statesmanship.

THE OBLIGATION ASSUMED

THE quantum of the achievement of the Pact depends largely upon the coöperation of the United States in peace measures and peace organization. An attack by nation A upon nation B has customarily found the United States neutral, insisting upon the neutral's profitable prerogative of trading with both belligerents. It is declared that a breach of the Pact would leave this situation unchanged. At the hearings before the Committee on Foreign Relations, Senator Walsh's question: "Supposing some other nation does break this treaty, why should we interest ourselves in it?" was met by the Secretary of State with "There is not a bit of reason." Senator Borah has declared himself opposed to "anything that savors of sanctions." A considerable body of official opinion would seek to guarantee neutral rights in war-time; Senator Reed (of Missouri) obtained the overwhelming support of the Senate to an amendment to the Cruiser Bill of 1929 which empowered the President to begin negotiations to this end.

Another body of opinion, mainly unofficial but articulate enough to make its influence felt on the Senate during the Pact discussions, argues that since an attack of one signatory Power on another would constitute a breach of a treaty to which the United States is a party, the state of mind generated would be inconsistent with American indifference to the origin of such an attack and with American insistence on the rights of trade. The Pact, in other words, is considered by this body of opinion as a sign that neutrality *per se* is in course of progressive renunciation with the renunciation of war as an established institution.

While there is no obligation imposed upon the parties to take any action in consequence of a breach of the treaty, the natural way of supporting a common interest is by counsel and a concerted program, and a community of interest naturally leads to a community of action.[9] There is precedent for this in contemporary American policy. A declaration of common interest in peace in the Pacific region was made in the Four Power Pacific Treaty signed at Washington, December 13, 1921, in which the United States, the British Empire, France, and Japan agreed

If there should develop between any of the High Contracting Parties a controversy arising out of any Pacific question and involving their said rights which is not satisfactorily settled by diplomacy and is likely to affect the harmonious accord now happily subsisting between them, they shall invite the other High Contracting Parties to a joint conference to which the whole subject will be referred for consideration and adjustment.[10]

[9] Article 11 of the Covenant provides—"Any war or threat of war, whether immediately affecting the members of the League or not, is hereby declared a matter of concern to the whole League, and the League shall take any action that may be deemed wise and effectual to safeguard the peace of nations."

[10] Shotwell, *op. cit.*, pp. 252 ff.

MODERN war arises as a consequence of policy rather than as its instrument. The man who has to face a crisis is not often the one who brought it into being, since the decisions of the past condition the acts of the present; Bethmann-Hollweg, Asquith, and Sazonoff had to make their decisions in July, 1914, in situations created for them by their predecessors.

The world is taking the first tentative steps in the process of withdrawing, in their early and malleable state, the problems out of which war arises from the arena of controversial struggle into the region of scientific examination and treatment. Meanwhile these problems are increasing in number. Many of them, essentially and originally domestic in character, such as tariffs, population, raw materials, and immigration, bristle with international complications caused by overlapping in modern world activities and the pressure of self-preservation. It is slowly dawning on public consciousness that the bases of self-preservation need to be recast into molds unmarked by frontiers. Europe in the course of time may come to see, for example, that through new economic and social policies which are not related to political boundaries it may help itself out of economic and social distress and diminish the possibility of future distress. Such a procedure would be the scientist's shift from cure to prevention.

No such scientific approach is possible until this public sense of security displaces the tribal fears which correspond to the principle of nationalism in its severely logical and extreme forms. Strategic considerations, as Philip Kerr observes, will condition policy as long as war is considered a contingency of national life. The conviction that war is "unthinkable" may therefore be helpful to the constructive measures which knit nations in peace organization. One of the procedures by which that conviction can be furthered is that of conference—conference thoroughly prepared, skilfully conducted, carefully followed up. Not every kind of conference will do this; the dispatch of delegates to infrequent *ad hoc* conventions whose resolutions remain unfulfilled, or the summoning of a hasty conference to avert a war when the war spirit has been mobilized, may be ineffectual. A system of regular and frequent meetings offers superior advantages: it prevents the feeling that a whole position must be established at a single throw, and makes it unnecessary and inadvisable for any nation to present the final expression of its desires—an ultimatum; it permits exploration of a subject and tentative proposals; it acquaints each party with the positions of the others and with an understanding of their genuine necessities; it develops personal affinities, and it allows of interim studies of deep-rooted problems. A calendar of unfinished business is often a wholesome factor in international relations.

At such regular conferences, munimented by portfolios, memoranda, experts, and secretaries, each man discovers new aspects of his problems; he comes in contact with reasonable hopes, fears, desires, and, indeed, necessities which in his domestic environment he would not have considered. On this account, as Professor Brierly remarks, the game cannot be played blindfold and is less like chess than poker; everyone comes persuaded of something of which he is a bit less sure after listening to the others; men gathered about a table are more apt to see that thorny problems can be better dealt with by conciliation and compromise than on the basis of theoretic, nationalistic, or obscurantist assumptions. At least ten thousand men in Europe today have had the experience of recurrent conference in their respective fields; few of them will ever in their domestic environment take up a piece of public business with international implications without reflecting how the matter will strike their "opposite numbers" dealing with the same subject in other countries.

The method of conference must of course take account of the differences between those conferences which attempt to regulate the activities of governments as political units and those which are concerned with the more multiple activities in which national life finds expression. "On the one hand there is the traditional conception of the diplomatic congress of representatives of independent states, surviving from the time when international intercourse was chiefly confined to the relations of states as political units. . . . In this case unanimity is obviously necessary in order to bind the parties, since in the absence of a 'meeting of the minds' there is no bargain. . . . On the other hand, there is the rapidly growing tendency to look upon international conferences as parliamentary assemblies, organized along the general lines of legislative bodies."[11] Since the reaching of unanimous agreement presents almost insuperable difficulties, there is thus an increasing tendency "to adopt some form of majority rule, in order to arrive at effective agreement. In this case, the deliberative body becomes a device for discovering the highest common factor of coincidence among the various diverging views of the community, and an organ for expressing this coincidence as the agreement of the whole community, including the dissenting minority."[12]

Conference does not in itself constitute a complete system of negotiation, and public conferences inadequately or unskilfully organized have special dangers of their own. Conferences on the subjects which easily rouse national feeling should usually be preceded by a period of careful international preparation. If on such subjects each of the participating governments has developed its own policy to the point of making a detailed and elaborate scheme; if it has constructed and buttressed its program by interdepartmental agreements and collaboration; if during the whole process of this national preparation there has been no contact with the other governments concerned; and if the complete schemes so prepared by the different countries are then announced to the national public before the conference or at its beginning, the task of securing agreement by conference will be immensely more difficult than it need have been, and may well be impossible. As soon as the different governments know the main outlines of their policies, and before they have published them, much less elaborated them, the responsible officials should explore one another's points of view in private meetings.

In this way the task of securing agreement in conference is limited to the essentials, all minor matters having been cleared away beforehand by preliminary meetings, and the chances of

11 F. S. Dunn, *Practice and Procedure of International Conference*, Johns Hopkins University Press, pp. 188, 123.
12 *Ibid.*, p. 124.

success made greater. Concessions, even in comparatively minor matters not touching the essential interests of the country, are difficult to make after a scheme has been proclaimed in public, for some question of national prestige then seems to be involved in any change. Preparatory meetings have the advantage of making it possible to decide with much greater certainty when a conference can be called with reasonable hope of success. A conference that fails is worse than a conference postponed or even cancelled, and this danger is greatly reduced by preparatory meetings.

The method of open diplomacy and of public conference, which is one illustration of open diplomacy, does not mean a substitution for the old and intricate system of the past of something which is simple and easy and requires no similar skill or care. On the contrary, the technique required for using open conference in proper relation to the formal or informal discussions and negotiations which must precede, accompany, and often follow it, requires care and skill which can scarcely be developed without considerable experience. The last ten years have produced much experience of this kind but there has been little attempt to study, generalize, and publish the results of this experience,[13] and of the technique which is being developed over a wide range of problems varying greatly in subject matter and character.

In 1925 the committee of experts appointed by the League of Nations for the progressive codification of international law determined to include the subject of conference procedure on the provisional list of subjects on international law "the regulation of which by international agreement would seem to be most desirable and realizable at the present moment." The proposal did not receive the support of a sufficient number of states (the United States, among others, "saw no real necessity for the regulation of these subjects by international agreement") and accordingly it was removed from the field of codification. The Assembly of the League of Nations on September 25, 1927, however, passed a resolution requesting the Council to instruct the Secretariat of the League to study the question, not as a topic of codification but as a subject whose study might produce valuable models.

[13] See, however, Dunn, *op. cit.*

The use of the conference process involves the compromises inherent in all coöperation; a determined aloofness from it results in a servitude to events shaped by the wills of others. The position of the United States in 1916, the limitations upon the choices then open to it, illustrate this kind of servitude.

III.

IMMIGRATION

INTRODUCTORY

A SEPARATE study of the American attitude toward immigration, developing under the influence of economic and political factors, such as the Irish potato famine, the European revolutionary movements of 1848, the building of American railroads and the opening of American coal-fields, the War hyphenates and the later flood of immigrants inexperienced in self-government, would examine their effect on the evolution of American political ideology. It would begin with the utterances, familiar to all but never commonplace, of the early American statesmen who regarded their country as an asylum for political refugees and the socially downtrodden, a land where the sun of freedom and of economic opportunity had forever dissipated the mists of religious bigotry, political obscurantism, and social oppression. Such a study would then seek to discover the qualities of the human beings who made up the extraordinary hegira—the independent and the enterprising, the ambitious, the restless and discontented, the destitute and the unsuccessful—and it would trace their mingled qualities in the history of American ideas and institutions.

The hospitality of the eighteenth and early nineteenth centuries had its basis in like-mindedness, in the ideas of "Sam" Adams, and "Tom" Paine, of Patrick Henry and Jefferson, which welcomed rebels against authority, and in sympathy of the masses for those who were escaping from the European and English caste systems; by the European standards of the time the ideas were subversive, and their exponents were "radicals." As the nineteenth century advanced, American wealth and numbers increased, and with the resolution of the slavery problem all barriers were removed from the road to phenomenal prosperity. Wealth then increasing faster than population, conservatism, prudence in political experiment, distrust of new ideas, and constitution-worship grew also.

After the World War the cooling of undiscriminating hospitality suddenly began to find legislative expression. Advantage was being or would be taken of it by newcomers out of a Europe which in its turn had become a land of agrarian governments, of socialistic heresies, and of the terrifying experiment of Bolshevism. The desire grew to reserve the enjoyment of material welfare and blessed institutions to the descendants of those who had created them, and who were thought to be most apt for maintaining their perfection. Much happened in the seventy years between the visit in 1851 of the Hungarian Kossuth, riding "Black Warrior" up Broadway from the Battery like a second Lafayette, to the applause of thousands, and the exclusion in 1928 of another Hungarian, Karolyi, by the State Department, without protest except from a few "intellectuals."

Such a study would relate primarily to American domestic ideology, and not to American foreign relations; a survey of those relations must content itself with a brief and objective treatment of the policies which have been the resultant of the multiplex forces of national life.

Increasing human migration in the past three centuries, culminating during the nineteenth century in a movement without parallel in world history,[1] has vitally affected the ethnic and economic characters of many modern nations. Changes in agricultural methods and in systems of landholding, growth of manufactures and of towns, extension of transportation facilities and an almost universal diffusion of information concerning opportunities in recently settled countries, have combined to give mobility to a large part of the world's population. Money wages and cheap land have aided in breaking down national boundaries and in weakening the bonds of home and native land as restraints on migration. As long as differences in living standards exist in various parts of the world, movement of population promises to continue, unless directly blocked by legislation guarding national frontiers.

The peopling of the North American continent has been one of the most dramatic chapters in the history of human migration. Thirty-six million people entered the United States in the nineteenth century to develop the country. This rapidity of expansion has been purchased at high cost. Resources have been wasted; losses in property and well-being have accompanied violent fluc-

---

[1] See the estimates by Professor Walter F. Willcox, cited in *Recent Economic Changes*, II, 843.

tuations in business conditions characteristic of rapid expansion; improvement in the living standard of workers commensurate with the increase in wealth has been retarded.

Absorption in the vision of a country populated from coast to coast made the social results of immigration seem of secondary importance. But the passing of the frontier changed the attitude of *laissez faire* toward a human invasion which had to a large extent determined American culture as well as American population. It brought about an immigration policy conditioned by the influence of the foreign-born on ways of life, political ideals, and national unity. The problem is now envisaged in terms of the right of a nation to isolation from the effects of foreign blood and foreign culture.

Inequalities in pressure of population and differences in living standards among nations have made labor migration a problem as full of international complications as the export of goods or capital, and a sound national policy must take these factors into consideration.

CHAPTER ONE

IMMIGRATION POLICY BEFORE THE WORLD WAR

U NTIL the World War the United States was regarded as a country of free entry. During the preceding decade gross immigration averaged approximately one million annually and net immigration about two-thirds of that number. The Chinese Exclusion Acts and the Gentlemen's Agreement with Japan had effectively limited the admission of Orientals, but the head tax and the provisions for excluding criminals, paupers, physical and mental defectives, and contract laborers had not seriously interrupted the human tide from Europe.

Free entry was based on the demand for more settlers and laborers than the natural increase in population could supply. Rapid exploitation of resources and settlement of lands depended on immigrants, whose availability in turn stimulated expansion. For almost three centuries the economic development of the United States offered livelihood to a continuous stream of newcomers.

Conditions Conducive to Migration.

The opportunities which attracted immigrants varied with the periods of American history. During colonial times immigrants were wanted for labor in the Middle Atlantic states and the South; the slave trade was an extreme example of "assisted immigration" for economic development. Lands beyond the coastal plain were available for settlement to persons of small means. Industrial opportunities were created by the growth of manufactures in New England and the Middle Atlantic states after the Napoleonic wars. Immigration was later encouraged by a federal law facilitating the importation of contract laborers. In 1862 the opening of the public domain to homesteaders created a demand for more homesteaders, and brought about social and economic advantages in closer settlement. The transcontinental railroads enlisted immigrants as laborers, as purchasers of railroad lands, and as producers and buyers of freight. Before the demand for people to fill the western lands declined, industry began to respond to the stimulus of an increased domestic market, and a call arose for laborers in coal and iron mining, in the smelting and refining of ore for steel, in the mechanical industries, and in almost every branch of manufacturing and mining.

Augmented production and widened markets, which increased the demand for labor, were accompanied by changes in the means of transportation facilitating travel. Steamship competition for the lucrative immigrant business produced effective methods in securing a continuous supply. Steamship agents were always on hand in countries suffering from social unrest or economic distress to sell passages to America. The western railroads coöperated with the steamship companies in offering through tickets to western lands, partly for the sake of the passage money, but mainly for the sake of settling the territory they served. Western states flooded Europe with literature containing alluring pictures of the advantages of life within their borders. Large corporations maintained agents abroad who recruited laborers by offering prepaid tickets.

The economic situation in Europe was also conducive to migration. Periodic famine under conditions of dense population and inadequate transport facilities, and the low living standards which accompanied these conditions, favored population movements. In northwestern Europe large migrations in the eighteenth and nineteenth centuries resulting from the displacement of agricultural workers by the introduction of farm machinery or change in the use of land from agriculture to grazing led to large holdings, increased land values, and decreased demand for farm labor. In England these changes were accompanied by new methods of manufacture in consequence of the invention of machinery and by shifts in the location of plants to places near water power or coal. The migration of individuals to factory villages oversupplied with labor was easily diverted overseas. From Great Britain, Ireland, and Germany came many paupers, their emigration financed by parishes liable for their support. After the industrialization of Germany and the Scandinavian countries in the eighties and nineties, increased opportunities at home reduced overseas migration; but in the same chain of economic events came the extension of transportation facilities into the agricultural countries of southern and eastern Europe, where the same economic conditions which had stimulated emigration from northwestern Europe at an earlier period proved equally effective. Frequently, political oppression, religious persecution, and catastrophes of war were important factors in motivating people to migrate, and brought to the United States groups with ideals other than those of economic betterment. But the great mass of American immigrants were displaced, impoverished, and maladjusted persons who moved in the hope of finding a better and easier living.

This was true even of the pre-Revolutionary period. The colonization of the Atlantic coast, undertaken by groups which chartered their own transportation facilities, and upon their arrival organized a set of institutions to govern their society, was fairly well accomplished in New England by the end of the seventeenth century and in the Middle Atlantic and southern colonies by the middle of the eighteenth century. For a full century before the Revolution, the chief migration was that of propertyless individuals who came under the redemptioner system. Large numbers of English agricultural laborers displaced by enclosures, of Scottish-Irish suffering from religious persecution and economic discrimination at the hands of England, of southern Irish oppressed by extortionate rents, of German peasants from the Palatinate suffering from European wars, were able to reach America as redemptioners. This migration was limited to the territory around embarkation ports in England and Holland which could be covered during the winter season by agents of vessels and from which travel to the coast was easy. The fact that the chief points of departure for America were also havens for political and religious refugees brought to the colonies groups of French Huguenots, Palatines, Hanoverians, Saxons, Austrians, and Swiss.

The American and French revolutions and the Napoleonic wars prevented much immigration between 1775 and 1815, but migration started immediately afterward on an unprecedented scale and continued to come in waves of increasing intensity and of varying ethnic composition until the outbreak of the World War.

Northwest European Immigration.

England was the main source of immigration before the Revolution. Between 1820 and 1890 immigration to the United States was predominantly Irish, German, and Scandinavian, owing in part to anti-English sentiment in the United States and in part to the British policy of diverting migration of its nationals to its own colonies. But despite the attraction of Australia and Canada for British immigrants with capital and the absorption by expanding British industries of the increasing labor population, large numbers of British industrial workers came to the United States and were absorbed, particularly by the textile and coal-mining industries. Although migration from Great Britain never approached the figures reached at the peak of the waves of Irish and German immigrations, it ranked third in importance through the century, and remained substantial between 1900 and 1914.

The migration from Ireland which constituted the largest single element before the Civil War came in part from the Scottish-Irish north, but in greater numbers from southern Ireland where absentee landlordism and increase in population had created a tenant peasantry continually on the verge of starvation. Destitution, combined with the political disabilities of Catholics, had started an emigration to the towns of northern Ireland and England which was diverted to America and greatly accelerated by the spread of information about the prosperity of the Irish settlers. When in the forties wet seasons stimulated the growth of a fungus which destroyed the potato crop for several successive years, migration presented the only escape from starvation in many sections of the country. Between 1845 and 1855 over a million persons left Ireland for the United States. Although the newly arrived Irish usually found employment in the growing industrial centers of the east, they gradually dispersed into less densely settled areas and became a ubiquitous element in the population. The "Know Nothing" movement of the fifties was a protest against the admission of these destitute hordes. Emigration and starvation so reduced the population of Ireland during the forties and fifties that Irish immigration to the United States fell to an annual average of less than fifty thousand during the sixties and seventies. Although it rose again to 81,486 in 1883, after 1890 it suffered a further decline owing to improvement in Irish living conditions.

The Germans, who contributed a larger number of immigrants during the nineteenth century than any other single group, included a mixed population of northwestern Protestant Prussians, southern Catholic Bavarians, Czechs, and Poles. Although not as destitute as the Irish peasant or the English "sturdy beggar," the early German immigrant was also motivated by adverse economic changes. A rise in the price of land as the result of the increased size of holdings and a surplus of agricultural labor were disorganizing rural life in Germany, and migration to the United States of whole villages with their pastors and teachers was not unusual. Crop failures on the continent in the late forties, suppression of the German liberal movement culminating in the revolution of 1848, and the exacting terms of compulsory military service required by the Prussian Government so stimulated emigration that German arrivals in 1854 numbered 215,009, only slightly less than the peak of Irish immigration in 1851. German migration was further stimulated by the demand for labor to operate the industries which started during the Civil War and to settle the public lands which were opened by the Homestead Law of 1862. Its peak in 1867 was 233,426. The third and last great German wave came in 1881 and 1882 when immigration for the two years was 461,-115. After 1882 the acceleration of economic changes in Germany under the stimulus of government protection of industry and agriculture resulted in the absorption of the domestic labor surplus. Trade-union action and social legislation so improved wages and conditions of employment in the fatherland that industrial opportunities in the United States became less attractive to German workers. Furthermore, the disappearance of free land in the United States, coincident with the increased prosperity of farmers in Germany, greatly reduced the influx to the United States for agricultural purposes. After the eighties an increasing proportion of German immigrants were industrial workers who settled in American industrial centers.

Scandinavian immigration did not become appreciable until the late sixties when news of free fertile lands diverted to the United States the slow migration to less settled and poor lands in the north and highlands of Norway and Sweden which had been going on for a century or more. The immigration of Scandinavians reached its high point in the eighties; during this decade the United States received 391,776 persons from Sweden, 176,586 from Norway, and 88,132 from Denmark. This stream began to decline in the late nineties with the disappearance of the public domain. Although it revived temporarily during the next decade, the opportunities for immigrants in American industrial centers and in extractive industries, unaccompanied by prospects of cheap lands, did not afford a tempting alternative to the increasing industrial opportunities at home.

South and East European Immigration.

Coincident with the decline in German and Scandinavian immigration was the increase in immigration from Italy, southeastern Europe, and Russia, which during the series of prosperous years following 1896 exceeded earlier streams from northwestern Europe. Before 1880 immigration from these sources had been negligible. With the decline in German emigration, German steamship lines began to solicit immigrants in Italy and southeastern Europe. Extension of railroads into these sections facilitated movement of the population, which had been stimulated by inducements of United States corporation agents and by letters from adventurous individuals who had already emigrated and who urged their relatives and friends to join them. The three predominant groups in this immigration were the Italians, Jews, and Poles. Between 1901 and 1910, 2,104,209 Italians, 976,263 Jews, and 873,-660 Poles were admitted to the United States. Other important ethnic groups admitted during this decade were 332,446 Slovaks, 318,674 Magyars, 309,727 Croatians and Slovenians, 210,794 Greeks, 158,089 Lithuanians, and 143,143 Ruthenians.

The economic background of the laborers from these recently opened areas differed only in minor details from the conditions which had stimulated emigration from northwestern Europe. For the most part they were a landless peasantry of farm workers and tenants, suffering from population pressure, oppressive landlords, and antiquated methods of agriculture. The notable exception to this was the Jewish immigration of tradesmen and town workers who had been kept from the land in most east European countries by legal disabilities and traditions or had been dispossessed during the persecutions which occurred in southeastern Europe and the Russian Empire after 1880. The non-Jewish immigration from

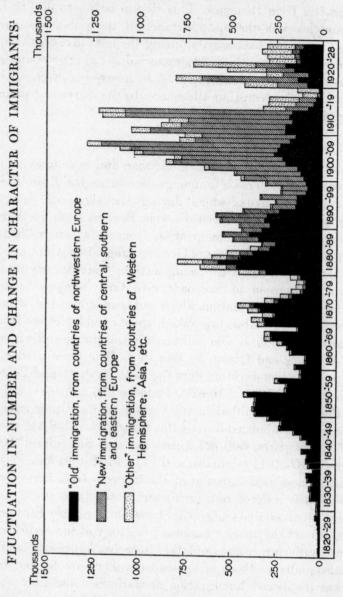

FLUCTUATION IN NUMBER AND CHANGE IN CHARACTER OF IMMIGRANTS[1]

"Old" immigration, from countries of northwestern Europe

"New" immigration, from countries of central, southern and eastern Europe

"Other" immigration, from countries of Western Hemisphere, Asia, etc.

[1] Compiled from data in United States Immigration Commission: Statistical Review of Immigration, 1820-1910, pp. 9-11; H. Jerome, *Migration and Business Cycles*, p. 35, and Annual Reports of Commissioner General of Immigration, 1925-1928.

southeastern Europe included many ethnic groups which had been repressed for centuries and which sought, in addition to economic betterment, an escape from social and political discrimination.

The distribution of these immigrants in the United States was determined by the opportunities for employment which tended to make them concentrate in the large manufacturing cities of the East, the new industrial towns of the north central states, and mining and smelting communities. They were numerous in new agricultural developments, such as the vineyards and vegetable farms of California, which attracted large numbers of Italians, and the sugar-beet fields, which depended on southeast Europeans for manual labor. The demand for agricultural labor, however, was numerically insignificant in comparison with that for industrial labor. Adapting itself to the needs of American economic life, the new immigration was predominantly adult male, mobile and flexible in supply. As a reserve of unskilled labor it became a part of the industrial system. Although restriction of immigration was advocated by an increasing group of persons, pre-war immigration legislation reflected the view that industrial growth depended on the continuance of a reservoir of unskilled European labor.

Colonial and State Regulation.

Before the War immigration was regulated to some extent. Exclusion of paupers, criminals, and diseased persons was accepted as good public policy even in the colonial period, and legislation based on this policy was enacted first by the states and in the quarter century before the War by the Federal Government.

Restrictions passed in the colonial period were intended primarily to stop the practices of sending criminals, a large percentage of whom were convicted of petty offenses or for political reasons, to the colonies as an alternative to capital punishment or imprisonment, of assisting paupers to emigrate and of disposing of dependent relatives by indenturing them to captains. The statutes usually prohibited the landing of undesirable classes or placed a head tax on certain groups, such as Irish servants in Pennsylvania. Attempts were also made to bar from admission religious sects which differed from those prevailing in any given colony. Some of these measures were disallowed by the home gov-

ernment, since it wished to encourage the emigration of unde-
sirables; others, though remaining on the statute books, were
nullified in effect by administrative difficulty in controlling transportation companies. At the outbreak of the Revolution opinion
on immigration was divided. The complaint of the Declaration
of Independence against George III for interfering with the
settlement of the colonies and preventing easy naturalization of
foreigners reflected southern opinion favoring liberal immigration. Jefferson, Franklin, and other leaders of the period expressed
grave concern over the mixed character of the population, predict-
ing that it would be disastrous to democratic government. A little
later the Continental Congress, dominated by the more densely
populated northern states which contained the immigrant-receiv-
ing ports, favored exclusion of convicts and recommended that
states fine shipowners who imported them.

For a half century after the Revolution the states led in legislation for the regulation of immigrants. Before 1847 but one federal
law had been passed, the Act of 1819, which resulted from protest
against the large immigration during the business depression in
the United States following the Napoleonic wars. Its only effective
provision was the requirement that passenger vessels furnish their
manifests as the basis of immigration statistics.

State legislation passed during the same crisis reduced immigration by abolishing the redemptioner system under which propertyless individuals had financed their passage by indenturing
themselves to sea captains who in turn indentured them upon arrival to United States employers who paid the cost of their passage.
The reduction proved to be only temporary, for by the end of the
twenties relatives already in the United States were in a position
to prepay the passages of such immigrants. When the problem of
a large immigrant labor supply during a period of unemployment
recurred in 1837, competition between native workers and new
arrivals led to the anti-Irish and anti-German riots which characterized the nativist movement of the later thirties and forties. The
growing trade unions began to agitate on economic grounds
against immigration. But the burden of supporting paupers in
public institutions, particularly those who were shipped to the
United States at the expense of their parishes, remained the most

general basis of appeal for restriction. In consequence, inadequate state legislation against criminals and paupers was supplemented by a head tax on immigrants in two of the important immigrant states, Massachusetts in 1837 and New York in 1848.

The imposition of a head tax raised the question of the constitutionality of state regulation. The power of the Federal Government to regulate immigration had been upheld by the Supreme Court on the ground that it was contemplated by the framers of the Constitution in the provision that "the migration or importation of such persons as any of the states now existing shall think proper to admit, shall not be prohibited by the Congress prior to the year 1808, but a tax or duty may be imposed on such importation, not exceeding ten dollars for each person." The question of whether the states had concurrent power remained open. In 1837 the United States Supreme Court held that the New York Passenger Act of 1824 which sought to exclude paupers, convicts, and diseased persons was a valid exercise of state police power.[2] In 1848, however, when the Supreme Court had before it the head tax provisions of the New York and Massachusetts acts, the primary concern of the Court was with the power such a tax gave to the states along the eastern coast to exclude immigrants on their way to western communities where they were wanted, and it declared that state head taxes were in effect taxes on foreign commerce and therefore unconstitutional.[3] But in the absence of federal restrictions, state inspection and care of pauper and diseased immigrants continued, and New York made two more attempts to finance this service by a tax on passengers.[4]

The legislation which Congress passed during this period tended to encourage rather than to discourage immigration. The Steerage Acts of 1847 and 1855 sought only to prevent overcrowding and to protect the health of steerage passengers. The contract labor law of 1864, a temporary war measure which was repealed in 1868, stimulated immigration by permitting immigrants to encumber

---

[2] *New York* v. *Miln,* 11 Pet. 101 (1837).

[3] *Smith* v. *Turner; Norris* v. *City of Boston* "Passenger cases," 7 Howard 283 (1849).

[4] By Acts of 1850 and 1881 which were declared unconstitutional in *Henderson* v. *Mayor of New York,* 92 U.S. 259 (1875), and in *People* v. *Compagnie Générale Transatlantique,* 107 U.S. 59 (1883).

their lands or assign their wages for a year in order to finance their passage. It provided also for an office in New York to make contracts for immigrants and to direct them to their destinations. Bills authorizing appointment of federal agents to solicit immigrants abroad were urged upon Congress, and although they failed to pass, the Federal Government published a bulletin describing the population and resources of the United States which was widely circulated in foreign countries by consular officers and agents of particularly interested states. Before 1882, the Steerage Acts, the legislation against coolie labor,[5] and a law excluding convicts and prostitutes, constituted the only federal restrictions on immigration.

Federal Regulation.

Following renewal of the controversy over state powers, opposition of the West and of manufacturing interests to restrictions by coast states, and a growing recognition of need for national regulation to relieve the congregation of undesirable and dependent persons in ports of arrival compelled the Federal Government to adopt a definite policy of excluding undesirable classes. The immediate situation out of which the 1882 act arose was the imposition, under a state act passed in 1881, of "head money" for inspection purposes on all persons entering New York. In view of previous court decisions New York justified its action on the ground that its residents should not be compelled to bear the expense of immigrant inspection necessary to protect public health and to support in state institutions dependent aliens whom the state was powerless to exclude. The unprecedented wave of immigration in 1880 and 1881 which occasioned the New York act created confusion and disturbance in all ports of arrival and it became clear that, if the states were incompetent to take action, the Federal Government would have to adopt some regulatory measures. While the New York law was still in the courts, Congress passed the Act of 1882.

Under the compromise policy adopted by Congress in this Act, the exclusion of convicts, lunatics, idiots, and persons likely to become public charges was a concession to the restrictionist opinion of the coast states, and the negligible amount of the head tax

[5] For discussion of legislation restricting immigration of Orientals see pp. 492 ff.

of 50 cents was a concession to western states and industrial interests which opposed anything resembling a property qualification. Responsibility for administration was vested in the Secretary of the Treasury, but examination of immigrants was to be carried out by state boards under contracts with the Treasury Department. Excluded aliens were to be returned at the ship's expense.

During the period between 1882 and the outbreak of the World War certain provisions of the Act were made more stringent; administration was centralized in the hands of a federal bureau; the classes of inadmissible persons were extended to include diseased persons, polygamists, anarchists, contract laborers, and Chinese; provision was made for deportation of aliens belonging to the excluded classes, and the head tax was gradually raised to $4.00 to meet increased cost of administration. Only two of these changes constituted a departure from the policy adopted in the Act of 1882 of excluding undesirable classes: the exclusion of the Chinese, discussed below, and the exclusion of contract laborers.

Under the Alien Contract Labor Law of 1885 and its amendments, trade unions sought to restrict the recruiting of cheap immigrant labor which was affecting wages and working conditions in basic industries. But the ease with which these laws could be evaded and the prevailing practice of having friends or relatives in this country finance the passage of immigrants made possible the continued immigration of unskilled laborers on informal promises of work. Corporations continued to recruit laborers by encouraging workers to send for their friends or by using immigrant agencies which made a business of recruiting workers, helping finance their passage, and steering them clear of the law. Successful prosecutions served only to change the methods of securing laborers and did not affect the number or kind of persons admitted.

The Act of 1882 was likewise limited in its effect by administrative difficulties and court interpretation of its provisions. Before examination by federal inspectors was established in 1891, the Act was practically unenforceable. Under federal examination the proportion of immigrants debarred gradually increased from one out of 268 in 1892 to one out of 43 in 1910. Prosecution of several steamship companies under acts of 1903 and 1907, which imposed a fine of $100 for the transportation of a person of the excluded classes, resulted in rejections at European ports by ships' doctors, and these in turn led to rejections at border control stations by Germany which sought to prevent congregation of rejected persons in German ports. The United States Immigration Commission estimated that in 1907 rejections in Europe amounted to approximately fifty thousand—almost five times the number debarred at United States ports of entry in the same year. Although these rejections were based chiefly on medical grounds and were usually made only in cases of idiocy, insanity, trachoma, or advanced tuberculosis, the probability of exclusion may have tended to discourage attempted emigration of other mental and physical defectives. The exclusion of large numbers of persons because they were likely to become public charges, amounting to fifteen thousand or about .7 per cent of the total number admitted in 1910, probably prevented the landing of helpless persons with no immediate means of support, but it did not reduce the total number of immigrants. Court interpretation of the clause prevented exclusion of persons likely to become public charges because they were destined for places where employment conditions were unfavorable; the courts assumed that able-bodied adults could support themselves and held that dependent persons who were otherwise admissible could be admitted on the bond of relatives.

Therefore, despite the improved immigration service made possible by the centralization of administration in a Bureau of Immigration under the Department of Labor, the organization of a trained staff of inspectors under civil service regulations, and the revision of statutory provisions which had permitted evasion of the laws, federal immigration regulations before the World War effected little selection or restriction of immigration. Administrative changes did not keep pace with the increased demands on the service created by increased immigration and corrupt practices. The fact that there was no border patrol along land boundaries makes it impossible to tell to what extent inadmissible classes escaped inspection by indirect entry. In its practical effect during the pre-war period immigration legislation was important chiefly for its provision of administrative machinery under federal auspices to prevent gross maltreatment of immigrants, and to exclude persons who were obviously diseased or mentally defective.

Character of Immigrants in the Geographical Divisions of the United States.

In selecting regions of origin which would indicate as nearly as possible in the limited space available the geographical distribution of various racial groups, the grouping of countries by the Census Bureau in its monograph "Immigrants and their Children" has been used. The countries included in the different groups are as follows:

Northwestern Europe	Central, Southern, and Eastern Europe	Elsewhere
England	Poland	Asia
Scotland	Czechoslovakia	Western Hemisphere
Wales	Austria	(The chief immigrants
Ireland	Hungary	from these regions have
Norway	Yugoslavia	been the French Cana-
Sweden	Russia	dians of New England,
Denmark	Lithuania	the Mexicans of the
Netherlands	Finland	west south central
Belgium	Rumania	states and the Orientals
Luxemburg	Bulgaria	of the Pacific Coast.)
Switzerland	Turkey in Europe	
France	Greece	
Germany	Albania	
	Italy	
	Spain	
	Portugal	

In the United States as a whole, 46.4 per cent of the foreign-born are natives of northwestern Europe, 40.2 per cent are natives of central, southern, and eastern Europe, and 13.4 per cent are natives of other countries. If these figures are taken as norms, the west north central and east south central states appear to have relatively high proportions of northwest Europeans; the middle Atlantic, east north central and south Atlantic states have relatively high proportions of central, south, and east Europeans, and New England, west south central, the mountain and Pacific states have a relatively high proportion of persons born in the Western Hemisphere and in Asia.

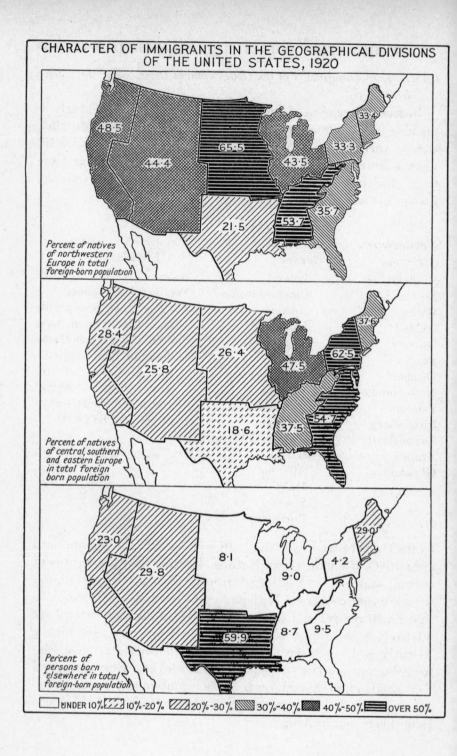

CHARACTER OF IMMIGRANTS IN THE GEOGRAPHICAL DIVISIONS
OF THE UNITED STATES, 1920

Percent of natives
of northwestern
Europe in total
foreign-born population

48·5
44·4
65·5
43·5
33·3
33·4
35·7
53·7
21·5

Percent of natives
of central, southern
and eastern Europe
in total foreign
born population

28·4
25·8
26·4
47·5
37·6
62·5
18·6
37·5
54·7

Percent of
persons born
"elsewhere" in total
foreign-born population

23·0
29·8
8·1
9·0
4·2
29·0
59·9
8·7
9·5

UNDER 10%   10%-20%   20%-30%   30%-40%   40%-50%   OVER 50%

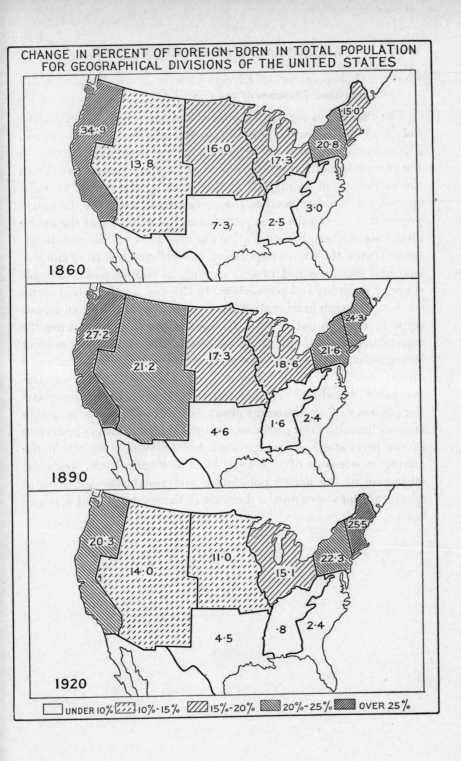

CHANGE IN PERCENT OF FOREIGN-BORN IN TOTAL POPULATION
FOR GEOGRAPHICAL DIVISIONS OF THE UNITED STATES

1860

34·9   16·0   17·3   20·8   15·0
13·8
7·3   2·5   3·0

1890

27·2   17·3   18·6   24·3
21·2   21·6
4·6   1·6   2·4

1920

20·3   11·0   25·5
14·0   15·1   22·3
4·5   ·8   2·4

UNDER 10% | 10%-15% | 15%-20% | 20%-25% | OVER 25%

Changes in Percentage of Foreign-born in Total Population for Geographical Divisions of the United States.

The changes in the distribution of the foreign-born population indicated in the accompanying maps are discussed elsewhere. For convenience, they are briefly explained here. The increase in the percentage of foreign-born in New England has resulted from the attraction of immigrant workers during the period of widespread industrial expansion, the westward migration of the native population during the same period, and the reduction of the native birth rate. Although immigration has been heavy in the middle Atlantic states, the native population has suffered less from emigration and has remained prolific enough to supply a considerable share of its industrial population. In the east north central states the large foreign immigration has been accompanied by an almost equal increase in native-born. In the west north central states the exhaustion of fertile public lands about 1890 checked subsequent immigration to this area. The south Atlantic states have remained almost untouched by immigration, owing partly to relatively unfavorable social and economic opportunities in agriculture, and the presence of an abundant cheap labor supply in its mountain regions for industrial purposes. In the mountain states the decline in the percentage of foreign-born has followed a decline in the mining enterprises of this area. On the Pacific coast, westward migration of the native population and restrictions on oriental immigration have effected a decrease in the percentage of foreign-born.

CHAPTER TWO

THE LITERACY TEST AND THE 1917 ACT

ALTHOUGH raised at all stages of economic development in the United States, objections to unrestricted immigration did not gain strength and become national in importance until after the disappearance of the frontier. Public opinion was affected by two considerations: the effect on American wages and living standards of the lack of free lands which had hitherto made labor scarce and wages high; and the effect of unrestricted immigration on the density and quality of population.

Agitation for Reduced Immigration.

The effect on wages of competition between native and alien workers was one of the objections to pauper immigrants against whom early state legislation had been directed, and also the basis of early labor opposition to unrestricted immigration resulting in Chinese exclusion and the alien contract labor legislation. But as long as demand for settlers in the interior continued, the free lands were considered an "insurance policy against want" for the industrial worker, and the remedy for low wages or unemployment in cities was thought to lie, not in reducing labor supply by restricting immigration, but in securing a better distribution of labor throughout the country. Despite the inducements to western settlement offered by state immigration bureaus and railroad land companies, a relatively small proportion of immigrants went direct from Europe to the West. Frequently, during periods of prosperity, immigrant settlers financed themselves by temporary employment at industrial labor in the cities, dispersing to agricultural areas in time of depression. The disappearance of the frontier checked this dispersion and led an increasing proportion of immigrants to remain permanently in cities as industrial workers. Industrial expansion not only absorbed for a time the existing labor supply but attracted immigrants in even larger numbers than at any preceding period. But the alleged maladjustment of wages to prices and the increasingly acute periods of unemployment which accompanied cyclical fluctuations in business caused national discontent among wage-earners.

At the same time, the effect of immigration on the quality and size of population began to arouse public interest. With natural resources recognized as limited, the advantages of an increasing population were less apparent. A decrease in living standards in the not too distant future as the result of an increase in population without a corresponding increase in national wealth became plausible. It was argued that the natural increase in population was sufficient to permit reasonable economic growth. Change in the source of immigration, moreover, began to excite comment. The south and east Europeans who predominated in the large immigrant waves which reached their peaks in 1907 and 1914 differed in physique, religion, economic background, and political and social tradition from the immigrant stocks which had become familiar and integral parts of the population. To an increasing number of persons from the older stocks the newcomers seemed not only economically unnecessary, but socially undesirable. Because of the poverty to which they had been accustomed in Europe, they were willing to accept wages which would not provide a laboring family with a living comparable to prevailing American standards. Frequently they came without families, worked long hours, spent only the minimum necessary for subsistence, and after a few years returned with their savings to their native lands. Those who remained and sent for their families lived for the most part in segregated communities where foreign traditions were perpetuated. In physique, mentality, and cultural attainments they were thought to be inferior to older stocks. The success of American democracy seemed to be threatened both by their indifference to the advantages of naturalization, and by their alleged abuse, undisciplined as they were in self-government, of the new privileges of citizenship when acquired. This sentiment was strongest in New England where population was particularly dense, where the highest percentage of foreign-born was to be found, and where instead of expanding, industries were beginning to suffer from competition with newer manufacturing centers. Consequently from New

England came the first organized effort to secure reduction in immigration.

Of the two most discussed methods of effecting a reduction—a head tax high enough to act as a property qualification and a literacy test which would eliminate the uneducated classes of southern and eastern Europe—the literacy test was selected by restrictionists as the more practical political expedient. In 1890 it was advocated at the hearings of the Joint Congressional Committee on Immigration, the next year it was introduced in Congress by Representative Lodge, and in 1894 the Immigration Restriction League was organized in Boston to fight for its passage. Political leaders advocated it as a remedy for the severe unemployment which prevailed in the middle nineties. During this crisis a measure providing for a reading and writing test for all immigrants who were not near relatives of persons already admitted found enough support among Congressmen from the East and West to pass both houses in 1896, only to be vetoed by President Cleveland. In 1898 the restrictionists won a slight advantage by securing the passage of a law which, by providing for the recording of immigration by race, made available statistics showing the changing character of immigration. Not until 1898 was an educational test indorsed by the American Federation of Labor. Although bills incorporating a literacy test passed one of the houses of Congress several times between 1897 and 1913, it was only in 1917 that the literacy test finally became law over the President's veto.

During these twenty years the United States changed from a preponderantly agricultural to a preponderantly industrial country; by 1920 the census report showed that 51.4 per cent of the total population of the United States was urban. Territorial expansion of industry changed the economic character of the east north central and Pacific states, which became predominantly urban and therefore developed sectional interests similar in some respects to those of New England and the middle Atlantic states. This change in economic activities focused public attention on the characteristics of business fluctuations on which immigration had an important bearing. The Industrial Commission of 1901, appointed to report to Congress on the effect of industrial expansion in general, made the following statement on the effects of immigration:

The great increase in the number of immigrants just at the time when employment is increasing, many of them expecting to return to their native land, furnishes an artificial supply of labor, and prevents those already at hand from demanding and securing that increase in wages which they could otherwise obtain. This, in turn, has serious ulterior effects on the duration of the period of prosperity. Employers are able both to expand more greatly their production for the immediate emergency, and to secure in the form of profits a greater share of the product than they would be able to do without this artificial increase of cheap labor. The result is a quick overproduction of commodities, owing to the inability of the working population, when prices have risen more than wages, to purchase and consume the same proportion of their product as that to which they have been accustomed.

These considerations lead to an important conclusion regarding the policy of restricting the number of immigrants as a protection to American labor. . . . But if immigration prevents American labor from advancing as rapidly as American capital in a period of prosperity, then restriction is needed at that time just as much, though not as plainly, as in a period of depression.[1]

Although the chairman personally favored the literacy test, the Commission as a whole recommended only administrative improvements in existing immigration laws and stated that the desirability of a head tax or a literacy test depended on "general opinion as to whether a large immigration is or is not a benefit to the country."[2]

The Immigration Commission of 1907.

Opinion on the desirability of a large immigration continued to be so heated and divided that the question was finally submitted to a special investigating commission appointed in accordance with a provision of the general Immigration Act of 1907 which had been passed as a substitute for the bitterly contested.

[1] United States Industrial Commission 1902, Final Report, XIX, 964.
[2] *Ibid.*, p. 1004.

literacy test. After four years of work, during which the Immigration Commission spent approximately $900,000 in conducting hearings in all parts of the country and employing a large staff of investigators, the findings and conclusions appeared in forty-one volumes. In its economic analysis of the relation between immigration and unemployment, the Immigration Commission came to a conclusion similar to that presented by the 1901 Industrial Commission:

Their numbers are so great and the influx is so continuous that even with the remarkable expansion of industry during the past few years there has been created an oversupply of unskilled labor, and in some of the industries this is reflected in a curtailed number of working days and a consequent yearly income among the unskilled workers which is very much less than is indicated by the daily wage rates paid; and while it may not have lowered in a marked degree the American standard of living, it has introduced a lower standard which has become prevalent in the unskilled industry at large.[3]

On the basis of its findings, the Commission recommended as a foundation for further immigration legislation the following principles:

1. While the American people, as in the past, welcome the oppressed of other lands, care should be taken that immigration be such both in quality and quantity as not to make too difficult the process of assimilation.
2. Since the existing law and further special legislation recommended in this report deal with the physically and morally unfit, further general legislation concerning the admission of aliens should be based primarily upon economic or business considerations touching the prosperity and economic well-being of our people.
3. The measure of the rational, healthy development of a country is not the extent of its investment of capital, its output of products, or its exports and imports, unless there is a corresponding economic opportunity afforded to the citizen dependent upon employment for his material, mental, and moral development.

[3] United States Immigration Commission 1907-1911, Abstract of Reports, I, 39.

4. The development of business may be brought about by means which lower the standard of living of the wage earners. A slow expansion of industry which would permit the adaptation and assimilation of the incoming labor supply is preferable to a very rapid industrial expansion which results in the immigration of laborers of low standards and efficiency, who imperil the American standard of wages and conditions of employment.[4]

The legislation recommended by the Commission included more effective exclusion of undesirable classes; more competent administration; measures to protect the immigrant against exploitation, to discourage sending savings abroad, to secure better distribution of aliens, to encourage permanent residence and naturalization, and to restrict the admission of unskilled labor. The Commission thought that in providing for restriction enough immigrants should be excluded to produce a marked effect upon the labor supply, that temporary immigration of adult males without families should be discouraged and that, as far as possible, "the aliens excluded should also be those, who, by reason of their personal qualities or habits, would least readily be assimilated or would make the least desirable citizens." A majority of the Commission favored "the reading and writing test as the most feasible single method of restricting undesirable immigration."

Although the Commission had investigated thoroughly the social aspects of immigration such as literacy, housing, and living standards, in its analysis it approached immigration primarily as an economic problem, and expressly stated that "further legislation should be based primarily on economic or business considerations." The questions with which it was chiefly concerned were the existence of an unskilled labor surplus, the effect of competition between native and immigrant workers, and the displacement of native workers by immigrants. The biological aspects of immigration, which have recently become the center of the immigration controversy, were studied for the Commission by Professor Franz Boas who found that "even those characteristics which modern science has led us to consider as most stable seem to be subject to thorough changes under the new environment, which would indi-

4 United States Immigration Commission 1907-1911, Abstract of Reports, I, 45.

cate that even racial physical characteristics do not survive under the new social and climatic environment of America."[5]

In this respect the attitude of the Commission differed from that of some leading restrictionist writers and of the Immigration Restriction League who were stressing the effect of immigration on American social and political life. In *Races and Immigrants*, published in 1908, John R. Commons urged restriction not only for economic reasons, but because the presence of immigrants had resulted in a decrease in birth rate of superior native strains in the population, because the general level of culture and political morals had deteriorated, and because immigrants had created heterogeneous communities in which control by the "ward boss" was the only practicable way of organizing the community politically. Soon after the Immigration Commission report was released this position was elaborated by Professor Ross in his *New Worlds for Old* and by Professor Fairchild in *The Melting Pot Mistake*. These writers agreed with the Commission in approving the literacy test as a means of excluding and reducing in number south and east European immigrants.

The Literacy Test.

The recommendations of the Commission, including the literacy test, were embodied in the Smith-Burnett bill which passed Congress in 1913 but was vetoed by President Taft. Although suspension of immigration and the increased business activity which followed the outbreak of the War practically eliminated the problem of unemployment for the time being, agitation for the bill continued. In 1915 it was passed again by Congress and vetoed by President Wilson on the ground that the literacy test was a test of opportunity, not one of character, that it was restrictive in purpose and was therefore contrary to cherished national principles.

By 1917 realignments had taken place on the immigration question. The industrial centers of the East which had been early champions of the literacy test began to modify their position as the new immigrant element in their population increased in number and in political influence. The South, on the other hand, was changing its attitude from one of almost solid opposition to the

[5] *Ibid.*, p. 44.

literacy test in 1896 to almost solid support. In the twenty intervening years it had given up hope of reorganizing its agriculture by diversification on the basis of a European peasantry, and, for its new industries, it had found in its mountain people a large labor reserve which was cheaper and easier to discipline than the foreign factory labor of the North. Strongly Protestant by tradition and predominantly Anglo-Saxon in origin, southern opinion was opposed to south and east European immigration. The conversion of the South to restriction more than compensated for the defections of some northern urban areas. In addition, the cause of restriction was helped by the World War. The activities of foreign-born groups in behalf of their belligerent fatherlands were thought to show the social dangers to which a nation is subject when many of its citizens are not assimilated. The anti-alien sentiment which these activities aroused contributed not a little to the strength of restrictionist agitation after the outbreak of the War. Consequently, when in 1917 the Smith-Burnett bill was again passed by Congress and again vetoed by President Wilson because of its literacy test provision, it received the two-thirds majority necessary to override the veto and became law.

The 1917 Immigration Act, known chiefly for its literacy test provision, was in fact a comprehensive law codifying and strengthening existing legislation. It added to excluded classes persons of "constitutional psychopathic inferiority," persons suffering from chronic alcoholism, vagrants and stowaways, and persons from an Asiatic barred zone, which included the larger number of Asiatics outside of Chinese and Japanese;[6] it strengthened deportation legislation by increasing the period during which aliens could be deported from three to five years and by including aliens convicted of crime; it increased the head tax from $4.00 to $8.00 but exempted children under sixteen. Public discussion, however, was centered almost exclusively on the literacy test provision which required of all immigrants ability to read thirty or forty words of print in some language—a requirement which was regarded at the time as a radical departure from the traditional immigration policy of the United States.

[6] For more complete discussion of this provision see Chapter VII, pp. 422 ff.

CHAPTER THREE

EMERGENCY QUOTA ACTS OF 1921 AND 1922 AND THE IMMIGRATION ACT OF 1924

T HE threat of an unprecedented immigration from the economically disorganized countries of Europe at the end of the War led to a demand for immediate and drastic restriction. The most fervent support for such legislation came from the intense nationalist feeling which survived the War in the form of a strong belief in domestic like-mindedness and a dread of pacifists and radicals, as well as antagonism to alien groups whose home ties had proved stronger than the new bonds of their adopted country. The preservation of foreign customs, of foreign tongues, lack of interest in national politics or political action which revealed solidarity of opinion within foreign groups, the congregation of immigrants in communities of their own, the patronage of business and professional persons of their own national origin, differences in religion and economic ideas—all these phenomena were cited as evidence that the foreign-born had not been fused by the American environment into a homogeneous population which could serve as a sound foundation for a nation. This feeling during the War had resulted in the Act of October, 1918, excluding and expelling "members of the anarchistic and similar classes," and the supplement to it passed in June, 1920, under which the theatrical "red" deportations took place. The popular association of all Slavic immigrants with Bolshevism intensified a hostility to south and east Europeans based on other social and economic grounds.

At the same time, post-war conditions created an economic emergency which led to demand for drastic restriction. It was generally felt that the unemployment which followed industrial demobilization and deflation would not act as an automatic safety valve in checking emigration from the starved countries of Europe. Nor did the literacy test provision of the 1917 Act promise effective restriction. Partly because of the low standard provided by the Act and partly because of poor enforcement, only about 1,500 persons were debarred annually for illiteracy between 1918 and 1921. By the end of 1920, when for the first time since the War normal conditions of travel in southeastern Europe had to some extent been restored, immigration began to approximate its pre-war volume and character. During the fiscal year ended June, 1921, 805,228 persons were admitted, 65 per cent of whom came from countries of southern and eastern Europe. Out of a total of 13,779 persons debarred during this fiscal year, only 1,450 had been debarred because of illiteracy. The literacy test was clearly not having the effect upon labor supply that the Immigration Commission had expected. The necessity for immediate and drastic restriction was implied in the following statement of the Commissioner of Immigration in his annual report for the fiscal year ended June, 1920:

Existing conditions in Europe and in the United States, and the vast number of people in the former and in other parts of the world who contemplate coming here, have caused it (the Bureau of Immigration) to give serious consideration to the possible effect which an influx of the dimensions promised will have, not only upon the people of our country but also upon the newcomers themselves. This consideration of the matter has forcibly suggested to it the need for further legislation, both selective and restrictive in nature, and it is believed that the early passage of such legislation is advisable.[1]

Emergency Quota Acts.

The immigration measures before Congress during the years immediately after the War reflected so many conflicting interests which had to be weighed and reconciled before agreement could be reached on a permanent restrictive policy that a temporary expedient was necessary. Proposals for complete suspension were abandoned and Congress finally adopted the quota system, a device which had been one of the possible methods of restriction reported by the 1907 Immigration Commission and had been the basis of a restrictive measure introduced by Senator Dillingham of Vermont in 1914. A proposal basing quotas on 3 per cent of the number of persons born in any given country and residing in the

[1] Annual Report of the Commissioner General of Immigration, 1920, p. 62.

United States at the time of the last available census (1910) was passed by Congress early in 1921, but was left unsigned by President Wilson when he went out of office. After President Harding's inauguration the 3 per cent limitation was reintroduced. A conflict in Congress which arose over liberal exemptions adopted by the House was finally resolved when exemption of victims of religious persecution (which would have given to Jews of eastern Europe and Greeks and Armenians of Anatolia claims to admission regardless of numbers) was abandoned by the House on condition that the Senate agree to exempt children of United States citizens. This Emergency Quota Act, which was to remain in force for a year, was approved on May 19 and took effect on June 3, 1921.

Since the permanent policy adopted in 1924 was based to a large extent on the experience gained during the operation of the Emergency Quota Act, its provisions were of great practical importance. The most striking feature of the new act was its numerical limitation of immigrants. Immigration from Europe and European colonies, except Canada and Newfoundland, was limited to 3 per cent of the number of persons born in any given country who were United States residents at the time of the 1910 census, with adjustments in census figures to take account of post-war changes in geographical boundaries.

Colonies of foreign countries separately enumerated in the 1910 census were treated as separate countries. The quota system was not applied to aliens with continuous residence for a year prior to admission in Canada, Newfoundland, Cuba, Mexico, countries of Central and South America or adjacent islands. Government officials and their households, aliens in transit, visitors on business or pleasure, and children of American citizens under eighteen were not to be counted in the quotas, and after the quotas were filled, aliens returning from a visit abroad, "professional actors, artists, lecturers, singers, nurses, ministers, professors, persons belonging to recognized learned professions, and servants," could still enter regardless of number. Within quotas preference was to be given to wives, parents, brothers, sisters, children under eighteen, and fiancées of citizens, of aliens who had applied for citizenship, and of World War veterans. The selective provi-

sions of earlier laws relating to health and literacy were not repealed and all persons admissible under the Emergency Quota Act
were subject to their restrictions.

The evidence which the Congressional committees on immigration were able to take during the year following the passage of the
1921 Act was so incomplete and inconclusive that in May, 1922,
the provisions of the Emergency Quota Act were extended for another two years, with the important amendment that quota exemption for immigrants from the western hemisphere should be limited
to persons who had resided in the countries specified for at least
five years.

Legislative History of 1924 Act.

The differences of opinion which were brought out in committee
hearings and debates on the floor of Congress and which seemed
to be concerned with methods of restriction were at bottom differences as to the desirability of drastic restriction. Continuation
of the quota system was supported by practically all restrictionists,
though a bitter dispute raged about the quota basis. Flexible immigration according to economic need, commonly referred to as "selective immigration," was the alternative advocated by opponents
of drastic restriction.

To prevent a labor scarcity an immigration policy, based on
economic need, was advanced by organized industrial interests
and supported by the Secretary of Labor. Groups of recent foreign-born immigrants indorsed it because more liberal admission
of their friends and relatives would thereby be permitted. The loos-
est form which this policy took was the proposal for a sliding scale
of immigration based on an index of employment. This was not a
precise measure of economic need in view of unsatisfactory employment statistics, and it provided no method for selection of the total
fixed by the sliding scale. Another proposal, similar to French
regulation of post-war immigration, provided for an estimate of
economic needs by the Department of Labor on the basis of information from employers indicating labor shortages and for the
issue of visas by consuls abroad in accordance with these labor demands, but no guarantees were proposed against misrepresenta-

tion by employers. Provision for more specific machinery based on experience with importation of contract labor was included in a proposal for the admission of immigrant labor upon the application of any employer on condition that labor of like kind could not be found unemployed in the United States and that the applicant would guarantee employment for one year. Even this proposal was felt to permit too wide administrative discretion to safeguard the American worker, since shortage of labor of a specific kind might be used as the ground for importing persons for labor which unskilled workers or unemployed workers in other trades might otherwise perform. The principle of selection according to economic need was opposed by organized labor as the basis of a permanent immigration policy because none of the proposals for flexibility permitted suspension of immigration in periods of severe unemployment.

The quota system offered at least some certainty of results, for it permitted comparatively little administrative discretion. Although the 3 Per Cent Limit Act had not meant a very drastic reduction in immigration, the large number of immigrant aliens admitted had clearly come in under the liberal exemptions of the Act. The total number of immigrant aliens rose to 522,919 during the fiscal year ended June, 1923, and to 706,896 during the following fiscal year; but of these, 335,480 in 1923 and 357,642 in 1924 were charged against the quota allotments, which were fixed at a total of 357,803 immigrants annually. By changing quotas and exempt classes immigration could be limited to any number desired. Probably this certainty more than any other factor secured for the quota method the indorsement of organized labor, which had adopted no fixed principles about the basis of restriction, and the support of eugenists and other persons interested in the character of immigration who since pre-war days had advocated restriction and selection on the basis of individual qualifications.

A general agreement on the quota method as a device for restriction did not preclude wide divergences in opinion as to the total to be admitted or the distribution of the total among the various emigrant countries. The vital issue was the racial character of future immigrants. The controversy centered around the quota basis and was less concerned with the total to be admitted. Extensive researches into the eugenic aspects of immigration were authorized by the House Committee on Immigration and Naturalization. In *An Analysis of the American Melting Pot*—the most widely read of these investigations—Dr. Harry H. Laughlin presented data supporting the view that recent immigrants came from stock biologically inferior to that of old immigrants and native-born. From statistics of state and federal penitentiaries and institutions for the feeble-minded, insane, epileptic, tubercular, blind, and dependent, and army tests of intelligence, he inferred that a higher proportion of recent immigrants than of old immigrants or native-born were "socially inadequate" persons who had "failed in comparison with normal persons to maintain themselves as useful members of the organized social state." This inferiority of new immigrants he attributed to their racial characteristics. In order to prevent further deterioration of stock he recommended a quota base which would give a predominantly northwest European immigration.

The scientific value of the report was attacked[2] on the ground that Dr. Laughlin made no adjustment in his computations for concentration of foreign-born in cities which are more highly institutionalized than rural areas, that in making allowances for the relative effects of environment and heredity his biological preconceptions had led him to resolve doubts in favor of heredity, and that "inadequacy" may depend upon pre-immigration environing conditions affecting the individual immigrant but not his offspring. Although in its final report the House Committee did not use the argument of biological inferiority of recent immigrants, the Laughlin report helped to crystallize the feeling which existed against south and east Europeans.

A slightly different reason for restriction of south and east European immigration was given during the Congressional hearings by John B. Trevor in a statement on the racial composition of the

[2] See *The Survey*, Dec. 15, 1923, "Undesirable Aliens," by H. S. Jennings; *American Journal of Sociology*, Aug., 1924, "Statistics and the Immigration Problem," by Joseph M. Gillman; and "Social Adequacy of Foreign Nationals in the United States," a critical review of "An Analysis of America's Modern Melting Pot," *Special Report No. 28* of the National Industrial Conference Board, 1924.

population of the United States which defended the preservation of the basic northwest European strain. The core of his argument, which was used verbatim in the report of the House Committee on Immigration and Naturalization to support its recommendation of the 1890 census as a quota basis, was as follows:

Since it is an axiom of political science that a government not imposed by external force is the visible expression of the ideals, standards, and social viewpoint of the people over which it rules, it is obvious that a change in the character or composition of the population must inevitably result in the evolution of a form of government consonant with the base upon which it rests. If, therefore, the principle of individual liberty, guarded by a constitutional government created on this continent nearly a century and a half ago, is to endure, the basic strain of our population must be maintained and our economic standards preserved.

With full recognition of the material progress which we owe to the races from southern and eastern Europe, we are conscious that the continued arrival of great numbers tends to upset our balance of population, to depress our standard of living, and to unduly charge our institutions for the care of the socially inadequate.

If immigration from southern and eastern Europe may enter the United States on a basis of substantial equality with that admitted from the older sources of supply, it is clear that if any appreciable number of immigrants are to be allowed to land upon our shores the balance of racial preponderance must in time pass to those elements of the population who reproduce more rapidly on a lower standard of living than those possessing other ideals.[3]

This position offered a justification for the comparatively large quotas for northwest European countries provided for in the Johnson Bill, which had been characterized in official protests by the Italian and Roumanian governments as an arbitrary and unjust discrimination against south and east Europeans.

In the bills finally enacted the two chambers of Congress adopted different methods for the determination of quotas. The House accepted the recommendation of its committee basing quotas on 2 per cent of the foreign-born at the time of the 1890 census, which

[3] Sixty-eighth Congress, First Session, House Report 350, March 24, 1924, pp. 13-14.

of all the methods proposed would secure the highest proportion of northwest Europeans. The Senate accepted as a quota base 2 per cent of the foreign-born at the time of the 1910 census, a base which had been favored by Secretary of State Hughes in order to avoid the charge of discrimination against south and east European countries, but with the amendment that after three years quotas were to be based on the national origins of the total population at the time of the 1920 census. This amendment, introduced by Senator Reed of Pennsylvania and supported by Senator Lodge, was an exact application of the principle set forth in Mr. Trevor's memorandum. It proposed to give to each country a proportion of the total quota equal to the proportion of the present population of the United States which was descended from persons born in that particular country. These proportions were to be determined not by tracing the ancestry of individuals but by the use of census and immigration statistics upon which had been based the racial analysis of the population prepared by the Census Bureau and presented by Mr. Trevor.[4] In the House the same amendment introduced by Mr. Rogers of Massachusetts had been overwhelmingly defeated in the course of debate. These differences were resolved in conference by a compromise which based quotas on 2 per cent of the foreign-born at the time of the 1890 census until July 1, 1927, when the base was to shift to the national origins of the whole population at the time of the 1920 census.

Other important points of controversy concerned Oriental immigration,[5] and the exempt classes. The large non-quota immigration under the Emergency Quota Acts had resulted chiefly from exemption of persons residing in the Western Hemisphere and from exemption of certain near relatives of citizens, persons who had applied for citizenship, and World War veterans. As it became more probable that a quota system would be adopted, opponents of drastic restriction made attempts to broaden these exemptions, to extend them to skilled laborers admitted under contract when labor of like kind was not to be found unemployed in the United

[4] A fuller description of how quotas are determined under the national origins provision is given on pp. 466-470.
[5] See pp. 509-511.

States, and to include skilled agriculturists in the skilled labor exemption. Not only were these attempts defeated, but the provisions finally adopted were more strict even than the recommendations of the House Committee.

Provisions of 1924 Act.

The Immigration Act of 1924, as finally passed on May 28, followed the early quota acts in the method of fixing numerical limits on immigration, but established two important departures in policy—the exclusion of Japanese and an apportionment of quotas based on racial selection.

The new quota provisions of the 1924 Act were as follows:

Sec. 11. (a) The annual quota of any nationality shall be 2 per centum of the number of foreign-born individuals of such nationality resident in continental United States as determined by the United States census of 1890, but the minimum quota of any nationality shall be 100.

(b) The annual quota of any nationality for the fiscal year beginning July 1, 1927, and for each fiscal year thereafter, shall be a number which bears the same ratio to 150,000 as the number of inhabitants in continental United States in 1920 having that national origin (ascertained as hereinafter provided in this section) bears to the number of inhabitants in continental United States in 1920, but the minimum quota of any nationality shall be 100.

(c) For the purpose of subdivision (b) national origin shall be ascertained by determining as nearly as may be, in respect of each geographical area which under section 12 is to be treated as a separate country (except the geographical areas specified in subdivision (c) of section 4) the number of inhabitants in continental United States in 1920 whose origin by birth or ancestry is attributable to such geographical area. Such determination shall not be made by tracing the ancestors or descendants of particular individuals, but shall be based upon statistics of immigration and emigration, together with rates of increase of population as shown by successive decennial United States censuses, and such other data as may be found to be reliable.

Within the quotas, preference up to 50 per cent of the quota of any country was to be given to unmarried children under twenty-one, parents, husbands and wives of resident United States citizens, and to skilled agriculturists and their wives and dependent children under sixteen. The act also established certain classes of immigrants who were to be admitted outside the quotas. The "non-quota immigrants" included unmarried children under eighteen and wives of resident United States citizens, immigrants previously admitted who were returning from a visit abroad, persons born in Canada, Newfoundland, Mexico, Cuba, Haiti, the Dominican Republic, the Canal Zone, or an independent country of Central or South America, with their wives and unmarried children under eighteen, ministers and professors, who had practiced their profession for two continuous years immediately preceding admission, with their wives and unmarried children under eighteen, and *bona fide* students under eighteen who entered solely for purposes of study. Other persons permitted to enter were the classes designated as "non-immigrants," who were not counted in the quotas, but who could not establish permanent residence here for purposes of naturalization—government officials with their families, attendants, servants, and employees, aliens visiting the United States temporarily for business or pleasure, aliens in transit, *bona fide* seamen who landed solely in pursuit of their calling, and aliens entitled to enter the United States solely to carry on trade under and in pursuance of existing treaties of commerce and navigation.

Another important feature of the 1924 Act was the establishment of administrative machinery which simplified and humanized earlier regulation under the quota system. In particular it stopped the rush of steamships into ports in order to land passengers in time to be counted in the monthly quotas by substituting for the practice of counting immigrants on landing the use of certificates of admission in the form of immigration visas which were to be issued by United States consuls. Under this system persons intending to migrate to the United States were to apply at a consulate for a quota number and visas were to be issued in the order of application to as many persons as the quota provisions permitted. The Act also made it possible to reduce rejections at United States ports and to prevent futile journeys by empowering the immigration service to examine immigrants abroad. Seasonal fluctuations and overcrowding at Ellis Island were to be eliminated as far as possible by the admission in any month of not more than one-tenth of the total annual quota. The act was signed by President Coolidge on May 28, 1924, and went into effect almost immediately.

CHAPTER FOUR

PROBLEMS ARISING OUT OF THE 1924 ACT

THE Act was effective in reducing the number of immigrants. After its passage total immigration dropped from 706,896 in 1924 to 294,314 in 1925, 304,448 in 1926, 335,175 in 1927, and 307,255 in 1928. It was equally effective in securing an immigration that was predominantly of northwest European origin. Though almost half of these immigrants were non-Europeans who came in outside of the quota, about two-thirds of that number came from Canada and were predominantly British in origin. The reduction in numbers and the use of immigrant visas have expedited examinations at ports of entry. With the permission of foreign governments medical examination of immigrants before departure was adopted in England, Germany, and Belgium, with satisfactory results, and has since been extended to most quota countries.

The 1924 Act has nevertheless given rise to serious problems of administration, has resulted in individual hardships, and the preference given particular racial strains and economic classes has led to agitation for revision.

Problems of Administration.

Administrative problems have changed considerably in character since the Act first went into effect. The crudest forms of organized smuggling of aliens by means of fraudulent visas, surreptitious coast landing and border crossing, which were widespread in 1924 and 1925, have been suppressed. Through coöperation with Canadian, Mexican, and Cuban authorities, the landing in their ports of European immigrants intending to pass illegally into continental United States has been made more difficult. Officials in charge of enforcement, however, believe that considerable smuggling of aliens as seamen and illegal crossing over land boundaries continue. In their opinion the border patrol which was established in 1924, and had a staff of 747 persons and an appropriation of $1,600,000 during the fiscal year 1928, is still inadequate to guard the long stretches of boundary between official border ports of entry. They feel that a stronger patrol is necessary to discourage and detect new smuggling enterprises and to secure more effective enforcement of the provisions applying to the large numbers of immigrants from Canada and Mexico who now evade the immigration authorities.

Similar questions arise in the administration of deportation legislation. To persons already deportable under the 1917 Act as members of excluded classes, the Quota Acts added all aliens who entered without proper immigration visas. Partly in order to secure strict observance of the 1924 Act, appropriations for deportations have been increased to more than $1,000,000 annually for the last few years. The results appear in the following increase in deportations since 1922:

1922—4,345	1925— 9,495
1923—3,661	1926—10,904
1924—6,409	1927—11,662
1928—11,625	

Almost half of the 1928 deportations were made on the ground of entry without proper visa. The Commissioner of Immigration has stated in recent annual reports that detection of deportable persons is limited by the size of the staff available for this purpose and that deportations have been prevented in a large number of cases because the Bureau has lacked funds, the average cost of deportation being approximately $84 per person. A more drastic deportation policy has for several years been supported by a majority of the House Committee on Immigration and Naturalization in the form of the Holaday Bill. This bill, the provisions of which would have added to the classes of deportable persons and facilitated deportation by placing the burden of proof entirely upon the alien in cases where it now rests on the Government, passed the House in 1926 and was favorably reported by the House Committee at both sessions of the Seventieth Congress. Some of its provisions, which mended loopholes in existing deportation legislation but did not incorporate the more drastic changes proposed, passed the Second Session of the Seventieth Congress as a Senate bill, to which the substance of the Holaday Bill had been added as an amendment and later deleted in conference.[1] Bills providing for registration of all aliens on penalty of deportation have also been advocated as a method of detecting persons who have entered illegally and of facilitating their deportation. The question of deportation involves the expatriation legislation of foreign countries which in some instances now makes it impossible for the United States to deport criminals or persons who have for a certain length of time resided outside the jurisdiction of the countries of their original allegiance.

Other administrative problems which may become increasingly important in the future are concerned with the selection of immigrants abroad. Questions have already been raised by the control exercised by foreign governments through their power to withhold passports without which immigrants cannot secure visas from United States consuls. Italy has used this power in such a way as to nullify preference within the quotas granted under the 1924 Act to families of United States citizens, giving preference in the granting of passports to adult male immigrants likely to send money to their families in Italy. Spain has pursued the reverse policy; it has given preference to women and children of Spanish residents in the United States, granting them priority in the issue of passports. Another aspect of the problem of selection abroad is the discretion which may be practiced in examinations at United States consulates by virtue of the final authority of consuls over the issue of visas. Decisions of inspectors in the United States have always been and still are subject to administrative and judicial review. For obvious reasons of expediency there is no provision in the 1924 Act for appeal by a person abroad from the decision of a United States consul, so that when an applicant has been rejected in a preliminary examination abroad and a visa has been refused the consul's act is final. This permits consuls to exercise more discretion than is possible for inspectors stationed in the United States. The clause excluding "persons of constitutional psychopathic inferiority" is particularly susceptible to differences of interpretation. Exercise of such administrative discretion on a

[1] S. 5094, approved March 4, 1929, Public No. 1018.

much wider scale is part of the accepted practice of such immigration countries as Canada, Australia, and France, but for the United States it marks a departure from a policy of granting a minimum of discretion to officials and of safeguarding this power against abuse by generous provisions for appeal. Since the consent of foreign governments is required for the conduct of examinations abroad, it may be expected that the exercise of any discretion will have to receive the sanction of the emigrant country. In this connection Secretary of Labor Davis has recommended that the United States refuse to accept emigrants from any country whose policies interfere with those laid down in United States legislation. Examples are Roumania and Russia, which have refused to accept deportees from the United States.

Separated Families.

The most sustained attack on the 1924 Act has been made on the ground that it has prevented families of United States residents from joining their breadwinners in this country. Though wives and unmarried children under eighteen of citizens are admitted outside the quota, and parents and unmarried children between eighteen and twenty-one of citizens are given preferred status within the quota, these provisions have been inadequate to permit reunion of families separated by the War, and the admission of the families of men who came in before the passage of the 1924 Act expecting to have their families follow them. The greatest pressure for places on the quotas naturally occurs in the countries of southern and eastern Europe from which have come the largest proportion of adult male immigrants, and which have suffered most from the quota restrictions. The 20,000 a year admissible under the quotas of countries in this geographical section was too small a number in 1926 to provide even for the preferred relatives of citizens who applied for visas. Because of the large number who might enter under a provision admitting families of all resident foreign-born and the desire to admit only the families of persons contemplating permanent residence, most proposals have been concerned with admission of families of alien declarants. Restrictionists who first opposed all such enlargements have recently favored a limited modification of the present law in order to remove just ground for objection to the Act lest the attack on some of its other features be strengthened and a general sentiment against its principle be increased. During the closing days of the first session of the Seventieth Congress a conservative measure[2] of relief was passed with the support of restrictionists. The new Act makes available for wives and unmarried minor children of aliens 50 per cent of the quota of each nationality and any portion of the remainder not used by other preferred classes. It also provides that non-quota status shall be granted to children of citizens between eighteen and twenty-one years of age and to husbands of United States citizens by marriages contracted before May 31, 1928, two classes which were formerly entitled to preference within the quota. Through this change approximately 10,000 additional persons may enter outside the quotas, thereby relieving to some extent the pressure for admission.

National Origins Provision.

Another feature of the 1924 Act which has met with serious opposition has been the national origins provision which enacted that beginning July 1, 1927, the basis of quotas should be changed from 2 per cent of the foreign-born of each nationality who were here in 1890 to that proportion of 150,000 which the number of persons of a given national origin residing in the United States in 1920 bears to its total population in 1920. The exact quotas were to be determined by the Secretaries of State, Commerce, and Labor jointly on the basis of census and immigration statistics and other reliable data and were to be reported to the President who should proclaim them on or before April 1, 1927.[3] If the proclamation were not made on or before that date, the new quotas were not to take effect until ninety days after they had been proclaimed. Provision was also made for the continuation of existing quotas based on the 1890 census if after the proclamation it appeared to the

[2] Senate Jt. Res. No. 5, approved May 29, 1928, Public Resolution No. 61.
[3] For the text of the national origins provision see p. 453.

officials and was proclaimed by the President that an error of fact had been made in the determination of quotas based on national origin.

This provision was inserted in the 1924 Act during the last stages of its legislative history. Introduced by Senator Reed of Pennsylvania early in March in the form of an amendment to a bill basing quotas on the foreign-born at the time of the 1910 census, it was supported in the Senate hearings by John B. Trevor. The Senate Committee, apparently through failure to reach an agreement on a quota base, had not reported on the bills before it when the House adopted its immigration act. The House bill, introduced by Representative Johnson, basing quotas on the 1890 census was not regarded with favor in the Senate because of its evident discrimination against south and east Europeans. The national origins provision, however, offered practically the same result and adopted a procedure which could be defended against charges of unfair discrimination. It was advocated by Senators Lodge and Reed as the only scientific basis for quotas that had been proposed and one which founded immigration policy on a broad principle. In April the amendment was accepted with little debate. In the House it was mentioned by Mr. Bacon of New York, a member of the House Immigration Committee, who had favored it but who had accepted the Johnson Bill because it achieved approximately the same result by a simpler method. During the debate on the floor the national origins provision had been presented in an amendment by Mr. Rogers of Massachusetts and rejected by a large majority. Later, as the result of compromises in the conference committee, it was incorporated in the act which passed both houses and was signed by President Coolidge.

An agitation for the repeal of the national origins provision sprang up among the German, Irish, and Scandinavian groups in the United States when they realized that it would greatly reduce the quotas for their mother countries as compared with existing quotas based on 2 per cent of the foreign-born at the time of the 1890 census. The provision has been one of the most controversial immigration measures since the passage of the 1924

Act. Associations of foreign-born which had been inactive since the War were revived in order to support the case for repeal, and United States history was rewritten to enhance the rôle of Irish and Germans in building up the nation. Societies were also organized to work for retention of the provision and a large number of articles appeared in its defense.

Supporters of the national origins provision argue that the national origins method is the only fair method of determining quotas because it takes into consideration all the present inhabitants of the United States, native-born as well as foreign-born. They believe that the principle of preserving the present racial composition of our population affords a scientific foundation for a permanent immigration policy. Selection of immigrants on this basis is justified on the ground that the culture which has taken root in this country during the first three centuries of its existence can be developed only by the people who founded it, and that the democratic character of our political institutions which is the outstanding feature of our national life can be preserved only if the ethnic strains from northwestern Europe with their tradition and aptitude for self-government continue to be predominant. Advocates of the national origins provision oppose the present quota basis, though it achieves approximately the same result, because it is arbitrary and subject to the charge of race discrimination. Under the national origins provision the most recent census is used, and all nationalities are given quotas which correspond as accurately as possible to their contribution to the racial stock of the country.

German, Irish, and Scandinavian groups feel that the provision is intended to favor immigrants from Great Britain and that the assumption behind it is that the British make better citizens than they. It is also argued that the national origins method of determining quotas can take account only of country of birth so that its purpose is achieved only in so far as country of birth is an index of race. The case against the provision, however, has rested primarily on the inadequacy of data for determining quotas by the national origins method and the uncertainty of the results obtained. It is held that quotas, based on the national origins of the whole population at the present time, are so difficult to calculate that the provision leaves the actual determination of numbers in the hands of administrative officials who can be accused of prejudice or of yielding to pressure.

In Congress the controversy over the provision has centered about the feasibility of determining quotas on the basis of national origins. The first estimates of quotas submitted by the Secretaries of State, Commerce, and Labor in January, 1927, varied in important respects from the unofficial estimates which had been presented to Congress in 1924, the most striking discrepancies being a reduction in the figure for Great Britain and North Ireland from 85,135 to 73,039 and an increase for Germany from 20,028 to 23,428 and for Ireland from 8,330 to 13,862. The report of the Secretaries to the President was accompanied by the statement that the "information available raises grave doubts as to the whole value of these computations for the purposes intended," and that "we therefore cannot assume responsibility for such conclusions under the circumstances." In order to give the experts more time to perfect their calculations, the Senate passed a resolution postponing the effective date of the provision until July 1, 1928. The House Committee on Immigration and Naturalization favored repeal of the provision on two grounds: first, that the possibility of such wide variations in estimates would leave quotas based on national origins open to continual dispute, and, secondly, that the provision was creating strife and feeling among different ethnic groups within this country. The House finally accepted the Senate resolution for postponement in order to prevent the new quotas from going into effect.

During the Seventieth Congress agitation for repeal of the provision continued. Upon the release by the Secretaries in February, 1928, of new figures, the House Committee on Immigration and Naturalization held hearings at which members of the Quota Board were asked to explain the provision and the procedure which had been adopted in determining the quotas. It was brought out that certain refinements in calculations had been left incomplete.

Partly in order to give the Quota Board more time, and partly to avoid making a decision on the eve of a presidential election, Congress passed, on March 31, 1928, a joint resolution which postponed for another year the date on which the provision was to take effect. During the 1928 campaign both major party candidates opposed the national origins provision. President Hoover indicated his position in his speech of acceptance, saying:

As a member of the commission whose duty it is to determine the quota basis under the national origins law I have found it impossible to do so accurately and without hardship. The basis now in effect carries out the essential principle of the law and I favor repeal of that part of the act calling for a new basis of quotas.

The second session of the Seventieth Congress, however, failed to pass a measure providing either for postponement or for repeal of the national origins provision. On the day before the adjournment of Congress the House of Representatives, by a vote of 191 to 152, passed a joint resolution postponing the date on which the provision should take effect to July 1, 1930. The Senate did not act on it. The Quota Board has testified that greater accuracy in results cannot be expected from an extension of time and has submitted its final report. President Hoover, on the advice of the Attorney-General that the proclamation of the quotas was mandatory upon him, proclaimed the quotas on March 22, 1929, stating:

While I am strongly in favor of restricted and selected immigration I have opposed the national origins basis. I therefore naturally dislike the duty of issuing the proclamation and installing the new basis; but the President of the United States must be the first to obey the law.

After the proclamation of the quotas, the President again voiced his objection to the provision through a recommendation in his message to the Special Sessions of the Seventy-first Congress for suspension of the national origins clause. The supporters of the bill in the Senate, however, were strong enough to prevent action, and the new quotas went into effect July 1, 1929.

COMPARISON OF OLD AND NEW QUOTA BASES

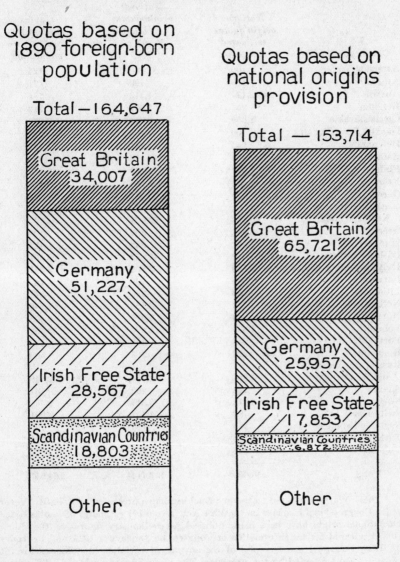

Quotas based on
1890 foreign-born
population

Total — 164,647

Great Britain
34,007

Germany
51,227

Irish Free State
28,567

Scandinavian Countries
18,803

Other

Quotas based on
national origins
provision

Total — 153,714

Great Britain
65,721

Germany
25,957

Irish Free State
17,853

Scandinavian Countries
6,872

Other

The figures for Great Britain include northern Ireland.

IMMIGRATION QUOTAS

Country or area	National origin quotas estimated in 1924[4]	National origin quotas proclaimed March 22, 1929	Quotas based on 1890 foreign-born population
Armenia	100	100	124
Australia	100	100	121
Austria	2,171	1,413	785
Belgium	251	1,304	512
Czechoslovakia	1,359	2,874	3,073
Danzig, Free City of	100	100	228
Denmark	945	1,181	2,789
Esthonia	325	116	124
Finland	517	569	471
France	1,772	3,086	3,954
Germany	20,028	25,957	51,227
Great Britain and Northern Ireland	85,135	65,721	34,007
Greece	384	307	100
Hungary	1,521	869	473
Irish Free State	8,330	17,853	28,567
Italy, including Dodecanese	5,716	5,802	3,845
Latvia	384	236	142
Lithuania	458	386	344
Netherlands	2,762	3,153	1,648
Norway	2,053	2,377	6,453
Poland	4,535	6,524	5,982
Portugal	236	440	503
Roumania	222	295	603
Russia, European and Asiatic	4,002	2,784	2,248
Spain	148	252	131
Sweden	3,072	3,314	9,561
Switzerland	783	1,707	2,081
Syria and the Lebanon	100	123	100
Turkey	100	226	100
Yugoslavia	591	845	671
Total	150,000[5]	153,714[6]	164,647[6]

[4] These figures are based on the unofficial estimates presented by John B. Trevor at the Congressional hearings on the 1924 Act. Two other estimates of quotas based on national origin have been made public—the preliminary figures of the Quota Board released for the information of Congress on January 7, 1927, and February 27, 1928. Following are examples of the amount of variation in estimates for the countries most affected by the provision. The possibility of such wide differences in figures for quotas was the reason most strongly urged by advocates of repeal of the national origins provision.

[5] Includes 16 minimum quotas of 100 each.

[6] Including 37 minimum quotas of 100 each.

	National origin quotas estimated in 1924	National origin quotas submitted Jan. 7, 1927	National origin quotas submitted Feb. 27, 1928	National origin quotas proclaimed March, 1929
Germany	20,028	23,428	24,908	25,957
Great Britain	85,135	73,039	65,894	65,721
Irish Free State	8,330	13,862	17,427	17,853
Norway	2,053	2,267	2,403	2,377
Sweden	3,072	3,259	3,399	3,314

Though this change in the quota basis is important primarily because of its political consequences, its feasibility has raised a real question owing to the uncertainties involved in the calculation of quotas by the national origins method. When the national origins provision was first proposed, provisional estimates presented to Congress had been based on an analysis of population composition made by the Census Bureau in a 1920 monograph entitled *A Century of Population Growth*. This study showed the national origin of the whole population and gave percentages for important nationality groups. In figuring the first estimates these percentages were brought up to date by taking account of the population increase since 1900 and making adjustments for post-war changes in national boundaries. The quota figures were secured by dividing the total of 150,000 among quota countries in accordance with these percentages. In specifying in the Act that national origin should be "based upon statistics of immigration and emigration, together with rates of increase of population as shown by successive decennial censuses, and such other data as may be found reliable" Congress intimated that it expected the quotas to be determined by a procedure similar to that used in the census study. But the board of experts intrusted with the detailed mathematical work had to take account of criticisms of the statistical methods and sources used by the Census Bureau.

In their calculations the Quota Board divided the population of the United States at the time of the 1920 census into three groups according to the data from which their totals were computed: (1) foreign-born and native-born of foreign parentage whose numbers are recorded in the 1920 census; (2) descendants of persons enumerated in the first federal census of 1790, referred to as "colonial stock"; and (3) the residue, composed of grandchildren of immigrants and earlier generations of "post-colonial stock" as distinguished from "colonial stock."[7] The figures obtained from these sources describe not the ancestry of individuals living in 1920, but the reservoirs of stock from which the population as a whole has been fed. The figure for "colonial stock," for instance, does not represent the number of persons descended from the 1790 population. Counting all individuals as of equal importance in the transmission of racial characteristics, it shows the total present population as containing a certain percentage of "colonial stock" and a certain percentage of "post-colonial stock." A person with two German grandparents and an English and Swedish grandparent would count as one-half German, one-fourth English, and one-fourth Swedish.

No difficulties arise with the first group, the foreign-born and native-born of foreign parentage, for they are enumerated in the 1920 census and classified by national origin; but in connection with the "colonial stock" and the grandchildren and earlier generations of "post-colonial stock," uncertainties arise. In determining the amount of "colonial stock" an estimate has to be made of the total amount of stock representing the descendants of the 1790 population, and its national origin has to be determined on the basis of surnames of heads of households listed in the first census. In the monograph of the Census Bureau, the total amount of "colonial stock" had been estimated by taking the rate of population increase for each decade, by assuming that native and foreign-born stocks increased at an equal rate and by applying the rate of increase to the population at the time of the 1790 census. By this method a total of approximately forty-seven million for "colonial stock" was secured. After the national origin of the 1790 population had been derived from a classification of surnames by country of origin, the percentage from each country was used as

[7] The designation used here is the one for which Dr. Hill, Assistant Director of the Census, expressed a preference in the hearings on the national origins provision held by the Senate Committee on Immigration in February, 1929. In previous publications of the Census Bureau and in previous committee hearings, these two groups were called "original native stock" and "immigrant stock."

the basis for apportioning the forty-seven million among European countries. The Quota Board did not follow this procedure but used a method of computing "colonial stock" suggested by a critic of the Census Bureau monograph. Instead of applying a rate of population increase to the early census, the Board computed its total on the basis of nativity statistics by age groups given in the censuses from 1890 to 1920. Beginning with the number of native-born of native parentage in each age group recorded in the 1920 census, the percentage of persons in each age group with native grandparents was computed by using the percentage of native-born in the age group which most probably represented the grandparents. The percentage of native-born with native great grandparents was then computed from the percentage of native-born in the age group which most probably represented the parents of the grandparents, etc. With some interpolation for the period between 1790 and 1820 the Quota Board arrived at an estimate of forty-one million for "colonial stock" in 1920, a figure less than the census monograph by six million. The first reduction which occurred in the estimates of the British quota is accounted for by this change in procedure. The second reduction of 10 per cent in the figure for Great Britain resulted from a new independent analysis of the 1790 census of surnames which took account of the origin and anglicizing of German and Irish names; in a predominantly German community, for instance, persons named Small, Little, or Cline, might be transferred from the English to the German group on the supposition that the family name had originally been Klein. Since the third group constituted the residue, the amount of stock it represented changed as alterations were made in the estimates of "colonial stock." The national origin of this group was determined by immigration statistics for the years during which the ancestors of these persons were presumed to have arrived.

Problems of statistics, however, are not peculiar to the determination of quotas under the national origins provision. Some of the present quotas probably contain substantial errors owing to the fact that the 1890 census records countries of birth in terms of pre-war geography. In determining quotas on the basis of the 1890 census it has been necessary to estimate the number of foreign residents of the United States in 1890 who were born in areas which have since been transferred from one sovereign power to another; the number of immigrants born in German Poland, for instance, has to be estimated, deducted from the number of German-born recorded in the 1890 census, and added to the number recorded as born in Poland; the number of immigrants who came from the Baltic provinces before 1890 has to be estimated and deducted from the totals for Russian-born and Polish-born persons as recorded in the 1890 census. According to the testimony of a State Department representative before the Senate Committee on Immigration in February, 1929, 14½ per cent of the total quota numbers are attributed to a quota country which differs in name from the census entry from which the quota is derived. About 43 per cent of the total quota numbers is allotted to countries whose boundaries have changed since 1890. For this reason Dr. Hill, Chairman of the Quota Board, believes that the national origin quotas are probably more accurate than the 1890 census basis for those countries whose boundaries have been materially changed by the War, but that for countries whose boundaries were not affected, they are not more accurate, and in some cases are less accurate.

Extension of Quota System to Countries in the Western Hemisphere.

The exemption from the quota provisions of the 1924 Act of persons born in Canada, Newfoundland, and independent countries of Central and South America, with their wives and unmarried children under eighteen, has also met with strong objection and has been the subject of proposed revision. This provision, under which almost half the total immigration of the past three years has been admitted, permits a flexibility in immigration desired by employers of labor but admits racial streams in proportions unwarranted by the principles on which the 1924 Act is based. The proposal to extend the quota to countries now exempt would reduce immigrants from the Western Hemisphere to approximately 15 per cent of their number admitted in 1927. Numerically the results would be as follows:

Countries	Immigration			Estimate of quotas based on 2 per cent of 1890 census[11]
	1926	1927	1928	
Total	144,393	161,872	124,114	23,309
Canada	91,019	81,506	54,691	19,619
Newfoundland	2,349	3,074	2,452	100
Mexico	43,316	67,721	58,188	1,557
Cuba	2,281	3,020	2,368	233[9]
Other West Indies	941[8]	999	1,076	200[10]
Central America	1,374[8]	1,771	1,684	600[10]
South America	3,107[8]	3,777	3,641	1,000[10]
Other	6	4	14	

On the Canadian border the free movement of population established under the Jay Treaty of 1793 has been advantageous to both countries and there has been little occasion to restrict it. Though the number of Canadian-born persons in the United States has exceeded one million since 1890, it decreased slightly between 1910 and 1920, despite an unusually large immigration from Canada. Between 1901 and 1910 only 179,226[12] immigrants were recorded; between 1910 and 1920, 742,185, and during the first eight years of the present decade, 792,810. The last two years, however, have shown a decline from the peak figure of 91,019 in 1926. The lack of a system of recording immigrants at land borders makes it impossible to tell how long-continued this migration has been. Canadian statistics indicate that net additions to the United States population from this exchange are probably no larger than half the number given above. Since the language, racial origin, and living standards of most of the present Canadian immigrants make them peculiarly adaptable to conditions in the United States, their immigration creates only such problems as attend the migration of population within national boundaries.

8 Figures include an insignificant immigration from foreign possessions in Central and South America.

9 Based on estimate of Cuban-born population in the U.S. in 1890.

10 Quota figures apply to independent countries only.

11 Estimates on the national origins basis, which went into effect on July 1, 1929, would show larger quotas, particularly in the case of Mexico.

12 Including between 2,000 and 3,000 persons from Newfoundland.

The difficulties which arose at the Detroit-Windsor border in 1927 were primarily administrative, involving Canadian residents who came daily to the United States to work, and were not the result of social and economic problems created by Canadian immigration. The use of some Canadian "commuters" in a Detroit strike resulted in action by trade unions in Detroit bringing to the attention of the immigration authorities the alleged illegal entry of these persons. A subsequent ruling by the Bureau of Immigration classified "commuters" as immigrants and ordered inspectors to request their compliance with the immigration laws including payment of head tax and visa fee amounting to $18. The Canadian Government declared that their classification as immigrants was improper since migration involved change of residence, and that the ruling violated provisions of the Jay Treaty, which granted the right to

His Majesty's subjects, and to the citizens of the United States, . . . also to the Indians dwelling on either side of the said boundary line, freely to pass and repass by land or inland navigation, into the respective territories and countries of the two parties.

The lower Federal courts supported the position of the Canadian Government but were overruled by the United States Supreme Court.[13] The final decision held that the Jay Treaty was no longer in force and that persons who entered daily to pursue an occupation did not fall within the exempt class of transients who enter temporarily for purposes of business and travel. Hereafter, Canadian residents desiring work in the United States can enter only if they qualify as immigrants and pay $18 for head tax and visa fee.

Free migration across the Mexican border has differed from that on the Canadian border in that it has brought into the United States individuals who differ from the rest of the population in racial origin and living standards. The shortage of cheap immigrant labor which existed during the War and which continued to some extent under the 1924 Immigration Act has increased the entry of Mexicans. Since they have become more widely dispersed

[13] *Karnuth* v. *U.S.*, April 8, 1929; 278 U.S.

within the United States, some writers have expressed alarm concerning their effect on racial purity and United States living standards. The demand for extension of the quota to countries of the Western Hemisphere is primarily an attempt to reduce this immigration to a negligible quantity.

Though Mexican laborers have always been used widely in Texas and New Mexico, where the Mexican strain has been longer established than the pure European strain, their influx did not become important until they were recruited for cultivation and harvesting in the new cotton areas opened in 1910 in California and Arizona. After the outbreak of the War Mexicans were brought into the coast and mountain states for work which had previously been done by south and east Europeans. The provisions of the 1917 Act subjecting all immigrants to the literacy test and the $8.00 head tax would have excluded, if strictly enforced, so large a proportion of Mexican immigrants that special regulations under war powers were issued exempting temporary Mexican contract laborers from provisions of the Act in order that they might work in sugar-beet fields, mining, and other essential war industries. Lack of adequate staff to enforce the law on the one hand, and the delay and expense incident to securing exempt laborers legally on the other, resulted in an organized "bootlegging" of Mexican laborers by recruiting agencies in the United States. This continued after the War with comparatively little interference from the insufficient immigration force. The border patrol, established in 1924 primarily to check the surreptitious entry of Europeans, reduced illegal entry of Mexicans and secured stricter enforcement of the literacy and health provisions of the 1917 Act. Partly because of rejections and partly because of lack of funds or fear of submitting themselves to examination, legal entry of Mexicans declined from 89,336 in 1924 to 32,964 in 1925; it rose to 67,721 in 1927, and dropped again to 59,016 in 1928. The unusually large cotton crop in 1926 made the reduction severely felt by large planters who began to agitate for a revision of the existing law in order to secure exemption of Mexican laborers from the literacy test and the payment of the head tax and visa fee. Border Chambers of Commerce, representatives of large-scale agriculturists, mining concerns, and railroads contended that since Mexican laborers came in only temporarily for the harvesting season they were not really immigrants, that their entry was essential to southwestern agriculture, and that the high head tax and visa fee encouraged illegal entries.

At the same time legislation restricting Mexican immigration by extending the quota system to Mexico was demanded by small planters of the southwest as protection against the increasingly disastrous competition of the large growers who used cheap Mexican labor. They asserted that the marked growth in the number of Mexican-born residents from 103,393 in 1900 to 495,418 in 1920 indicated that though Mexicans came in to do seasonal labor, a large proportion of them remain in this country, where they enter industrial occupations and with their low living standards undermine the wages of the native population. Additional support for the extension of the quota system to Mexico has come from restrictionists, who wish to exclude Mexicans because of the fear that they will not form a desirable element in the population and will create a social situation in the communities in which they settle inimical to the democratic character of United States institutions.

The dispersion of Mexican laborers throughout industrial centers west of the Mississippi and in some industrial cities as far east as Pittsburgh has brought the Mexican into direct competition with non-agricultural workers. His economic position at present is similar to that of the south and east European laborer before the World War. In meeting this problem the American Federation of Labor has been affected by its cordial relations with the Mexican Federation and for several years has refused to indorse extension of the quota to Mexico in the hope that a satisfactory solution could be worked out through voluntary action on the part of the Mexican Government and the Mexican labor movement. The Mexican Government has been anxious to stem the tide of migration because it is diverting the population needed to regenerate the land. Mexican land reform, however, has failed to counteract the attractions of material prosperity offered by work in the United States, and despite efforts to stop organized recruiting the Government has been powerless to prevent emigration. At its 1929 convention the American Federation of Labor finally indorsed restriction of Mexicans and other immigrants from the Western Hemisphere by adopting a declaration that "restriction against entry of aliens in the United States should be more rigid in character, though tempered with humane considerations, and applicable to all aliens."

The setback in Mexican immigration during the fiscal year 1928 can hardly be expected to appease the demands of American labor for restriction of unskilled laborers from this source, since the decrease of 8,705 has been attributed[14] in large part to an oversupply of Mexicans in certain areas. The release of laborers by the lumber industry of the Northwest, the reduction in acreage of sugar-beet production, and the low seasonal demand for labor on southwestern railroads have discouraged Mexicans from seeking employment in the United States.

The difficulty of restricting Mexican immigration without either interfering with free movement of labor across the Canadian border or expressly discriminating against Mexicans as such explains in part the reluctance of Congress to take action on the bills extending the quota to countries of the Western Hemisphere. Another objection to Mexican restriction has been the argument that the enforcement of the literacy and health tests would restrict the number and improve the quality of immigrants entering under existing legislation. In fact the obstacles in the way of enforcing relatively stricter measures than at present may be insurmountable along a land and river boundary which is easy to cross and hard to police. On the whole, however, sentiment favoring restriction seems to be increasing. After several lengthy hearings during the past nine years, the Senate Committee on Immigration during the second session of the Seventieth Congress declared itself in favor of extending the quota to Mexico.[15]

[14] By the Commissioner General of Immigration in his Annual Report for 1928, p. 10.
[15] Seventieth Congress, Second Session, Senate Report No. 1343.

CHAPTER FIVE

ECONOMIC ASPECTS OF RESTRICTION

FROM a pre-war annual figure of approximately a million, immigration has declined to about three hundred thousand annually since 1924. Net immigration for these years has dropped from an annual average of 663,656 to an annual average of 230,297. The increase in the proportion of women, children, and elderly persons has meant a decrease in the percentage of wage-earners. But on the whole, restriction of immigration seems to have caused no acute shortage in the labor supply. This has been accounted for by a number of factors. During the World War the war industries not only absorbed the surplus of unskilled labor which had been observed by the Immigration Commission in 1911-1914, but also increased negro migration to northern industrial districts and stimulated migration of rural population to urban areas. Other adjustments in the demand for labor have resulted from the migrations of industry itself. The striking increase in the number of southern textile mills has brought about full-time employment of a larger proportion of the southern rural population, and has thrown out of work communities of textile laborers in New England. Shifts in the coal-mining industry and in the centers of shoe and clothing manufacture have also tended to create regional unemployment.

To what extent a decrease in immigration figures since 1914 has been offset, and the demand for labor in new industrial areas has been supplied by surreptitious entries cannot be accurately estimated. Labor has become available from countries of the Western Hemisphere not subject to quota restrictions. Throughout the West, and to a less extent in the north central states, Mexicans are being employed in unskilled jobs formerly held by south and east Europeans. The absorption of immigrants from adjacent territory has led a foreign observer[1] to the conclusion that restriction of European immigration by the United States on economic grounds was premature. Records show, however, that the annual

[1] André Siegfried, *America Comes of Age*, p. 124.

immigration from the Western Hemisphere for the past eight years has varied only slightly from 150,000, except for the year 1924, when it mounted to 318,855. Increased vigilance at border points of entry, examination, and payment of head tax and visa fee have undoubtedly driven immigrants to attempt surreptitious entry all along the borders. At the same time, the organization of the border patrol in 1924 diminished "bootlegging" of immigrants. To some extent, unrecorded immigration has been offset by an unascertainable flow of Mexicans to their native land, and of Canadians and Americans to the western provinces of Canada. Although the net result of these various movements, if known, would probably be somewhat in excess of the recorded immigration, the net additions would not approach the annual inflow of labor which the United States received, on the average, from Europe in pre-war years.

The most important factor counterbalancing the diminished European labor supply has been an increase in the rate of mechanization and greater efficiency throughout American industry. In manufacturing, the total gains in output per worker during the four years following 1921 amounted to more than 35 per cent. This unusual increase can be partially explained as a recovery from abnormally low per-capita output during the preceding years, but a substantial portion represents a net gain in productivity over any preceding period. During the sixteen years from 1909 to 1925, productivity increased 33 per cent. Two-thirds of this increase occurred between 1916 and 1925. This is a rate of gain more than double that of 1899-1909.[2] In other branches of industry, also, output per worker has risen; between 1918 and 1926 it increased 27 per cent in mining, 20 per cent in agriculture, and 9 per cent in railways.[3] During 1926 and 1927 changes in productivity seem to be relatively insignificant. Recent studies suggest, indeed, that not only can the present population for the time being adequately fill the needs of United States industry as far as numbers are concerned, but that during 1928 there were indica-

[2] *Recent Economic Changes*, National Bureau of Economic Research, 1929, p. 456.
[3] *Ibid.*, p. 452.

tions of serious unemployment. This is remarkable because unemployment, in this instance, was not coincident with business depression. In the most recent estimate of unemployment, computed by subtracting the number of persons actually employed from the number "desiring and habitually dependent upon employment," the number of persons in non-agricultural pursuits out of work in 1927 was placed at a minimum of 2,055,000.[4] In 1928 unemployment was more severe for a time; but some, if not all, of the slack has been taken up during 1929. This coincidence of increased production and unemployment is described as "technological" unemployment and is attributed to a rate of mechanization so high that workers are displaced from the industries affected more rapidly than they can be reabsorbed by other occupations.

The decline from 1920 to 1927 in the number of persons actually at work in manufacturing enterprises is put at 825,000 but the number of *unemployed* among the people who depended on factory work for a living increased only 240,000 between 1920 and 1927, according to the best figures available . . . [in other words,] 71 per cent of the workers displaced had attached themselves to new trades by 1927.[5]

This does not mean that all who left factory employment to seek work elsewhere secured jobs, for the net increase in unemployment between 1920 and 1927 has been more than 650,000.

Mechanization in agriculture is still in its early stages but is rapidly being advanced, as in industry, by the high price of labor, to which migration from country to town is a contributing factor. The general movement toward mechanization has been reinforced by other factors coincident with the maintenance of high wages, such as the price decline in producers' goods and in long-time interest rates, which invite the use of relatively more capital than labor. As mechanization proceeds, some additional farm labor will doubtless be released for other employments. If, for example, the machinery for harvesting cotton now being developed should become commercially practicable, the Southwest will no longer be so dependent on a large annual immigration of Mexicans. But the

---

[4] *Recent Economic Changes*, p. 478.   [5] *Ibid.*, p. 878.

number of farm laborers who sought a livelihood elsewhere is small in proportion to the total increase in the number of all employees who between 1920 and 1927 were seeking non-agricultural jobs.

The 1928-29 unemployment problem would seem to be one of shifts in employment, irksome to the large groups affected but transitory in character. The economic effects of the 1924 Immigration Act are somewhat obscured in this complex situation. The whole history of the factory system in a competitive economy shows the steady pressure to reduce unit cost by increasing the output per worker. The severe post-war depression reinforced this tendency and gave a special incentive to mechanization and more efficient management. A study of productivity[6] reaches the conclusion that the tendency toward mechanization was intensified by the absence of immigration after 1914, when the War closed the Atlantic to travel, and by the post-war legal restrictions on immigration.

The effects of restriction on population accretion are not yet fully evident. Many of the immigrant groups who arrived before 1914, especially those who came as children, probably still show a higher reproduction rate than the average of the native population; this secondary effect of a large immigration did not stop when immigration was checked by the new policy, but will run out gradually over a period of years. The fall in the mortality rate, which is accompanied by a decrease in the birth rate, is another factor which must be considered.

Combined, the birth-rate and death-rate changes and the changes in immigration reduced the average annual increase of population from 1,800,000 in 1920-1925 to 1,545,000 in 1925-1928.[7]

With a normal increase in birth rates and an annual average net pre-war immigration of over half a million,

the national income would be rising faster than it is; but per capita income would be growing slower than it is. Since birth-rate restriction seems to be voluntary, and since immigration restriction certainly is, we must conclude that Americans are preferring to raise

6 H. Jerome, *American Economic Review,* Supplement, March, 1927, p. 128.
7 *Recent Economic Changes,* p. 885.

the economic level of average life rather than to maximize national wealth.[8]

The effect of immigration restriction upon wages is likewise difficult to estimate. Throughout United States history the belief has been widely held that new immigrants depressed wages in the communities in which they settled and that restriction would be followed by a rise in the wage level of unskilled and semi-skilled workers. But the flow of new immigrant labor to our expanding labor market is only a part of the supply side of the problem, and the demand from active industrial growth may fully absorb this element of the supply. Indeed, wage increases in leading centers of immigration may be secured by energetic immigrant trade unions, as has been done in the clothing industry, while wage decreases may be suffered by immigrant workers, such as the New England textile employees, through competition with more poorly paid native white workers in the South. Moreover the assumption that the restriction of unskilled immigrant labor would mean the gradual absorption of the labor reserve, which had at times been used to stave off wage increases, has been nullified by two factors: mechanization which has released unexpected supplies of labor, and the 1924 Immigration Act which has permitted the immigration of unskilled workers from adjacent countries. Although wages as a whole have increased since restriction, no marked change in the difference in wage level between unskilled and skilled workers has taken place.

It would seem, then, that recent immigration policy cannot be regarded as a major cause but only as one of the many factors influencing the recent advance in the productive organization of industry.

[8] *Recent Economic Changes*, p. 886.

CHAPTER SIX

AN ANALYSIS OF ETHNIC DISCRIMINATION

THE ethnic controversy provoked by the problem of assimilating immigrant population did not abate with the passage of the 1924 Immigration Act. Although this Act reduced south and east European immigration to a negligible quantity, it permitted and stimulated immigration from Latin-American countries and has thus introduced a new element into the controversy.

Criticism of the traditional concept of the American "melting pot" is sometimes based on the contention that different cultures cannot be harmonized. "Contact of diverse nationalities," observes Professor Fairchild, "far from tending to produce a coalescing, actually tends to accentuate the differences and to intensify the unreasoning tenacity with which each group clings to its own particular traits."[1] Culture traits persist, he holds, by reason of their biological basis or their acquisition through habits fixed in early childhood; immigration of diverse ethnic strains, therefore, results only in the coexistence of several independent, conflicting cultures which struggle for predominance. True "assimilation" would require foreign elements to divest themselves completely of their alien traits and effect no change in the receiving nationality. Such adaptation on the part of adult immigrants is not to be expected, and yet without it the development and flowering of a distinctive national culture in the United States will be retarded. The line between assimilable and unassimilable elements, in this strict sense of the term, cannot be drawn precisely, but the writers who take this point of view agree that the peoples of northwestern Europe are sufficiently homogeneous in racial origin and cultural heritage to live together in one nation. They believe that a specialized American type has been developed of predominantly Nordic blood, with a small admixture of Mediterranean and Alpine stocks—a type which is decidedly limited in variety and combined in characteristic proportions, and which has pro-

[1] H. P. Fairchild, *The Melting Pot Mistake*, 1924 ed., p. 151.

duced a distinct culture, not necessarily a culture superior to others but one which it is desirable to preserve. The survival of this culture is now threatened by the millions of predominantly Mediterranean and Alpine stock with radically different cultures who have migrated to the United States within the last fifty years. The modern stress is thus not upon discrimination *per se* but upon the necessity of preserving "like-mindedness." In their view race mixture is undesirable because it destroys specialized types and produces a "mongrel" population in which the excellences of all types are likely to be lost and the less desirable qualities are likely to survive and predominate.[2]

The "foreign colonies" in which "new" immigrants generally settle upon their arrival in the United States have facilitated the transplanting of alien culture traits. Unlike the "old" immigrants from northwestern Europe the "new" immigrants have tended to drift to industrial centers and to form groups of the same racial origin which have preserved such aspects of communal village life as could be adapted to American urban conditions. Frequently they have started schools, social and political clubs, newspapers, stores, banks, and other social and business enterprises, thereby eliminating many opportunities for contact with native persons and institutions. The tendency toward intermarriage within such segregated groups has helped to perpetuate both the racial types and the culture traits of the "new" immigrants. Some foreign countries, such as Italy, have fostered the home ties of emigrants in order to encourage them to send back their savings, to develop an export market, and to enhance the influence of the nation in the United States.

The critics of the "new" immigrants have been particularly concerned with the effect of south and east European immigration upon democratic political institutions. The corruption of American political life by unscrupulous political machines has been attributed to the large purchasable vote of foreign elements unaccustomed to the exercise of political power, and yet endowed with privileges of citizenship. Where outright corruption does not

[2] See introduction to *Immigrant Backgrounds,* by H. P. Fairchild, and *America: Nation or Confusion,* by Edward R. Lewis.

exist, the foreign vote is considered harmful because it has injected foreign issues into American politics and has been exploited by politicians in order to confuse or evade domestic problems. To this end the foreign language press has been instrumental in centering interest upon the affairs of the old country and in translating American issues into terms of European politics. On the other hand, non-participation in politics, which is indicated by the large percentage of south and east Europeans who have failed to acquire citizenship, has not been less harmful than corruption and perversion of issues; for it has prevented the development of a sense of responsibility for government and confidence in it as a remedial agency for social wrongs. Direct economic action through violent strikes, and social revolution, are believed to be concepts tenable only by a citizenry which fails to appreciate the power and value of political action.

The most serious indictment against the "new" immigrant, and the most provocative, has been the assertion of his inferiority to the older stocks in moral and intellectual qualities. In Laughlin's *Analysis of the American Melting Pot*[3] and McDougall's *Is America Safe for Democracy?* statistics supporting this contention have been assembled. They show a higher percentage of crime and social dependency and a lower intelligence level as measured by intelligence tests[4] among "new" immigrants than among "old" immigrants and native-born. Since the writers assume that character and intelligence are determined primarily by inherited traits, their conclusion is that amalgamation of the "new" and "old" stocks through intermarriage will inevitably lead to racial deterioration, particularly in view of the higher birth rate of the "new" stocks.

Case against Ethnic Discrimination.

Most of the arguments opposing a policy of racial selection are based on the assumption that freedom of migration is sound in principle, both socially and economically, and that it should be restricted only if it clearly harms the receiving country. The posi-

[3] See *supra*, p. 450 for a detailed discussion of this report.
[4] See also Carl Campbell Brigham, *A Study of American Intelligence*.

tive case in favor of the "new" immigrant rests upon the theory that contact of different cultures enriches civilization and promotes cultural progress. The result may be fusion into a new national culture or the development of a variety of cultures which would give expression to widely different personalities. According to H. M. Kallen[5] such an expression is not only compatible with democracy but is its very essence. It is therefore not necessary or desirable that foreign culture traits should be destroyed. What is needed is an atmosphere of toleration in which they may freely adapt themselves and grow into expressions of American life.

The social evils charged against the "new" immigrants are questioned or denied. It is asserted that they result primarily from the urbanization of a rural population and would arise even in the absence of immigration. Immigrant "colonies" have helped to solve rather than to create these problems. They have tended to preserve moral restraints which counteract the disintegrating influences of city environment upon family relations and standards of social conduct, and they have created spontaneously an urban community life which is socially desirable and is lacking in most native-born sections of American cities. The perpetuation of alien traits in the foreign-born "colony" is doubted. In the isolated instances in which foreign-born groups have consciously attempted to organize societies of their own through colonization, the societies that have been created have acquired the characteristics of surrounding American communities. The colonies of Swedes in Minnesota, of Germans in Wisconsin, the isolated Bohemian and Dutch colonies on Long Island have failed to preserve an identity, although some of their activities can be explained in terms of their origin. The urban communities, against which criticism is usually directed, are accidental and temporary congregations of immigrant workers who ordinarily stay in the "colony" only until they acquire use of the English language and experience with American customs and until more attractive economic opportunities are presented. The continuity of the colonies depends upon a constant stream of new recruits. These seemingly

[5] H. M. Kallen, *Culture and Democracy*, and Julius Drachsler, *Democracy and Assimilation*.

fixed groups are, therefore, often the catch-basins of immigration from which distribution and assimilation take place. The cultural peculiarities which these groups tend to preserve are believed by some to be destined to disappear with the dispersion of "new" immigrants throughout the country and with the education of their children in the public schools. Others hope that some of this culture may be preserved to enrich American civilization.

Many of the characteristics for which the "new" immigrants are criticized are asserted to arise not from their foreign origin but from the circumstances of American life. Thus their concentration in urban areas is attributed not to ineptitude for agricultural settlement but to the economic opportunities open to the propertyless at the time of their admission. The settlement of Polish industrial workers on the tobacco and onion farms of the Connecticut Valley, the migration of Slovak miners to the farms of Arkansas, and the wide dispersion of Italians in truck garden areas indicate a leaning toward agricultural pursuits among some of the "new" immigrants. So far as naturalization is concerned, the statistics showing a higher percentage of naturalized persons among immigrants of the "old" than of the "new" type are declared to be misleading because of the longer residence period of the "old" immigrants.[6] It has been estimated that "new" immigrants become naturalized after a shorter period of residence, and that if declarations of intention are considered and account is taken of the increasing strictness of naturalization procedure, the statistics do not show a tendency on the part of new immigrants to form large permanently alien groups in the United States.[7] The difference in period of residence helps to explain also the low percentage of "new" immigrants who marry native-born persons. Many mixed marriages among "old" immigrants are marriages between the first and second generation of the same racial group. Intermarriage is more likely to occur, moreover, between groups which have been in the country longest, are similar in religion and language, and with which, on account of territorial distribution and occupation, natives have the closest contacts. The percentage

---

6 John Palmer Gavit, *Americans by Choice.*

7 *Immigrants and Their Children,* 1920. Census Monographs VII, p. 266.

of mixed marriages among recent immigrant groups is expected to increase with their length of residence, and as dispersion broadens their contacts with other groups. Fusion of all native and immigrant groups, however, cannot take place as long as religious differences, prejudice against certain ethnic groups, and stratification of racial groups along occupational lines continue to exist and to influence mate selection.[8]

It has also been argued that traits by which "new" immigrants have been judged to be biologically inferior to "old" immigrants and native-born are determined not by racial origin but by the American environment. The higher percentage of social dependency and crime among "new" immigrants is attributed in part to the fact that a larger proportion of "new" immigrants than of native-born and "old" immigrants resides in cities where social dependency and criminality are more highly institutionalized than in rural areas. A study which took this fact into consideration showed there was not "undue" crime among immigrants.[9] The greater economic insecurity in city life and the comparatively low income level of "new" immigrants also help to account for greater social dependency among them. The significance of intelligence tests has been questioned on the ground that they test not native mental qualities but mental qualities developed under conditions which vary with the cultural background, familiarity with English, money income, and other opportunities of the individual.

In brief, it is argued that assimilation presents no national problem. With the passage of time "foreign colonies" and the foreign language press will cease to exist; the "new" immigrants will disperse throughout the country; their peculiarities will die with first-generation immigrants; and the alien population will gradually become naturalized. Social dependency and crime are not primarily eugenic problems for which the "new" immigration is responsible. The question, this school asserts, is whether foreign culture traits should be condemned and discouraged, thereby foster-

8 *Immigrants and Their Children*, p. 246.
9 E. H. Sutherland, "Is There Undue Crime Among Immigrants?" National Conference for Social Work, *Proceedings,* 1927, p. 572.

ing intolerance and an ethnic conflict, or whether these traits should be permitted to develop and enrich American civilization.

Scientific Contributions to the Race Question.

To a certain extent the disparity between these two sets of ideas can be reduced to differences in scientific assumptions which are briefly reviewed below in order to show the nature of the evidence on which they rest. The "Nordic race" doctrine, on which the validity of the case against the south and east European originally rested, has grown out of an early nineteenth-century idea popularized by Gobineau in *The Inequality of Races*. In this book the responsibility for all great civilizations of the past was attributed to the spread of "Aryan" blood through the migration of this race. The rise and fall of cultures depended on the amount of "Aryan" blood in the populations which produced them. Later, when the old classification of races, which had been based primarily on a study of languages, was revised during the middle of the century in the light of measurements of head form, height, and skin and eye color, and the white race was divided into Nordics, Alpines, and Mediterraneans, the Nordics were credited with the qualities which had formerly been attributed to the Aryan race. A series of writers beginning with Houston Stewart Chamberlain adopted this theory in tracing the development of Great Britain's political institutions, and popularized the idea that democracy is the product of the racial genius of the "Teutons" for self-government. The theory was also applied by German sociologists in considering changes in physical characteristics in the population of western Europe. From their statistics of cephalic indices, which showed that the proportion of round-headed individuals was increasing, they concluded that the long-headed Nordic elements, which they considered superior, were disappearing.

These ideas, translated into terms of "new" and "old" immigrant stocks and native stocks, have been diffused in the United States by Madison Grant, Lothrop Stoddard, William McDougall and others. In its application to the United States this theory has been reinforced by tests of "Nordic" superiority—intelligence tests of army recruits and school children, and quotas of "social adequacy"[10]—and by statistics which show that the fecundity of new immigrant stocks threatens the predominance of the "Nordic" element in the population.

Biologists and eugenists who deal with problems of heredity and are inclined to attach greater importance to inheritance than to environment frequently support this point of view. The results of experiments in animal breeding, which show that "mongrelization" destroys the qualities in which the specialized breeds excel and perpetuates the less desirable qualities of the original breeds, have been used as evidence against the desirability of "race" mixture. Eugenists have concluded that since character traits such as drunkenness, dishonesty, criminal tendency, delinquency, social failure, intellectual brilliance, or stupidity recur in given families, they result from qualities transmitted by inheritance. From this they argue that racial groups which contain an undue number of individuals with such character traits are biologically inferior and should be prevented as far as possible from contributing an increasing share to the population.

With this position and the other assumptions of the "Nordic" school, Professor Boas and some other anthropologists take issue. Professor Boas holds that the argument from family traits to racial groups is unsound. The inherited variations within a single population are much greater than the differences between "racial" groups, at least so far as branches of the white race are concerned. "Eugenists" have confused racial groups with genealogical lines. All European peoples have some common genealogical lines and therefore have inherited some common traits. "Racial" selection, whether it happens through migration, selective mating, or differences in birth or mortality rates, therefore results not in a change of genealogical lines but only in the preponderance of certain genealogical lines. Moreover, he maintains that the significance of the traits determined by inheritance is not so great as is commonly believed, because the functions of the body, physiological as well as mental, are determined by environment more than by anatomy. This conclusion was supported by a study of racial char-

10 Laughlin report, cf. p. 450.

acteristics of immigrants which Professor Boas made for the 1907 Immigration Commission. His report indicated that the descendants of European immigrants changed in type even in the first generation; modifications were found in all physical characteristics, even in the head form, which had been considered one of the most permanent hereditary features.

The study of cultural processes by anthropologists, while offering no conclusive evidence as to the superiority or inferiority of certain races, has revealed facts which bear on the question. The complexity of grammatical forms found in primitive languages and the independent invention of the zero in mathematics by American Indians before its use by Europeans indicate a high degree of mental activity on the part of primitive peoples. As culture is spread from group to group by diffusion, the existence of a culture may be no test of the inventive genius of the people who possess it. The occurrence of marked cultural changes in past civilizations during periods in which there is no evidence of racial changes suggests that factors other than biological stock may have been crucial in cultural growth.

Professor Goldenweiser, who takes an extreme position in this respect, believes that "man is one but civilizations are many," that races do not differ significantly in psychological endowment, and that the characteristics of a particular civilization are to be explained in terms of its history rather than of its racial composition. In the opinion of Professor Kroeber, cultural achievements, in so far as they are an index to ability, do not indicate the superiority of the Nordic stock among the white races, and "any fears of arrest or decay of human progress if a particular race should lose in fertility or become absorbed in others, are unfounded."

A position between that of the "Nordicists" and the cultural anthropologists has been taken by Professor Hankins in his recent *Racial Basis of Civilization*. He disagrees with the cultural anthropologists who believe that culture begets culture and that cultural contacts and history are more important than any possible biological differences between racial stocks. Although he grants that "acculturation" is an essential factor in the development of culture, and that environment may set limits to cultural progress or determine its direction to a certain degree, the reaction of human beings to a given culture is, in his opinion, determined primarily by their biological make-up. As individuals in the same environment will make widely different uses of the opportunities open to them so will social groups develop cultures in accordance with their racial traits. Believing that primary racial traits persist in existing social groups despite the disappearance of "pure" racial types through thousands of years of commingling, he would define a race as any group set apart from others by physical differences which are distinctive hereditary traits and are inherited together within a limited range of variability. This concept of race permits considerable overlapping between racial groups and accounts for the fact that in any given "race" comparatively few individuals will conform to the "racial type." He does not, however, believe that comparatively homogeneous hybrids such as the English possess sufficiently distinctive traits to be considered races. Moreover, since all "races" are mixed, variations among them are differences in degree, and superiority and inferiority exist only in respect of specific traits.

The quality of a population, therefore, depends on the quality of its stock rather than on its racial composition. This does not mean that racial composition is not important, for it will determine what racial traits will predominate in a population. For a rich and complex culture a variety of aptitudes is necessary, and Professor Hankins thinks that a population of hybrids is more likely to produce a high civilization than one composed of a single racial unit. The history of civilizations suggests that migration and race commingling have preceded every great "flowering period" of culture in the past. The theory that race crossing widens variability and at least temporarily enhances racial vigor leads him to the conclusion that cultural progress has been due to the effects of race crossing. This theory he further supports by stating that there is no record of a high civilization developed in an area characterized by racial "purity." Believing that race mixture, in addition to increasing the versatility of talents in the population generally, makes more probable the rare combination of genetic factors which produce genius, and attributing the rise and fall of civilizations to relative frequency in the occurrence and preservation of genius, he suggests that civilization depends on the development of conditions favorable to race mixtures.

Although Professor Hankins is not directly concerned with either past or present immigration policy, he does not ignore the effect of immigration upon the quality of population and the need for exercising some control over biological stock. With him the problem is to get good stock of the various races; since recent improvements in transportation facilities and industrial opportunities have broken down early selective barriers to immigration, the scientific solution lies not in the exclusion of later immigrant stocks but in the selection of individuals on the basis of their merits regardless of race.

The basis on which immigrants are chosen is of more than theoretical interest because it crystallizes an attitude toward immigrants which affects the problem of assimilation. Legal discriminations may help to intensify and perpetuate attitudes which determine the social contacts of immigrants, their conception of American institutions and ideals, the extent of their intermarriage with other stocks, and the economic opportunities open to them.

CHAPTER SEVEN

ORIENTAL EXCLUSION

WHILE on the Atlantic coast the United States has until recently permitted a relatively free European immigration, the problem was different on the Pacific coast where immigration was largely Asiatic. Despite the universal agreement among nations that control of immigration is a purely domestic matter, this difference in treatment of Asiatics and Europeans has led to international difficulties which have given Oriental immigration an importance disproportionate to its numerical significance.

The total recorded Asiatic immigration to the United States during the last century amounted to slightly less than 900,000, a figure below the average annual European immigration during the decade preceding the War. Of these, about 20 per cent came from the Near East, 70 per cent or about 650,000 from China and Japan, and 10 per cent from the rest of Asia. Immigration from China has been approximately 375,000, from Japan about 275,-000. The net contribution of Orientals to the population measured by census statistics of race has been considerably less than the immigration figures would suggest; the 1920 census reports only 61,639 of the Chinese and 110,010 of the Japanese race. Chinese laborers have been excluded by United States legislation since 1882, and Japanese by action of their own Government between 1907 and 1924, and by restrictions of the United States since that date. The number of Chinese in the United States decreased after the Exclusion Act from 107,488 in 1890 to 61,639 in 1920. Although the Japanese increased 54 per cent between 1910 and 1920, the fact that in Hawaii, where economic opportunities have been less favorable than those in the United States, the Japanese population is almost as large as that in continental United States suggests that effective controls were operating to check Japanese immigration to the mainland.

Restriction of Oriental immigration has led to international friction because discrimination on grounds of race has been considered by Oriental countries to be contrary to the accepted international practice of guaranteeing to all friendly powers similar treatment of their nationals. To avoid violation of this practice the United States attempted to come to an agreement with Oriental countries—in the case of China by treaties consenting to discriminatory legislation, and in the case of Japan by arrangements under which the latter assumed responsibility for restriction of its emigrants. Neither China nor Japan has insisted on the right of its nationals to enter the United States, and neither seems to have entertained the idea of a large emigration to the Pacific coast as a measure of relief from population pressure. Both have protested against legislation which in their opinion violated treaty provisions or other international rights, and Japan, in addition, has protested against an immigration policy based on race discrimination, although it is willing to accept restriction based on economic and social grounds.

Recognized by the State Department in diplomatic negotiations, these international considerations were at first accepted by Congress as important factors in determining immigration policy. Later they were rejected, at least in part because executive agreements deprived Congress of its exclusive jurisdiction over immigration. Objection to presidential encroachment on the powers of Congress, through extensive use of treaties and executive agreements, was probably a more important factor in the adoption by Congress of the exclusion provisions of the 1924 Act than the theory that policies of the United States should be determined without reference to the desires of foreign powers.

Discriminatory Legislation against Chinese by State Governments.

Chinese immigration began with the early settlement of California. Between 1850 and 1860 almost fifty thousand Chinese were lured to the Pacific coast by gold-mining ventures and their ancillary enterprises. Competition with the white settlers and failure to conform to the customs and standards of the white population provoked a strong anti-Chinese sentiment, which resulted in crimes against Chinese persons and property and in state and municipal legislation. In 1855 California sought to limit Chinese immigration by a head tax of $55 on Chinese immigrants and in 1858 to exclude Chinese altogether. Attempts to discourage business enterprise by Chinese residents during the late fifties and early sixties included a state tax on foreign miners which was enforced only against Chinese, and a state head tax of $2.50 a month on all Chinese residents. City ordinances discriminated against Chinese laundries, vegetable vendors, and tenements. Through the so-called "queue ordinance," which required persons convicted of criminal offenses to have their hair cut to within an inch of the head, personal humiliation was inflicted. Practically all these disabilities were declared invalid by decisions of the highest state court, and state regulation of Chinese immigration was declared unconstitutional by the United States Supreme Court.[1]

Regulation of Chinese Immigration by Treaty and by Early Federal Laws.

Local public opinion, which made this discriminatory legislation possible, supported an economic and social boycott of Chinese which might have reduced immigration substantially had not a new demand for labor on the Pacific coast been created by the undertaking of a transcontinental railroad in 1861. Coolie labor was well adapted to construction work in the wilderness; ocean transport from China was more convenient and less expensive than land transport from the East; Chinese laborers required comparatively little food and shelter; Chinese emigration companies simplified labor problems by assuming responsibility for recruiting and supervising workers. A large percentage of the sixty-five thousand Chinese who came to the United States during the sixties were brought in for railroad construction. Acts passed by Congress in 1862, forbidding the transportation of involuntary coolie laborers, do not seem to have had much practical effect on the number or character of Chinese immigrants.

Chinese migration became the subject of treaty negotiations before the completion of the Southern Pacific Railway in 1869. Independent attempts had been made by Chinese provincial governors to prevent emigration and by California to prevent immi-

[1] *Soon Hing* v. *Crowley*, 113 U.S. 703 (1885). *Yick Wo* v. *Hopkins*, 118 U.S. 356 (1886).

gration, but these restrictions did not represent national policies; the rights and privileges of migrants had not been defined by treaty. The Burlingame Treaty of 1868 met this need; it condemned involuntary emigration and bound both parties to its prohibition. This was intended to discourage the practice of coerced emigration organized by recruiting companies which had been indirectly prohibited by the Federal Act of 1862. In so far as the Treaty otherwise dealt with the migration of Chinese it committed the United States to a policy of free immigration and committed China to a policy of free emigration. The terms of the treaty suggest that the State Department conceded the right of immigration to all Chinese laborers, except contract laborers, in exchange for privileges granted to United States commercial interests in China.

A national demand for restriction of Chinese immigration arose within two years of the signing of the Burlingame Treaty. The completion of the Southern Pacific Railroad in 1869 made possible the use of Chinese laborers to break a Massachusetts strike in 1870, an incident which resulted in a strong declaration by the National Labor Union in favor of abrogation of the Burlingame Treaty and effective exclusion of coolie labor. In the face of depression caused by the flood of eastern goods and eastern labor brought in by the new railroad in the seventies, manufacturers, farmers, and merchants in California became acutely aware of the competition of Chinese, who had established independent enterprises and could operate on margins which drove white men out of business. An increasing number of these economic classes joined in the anti-Chinese agitation.

The rapid dispersion of Chinese through the coast and mountain states raised fears of an Asiatic invasion which would swamp the sparse white population. In addition to antagonism aroused by their successful competition, their concentration in isolated communities, their racial characteristics, and their tenacity in preserving their national customs made them a clearly distinguishable class susceptible to ridicule, contempt, and attack. The feeling that they were undermining labor standards and could never become assimilated in an American community became national.

Since the states were not legally competent to deal with Chinese immigration, proponents of exclusion demanded federal action. In response to the anti-Chinese agitation both political parties during the 1870 Congressional elections advocated restriction of Chinese immigration. In his message to Congress in 1874 President Grant characterized Chinese immigrants as involuntary contract laborers and prostitutes, and recommended legislation against them. An act passed in 1875 prohibited importation of prostitutes and criminals, transportation of Asiatics without their consent, and contracting for coolie labor. These restrictions were as drastic as the Burlingame Treaty allowed, but they satisfied neither organized labor nor the Californians who were bent on getting rid of the Chinese and to this end were demanding total exclusion. The question assumed such importance as a political issue that in 1876 the State Department expressed itself in favor of some modification of the "settled principles of international law" in the case of Chinese immigrants because of their cultural isolation and the temporary character of their residence. A joint investigating committee, appointed by Congress to visit the coast, returned with a recommendation for modification of the Burlingame Treaty and drastic restriction of Asiatic immigration. Action on the report was postponed until after the election of 1876.

In 1879 Congress passed an act that practically excluded Asiatics, but President Hayes vetoed it because it violated treaty provisions, and his veto message proposed to remedy the evil through the "proper course of diplomatic negotiations." In the following year a commission, sent to China to revise the treaty, secured China's consent to the "reasonable regulation, suspension and limitation of immigration of Chinese laborers" whenever their coming "affects or threatens to affect the interests . . . or to endanger the good order" of the United States. Immigration for trade, travel, and study was not to be restricted. China refused to consent to absolute "prohibition" of laborers.

The Exclusion Acts.

In accordance with the 1880 treaty Congress passed the Exclusion Act of 1882, prohibiting immigration of Chinese laborers for ten years, though exempting former United States residents, providing for deportation of illegally entered Chinese, and denying to Chinese the privilege of naturalization.[2] In 1884 changes were made in the administrative provisions of the Act in order to prevent frauds and smuggling across the land frontiers. Following this legislation the recorded immigration dropped from an annual average of 15,975 during the decade preceding the Act to 1,453 during the decade following its passage. Considerable illicit immigration continued, but the census figures show an increase of only 2,000 Chinese residents in the United States between 1880 and 1890 and a substantial decline in subsequent decades.

The Exclusion Act of 1882 did not, however, eliminate the "Chinese problem." Anti-Chinese demonstrations occurred after its passage. A number of Chinese were killed and considerable Chinese property was destroyed. A particularly violent incident in Wyoming brought forth protests by the Chinese Government and an announcement in 1886 that it intended to prohibit emigration of all Chinese laborers—even those who were in China on a temporary visit and were legally entitled to reëntry into the United States— "in order that Chinese laborers may gradually be reduced in number and causes of danger to lives averted." To maintain friendly diplomatic relations the Federal Government appropriated funds to pay the indemnity Wyoming refused to honor, and to pacify domestic feeling concluded a new treaty in 1888. Its terms secured China's consent to and coöperation in exclusion of all laborers for twenty years. Exceptions were made for those who had families, property, or debts in this country; admission of new immigrants was confined to officials, students, teachers, merchants, and travelers; provision was made for renewal for another twenty years on the consent of both parties. The chief change intended by this treaty was the exclusion of former residents who had no substantial property rights in this country; presumably this would have prevented the return of common laborers. China's coöperation would

2 Chinese had never been clearly eligible to citizenship under United States naturalization laws which from their beginning (1795 and 1802) limited naturalization to "free white persons" and were later modified to permit naturalization of negroes and American Indians. The Act of 1882 avoided further court controversy as to whether the Chinese came within the meaning of the term "white person."

have meant that they would be denied passports for the United States. In approving the treaty the Senate made amendments which, regardless of reëntry permits, prohibited the return of laborers who were at that time out of the country, and which made certificates of entry a condition of Chinese admission. While action by China was pending owing to delay caused by discussion of the Senate amendments, Congress passed legislation incorporating the treaty provisions. Later, on the basis of an unofficial rumor that China had rejected the treaty, Congress went further and excluded all Chinese laborers regardless of previous residence or reëntry permits. The Act was signed by the President after it became clear that China would not accept the treaty without substantial modification. China lodged a formal protest on the ground that the legislation violated existing treaty provisions; the United States appropriated money to compensate Chinese residents for damages inflicted by its nationals; and with this interchange the incident was temporarily closed as a subject of diplomatic negotiation.

On the expiration of the Act of 1882 all the exclusion laws were renewed in 1892 for another ten years and provision was made for compulsory registration under penalty of deportation. On this occasion China started negotiations which resulted in a new treaty in 1894. In this the Chinese Government consented to the exclusion of laborers, but the reëntry of persons with families or property in the United States was permitted. These changes brought the treaty provisions into conformity with the provisions of the Exclusion Acts. Subsequent to the new treaty Congress further restricted Chinese entries to the United States by extending the Exclusion Acts to Hawaii in 1896 and by providing in 1900 for registration of Hawaiian Chinese.

Anti-Chinese sentiment diminished with the decline in the Chinese population and the acceptance by the Chinese of inferior social status and a limited sphere of economic activity in which they did not compete with the white population. No relaxation of the exclusion laws was considered, however, and they became accepted as permanent policy. As the second decade of their validity drew to a close, Roosevelt in 1901 recommended that they be reënacted with strengthened provisions. The Chinese, on their part, proposed an adjustment that they contended would be more in harmony with friendly relations than was the 1894 treaty. Pending negotiation of a new treaty the exclusion laws were reënacted in 1902 and extended to the Philippines as well as to Hawaii. When in 1904 China refused to continue the treaty of 1894, the 1902 Act was reenacted without any time limits. Whereas in earlier acts attempts had been made to stay within the letter of the existing treaties the permanent exclusion legislation of 1904 definitely repudiated any treaty provisions qualifying the right of the United States to exclude Chinese laborers.

The Immigration Act of 1924 excluded all aliens ineligible to citizenship and applied to the entry of exempt classes the general administrative provisions of the Act. Since it repealed only such provisions of the Exclusion Acts as were inconsistent with it, Chinese laborers are still subject to important restrictions not imposed on other immigrant groups—notably denial of reëntry permits except in the case of persons with families or property in this country, and the possibility of deportation in the absence of registration.[3]

That China has made no further protests has been due to the futility of such action from a country so weak internationally rather than to China's acceptance of United States policy as according with treaty provisions. Although recent active anti-Japanese agitation has made the problem of the Chinese comparatively insignificant, certain aspects of Chinese migration still constitute important problems in United States immigration policy. Most acute among these have been the detection and deportation of illegally entered persons and the admission of exempt classes, particularly merchants and their wives, whose entry is legal under United States legislation and is guaranteed by treaty. After forty years of varying success in control of sur-

[3] The compulsory registration feature of the Exclusion Acts was in force only for six months in 1893 and 1894, but the statute of limitations did not apply to the deportation of unregistered persons. Chinese laborers who are now unregistered are liable to deportation for they have either violated the expired registration act or have entered illegally. In recent years, failure to register has only occasionally been used as ground for deportation of Chinese.

reptitious Chinese entries, the establishment of a border patrol to prevent migration across land borders in violation of the 1924 Act is reducing the smuggling of Chinese. The main problem now arises in connection with persons who claim to be United States citizens by birth or parentage, of whom over three thousand apply for admission annually. Attempts of the Labor Department to exclude persons of Chinese birth who could not offer satisfactory proof that their parents were United States citizens have been frustrated to some extent by court decisions overruling the Department's decisions on the ground that evidence was so unsubstantial as to render them arbitrary.[4] In the case of one ruling, however, which declared grandsons of native-born Chinese were not citizens if their fathers had never lived in the United States, the Department has been upheld by the courts.[5] The task remains of weeding out the illegally entered, criminal, and unregistered Chinese subject to deportation. The registration law, by which it was hoped to facilitate ridding the country of Chinese laborers, has never been very effective. The enforcement of Chinese deportation legislation has been a question of practical administrative difficulties and inadequate appropriations rather than one of policy.

In its attempt to enforce Chinese exclusion laws the immigration force has been accused of suspecting all Chinese and of excluding a large proportion of admissible merchants and their wives by humiliating and exacting administrative procedure. Suspicion has been aroused because persons securing exemption as merchants have so frequently changed their status after entry or have engaged in pursuits held by immigration officers to fall outside the legitimate field of the foreign merchant privileged to enter to carry on trade,[6] though of a kind commonly classed as mercantile. This departure of practice from expressed policy presents another important administrative problem—the adoption of a procedure

4 *Weedin* v. *Chin Bow*, 274 U.S. 657 (1927).

5 *Annual Report of the Commissioner General of Immigration*, 1928, p. 16.

6 Change in status and pursuit of usual mercantile enterprises is legal in the case of persons entering before July 1, 1924, though contrary to the spirit and purposes of the exclusion laws. For juridical status of Chinese merchants see A. W. Parker, Jan., 1925, "Ineligible to Citizenship Provisions of Immigration Act of 1924," *American Journal of International Law*, XIX, 23.

which will be effective in enforcing exclusion of Chinese laborers without discouraging international trade and creating international ill will.

The Japanese.

One of the results of the exclusion and dispersion of the Chinese was the Japanese migration which became important in the nineties. Japan's policy of political and social isolation, although broken down for trade purposes by Perry's expedition in 1853, prevented any considerable emigration until 1885. Emigration was then legalized on condition that Japanese allegiance was retained. This change in Japanese law was followed by a large migration of Japanese laborers to Hawaii and the Philippines, recruited and controlled by emigration companies. Japanese migrants to the United States first came indirectly from Hawaii to work on plantations in sections of California where the tropical climate was considered unsuited to the labor of white persons. With the decrease in Chinese laborers, increase in large-scale agricultural enterprise and industrial expansion, Japanese emigration companies found the Pacific coast an excellent market for their services. Between 1890 and 1900 they brought in about twenty thousand laborers, some of them from Hawaii but an increasing number direct from Japan.

The Treaty of Commerce and Navigation between the United States and Japan signed in 1894 stated that "the citizens or subjects of each of the High Contracting Parties shall have full liberty to enter, travel, or reside in any part of the territories of the other Contracting Party, and shall enjoy full and perfect protection for their persons and property." This guarantee was qualified, however, in that the privileges granted by it were declared not "in any way to affect the laws, ordinances, and regulations with regard to trade, the immigration of laborers, police and public security which are in force or may hereafter be enacted in either of the two countries." As in the case of the Burlingame Treaty with China, there seems to have been an early disposition to concede to the Japanese the right of immigration as the condition of securing rights for United States nationals in Japan. In the Japanese treaty, however, the United States secured qualifications which would permit it to restrict Japanese migration should it so desire.

Though Japanese laborers were found to be efficient, industrious, orderly, and obedient; they very soon fell heir to the racial antagonism that already existed against the Chinese. Organized labor kept them out of the skilled trades and the memory of the boycott against manufacturers employing Chinese was effective in preventing employment of Japanese in industries generally. In salmon canning, construction work, and agriculture, however, they were employed extensively. They usually accepted wages below those of southeast European immigrants, and their initiative made them particularly keen competitors. Although outrages comparable to those which characterized the anti-Chinese riots in frontier days were not repeated against the Japanese, demonstrations of anti-Japanese sentiment were strong enough to suggest such a critical social situation that in 1900 Japan announced its intention to stop organized emigration of laborers and to refuse passports to laborers bound for the United States and Canada. This action did not appreciably reduce immigration because law-evading Japanese emigration companies continued to bring in laborers indirectly through Hawaii.

The Gentlemen's Agreement.

To insure more effective restriction the Japanese and Korean Exclusion League was organized in 1906 in San Francisco. Its first achievement was the adoption of a ruling by the San Francisco School Board requiring Japanese children to attend the Oriental school in Chinatown, though at the time only ninety-three of the twenty-five thousand school children of San Francisco were Japanese. Japan protested, and its protest commanded respect because of its increased prestige after its victory in the Russo-Japanese War. On assurances from President Roosevelt that effective Japanese restriction would be secured if the ruling were rescinded, the School Board changed its position.

Based on economic reasons, Roosevelt's policy was to effect Japanese exclusion by arrangement with Japan and to put Japanese residents in the United States on an equality with other aliens in all respects, including the privileges of naturalization, but this he was unable to carry out. In pursuance of the former part of his policy he secured a provision in the 1907 Immigration Act empowering the President to exclude laborers with passports issued for destinations other than continental United States and to negotiate treaties dealing with immigration. Under this law he issued in 1907 an executive order[7] excluding Japanese and Korean laborers with passports for Mexico, Canada, or Hawaii and made an arrangement with Japan for restriction of direct migration of Japanese laborers. This arrangement became known as the Gentlemen's Agreement. The provisions of the Agreement had been made public only to the extent of a brief announcement in the Secretary of Labor's 1908 report of "a general understanding between the governments of the United States and Japan, in accordance with which the latter government is continuing its policy of discouraging the migration of its laborers to this country," and a more specific statement in the report of the Commissioner of Immigration for the same year that the law and proclamation of 1907 had been "supplemented by a general understanding with Japan contemplating that the Japanese Government shall issue passports to continental United States only to such of its subjects as are non-laborers or are laborers, who, in coming to the continent seek to resume a formerly acquired domicile, to join a parent, wife or children residing therein, or to resume active control of an already possessed interest."

In accordance with the Gentlemen's Agreement, Japan stopped the recruiting of labor by emigration companies, and Japanese immigration declined from an annual average of 12,587 during the decade preceding the Agreement to an annual average of 7,017 during the decade following it. This reduction did not satisfy Californians who wanted total exclusion; they compared this decrease with the severe drop in Chinese immigration which had followed the Exclusion Acts. The 1910 census statistics added to their dissatisfaction by showing that the total Japanese popula-

[7] In 1913 the wording of this order was made general, so as not to discriminate specifically against Japanese and Koreans.

tion had increased from 24,326 in 1900 to 72,157 in 1910 and that the number of female Japanese had increased from 985 to 9,087 during the decade. The fact that this increase in women, which added to the labor force and made possible a growing population of native-born Japanese, was legitimate under the Gentlemen's Agreement constituted one of the most serious objections to it.

While the demand for total exclusion of Japanese was becoming more articulate, Japan, on the strength of its increased international prestige, began to seek revision of the 1894 treaty which bound it to consent to any restrictive legislation that the United States might pass, especially since it became clear that such legislation would probably put Japan in a class with China and apart from European Powers. Negotiations resulted in a new treaty in 1911 which is still in force. Under its terms the provisions of the 1894 treaty offensive to the Japanese were omitted, but the privileges guaranteed by treaty were limited to persons entering to carry on trade. The section of the 1911 treaty which has been the subject of controversy in connection with subsequent legislation reads:

The citizens or subjects of each of the High Contracting Parties shall have the liberty to enter, travel, and reside in the territories of the other to carry on trade, wholesale and retail, to own or lease and occupy houses, manufactories, warehouses and shops, to employ agents of their own choice, to lease land for residential and commercial purposes, and generally to do anything incident to or necessary for trade upon the same terms as native citizens or subjects, submitting themselves to the laws and regulations.[8]

It was understood by both parties that the new treaty did not affect the provisions of the 1907 Act, and in approving it Japan agreed to continue its restrictions on emigration of laborers. Thus, although Japan was no longer bound to recognize the right of the United States to exclude Japanese, the right of Japanese other than traders to migrate to the United States in the absence of restrictive legislation and to enjoy the usual privileges of resident aliens was no longer recognized by the United States as a treaty obligation.

[8] R. L. Buell, *Japanese Immigration*, "World Peace Pamphlets," 1924, III, 289.

This change in treaty provisions did not decrease the demand for discriminatory legislation on the Pacific coast. Popular feeling was high in California owing to the tendency of the Japanese to rise above the customary social and economic status of Orientals by becoming successful competitors of white landowners. The discriminations against Japanese in industry made them turn to agriculture where, as laborers working on piece rates, their skill and endurance, combined with their natural aptitude for labor which required squatting, brought wages equal to and frequently higher than those of white laborers, and where their rise to the position of landowners depended solely on their own enterprise. By employing all the members of their families in agricultural labor, and by other sacrifices that white farmers were unwilling to make, they were able to offer high rentals and purchase prices. In a remarkably short time large numbers of Japanese laborers were working under crop shares, crop leases, cash leases, or on their own lands. Predominantly Japanese communities sprang up, particularly in the Imperial and San Joaquin valleys where the intensive cultivation and continual stooping required in the culture of strawberries, celery and asparagus, onions, cantaloupes, and other fruits and vegetables, gave the Japanese an advantage over white farmers. The complaints of the farmers who came into direct competition with Japanese were capitalized by organized labor, by politicians in 1912, and by newspapers. Though the Japanese at no time owned more than 1.5 per cent of the total arable land of the state, apprehension extended to parts of the state which had no contact with Japanese and the demand for prohibiting landownership by Japanese became general.

Alien Land Laws and Other Discriminatory Measures.

The California legislature elected in 1912 was pledged to pass land legislation prohibiting Japanese ownership. Japan protested, President Wilson attempted to check action, and a personal visit from Secretary of State Bryan failed to deter the legislature; in 1913 the Alien Land Law was passed. By its provisions aliens ineligible to citizenship were permitted to own or lease land only to the extent and for purposes prescribed by treaty, though leasing for three years for any purpose was permitted. In this legislation the classification "aliens ineligible to citizenship" was used for the first time to discriminate against Orientals. Japanese had never been specifically denied the privilege of naturalization, as had the Chinese,[9] but it was established by court decision that they did not fall within the classes of persons on whom Congress had bestowed this privilege. Consequently, since the 1911 treaty guaranteed landownership to alien Japanese only for residential and commercial purposes, ownership for agricultural purposes was prohibited under the law. In a formal protest in June, 1913, Japan contended that the law was contrary to the spirit and letter of the treaty of 1911 and "at variance with the accepted principles of just and equal treatment upon which good relations between friendly nations must, in the last analysis, so largely depend." Japan felt that eligibility to citizenship was a purely domestic matter but it refused to recognize the right of the United States to deprive Japanese of civil rights that were granted to other aliens. The Federal Government took no steps to nullify this legislation and in 1923 it was upheld by the United States Supreme Court.[10]

In the meantime evasion of the 1913 law by Japanese, who continued to cultivate land held in trust by them for their American-born minor children or owned by corporations in which Japanese controlled stock, led in 1920 to an "initiative" measure in California forbidding these practices. Furthermore, California land legislation had caused a dispersion of Japanese to other states. The result was a series of laws on the California model passed by Washington, Arizona, New Mexico, Texas, Louisiana, Delaware, and other states. Some of these permitted aliens who had declared their intention to become citizens to acquire land on the same basis as citizens, a provision which in wording was not as directly based on racial distinction as was the classification "ineligible to citizen-

---

[9] By Act of 1882. See R. Malcolm, *American Citizenship and the Japanese; Annals of American Academy of Political and Social Science*, 1921, XCIII, 77.

[10] *Terrace* v. *Thompson*, 263 U.S. 197 (1923); *Porterfield* v. *Webb*, 263 U.S. 225 (1923); *Webb* v. *O'Brien*, 263 U.S. 313 (1923); *Frick* v. *Webb*, 263 U.S. 326 (1923).

ship" but which was equally effective in prohibiting Japanese land-ownership.

The alien land laws of 1913 and 1920 were accompanied by other discriminatory measures in California. A later act further restricted Japanese cultivation by prohibiting croppage contracts by Japanese. Other discriminations were state laws passed in 1921 which provided for drastic regulation of foreign language schools and permitted school boards to establish separate schools for Orientals. The abolition of foreign language schools was prevented only by a veto of the governor on grounds of unconstitutionality. An alien poll tax, aimed at the Japanese, was also declared unconstitutional. In addition to legal disabilities, Japanese were subjected to social and economic discriminations, attended by occasional violence; a few isolated cases of arson, blackmail, and coerced departure of Japanese workers who underbid white workers were reported.

The opinion behind these measures, though apparently irresistible, did not represent all classes and was not occasioned entirely by the local economic situation. Chambers of Commerce never supported it; in Oregon they openly opposed it because of its probable effects upon Japanese trade. On the other hand Japanese absorption of Korea gave the press and politicians an occasion to criticize the militaristic institutions which were alleged to be part of the culture Japanese immigrants brought with them.

The tendency of the President and the State Department after 1913 was to oppose a federal exclusion measure but to refrain from interfering with state legislation, though in 1919 Secretary Lansing wired to California from Paris requesting that the legislature take no action which might interfere with peace negotiations. Concerted efforts throughout the Pacific coast failed to secure exclusion of Japanese in the 1917 Immigration Act and the Emergency Quota Acts. In the 1917 Act[11] the "barred zone" erected for the specific purpose of excluding Asiatics did not include Japanese territory. Later, in the Emergency Quota Acts, Japan was again made an exception by a section[12] making quota

11 1917 Immigration Act, Sec. 3.
12 1921 Emergency Quota Act, Sec. 2 (a), 5.

provisions inapplicable to "aliens from countries immigration from which is regulated in accordance with treaties or agreements relating solely to immigration." In order to change this Federal policy California supported the numerous resolutions of the legislature, urging Congress to exclude Japanese, with a report on "California and the Oriental," prepared by the State Board of Control. In submitting it to the Secretary of State, the Governor explained that

the people of California . . . are determined to exhaust every power in their keeping to maintain this state for its own people. This determination is based fundamentally upon the ethnological impossibility of assimilating the Japanese people and the consequential alternative of increasing a population whose very race isolation must be fraught with the gravest consequences.[13]

The report presented statistics showing continued increase in Japanese population through immigration, an exceptionally high birth rate and illegal entry—an increase which it had been the purpose of the Gentlemen's Agreement to prevent. The chief reason for this increase, and therefore the chief source of grievance, was the admission of wives of resident laborers, facilitated by a Japanese law permitting marriage by proxy. The women thus married were called "picture brides." Japan's action was held by the State Board of Control to show "lack of entire good faith in carrying out the Agreement," though the United States Department had accepted it as consistent with the arrangements existing between the two governments and the Bureau of Immigration regulations had entitled "picture brides" to admission. The other important source of complaint was the grant of passports by Japan to persons of the exempt classes who became laborers. Such change of status was held to be legal by the United States courts and deportation was forbidden. The Federal Government was blamed for conceding to Japan the right of determining who were laborers and for failing to take adequate steps to stop smuggling and to deport illegally entered Japanese.

Japan seems to have been disposed to remove some of these

13 California State Board of Control, *California and the Oriental,* 1920, p. 10.

charges. In 1920 it stopped issuing passports to "picture brides," but almost as much resentment was felt against it for extending the period of immunity from military service in the case of emigrants who returned to Japan temporarily to secure a bride. In subsequent statements[14] Japan declared that it always stood willing to make any adjustments in the Agreement which might be considered necessary to carry out its purpose. The State Department on several occasions[15] announced its satisfaction with the functioning of the Agreement.

The "Grave Consequences" Incident.

When legislation to take the place of the Emergency Quota Act upon its expiration was under discussion in Congress in 1924, Mr. Albert Johnson of the state of Washington, chairman of the House Committee on Immigration and Naturalization, presented the case of the Pacific coast to Congress. Under his leadership the House Committee favored a provision to exclude aliens ineligible to citizenship. All the classes admitted under the Gentlemen's Agreement were exempted in the bill, so that the change was primarily in method of enforcement. To meet the objection of Secretary of State Hughes that temporary admission for business or pleasure did not fully meet existing treaty obligations, a provision was added exempting alien merchants entering in accordance with a treaty. The Committee in its report gave as grounds for its position the unwisdom of permitting the formation of colonies of persons ineligible to citizenship and the logic of putting Japan on the same basis as other Oriental countries. In considering international obligations toward Japan under the Gentlemen's Agreement the Committee was further influenced by the secrecy of its provisions, by failure of the agreement to prevent an increase in the Japanese population, and by objection to regulating immigration by treaty. Congress desired to control immigration policy and not to leave control to the executive. The Committee stated in its report that "the congressional prerogative of regulating im-

14 Japanese Protest of May 31, 1924; Buell, *op. cit.*, p. 375.
15 Letter of August, 1919, from Hon. William Phillips, acting Secretary of State, to Senator Phelan; California State Board of Control, *California and the Oriental*, 1920, p. 142.

migration from Japan has been surrendered to the Japanese Government. That condition, coupled with the fact that the terms of the agreement are secret, would justify immediate cancellation of the agreement." The House adopted the exclusion clause on April 17, with a vote of 323 to 71 (37 not voting) and with a protest only from Congressman Burton of Ohio.

The report of the Senate Committee supported the proposal of Secretary Hughes to except from the provision excluding aliens "ineligible to citizenship" "aliens entitled to enter the United States under provisions of a treaty or an agreement relating solely to immigration." This language would have covered the Gentlemen's Agreement and put Japan on the same basis as European countries with a quota of 146. That Japan would continue its co-operation in enforcing such a provision was considered probable. Objection was raised in debate by Senator McKellar against a "principle by which in the future Japanese can come in here as the subjects of other nations come in. To that I am opposed. I am opposed to it not because I do not believe the Japanese are a great people, for they are a great people, but because we can never assimilate that race of people with ours."[16] On April 10 Mr. Hughes sent to the Senate a note from Ambassador Hanihara protesting against exclusion in which it was stated that "grave consequences" to the "otherwise happy and mutually advantageous relations between Japan and the United States" would result from such action; it was common knowledge on Capitol Hill that the Hanihara Note had been written with the advice of the State Department and that the note was acceptable to that office. Senator Lodge announced a few days later that the note contained a "veiled threat" which compelled him to oppose the Committee's recommendation and to support the provision for exclusion; at the same time Senator Reed of Missouri, who had previously defended the quota provision, announced a change of opinion. After discussion, centering chiefly on the Hanihara Note, the amendment to put Japan under a quota was rejected by the Senate. A denial by Mr. Hanihara of any implied threat on his part and a statement by Mr. Hughes that he had not understood the Japanese

[16] *Congressional Record,* April 9, 1924, LXV, 5958.

ambassador's language to be threatening were ignored by Congress.

While the bill was under discussion by a conference committee of both houses, President Coolidge attempted to secure amendments postponing the operation of the exclusion clause until March 1, 1926, and providing for regulation of Japanese immigration by treaty. The conference committee did recommend postponement until March 1, 1925, in order to permit the President to negotiate a new treaty in conformity with Congressional policy, but even this compromise met opposition. Characteristic of the attitude of Congress in such matters was the statement of Senator Robinson of Arkansas that to permit regulation of Japanese immigration by treaty "would seem to constitute a recognition of the immigration question as a proper subject for international negotiations" and it constitutes a "distinct recognition of the force of the Gentlemen's Agreement as superior to the right of Congress to legislate upon the subject."[17] Fearing that postponement of exclusion might lead to a treaty inconsistent with the proposed legislation, the House recommitted the bill with instructions not to agree to postponement and the bill as finally reported by the conference committee and passed by Congress fixed July 1, 1924, as the effective date. In signing it President Coolidge deplored the provision for Japanese exclusion:

. . . we have had for many years an understanding with Japan by which the Japanese Government has voluntarily undertaken to prevent the emigration of laborers to the United States and in view of this historic relation and of the feeling which inspired it, it would have been much better, in my judgment, and more effective in the actual control of immigration, if we had continued to invite that coöperation which Japan was ready to give and had thus avoided creating any ground for misapprehension by an unnecessary statutory enactment. That course would not have derogated from the authority of the Congress to deal with the question in any exigency requiring its action. There is scarcely any ground for disagreement as to the result we want, but this method of securing it is unnecessary and deplorable at this time. If the exclusion provision stood alone, I should disapprove it without hesitation, if sought in this way at this time. . . .

[17] *Congressional Record,* May 8, 1924, LXV, 8086.

Effects of Japanese Exclusion.

Passage of the act led to a formal protest by Japan:

while reserving for another occasion the presentation of the question of legal technicality, whether and how far the provisions of Section 13 (c) of the Immigration Act of 1924 are inconsistent with the terms of the Treaty of 1911, the Japanese Government desire now to point out that the new legislation is in entire disregard of the spirit and circumstances that underlie the conclusion of the Treaty.

The general foundation of its protest was that

international discriminations in any form and on any subject, even if based on purely economic reasons, are opposed to the principles of justice and fairness upon which the friendly intercourse between nations must, in its final analysis, depend. To these very principles the doctrine of equal opportunity now widely recognized, with the unfailing support of the United States, owes its being. Still more unwelcome are discriminations based on race.

Although not denying the right of a sovereign power to control immigration, it did maintain that

when, in the exercise of such right, an evident injustice is done to a foreign nation in disregard of its proper self-respect, of international understandings or of ordinary rules of comity, the question necessarily assumes an aspect which justifies diplomatic discussion and adjustment.

Accordingly, the Japanese Government consider it their duty to maintain and to place on record their solemn protest against the discriminatory clause in section 13 (c) of the Immigration Act of 1924 and to request the American Government to take all possible and suitable measures for the removal of such discrimination.[18]

The ambassadors of both countries resigned almost immediately after the enactment of the exclusion provisions. Anti-American demonstrations in Japan reflected an intensity of feeling which rivaled that on the Pacific coast, expressed in a boycott of American goods, American society, and Christian churches, mutilation of the United States embassy flag, hero worship of a student, who,

[18] Japanese Protest of May 31, 1924; Buell, *op. cit.*, p. 372.

according to custom, committed suicide as an extreme protest against United States action; these incidents ceased only after a proclamation of the Tokyo prefect of police requesting subordination of personal feeling to national interest. Editorial comment and public discussion of the affair in Japan have not yet stopped. As far as Japan is concerned, Japanese exclusion injects itself into every aspect of international relations between the two countries; to the average Japanese, American relations still mean the Exclusion Act. Japanese who are friendly to the United States hope that through "the traditional sense of justice and fair play on the part of the American people . . . in due course of time this wrong will be righted with honor to both nations."[19] For the present they propose only to promote a better understanding between the two nations. Thus, Foreign Minister Shidehara in addressing the Imperial Diet in January, 1927, said:

I regret that the question of discriminatory treatment involved in the United States Immigration Act of 1924 remains unadjusted.

I have nothing to say at present that would modify or supplement the observations I have made on many previous occasions, but to point out the evident welcome fact that on this, and on all matters of common interest, the true knowledge and sympathetic understanding of Japan have grown considerably in the United States in recent years, and that the wild reports circulated at one time discrediting Japan's pacific intentions now are receiving the general condemnation of an enlightened public opinion there.

In our turn, for the correct estimation of the question, we should also fully appreciate the national institutions and conditions which characterize the United States.

A mutual understanding is the first essential step for the settlement of all international questions, and I am firmly convinced that the two nations, conscious of their important missions of guardians of the peace of the Pacific will stand side by side for all time in friendly accord for the fulfillment of such responsibilities.

Exclusion by the United States has for the Japanese an aspect other than resentment at being rated inferior, for it sets a precedent for official exclusion by other white immigrant countries. To

[19] Mr. Sawayanagi in a speech before the Institute of Pacific Relations, 1925.

establish rights of migration and residence equal to those of European peoples has been one of Japan's international aims. Restriction by administrative discretion and by use of a literacy test existed in Australia and Africa, and restriction by international arrangements similar to the former Gentlemen's Agreement with the United States exists in Canada, but there was no statutory discrimination against Japanese on the ground of race. Japanese exclusion by the United States ended recognition of the superiority of Japanese over other Orientals.

The immediate economic effect upon Japan was negligible because of the reasonably effective control it had already been exercising over emigration. In the United States, Japanese exclusion seems to be accepted for the present as part of a permanent immigration policy based on the principle of preserving American institutions and protecting American living standards. Ineligibility to citizenship of the Japanese is sometimes justified on the ground that Japan does not recognize renunciation of allegiance without its expressed consent and that consequently Japanese cannot give an unqualified allegiance to the United States. Although Japan's expatriation laws have not been liberalized as rapidly as those of other countries, an act was passed in 1924 which permitted voluntary expatriation of Japanese nationals born abroad.[20] Exclusion has to some extent fulfilled the expectations of its advocates; the following reduction in the number of immigrants born in Japan has taken place:

1922—6,178	1925—723
1923—5,809	1926—654
1924—8,801	1927—723
1928—550	

Nevertheless a gradual decline of the total resident Japanese population does not seem likely. Although emigrants have exceeded immigrants, the entry of approximately two thousand non-immigrant Japanese a year, many of whom can establish permanent residence here as merchants, has prevented a net decrease in Japanese residents. The exclusion of wives of resident Japanese immigrants may result in a decline in the natural increase of the

[20] Buell, *op. cit.*, p. 303.

Japanese population in the United States, but this effect may be partly offset by the immigration of American-born Japanese women from Hawaii who are admissible as citizens of the United States. The disappearance of anti-Japanese agitation which it was hoped would follow a decline in the Japanese population may come about as the result of their dispersion since the enactment of the land laws. Their disinclination to accept fixed economic status and their deliberate attempt to become assimilated may prevent the segregation which has facilitated the social and economic discrimination against the Chinese. There seems to be no prospect, however, of a tolerance that promises to the second generation of Japanese, of whom an extraordinarily large percentage are highly educated, opportunities equal to those open to educated persons of European origin. The attitude toward these Japanese and toward all relations with Japan will be affected by the suspicion of Japan as a nation which has been fomented in the United States as a legacy of the whole controversy.

CHAPTER EIGHT

INTERNATIONAL IMPLICATIONS

THE undisputed right of nations to regard immigration as a matter for domestic control has not prevented migration problems from becoming subjects of international conflict and negotiation. Allusion has been made to the international crisis which was provoked by discrimination against Japanese immigrants under the exclusion clause of the 1924 Act and to the official protests of Roumania and Italy against its selective features. Attempts of emigrant countries to determine the character of emigrants and to control their activities abroad have also led to conflicts, though these have not become subjects of official protests.

International conferences have attempted to resolve some of the differences in policy between immigrant and emigrant countries but have not succeeded in bringing about agreement on fundamental principles. The International Emigration Commission of 1921, established under the auspices of the League of Nations, avoided controversy by limiting itself to discussion of measures dealing with protection of migrants during passage and with the treatment of alien workers. At the Rome Conference on Emigration and Immigration called by Italy in 1924 questions concerning national policies arose in the discussion of migration treaties. Italy attempted to secure support for its policy of systematic colonization of emigrants under bilateral treaties and took the position that workers entering a country for temporary residence should be regarded as immigrants. The conference finally agreed on a resolution favoring freedom of migration except where undesirable elements or a surplus of labor made restriction necessary. During the interval between the Rome Conference and its sequel held at Havana in March, 1928, Italian emigration policy met with so much opposition in immigrant countries that the Italian delegation in 1928 did not resume the aggressive position it had taken in 1924. At the Havana conference, therefore, only strictly non-controversial subjects were presented in resolutions and the conference adjourned without making provision for future meetings or for permanent organization, with the result that future international action on migration now depends on the International Labor Office.

Although the International Labor Office does not attempt to handle problems of immigration, its dealing with the passage of workers from country to country permits it to assemble information and to call conferences. It has already passed four recommendations dealing with migration. Two of the resolutions of the unemployment conference held at Washington in 1919 affect migration—those dealing with reciprocity to alien workers in regard to social insurance and with national unemployment exchanges. In 1922 the International Labor Office requested authorization to secure and compile information on statistics of migration and migration laws and treaties. In 1925 it approved a draft convention on equality of treatment of alien workers in regard to workmen's compensation, and in 1926 it approved a draft convention on simplification of inspection of immigrants aboard ship. Some of these conventions constitute an integral part of the system of arrangements which control most continental European migration and an increasing proportion of overseas migration. The arrangements are made through bilateral or multilateral treaties fixing conditions of work and wage payment, prescribing methods of recruiting, and defining rights of emigrants. These treaties are based on community of interest between the two contracting parties to the extent at least that one country desires immigrants and the other desires relief from overpopulation; they have not been made in order to check migration from overpopulated countries, except in the case of Oriental countries, and have not, therefore, been instrumental in resolving the fundamental conflict between overpopulated countries which seek an outlet, and rich, sparsely populated countries which wish to restrict population in order to retain their economic advantage. At the World Population Conference in 1927, M. Albert Thomas of the International Labor Office suggested that amicable settlement of the difficulties arising from the defective distribution of population depended on an international tribunal with power to determine when territory within the boundaries of national states should be open to immigration. At international discussions the United States has continually asserted the right of a nation to control its immigration according to its national interests only, and no opposing attitude is likely to secure serious consideration; yet the assertion of the right to sole national control does not dispose of the international consequences of national action, and it is likely that the migration question, like tariffs, will in the future continue to occupy part of the field of international problems.

APPENDIX

CONTENTS OF AMERICAN FOREIGN RELATIONS, 1928

INDEX

Accessory Transit Company, 220.

Acosta, Julio, 226, 227.

Adams, Brooks, quoted, 317.

Adams, John Quincy, 5, 275.

Adams, Samuel, 417.

Administration, problems of, 311–319; by different departments, 137–138, 312–313.

Advisory opinions of World Court, 336–337, 337, 337–339, 345, 351, 355, 364, 365–366, 373–381; and non-members of League, 339–341, 357, 371; publicity of, 339, 350, 358, 361, 364, 367, 374, 382, 385; and United States interests, 348, 349, 350, 352, 356, 357–359, 361, 362, 363, 365, 366–367, 369, 370–371, 375–378, 380, 381, 383, 385–386.

Afghanistan, 400.

Africa, 514.

Agriculture, and tariff, 290.

Air routes, 288.

Alexis, Nord, 117.

Amador Guerrero, Manuel, 210.

American Bar Association, 346, 352.

American Federation of Labor, and immigration, 439, 474–475; and World Court, 346, 352. *See also* Labor, organized.

American Foreign Banking Corporation, 141.

Amory concession, 227–228.

Anzilotti, Dionisio, 370.

Arbitration, 11, 68, 209, 240, 323, 324, 333–335, 387 n.; in Central America, 211–212, 212–214, 233–235, 235–236, 244, 253, 253–254; compulsory, 336, 340; financial, 78, 119, 122, 228, 232–233, 233 n., 241, 258, 259, 310–311, 322, 323, 328, 329; Pan-American treaty of (1929), 68, 309–310, 326–329; treaties of, 68, 218, 235, 236, 268, 308–309, 309–310, 326–329, 361, 389. *See also* Conciliation; Hague Permanent Court of Arbitration; Inquiry, commissions of; Mediation.

Argentina, 100, 213, 292, 298, 308.

Arias, Desiderio, 86, 89, 90.

Arizona, 473; alien laws of, 506.

Armament, limitation of, 268, 400.

Armenians, immigration of, 447, 466.

Arms, embargo on, 188, 191, 251, 307–308.

Arosemena, F. H., 218.

Asquith, Herbert H., 409.

Asylum for political refugees, 124, 229–230, 243, 243 n., 255.

Australia, 393, 399, 402, 423, 459, 466, 514.

Austria, emigration from, 422, 466.

Babcock, Orville E., 75.

Bacon, Robert, 25, 26, 30, 32; quoted, 25.

Bacon, Robert L., 461.

Baez, Buenaventura, 75, 76, 87.

Baez, Rámon, 87.

Bahía Honda, 23–24.

Baker, Capt., 270, 271.

Baldwin, Stanley, 388.

Bananas, 169–170, 171, 242, 253, 269, 270–272, 280.

Barquero, F. A., 227.

Barrios, José Rufino, 230–231, 255, 262.

Barrundia, J. M., 243 n., 256.

Basle, Treaty of (1795), 71.

Bay Islands, 174.

Beard, Charles and Mary, 315 n.

Belgium, 78, 79, 80, 118, 192, 257, 365, 389, 390, 394, 399, 456, 466.

Belknap, R. R., 41.

Beneš, Edouard, 393–394; quoted, 393, 394.

Bertrand, Francisco, 245.

Bethmann-Hollweg, Theobald von, 409.

Bishop, J. B., 280 n.

Blaine, James G., 243 n.

Bliss, Tasker H., 23.

Boas, Franz, 488–489; quoted, 442–443.

Bolivar, Simon, 116.

Bolivia, 406.

Bolshevism, 417, 445.

Bondholders, Council of Foreign, 245–246, 257, 259.

Bonilla, Manuel, 235, 244, 245, 247.

Bonilla, Policarpo, 242.

Borah, William E., 182, 343, 344, 348, 349–350, 350, 354, 360, 369, 405, 407; quoted, 349–350.

Borchard, Edwin M., 325; quoted, 323, 323–324.